Memoirs Of The Life And Writings Of Benjamin Franklin......

Benjamin Franklin, William Temple Franklin

PHILOSOPHICAL.

ESSAYS

AND

CORRESPONDENCE.

THE

WORKS

OF

BENJAMIN FRANKLIN.

VOLUME III.

PHILADELPHIA:

PRINTED AND PUBLISHED BY WILLIAM DUANE.

1809.

THE

WORKS

OF

DR. BENJAMIN FRANKLIN,

IN

PHILOSOPHY, POLITICS, AND MORALS:

CONTAINING, BESIDE ALL THE WRITINGS PUBLISHED
IN FORMER COLLECTIONS, HIS

DIPLOMATIC CORRESPONDENCE,

AS MINISTER OF THE UNITED STATES, AT
THE COURT OF VERSAILLES;

A VARIETY OF LITERARY ARTICLES;

AND

EPISTOLARY CORRESPONDENCE,

NEVER BEFORE PUBLISHED.

WITH

MEMOIRS AND ANECDOTES OF HIS LIFE.

VOL. III.

PHILADELPHIA: PRINTED AND PUBLISHED BY WILLIAM DUANE.

1808.

CONTENTS.

VOL. III.

LETTERS AND PAPERS ON ELECTRICITY.

CONTENTS.

LETTERS AND PAPERS ON PHILOSOPHICAL SUBJECTS.

REFERENCES TO THE PLATES.

Vol. III.

PHILOSOPHICAL.

ESSAYS AND CORRESPONDENCE.

ELECTRICITY.

TO PETER COLLINSON, ESQ. F. R. S. LONDON.

Philadelphia, March 28, 1747.

SIR,

YOUR kind present of an electric tube, with directions for using it, has put several of us[1] on making electrical experiments, in which we have observed some particular phenomena that we look upon to be new. I shall therefore communicate them to you in my next, though possibly they may not be new to you, as among the numbers daily employed in those experiments on your side the water, it is probable some one or other has hit on the same observations. For my own part, I never was before engaged in any study that so totally engrossed my attention and my time as this has lately done; for what with making experiments when I can be alone, and repeating them to my friends and acquaintance, who, from the novelty of the thing, come continually in crouds to see them, I have, during some months past, had little leisure for any thing else.

I am, &c.

B. FRANKLIN.

---

[1] The *Library-Company*, an institution of the author's, founded in 1730. To which company the present was made

† Where notes occur without a signature, in the Philosophical, or other papers, they are generally notes of the author.

TO PETER COLLINSON, ESQ. F. R. S. LONDON.

Wonderful Effect of points.—Positive and negative Electricity.—Electrical Kiss.—Counterfeit Spider.—Simple and commodious electrical Machine.

Philadelphia, July 11, 1747.

SIR,

IN my last I informed you that, in pursuing our electrical enquiries, we had observed some particular phenomena, which we looked upon to be new, and of which I promised to give you some account, though I apprehended they might not possibly be new to you, as so many hands are daily employed in electrical experiments on your side the water, some or other of which would probably hit on the same observations.

The first is the wonderful effect of pointed bodies, both in *drawing off* and *throwing off* the electrical fire. For example.

Place an iron shot of three or four inches diameter on the mouth of a clean dry glass bottle. By a fine silken thread from the cieling, right over the mouth of the bottle, suspend a small cork-ball, about the bigness of a marble; the thread of such a length, as that the cork-ball may rest against the side of the shot. Electrify the shot, and the ball will be repelled to the distance of four or five inches, more or less, according to the quantity of electricity.—When in this state, if you present to the shot the point of a long, slender, sharp bodkin, at six or eight inches distance, the repellency is instantly destroyed, and the cork flies to the shot. A blunt body must be brought within an inch, and draw a spark to produce the same effect. To prove that the electrical fire is *drawn off* by the point, if you take the blade of the bodkin out of the wooden handle, and fix it in a stick of sealing-wax, and then present it at the distance aforesaid, or if you bring it very near, no such effect follows; but sliding one finger along the wax till you touch the blade, and the ball flies to the shot immediately.—If you present the point in the dark, you will see, sometimes at a foot distance and more, a light gather upon it, like that of a fire-fly, or glow-worm ; the less sharp the point, the nearer you must bring it to observe the light ; and at whatever distance you see the light, you may draw off the electrical fire, and destroy the repellency.—If a cork-ball so suspended be repelled by the tube, and a point be presented quick to it, though at a con-siderable distance, it is surprising to see how suddenly it flies back to the tube. Points of wood will do near as well as those of iron, provided the wood is not dry ; for per-fectly dry wood will no more conduct electricity than seal-ing-wax.

To shew that points will *throw off*[2] as well as *draw off* the electrical fire ; lay a long sharp needle upon the shot, and you cannot electrise the shot so as to make it repel the cork-ball.—Or fix a needle to the end of a suspended gun-barrel, or iron-rod, so as to point beyond it like a little bayonet[3] ; and while it remains there, the gun-barrel, or rod, cannot by applying the tube to the other end be elec-trised so as to give a spark, the fire continually running out silently at the point. In the dark you may see it make the same appearance as it does in the case before-mentioned.

The repellency between the cork-ball and the shot is like-wise destroyed. 1. By sifting fine sand on it ; this does it gradually. 2. By breathing on it. 3. By making a smoke about it from burning wood[4]. 4. By candle-light, even though the candle is at a foot distance : these do it suddenly.—The light of a bright coal from a wood fire, and the light of a red-hot iron do it likewise ; but not at so great a distance. Smoke from dry rosin dropt on hot iron,

---

2 This power of points to *throw off* the electrical fire, was first communi-cated to me by my ingenious friend Mr. Thomas Hopkinson, since deceased, whose virtue and integrity, in every station of life, public and private, will ever make his memory dear to those who knew him, and knew how to value him.

3 This was Mr. Hopkinson's experiment, made with an expectation of draw-ing a more sharp and powerful spark from the point, as from a kind of focus, and he was surprised to find little or none.

does not destroy the repellency; but is attracted by both shot and cork-ball, forming proportionable atmospheres round them, making them look beautifully, somewhat like some of the figures in Burnet's or Whiston's Theory of the Earth.

N. B. This experiment should be made in a closet, where the air is very still, or it will be apt to fail.

The light of the sun thrown strongly on both cork and shot by a looking-glass for a long time together, does not impair the repellency in the least. This difference between fire-light and sun-light is another thing that seems new and extraordinary to us[5].

We had for some time been of opinion, that the electrical fire was not created by friction, but collected, being really an element diffused among, and attracted by other matter, particularly by water and metals. We had even discovered and demonstrated its afflux to the electrical sphere, as well as its efflux, by means of little light wind-mill-wheels made of stiff paper vanes, fixed obliquely, and turning freely on fine wire axles. Also by little wheels of the same matter, but formed like water-wheels. Of the disposition and application of which wheels, and the various phenomena resulting, I could, if I had time, fill you a sheet[6]. The impossibility of electrising one's self (though standing on wax) by rubbing the tube, and drawing the fire from it; and the manner of doing it, by passing the tube near a person or thing standing on the floor, &c. had also

---

4 We suppose every particle of sand, moisture, or smoke, being first attracted and then repelled, carries off with it a portion of the electrical fire; but that the same sti 1 subsists in those particles, till they communicate it to something else, and that it is never really destroyed. So when water is thrown on common fire, we do not imagine the element is thereby destroyed or annihilated, but only dispersed, each particle of water carrying off in vapour its portion of the fire, which it had attracted and attached to itself.

5 This different effect probably did not arise from any difference in the light, but rather from the particles separated from the candle, being first attracted and then repelled, carrying off the electric matter with them; and from the rarefy-ing of the a r, between the glowing coal or red-hot iron, and the electrised shot, through which rarefied air the electric fluid could more readily pass.

occurred to us some months before Mr. Watson's ingenious *Sequel* came to hand, and these were some of the new things I intended to have communicated to you.—But now I need only mention some particulars not hinted in that piece, with our reasonings thereupon : though perhaps the latter might well enough be spared.

1. A person standing on wax, and rubbing the tube, and another person on wax drawing the fire, they will both of them (provided they do not stand so as to touch one another) appear to be electrised, to a person standing on the floor; that is, he will perceive a spark on approaching each of them with his knuckle.

2. But if the persons on wax touch one another during the exciting of the tube, neither of them will appear to be electrised.

3. If they touch one another after exciting the tube, and drawing the fire as aforesaid, there will be a stronger spark between them than was between either of them and the person on the floor.

4. After such strong spark, neither of them, discover any electricity.

These appearances we attempt to account for thus : We suppose, as aforesaid, that electrical fire is a common element, of which every one of the three persons abovementioned has his equal share, before any operation is begun with the tube. *A*, who stands on wax and rubs the tube, collects the electrical fire from himself into the glass; and his communication with the common stock being cut off by the wax, his body is not again immediately supplied. *B*, (who stands on wax likewise) passing his knuckle along near the tube, receives the fire which was collected by the glass from *A;* and his communication with the common stock being likewise cut off, he retains the additional quantity re-

6 These experiments with the wheels, were made and communicated to me by my worthy and ingenious friend Mr. Philip Syng; but we afterwards discovered that the motion of those wheels was not owing to any afflux or efflux of the electric fluid, but to various circumstances of attraction and repulsion. 1750.

ceived.—To *C*, standing on the floor, both appear to be electrised : for he having only the middle quantity of electrical fire, receives a spark upon approaching *B*, who has an over quantity ; but gives one to *A*, who has an under quantity. If *A* and *B* approach to touch each other, the spark is stronger, because the difference between them is greater : After such touch there is no spark between either of them and *C*, because the electrical fire in all is reduced to the original equality. If they touch while electrising, the equality is never destroyed, the fire only circulating. Hence have arisen some new terms among us; we say *B*, (and bodies like circumstanced) is electrised *positively*; *A*, *negatively*. Or rather, *B* is electrised *plus*; *A*, *minus*. And we daily in our experiments electrise bodies *plus* or *minus*, as we think proper.—To electrise *plus* or *minus*, no more needs to be known than this, that the parts of the tube or sphere that are rubbed, do, in the instant of the friction, attract the electrical fire, and therefore take it from the thing rubbing : the same parts immediately, as the friction upon them ceases, are disposed to give the fire they have received, to any body that has less. Thus you may circulate it, as Mr. Watson has shewn; you may also accumulate or subtract it, upon, or from any body, as you connect that body with the rubber or with the receiver; the communication with the common stock being cut off. We think that ingenious gentleman was deceived when he imagined (in his *Sequel*) that the electral fire came down the wire from the ceiling to the gun-barrel, thence to the sphere, and so electrised the machine and the man turning the wheel, &c. We suppose it was *driven off*, and not brought on through that wire; and that the machine and man, &c. were electrised *minus*; *i. e.* had less electrical fire in them, than things in common.

As the vessel is just upon sailing, I cannot give you so large an account of American electricity as I intended : I shall only mention a few particulars more.—We find granulated lead better to fill the phial with, than water, being

easily warmed, and keeping warm and dry in damp air.—
We fire spirits with the wire of the phial.—We light candles just blown out, by drawing a spark among the smoke
between the wire and snuffers.—We represent lightning,
by passing the wire in the dark, over a china plate that has
gilt flowers, or applying it to gilt frames of looking-glasses,
&c.—We electrise a person twenty or more times running,
with a touch of the finger on the wire, thus: he stands on
wax; give him the electrised bottle in his hand; touch
the wire with your finger, and then touch his hand or face;
there are sparks every time[7].—We encrease the force of the
electrical kiss vastly, thus: let _A_ and _B_ stand on wax; or
_A_ on wax, and _B_ on the floor; give one of them the electrised phial in hand; let the other take hold of the wire;
there will be a small spark; but when their lips approach,
they will be struck and shocked: the same if another gentleman and lady, _C_ and _D_, standing also on wax, and joining hands with _A_ and _B_, salute or shake hands. We suspend by fine silk thread a counterfeit spider, made of a
small piece of burnt cork, with legs of linen thread, and
a grain or two of lead stuck in him, to give him more
weight; upon the table, over which he hangs, we stick a
wire upright, as high as the phial and wire, four or five
inches from the spider; then we animate him, by setting
the electrified phial at the same distance on the other side
of him; he will immediately fly to the wire of the phial,
bend his legs in touching it, then spring off, and fly to the
wire on the table, thence again to the wire of the phial,
playing with his legs against both, in a very entertaining
manner, appearing perfectly alive to persons unacquainted:
he will continue this motion an hour or more in dry weather. We electrify, upon wax in the dark, a book that has
a double line of gold round upon the covers, and then apply a knuckle to the gilding; the fire appears every where

---

7 By taking a spark from the wire, the electricity within the bottle is diminished; the outside of the bottle then draws some from the person holding
it, and leaves him in the negative state. Then when his hand or face is touched
an equal quantity is restored to him from the person touching.

upon the gold like a flash of lightning: not upon the leather, nor, if you touch the leather instead of the gold.
We rub our tubes with buckskin, and observe always to
keep the same side to the tube, and never to sully the tube
by handling; thus they work readily and easily, without the
least fatigue, especially if kept in tight pasteboard cases,
lined with flannel, and sitting close to the tube[8]. This I
mention, because the European papers on electricity frequently speak of rubbing the tube as a fatiguing exercise.
Our spheres are fixed on iron axles, which pass through
them. At one end of the axis there is a small handle, with
which you turn the sphere like a common grindstone. This
we find very commodious, as the machine takes up but little room, is portable, and may be enclosed in a tight box,
when not in use. It is true, the sphere does not turn so
swift as when the great wheel is used: but swiftness we
think of little importance, since a few turns will charge the
phial, &c. sufficiently[9].

I am, &c.

B. FRANKLIN.

TO PETER COLLINSON, LONDON.

*Observations on the Leyden Bottle, with Experiments proving the
different electrical State of its different Surfaces.*

Philadelphia, Sept. 1, 1747.

SIR,

THE necessary trouble of copying long letters, which,
perhaps, when they come to your hands, may contain nothing new, or worth your reading, (so quick is the progress made with you in electricity) half discourages me from
writing any more on that subject. Yet I cannot forbear
adding a few observations on M. Muschenbroek's wonderful
bottle.

---

8 Our tubes are made here of green glass, 27 or 30 inches long, as big as can
be grasped.

9 This simple easily-made machine was a contrivance of Mr. Syng's.

1. The non-electric contained in the bottle differs, when electrised, from a non-electric electrised out of the bottle, in this; that the electrical fire of the latter is accumulated *on its surface*, and forms an electrical atmosphere round it of considerable extent; but the electrical fire is crowded *into the substance* of the former, the glass confining it[1].

2. At the same time that the wire and the top of the bottle, &c. is electrised *positively* or *plus*, the bottom of the bottle is electrised *negatively* or *minus*, in exact proportion; *i. e.* whatever quantity of electrical fire is thrown in at the top, an equal quantity goes out of the bottom[2]. To understand this, suppose the common quantity of electricity in each part of the bottle, before the operation begins, is equal to 20; and at every stroke of the tube, suppose a quantity equal to 1 is thrown in; then, after the first stroke the quantity contained in the wire and upper part of the bottle will be 21, in the bottom 19. After the second, the upper part will have 22, the lower 18, and so on, till, after 20 strokes, the upper part will have a quantity of electrical fire equal to 40, the lower part none: and then the operation ends: for no more can be thrown into the upper part, when no more can be driven out of the lower part. If you attempt to throw more in, it is spewed back through the wire, or flies out in loud cracks through the sides of the bottle.

3. The equilibrium cannot be restored in the bottle by *inward* communication or contact of the parts; but it must be done by a communication formed *without* the bottle, between the top and bottom, by some non-electric, touching or approaching both at the same time; in which case it is restored with a violence and quickness inexpressible; or, touching each alternately, in which case the equilibrium is restored by degrees.

---

1 See this opinion rectified in Sect. 16 and 17 of the next letter. The fire in the bottle was found by subsequent experiments not to be contained in the non-electric, but *in the glass.* 1748.

2 What is said here, and after, of the *top* and *bottom* of the bottle, is true of the *inside* and *outside* surfaces, and should have been so expressed.

4. As no more electrical fire can be thrown into the top of the bottle, when all is driven out of the bottom, so in a bottle not yet electrised, none can be thrown into the top, when none *can* get out at the bottom; which happens either when the bottom is too thick or when the bottle is placed on an electric *per se*. Again, when the bottle is electrised, but little of the electrical fire can be *drawn out* from the top, by touching the wire, unless an equal quantity can at the same time *get in* at the bottom[3]. Thus, place an electrised bottle on clean glass or dry wax, and you will not, by touching the wire, get out the fire from the top. Place it on a non-electric, and touch the wire, you will get it out in a short time; but soonest when you form a direct communication as above.

So wonderfully are these two states of electricity, the *plus* and *minus*, combined and balanced in this miraculous bottle! situated and related to each other in a manner that I can by no means comprehend! If it were possible that a bottle should in one part contain a quantity of air strongly comprest, and in another part a perfect vacuum, we know the equilibrium would be instantly restored *within*. But here we have a bottle containing at the same time a *plenum* of electrical fire, and a *vacuum* of the same fire; and yet the equilibrium cannot be restored between them but by a communication *without!* though the *plenum* presses violently to expand, and the hungry vacuum seems to attract as violently in order to be filled.

5. The shock to the nerves (or convulsion rather) is occasioned by the sudden passing of the fire through the body in its way from the top to the bottom of the bottle. The fire takes the shortest[4] course, as Mr. Watson justly observes: but it does not appear from experiment, that in order for a person to be shocked, a communication with the floor is necessary: for he that holds the bottle with one hand, and touches the wire with the other, will be shocked

---

3 See the preceding note, relating to *top* and *bottom*.
4 Other circumstances being equal,

Fig. 4.

.3.

Page 14.

Fig. 7.

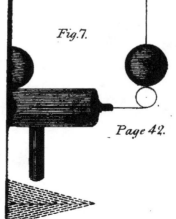

Page 42.

as much, though his shoes be dry, or even standing on wax, as otherwise. And on the touch of the wire, (or of the gun-barrel, which is the same thing) the fire does not proceed from the touching finger to the wire, as is supposed, but from the wire to the finger, and passes through the body to the other hand, and so into the bottom of the bottle.

Experiments confirming the above.

EXPERIMENT I.

Place an electrised phial on wax ; a small cork-ball suspended by a dry silk thread held in your hand, and brought near to this wire, will first be attracted, and then repelled : when in the state of repellency, sink your hand, that the ball may be brought towards the bottom of the bottle ; it will be there instantly and strongly attracted, till it has parted with its fire.

If the bottle had a *positive* electrical atmosphere, as well as the wire, an electrified cork would be repelled from one as well as from the other.

EXPERIMENT II.

Fig. 1. From a bent wire *(a)* sticking in the table, let a small linen thread *(b)* hang down within half an inch of the electrised phial *(c)*. Touch the wire or the phial repeatedly with your finger, and at every touch you will see the thread instantly attracted by the bottle. (This is best done by a vinegar cruet, or some such bellied-bottle.) As soon as you draw any fire out of the upper part, by touching the wire, the lower part of the bottle draws an equal quantity in by the thread.

EXPERIMENT III.

Fig. 2. Fix a wire in the lead, with which the bottom of the bottle is armed *(d)* so as that bending upwards, its ring-end may be level with the top or ring-end of the wire in the cork *(e)* and at three or four inches distance. Then electrise the bottle, and place it on wax. If a cork suspended by a silk thread *(f)* hang between these two wires,

it will play incessantly from one to the other, till the bottle
is no longer electrised ; that is, it fetches and carries fire
from the top to the bottom[5] of the bottle, till the equilibrium is restored.

EXPERIMENT IV.

FIG. 3. Place an electrised phial on wax; take a wire
(g) in form of a C, the ends at such a distance when bent,
(as that the upper may touch the wire of the bottle, when
the lower touches the bottom : stick the outer part on a
stick of sealing-wax (h), which will serve as a handle ;
then apply the lower end to the bottom of the bottle, and
gradually bring the upper end near the wire in the cork.
The consequence is, spark follows spark till the equilibrium
is restored.   Touch the top first, and on approaching the
bottom with the other end, you have a constant stream of
fire from the wire entering the bottle.   Touch the top and
bottom together, and the equilibrium will instantly be
restored, the crooked wire forming the communication.

EXPERIMENT V.

FIG. 4. Let a ring of thin lead, or paper, surround a
bottle (i) even at some distance from or above the bottom.
From that ring let a wire proceed up, till it touch the wire
of the cork (k).   A bottle so fixt cannot by any means be
electrised : the equilibrium is never destroyed : for while
the communication between the upper and lower parts of
the bottle is continued by the outside wire, the fire only
circulates : what is driven out at bottom, is constantly supplied from the top[6].   Hence a bottle cannot be electrised
that is foul or moist on the outside, if such moisture continue up to the cork or wire.

EXPERIMENT VI.

Place a man on a cake of wax, and present him the wire
of the electrified phial to touch, you standing on the floor,
and holding it in your hand.   As often as he touches it, he
will be electrified *plus* ; and any one standing on the floor

---

5 *i. e.* From the inside to the outside.
6 See the preceding note, relating to *top* and *bottom*.

may draw a spark from him. The fire in this experiment passes out of the wire into him ; and at the same time out of your hand into the bottom of the bottle.

EXPERIMENT VII.

Give him the electrical phial to hold ; and do you touch the wire ; as often as you touch it he will be electrified *minus*, and may draw a spark from any one standing on the floor. The fire now passes from the wire to you, and from him into the bottom of the bottle.

EXPERIMENT VIII.

Lay two books on two glasses, back towards back, two or three inches distant. Set the electrified phial on one, and then touch the wire ; that book will be electrified *minus ;* the electrical fire being drawn out of it by the bottom of the bottle. Take off the bottle, and holding it in your hand, touch the other with the wire ; that book will be electrified *plus ;* the fire passing into it from the wire, and the bottle is at the same time supplied from your hand. A suspended small cork-ball will play between these books till the equilibrium is restored.

EXPERIMENT IX.

When a body is electrified *plus*, it will repel a positively electrified feather or small cork-ball. When *minus* (or when in the common state) it will attract them, but stronger when *minus* than when in the common state, the difference being greater.

EXPERIMENT X.

Though, as in *Experiment* VI, a man standing on wax may be electrised a number of times by repeatedly touching the wire of an electrised bottle (held in the hand of one standing on the floor) he receiving the fire from the wire each time ; yet holding it in his own hand, and touching the wire, though he draws a strong spark, and is violently shocked, no electricity remains in him ; the fire only passing through him, from the upper to the lower part of the bottle. Observe, before the shock, to let some one on the floor touch him to restore the equilibrium in his body ; for in taking hold of the bottom of the bottle, he sometimes becomes a little electrised *minus*, which will continue after the shock, as would also any *plus* electricity, which he might have given him before the shock. For restoring the equilibrium in the bottle, does not at all affect the electricity, in the man through whom the fire passes ; that electricity is neither increased nor diminished.

EXPERIMENT XI.

The passing of the electrical fire from the upper to the lower part[7] of the bottle, to restore the equilibrium, is rendered strongly visible by the following pretty experiment. Take a book whose covering is filletted with gold ; bend a wire of eight or ten inches long, in the form of *(m)* Fig. 5 ; slip it on the end of the cover of the book, over the gold line, so as that the shoulder of it may press upon one end of the gold line, the ring up, but leaning towards the other end of the book. Lay the book on a glass or wax[8], and on the other end of the gold lines set the bottle electrised : then bend the springing wire, by pressing it with a stick of wax till its ring approaches the ring of the bottle wire, instantly there is a strong spark and stroke, and the whole line of gold, which completes the communication, between the top and bottom of the bottle, will appear a vivid flame, like the sharpest lightning. The closer the contact between the shoulder of the wire, and the gold at one end of the line, and between the bottom of the bottle and the gold at the other end, the better the experiment succeeds. The room should be darkened. If you would have the whole filletting round the cover appear in fire at once, let the bottle and wire touch the gold in the diagonally opposite corners.

I am, &c.

B. FRANKLIN.

---

7 *i. e.* From the *inside* to the *outside*.

8 Placing the book on glass or wax is not necessary to produce the appearance ; it is only to shew that the visible electricity is not brought up from the common stock in the earth.

TO PETER COLLINSON, LONDON.

Farther Experiments confirming the preceding Observations.—Leyden Bottle analysed.—Electrical Battery.—Magical Picture.—Electrical Wheel or Jack.—Electrical Feast.

Philadelphia, 1748.

SIR,

§ 1. THERE will be the same explosion and shock if the electrified phial is held in one hand by the hook, and the coating touched with the other, as when held by the coating, and touched at the hook.

2. To take the charged phial safely by the hook, and not at the same time diminish its force, it must first be set down on an electric *per se.*

3. The phial will be electrified as strongly, if held by the hook, and the coating applied to the globe or tube ; as when held by the coating, and the hook applied[9].

4. But the *direction* of the electrical fire being different in the charging, will also be different in the explosion. The bottle charged through the hook, will be discharged through the hook ; the bottle charged through the coating, will be discharged through the coating, and not otherways ; for the fire must come out the same way it went in.

5. To prove this, take two bottles that were equally charged through the hooks, one in each hand : bring their hooks near each other, and no spark or shock will follow ; because each hook is disposed to give fire, and neither to receive it. Set one of the bottles down on glass, take it up by the hook, and apply its coating to the hook of the other ; then there will be an explosion and shock, and both bottles will be discharged.

6. Vary the experiment, by charging two phials equally, one through the hook, the other through the coating : hold that by the coating which was charged through the hook ; and that by the hook which was charged through the coating : apply the hook of the first to the coating of the other,

---

[9] This was a discovery of the very ingenious Mr. Kinnersley, and by him communicated to me.

C

and there will be no shock or spark. Set that down on glass which you held by the hook, take it up by the coating, and bring the two hooks together: a spark and shock will follow, and both phials be discharged.

In this experiment the bottles are totally discharged, or the equilibrium within them restored. The *abounding* of fire in one of the hooks (or rather in the internal surface of one bottle) being exactly equal to the *wanting* of the other: and therefore as each bottle has in itself the *abounding* as well as the *wanting*, the wanting and abounding must be equal in each bottle. See § 8, 9, 10, 11. But if a man holds in his hands two bottles, one fully electrified, the other not at all, and brings their hooks together, he has but half a shock, and the bottles will both remain half electrified, the one being half discharged, and the other half charged.

7. Place two phials equally charged on a table at five or six inches distance. Let a cork-ball, suspended by a silk thread, hang between them. If the phials were both charged through their hooks, the cork, when it has been attracted and repelled by the one, will not be attracted, but equally repelled by the other. But if the phials were charged, the one through the hook, and the other [1] through the coating, the ball, when it is repelled from one hook, will be as strongly attracted by the other, and play vigorously between them, fetching the electric fluid from the one, and delivering it to the other, till both phials are nearly discharged.

8. When we use the terms of *charging* and *discharging* the phial, it is in compliance with custom, and for want of others more suitable. Since we are of opinion that there is really no more electrical fire in the phial after what is called its *charging*, than before, nor less after its *discharging*; excepting only the small spark that might be

---

[1] To charge a bottle commodiously through the coating, place it on a glass stand; form a communication from the prime conductor to the coating, and another from the hook to the wall or floor. When it is charged, remove the latter communication before you take hold of the bottle, otherwise great part of the fire will escape by it.

given to, and taken from the non-electric matter, if separated from the bottle, which spark may not be equal to a five hundredth part of what is called the explosion.

For, if on the explosion, the electrical fire came out of the bottle by one part, and did not enter in again by another, then, if a man, standing on wax, and holding the bottle in one hand, takes the spark by touching the wire hook with the other, the bottle being thereby *discharged*, the man would be *charged;* or whatever fire was lost by one, would be found in the other, since there was no way for its escape : but the contrary is true.

9. Besides, the phial will not suffer what is called a *charging*, unless as much fire can go out of it one way, as is thrown in by another. A phial cannot be charged standing on wax or glass, or hanging on the prime conductor, unless a communication be formed between its coating and the floor.

10. But suspend two or more phials on the prime conductor, one hanging on the tail of the other ; and a wire from the last to the floor, an equal number of turns of the wheel shall charge them all equally, and every one as much as one alone would have been. What is driven out at the tail of the first, serving to charge the second ; what is driven out of the second, charging the third ; and so on. By this means a great number of bottles might be charged with the same labor, and equally high, with one alone ; were it not that every bottle receives new fire, and loses its old with some reluctance, or rather gives some small resistance to the charging, which in a number of bottles becomes more equal to the charging power, and so repels the fire back again on the globe, sooner in proportion than a single bottle would do.

11. When a bottle is charged in the common way, its *inside* and *outside* surfaces stand ready, the one to give fire by the hook, the other to receive it by the coating ; the one is full, and ready to throw out, the other empty and extremely hungry ; yet as the first will not *give out*, unless the other can at the same instant *receive in;* so neither will

the latter receive in, unless the first can at the same instant
give out.   When both can be done at once, it is done with
inconceivable quickness and violence.

12. So a straight spring (though the comparison does not
agree in every particular) when forcibly bent, must, to
restore itself, contract that side which in the bending
was extended, and extend that which was contracted; if
either of these two operations be hindered, the other cannot
be done.   But the spring is not said to be *charged* with
elasticity when bent, and discharged when unbent; its
quantity of elasticity is always the same.

13. Glass in like manner, has, within its substance, always the same quantity of electrical fire, and that a very
great quantity in proportion to the mass of glass, as shall
be shewn hereafter.

14. This quantity, proportioned to the glass, it strongly
and obstinately retains, and will have neither more nor less,
though it will suffer a change to be made in its parts and
situation; *i. e.* we may take away part of it from one of
the sides, provided we throw an equal quantity into the
other.

15. Yet when the situation of the electrical fire is thus
altered in the glass; when some has been taken from one
side, and some added to the other, it will not be at rest or
in its natural state, till it is restored to its original equality.
And this restitution cannot be made through the substance
of the glass, but must be done by a non-electric communication formed without, from surface to surface.

16. Thus, the whole force of the bottle, and power of
giving a shock, is in the GLASS ITSELF; the non-electrics
in contact with the two surfaces, serving only to *give* and
receive to and from the several parts of the glass; that is,
to give on one side, and take away from the other.

17. This was discovered here in the following manner:
Purposing to analyse the electrified bottle, in order to find
wherein its strength lay, we placed it on glass, and drew
out the cork and wire which for that purpose had been
loosely put in.   Then taking the bottle in one hand, and

bringing a finger of the other near its mouth, a strong spark came from the water, and the shock was as violent as if the wire had remained in it, which shewed that the force did not lie in the wire. Then to find if it resided in the water, being crowded into and condensed in it, as confined by the glass, which had been our former opinion, we electrified the bottle again, and placing it on glass, drew out the wire and cork as before; then taking up the bottle, we decanted all its water into an empty bottle, which likewise stood on glass; and taking up that other bottle, we expected, if the force resided in the water, to find a shock from it; but there was none. We judged then that it must either be lost in decanting, or remain in the first bottle. The latter we found to be true; for that bottle on trial gave the shock, though filled up as it stood with fresh unelectrified water from a tea-pot. To find, then, whether glass had this property merely as glass, or whether the form contributed any thing to it; we took a pane of sash-glass, and laying it on the hand, placed a plate of lead on its upper surface; then electrified that plate, and bringing a finger to it, there was a spark and shock. We then took two plates of lead of equal dimensions, but less than the glass by two inches every way, and electrified the glass between them, by electrifying the uppermost lead; then separated the glass from the lead, in doing which, what little fire might be in the lead was taken out, and the glass being touched in the electrified parts with a finger, afforded only very small pricking sparks, but a great number of them might be taken from different places. Then dextrously placing it again between the leaden plates, and completing a circle between the two surfaces, a violent shock ensued.—Which demonstrated the power to reside in glass as glass, and that the non-electrics in contact served only, like the armature of a loadstone, to unite the force of the several parts, and bring them at once to any point desired: it being the property of a non-electric, that the whole body instantly receives or gives what electrical fire is given to or taken from any one of its parts.

18. Upon this we made what we called an *electrical-battery*, consisting of eleven panes of large sash-glass, armed

with thin leaden plates, pasted on each side, placed verti-
cally, and supported at two inches distance on silk cords,
with thick hooks of leaden wire, one from each side, standing upright, distant from each other, and convenient communications of wire and chain, from the giving side of one
pane, to the receiving side of the other; that so the whole
might be charged together, and with the same labor as one
single pane; and another contrivance to bring the giving
sides, after charging, in contact with one long wire, and the
receivers with another, which two long wires would give
the force of all the plates of glass at once through the body
of any animal forming the circle with them. The plates
may also be discharged separately, or any number together
that is required. But this machine is not much used, as
not perfectly answering our intention with regard to the
ease of charging, for the reason given, *Sec.* 10. We made
also of large glass panes, magical pictures, and self-moving
animated wheels, presently to be described.

19. I perceive by the ingenious Mr. Watson's last book,
lately received, that Dr. Bevis had used, before we had,
panes of glass to give a shock[2]; though, till that book came
to hand, I thought to have communicated it to you as a novelty. The excuse for mentioning it here is, that we tried
the experiment differently, drew different consequences
from it (for Mr. Watson still seems to think the fire *accumulated on the non-electric* that is in contact with the glass,
p. 72) and, as far as we hitherto know, have carried it farther.

20. The magical picture[3] is made thus : Having a large
mezzotinto with a frame and glass, suppose of the KING,
take out the print, and cut a pannel out of it near two
inches distant from the frame all round. If the cut is
through the picture it is not the worse. With thin paste,
or gum water, fix the border that is cut off on the inside

---

2 I have since heard that Mr. Smeaton was the first who made use of
panes of glass for that purpose.

3 Contrived by Mr. Kinnersley.

the glass, pressing it smooth and close ; then fill up the vacancy by gilding the glass well with leaf-gold, or brass. Gild likewise the inner edge of the back of the frame all round, except the top part, and form a communication between that gilding and the gilding behind the glass : then put in the board, and that side is finished. Turn up the glass, and gild the foreside exactly over the back gilding, and when it is dry, cover it, by pasting on the pannel of the picture that hath been cut out, observing to bring the correspondent parts of the border and picture together, by which the picture will appear of a piece, as at first, only part is behind the glass, and part before. Hold the picture horizontally by the top, and place a little moveable gilt crown on the king's head. If now the picture be moderately electrified, and another person take hold of the frame with one hand, so that his fingers touch its inside gilding, and with the other hand endeavor to take off the crown, he will receive a terrible blow, and fail in the attempt. If the picture were highly charged, the consequences might perhaps be as fatal[4] as that of high treason, for when the spark is taken through a quire of paper laid on the picture by means of a wire communication, it makes a fair hole through every sheet, that is, through forty-eight leaves, though a quire of paper is thought good armour against the push of a sword, or even against a pistol bullet, and the crack is exceeding loud. The operator, who holds the picture by the upper end, where the inside of the frame is not gilt, to prevent its falling, feels nothing of the shock, and may touch the face of the picture without danger, which he pretends is a test of his loyalty.——If a ring of persons take the shock among them, the experiment is called, *The Conspirators.*

21. On the principle, in *Sec. 7,* that hooks of bottles, differently charged, will attract and repel differently, is made an electrical wheel, that turns with considerable

---

4 We have since found it fatal to small animals, though not to large ones. The biggest we have yet killed is a hen. 1750.

strength. A small upright shaft of wood passes at right angles through a thin round board, of about twelve inches diameter, and turns on a sharp point of iron, fixed in the lower end, while a strong wire in the upper end, passing through a small hole in a thin brass plate, keeps the shaft truly vertical. About thirty *radii* of equal length, made of sash-glass, cut in narrow strips, issue horizontally from the circumference of the board, the ends most distant from the centre, being about four inches apart. On the end of every one, a brass thimble is fixed. If now the wire of a bottle electrified in the common way, be brought near the circumference of this wheel, it will attract the nearest thimble, and so put the wheel in motion; that thimble, in passing by, receives a spark and thereby being electrified is repelled, and so driven forwards; while a second being attracted, approaches the wire, receives a spark, and is driven after the first, and so on till the wheel has gone once round, when the thimbles before electrified approaching the wire, instead of being attracted as they were at first, are repelled, and the motion presently ceases.——But if another bottle, which had been charged through the coating, be placed near the same wheel, its wire will attract the thimble repelled by the first, and thereby double the force that carries the wheel round; and not only taking out the fire that had been communicated to the thimbles by the first bottle, but even robbing them of their natural quantity, instead of being repelled when they come again towards the first bottle, they are more strongly attracted, so that the wheel mends its pace, till it goes with great rapidity twelve or fifteen rounds in a minute, and with such strength, as that the weight of one hundred Spanish dollars with which we once loaded it, did not seem in the least to retard its motion—This is called an electrical jack; and if a large fowl were spitted on the upright shaft, it would be carried round before a fire with a motion fit for roasting.

22. But this wheel, like those driven by wind, water, or weights, moves by a foreign force, to wit, that of the bottles. The self-moving wheel, though constructed on the same

principles, appears more surprising. It is made of a thin round plate of window-glass, seventeen inches diameter, well gilt on both sides, all but two inches next the edge. Two small hemispheres of wood are then fixed with cement to the middle of the upper and under sides, centrally oppo-site, and in each of them a thick strong wire eight or ten inches long, which together make the axis of the wheel. It turns horizontally on a point at the lower end of its axis, which rests on a bit of brass cemented within a glass salt-cellar. The upper end of its axis passes through a hole in a thin brass plate cemented to a long strong piece of glass, which keeps it six or eight inches distant from any non-electric, and has a small ball of wax or metal on its top, to keep in the fire. In a circle on the table which supports the wheel, are fixed twelve small pillars of glass, at about four inches distance, with a thimble on the top of each. On the edge of the wheel is a small leaden bullet, commu-nicating by a wire with the gilding of the *upper* surface of the wheel; and about six inches from it is another bul-let, communicating in like manner with the *under* surface. When the wheel is to be charged by the upper surface, a com-munication must be made from the under surface to the table. When it is well charged it begins to move; the bullet nearest to a pillar moves towards the thimble on that pillar, and passing by electrifies it, and then pushes itself from it; the succeeding bullet, which communicates with the other sur-face of the glass, more strongly attracts that thimble, on ac-count of its being before electrified by the other bullet; and thus the wheel encreases its motion till it comes to such a height as that the resistance of the air regulates it. It will go half an hour, and make one minute with another twenty turns in a minute, which six hundred turns in the whole; the bullet of the upper surface giving in each turn twelve sparks to the thimbles, which makes seven thousand two hundred sparks: and the bullet of the under surface re-ceiving as many from the thimbles; those bullets moving in the time near two thousand five hundred feet.——The thim-bles are well fixed, and in so exact a circle, that the bullets

D

may pass within a very small distance of each of them.—If instead of two bullets you put eight, four communicating with the upper surface, and four with the under surface, placed alternately, with eight, at about six inches distance, completes the circumference, the force and swiftness will be greatly increased, the wheel making fifty turns in a minute ; but then it will not continue moving so long.—These wheels may be applied, perhaps, to the ringing of chimes [4], and moving of light-made orreries.

23. A small wire bent circularly, with a loop at each end ; let one end rest against the under surface of the wheel, and bring the other end near the upper surface, it will give a terrible crack, and the force will be discharged.

24. Every spark in that manner drawn from the surface of the wheel, makes a round hole in the gilding, tearing off a part of it in coming out ; which shews that the fire is not accumulated on the gilding, but is in the glass itself.

25. The gilding being varnished over with turpentine varnish, the varnish though dry and hard, is burnt by the spark drawn through it, and gives a strong smell and visible smoke. And when the spark is drawn through paper, all round the hole made by it, the paper will be blacked by the smoke, which sometimes penetrates several of the leaves. Part of the gilding torn off is also found forcibly driven into the hole made in the paper by the stroke.

26. It is amazing to observe in how small a portion of glass a great electral force may lie. A thin glass bubble, about an inch diameter, weighing only six grains, being half filled with water, partly gilt on the outside, and furnished with a wire hook, gives, when electrified, as great a shock as a man can well bear. As the glass is thickest near the orifice, I suppose the lower half, which being gilt was electrified and gave the shock, did not exceed two grains ; for it appeared, when broken, much thinner than the upper half.—If one of these thin bottles, be electrified by the coating, and the spark taken out through the gilding, it

---

4 This was afterwards done with success by Mr. Kinnersley.

will break the glass inwards, at the same time that it breaks the gilding outwards. ·

27. And allowing (for the reasons before given, § 8, 9, 10,) that there is no more electral fire in a bottle after charging, than before, how great must be the quantity in this small portion of glass! It seems as if it were of its very substance and essence. Perhaps if that due quantity of electral fire so obstinately retained by glass, could be separated from it, it would no longer be glass; it might lose its transparency, or its brittleness, or its elasticity.—Experiments may possibly be invented hereafter, to discover this.

28. We were surprised at the account given in Mr. Watson's book, of a shock communicated through a great space of dry ground, and suspect there must be some metalline quality in the gravel of that ground; having found that simple dry earth, rammed in a glass tube, open at both ends, and a wire hook inserted in the earth at each end, the earth and wires making part of a circuit, would not conduct the least perceptible shock, and indeed when one wire was electrified, the other hardly shewed any signs of its being in connection with it[5]. Even a thoroughly wet packthread sometimes fails of conducting a shock, though it otherwise conducts electricity very well. A dry cake of ice, or an icicle held between two in a circle, likewise prevents the shock, which one would not expect, as water conducts it so perfectly well.—Gilding on a new book, though at first it conducts the shock extremely well, yet fails after ten or a dozen experiments, though it appears otherwise in all respects the same, which we cannot account for[6].

29. There is one experiment more which surprises us, and is not hitherto satisfactorily accounted for; it is this:

---

5 Probably the ground is never so dry.

6 We afterwards found that it failed after one stroke with a large bottle; and the continuity of the gold appearing broken, and many of its parts dissipated, the electricity could not pass the remaining parts without leaping from part to part through the air, which always resists the motion of this fluid, and was probably the cause of the gold's not conducting so well as before; the number of interruptions in the line of gold, making, when added together, a space larger, perhaps, th the striking distance.

place an iron shot on a glass stand, and let a ball of damp cork, suspended by a silk thread, hang in contact with the shot. Take a bottle in each hand, one that is electrified through the hook, the other through the coating: apply the giving wire to the shot, which will electrify it *positively*, and the cork shall be repelled : then apply the requiring wire which will take out the spark given by the other ; when the, cork will return to the shot: apply the same again, and take out another spark, so will the shot be electrified *negatively*, and the cork in that case shall be repelled equally as before. Then apply the giving wire to the shot, and give the spark it wanted, so will the cork return : give it another which will be an addition to its natural quantity, so will the cork be repelled again : and so may the experiment be repeated as long as there is any charge in the bottles. Which shews that bodies, having less than the common quantity of electricity, repel each other, as well as those that have more.

Chagrined a little that we have been hitherto able to produce nothing in this way of use to mankind ; and the hot weather coming on, when electrical experiments are not so agreeable, it is proposed to put an end to them for this season, somewhat humorously, in a party of pleasure, on the banks of *Schuylkill*[7]. Spirits at the same time, are to be fired by a spark sent from side to side through the river, without any other conductor than the water ; an experiment which we some time since performed, to the amazement of many[8].

---

7 The river that washes the west side of Philadelphia, as the Delaware does the east side.

8 As the possibility of this experiment has not been easily conceived, I shall here describe it.—Two iron rods, about three feet long, were planted just within the margin of the river, on the opposite sides. A thick piece of wire, with a small round knob at its end, was fixed on the top of one of the rods, bending downwards, so as to deliver commodiously the spark upon the surface of the spirit. A small wire fastened by one end to the handle of the spoon, containing the spirit, was carried across the river, and supported in the air by the rope commonly used to hold by, in drawing the ferry-boats over. The other end of this wire was tied round the coating of the bottle ; which being charged, the spark was delivered from the hook to the top of the rod standing in the water on that side. At the same instant the rod on the other side delivered a spark into the spoon, and fired the spirit ; the electric fire returning to the coating of the bottle, through the handle of the spoon and the supported wire connected with them

A turkey is to be killed for our dinner by the *electrical shock*, and roasted by the *electrical jack*, before a fire kindled by the *electrified bottle:* when the healths of all the famous electricians in England, Holland, France, and Germany are to be drank in *electrified bumpers*[9], under the discharge of guns from the *electrical battery*.

TO PETER COLLINSON, LONDON.

Observations and suppositions, towards forming a new Hypothesis for explaining the several Phenomena of Thunder-gusts .

SIR,

1. NON-ELECTRIC bodies, that have electric fire thrown into them, will retain it till other electrics, that have less, approach ; and then it is communicated by a snap, and becomes equally divided.

2. Electrical fire loves water, is strongly attracted by it, and they can subsist together.

3. Air is an electric *per se*, and when dry will not conduct the electrical fire ; it will neither receive it, nor give it to other bodies ; otherwise no body surrounded by air, could be electrified positively and negatively: for should it be attempted positively, the air would immediately take away the overplus ; or negatively, the air would supply what was wanting.

4. Water being electrified, the vapors arising from it will be equally electrified ; and floating in the air, in the

---

* That the electric fire thus actually passes through the water, has since been satisfactorily demonstrated to many by an experiment of Mr. Kinnersley's, performed in a trough of water about ten feet long. The hand being placed under water in the direction of the spark (which always takes the strait or shortest course, if sufficient, and other circumstances are equal) is struck and penetrated by it as it passes.

9 An *Electrified bumper* is a small thin glass tumbler, nearly filled with wine and electrified as the bottle. This when brought to the lips gives a shock, if the party be close shaved, and does not breath on the liquor. April 29, 1749.

1 Thunder-gusts are sudden storms of thunder and lightning, which are frequently of short duration, but some times produce mischievous effects.

form of clouds, or otherwise, will retain that quantity of electrical fire, till they meet with other clouds or bodies not so much electrified, and then will communicate as before-mentioned.

5. Every particle of matter electrified is repelled by every other particle equally electrified. Thus the stream of a fountain, naturally dense and continual, when electrified, will separate and spread in the form of a brush, every drop endeavoring to recede from every other drop. But on taking out the electrical fire they close again.

6. Water being strongly electrified (as well as when heated by common fire) rises in vapors more copiously ; the attraction of cohesion among its particles being greatly weakened, by the opposite power of repulsion introduced with the electrical fire ; and when any particle is by any means disengaged, it is immediately repelled, and so flies into the air.

7. Particles happening to be situated as *A* and *B*, (FIG. VI. *representing the profile of a vessel of water*) are more easily disengaged than *C* and *D*, as each is held by contact with three only, whereas *C.* and *D.* are each in contract with nine. When the surface of the water has the least motion, particles are continually pushed into the situation represented by *A.* and *B.*

8. Friction between a non-electric and an electric *per se* will produce electrical fire ; not by *creating* but *collecting* it ; for it is equally diffused in our walls, floors, earth, and the whole mass of common matter. Thus the whirling glass globe, during its friction against the cushion, draws fire from the cushion, the cushion is supplied from the frame of the machine, that from the floor on which it stands. Cut off the communication by thick glass or wax, placed under the cushion, and no fire can be *produced*, because it cannot be *collected.*

9. The ocean is a compound of water, a non-electric, and salt an electric *per se.*

10. When there is a friction among the parts near its surface, the electrical fire is collected from the parts below. It is then plainly visible in the night ; it appears in the stern

and in the wake of every sailing vessel ; every dash of an oar shews it, and every surf and spray : in storms the whole sea seems on fire.—The detached particles of water then repelled from the electrified surface, continually carry off the fire as it is collected; they rise and form clouds, and those clouds are highly electrified, and retain the fire till they have an opportunity of communicating it.

11. The particles of water, rising in vapors, attach them. selves to particles of air.

12. The particles of air are said to be hard, round, separate and distant from each other; every particle strongly repelling every other particle, whereby they recede from each other, as far as common gravity will permit.

13. The space between any three particles, equally repelling each other, will be an equilateral triangle.

14. In air compressed, these triangles are smaller; in ratified air they are larger.

15. Common fire, joined with air, increases the repulsion, enlarges the triangles, and thereby makes the air specifically lighter. Such air, among denser air, will rise.

16. Common fire, as well as electrical fire, gives repulsion to the particles of water, and destroys their attraction of cohesion ; hence common fire, as well as electrical fire, assists in raising vapors.

17. Particles of water, having no fire in them, mutually attract each other. These particles of water then, being attached to the three particles of a triangle of air, would, by their mutual attraction operating against the air's repulsion, shorten the sides and lessen the triangle, whereby that portion of air made denser, would sink to the earth with its water, and not rise to the formation of a cloud.

18. But if every particle of water attaching itself to air brings with it a particle of common fire, the repulsion of the air being assisted and strengthened by the fire, more than obstructed by the mutual attraction of the particles of water, the triangle dilates, and that portion of air, becoming rarer and specifically lighter, rises.

19. If the particles of water bring electrical fire when they attach themselves to air, the repulsion between the

particles of water electrified, joins with the natural repulsion of the air, to force its particles to a greater distance,
whereby the triangles are dilated, and the air rises, carrying
up with it the water.

20. If the particles of water bring with them portions
of *both sorts* of fire, the repulsion of the particles of air is
still more strengthened and increased, and the triangles farther enlarged.

21. One particle of air may be surrounded by twelve
particles of water of equal size with itself, all in contact
with it; and by more added to those.

22. Particles of air, thus loaded, would be drawn nearer
together by the mutual attraction of the particles of water,
did not the fire, common or electrical, assist their repulsion.

23. If air, thus loaded, be compressed by adverse winds,
or by being driven against mountains, &c. or condensed by
taking away the fire that assisted it in expanding; the triangles contract, the air with its water will descend as a dew;
or, if the water surrounding one particle of air comes in
contact with the water surrounding another, they coalesce
and form a drop, and we have rain.

24. The sun supplies (or seems to supply) common fire
to vapors, whether raised from earth or sea.

25. Those vapours, which have both common and electrical fire in them, are better supported than those which
have only common fire in them; for when vapors rise into
the coldest region above the earth, the cold will not diminish the electrical fire, if it doth the common.

26. Hence clouds, formed by vapors raised from fresh
waters within land, from growing vegetables, moist earth,
&c. more speedily and easily deposite their water, having
but little electrical fire to repel and keep the particles separate. So that the greatest part of the water raised from the
land, is let fall on the land again; and winds blowing from
the land to the sea are dry; there being little use for rain
on the sea, and to rob the land of its moisture, in order to
rain on the sea, would not appear reasonable.

27. But clouds, formed by vapors raised from the sea, having both fires, and particularly a great quantity of the electrical, support their water strongly, raise it high, and being moved by winds, may bring it over the middle of the broadest continent from the middle of the widest ocean.

28. How these ocean clouds, so strongly supporting their water, are made to deposite it on the land where it is wanted, is next to be considered.

29. If they are driven by winds against mountains, those mountains being less electrified attract them, and on contact take away their electrical fire (and being cold, the common fire also;) hence the particles close towards the mountains and towards each other. If the air was not much loaded, it only falls in dews on the mountain tops and sides, forms springs, and descends to the vales in rivulets, which, united, make larger streams and rivers. If much loaded, the electrical fire is at once taken from the whole cloud; and, in leaving it, flashes brightly and cracks loudly; the particles instantly coalescing for want of that fire, and falling in a heavy shower.

30. When a ridge of mountains thus dams the clouds, and draws the electrical fire from the cloud first approaching it; that which next follows, when it comes near the first cloud, now deprived of its fire, flashes into it, and begins to deposite its own water; the first cloud again flashing into the mountains; the third approaching cloud, and all succeeding ones, acting in the same manner as far back as they extend, which may be over many hundred miles of country.

31. Hence the continual storms of rain, thunder, and lightning on the east side of the Andes, which running north and south, and being vastly high, intercept all the clouds brought against them from the Atlantic ocean by the trade winds, and oblige them to deposite their waters, by which the vast rivers Amazons, La Plata, and Oroonoko are formed, which return the water into the same sea, after having fertilized a country of very great extent.

E

32. If a country be plain, having no mountains to intercept the electrified clouds, yet it is not without means to make them deposite their water. For if an electrified cloud, coming from the sea, meets in the air a cloud raised from the land, and therefore not electrified; the first will flash its fire into the latter, and thereby both clouds shall be made suddenly to deposite water.

33. The electrified particles of the first cloud close when they lose their fire; the particles of the other clouds close in receiving it: in both, they have thereby an opportunity of coalescing into drops.—The concussion, or jerk given to the air, contributes also to shake down the water, not only from those two clouds, but from others near them. Hence the sudden fall of rain immediately after flashes of lightning.

34. To shew this by an easy experiment: Take two round pieces of pasteboard two inches diameter; from the centre and circumference of each of them suspend by fine silk threads eighteen inches long, seven small balls of wood, or seven peas equal in goodness: so will the balls appending to each pasteboard, form equal equilateral triangles, one ball being in the centre, and six at equal distances from that, and from each other; and thus they represent particles of air. Dip both sets in water, and some adhering to each ball, they will represent air loaded. Dexterously electrify one set, and its balls will repel each other to a greater distance, enlarging the triangles. Could the water supported by seven balls come into contact, it would form a drop or drops so heavy as to break the cohesion it had with the balls, and so fall. Let the two sets then represent two clouds, the one a sea cloud electrified, the other a land cloud. Bring them within the sphere of attraction, and they will draw towards each other, and you will see the separated balls close thus; the first electrified ball that comes near an unelectrified ball by attraction joins it, and gives it fire; instantly they separate, and each flies to another ball of its own party, one to give, the other to receive fire; and so it proceeds through both sets, but so quick as to be in a man-

ner instantaneous. In the cohesion they shake off and drop their water, which represents rain.

35. Thus when sea and land clouds would pass at too great a distance. for the flash, they are attracted towards each other till within that distance; for the sphere of electrical attraction is far beyond the distance of flashing.

36. When a great number of clouds from the sea meet a number of clouds raised from the land, the electrical flashes appear to strike in different parts; and as the clouds are jostled and mixed by the winds, or brought near by the electrical attraction, they continue to give and receive flash after flash, till the electrical fire is equally diffused.

37. When the gun-barrel, (in electrical experiments) has but little electrical fire in it, you must approach it very near with your knuckle before you can draw a spark. Give it more fire, and it will give a spark at a greater dis- tance. Two gun-barrels united, and as highly electrified, will give a spark at a still greater distance. But if two gun-barrels electrified will strike at two inches distance, and make a loud snap, to what a great distance may 10,000 acres of electrified cloud strike and give its fire, and how loud must be that crack?

38. It is a common thing to see clouds at different heights passing different ways, which shews different currents of air one under the other. As the air between the tropics is rarified by the sun, it rises, the denser northern and southern air pressing into its place. The air so rarified and forced up, passes northward and southward, and must descend in the polar regions, if it has no opportunity before, that the circulation may be carried on.

39. As currents of air, with the clouds therein, pass dif- ferent ways, it is easy to conceive how the clouds, passing over each other, may attract each other, and so come near enough for the electrical stroke. And also how electrical clouds may be carried within land very far from the sea, before they have an opportunity to strike.

When the air, with its vapors raised from the ocean between the tropics, comes to descend in the polar regions and to be in contact with the vapors arising there, the electrical fire they brought begins to be communicated, and is seen in clear nights, being first visible where it is first in motion, that is, where the contact begins, or in the most northern part; from thence the streams of light seem to shoot southerly, even up to the zenith of northern countries. But though the light seems to shoot from the north southerly, the progress of the fire is really from the south northerly, its motion beginning in the north, being the reason that it is there seen first.

For the electrical fire is never visible but when in motion, and leaping from body to body, or from particle to particle through the air. When it passes through dense bodies it is unseen. When a wire makes part of the circle, in the explosion of the electrical phial, the fire, though in great quantity, passes in the wire invisibly; but in passing along a chain, it becomes visible as it leaps from link to link. In passing along leaf gilding it is visible: for the leaf-gold is full of pores; hold a leaf to the light and it appears like a net, and the fire is seen in it leaping over the vacancies.— And as when a long canal filled with still water is opened at one end, in order to be discharged, the motion of the water begins first near the opened end, and proceeds towards the close end, though the water itself moves from the close towards the opened end: so the electrical fire discharged into the polar regions, perhaps from a thousand leagues length of vaporised air, appears first where it is first in motion, *i. e.* in the most northern part, and the appearance proceeds southward, though the fire really moves northward. This is supposed to account for the *aurora borealis.*

41. When there is great heat on the land, in a particular region (the sun having shone on it perhaps several days, while the surrounding countries have been screened by clouds) the lower air is rarified and rises, the cooler denser air above descends; the clouds in that air meet from all sides, and join over the heated place; and if some are electrified, others not, lightning and thunder succeed, and

showers fall. Hence thunder-gusts after heats, and cool air after gusts; the water and the clouds that bring it, coming from a higher and therefore a cooler region.

42. An electrical spark, drawn from an irregular body at some distance is scarcely ever strait, but shows crooked and waving in the air. So do the flashes of lightning; the clouds being very irregular bodies.

43. As electrified clouds pass over a country, high hills and high trees, lofty towers, spires, masts of ships, chimneys, &c. as so many prominencies and points, draw the electrical fire, and the whole cloud discharges there.

44. Dangerous, therefore, is it to take shelter under a tree, during a thunder-gust. It has been fatal to many, both men and beasts.

45. It is safer to be in the open field for another reason. When the clothes are wet, if a flash in its way to the ground should strike your head, it may run in the water over the surface of your body; whereas, if your clothes were dry, it would go through the body, because the blood and other humors, containing so much water, are more ready conductors.

Hence a wet rat cannot be killed by the exploding electrical bottle, when a dry rat may[2].

46 Common fire is in all bodies, more or less, as well as electrical fire. Perhaps they may be different modifications of the same element; or they may be different elements. The latter is by some suspected.

47. If they are different things, yet they may and do subsist together in the same body.

48. When electrical fires strikes through a body, it acts upon the common fire contained in it, and puts that fire in motion; and if there be a sufficient quantity of each kind of fire, the body will be inflamed.

49. When the quantity of common fire in the body is small, the quantity of the electrical fire (or the electrical

2 This was tried with a bottle, containing about a quart. It is since thought that one of the large glass jars, mentioned in these papers, might have killed him, though wet.

stroke) should be greater: if the quantity of common fire be great, less electrical fire suffices to produce the effect.

50. Thus spirits must be heated before we can fire them by the electrical spark[3]. If they are much heated, a small spark will do; if not, the spark must be greater.

51. Till lately we could only fire warm vapors; but now we can burn hard dry rosin. And when we can procure greater electrical sparks, we may be able to fire not only unwarmed spirits, as lightning does, but even wood, by giving sufficient agitation to the common fire contained in it, as friction we know will do.

52. Sulphureous and inflammable vapors, arising from the earth, are easily kindled by lightning. Besides what arise from the earth, such vapors are sent out by stacks of moist hay, corn, or other vegetables, which heat and reek. Wood, rotting in old trees or buildings, does the same. Such are therefore easily and often fired.

53. Metals are often melted by lightning, though perhaps not from heat in the lightning, nor altogether from agitated fire in the metals.——For as whatever body can insinuate itself between the particles of metal, and overcome the attraction by which they cohere (as sundry *menstrua* can) will make the solid become a fluid, as well as fire, yet without heating it: so the electrical fire, or lightning, creating a violent repulsion between the particles of the metal it passes through, the metal is fused.

54. If you would, by a violent fire, melt off the end of a nail, which is half driven into a door, the heat given the whole nail, before a part would melt, must burn the board it sticks in; and the melted part would burn the floor it dropped on. But if a sword can be melted in the scabbard, and money in a man's pocket by lightning, without burning either, it must be a cold fusion[4].

---

3 We have since fired spirits without heating them, when the weather is warm. A little, poured into the palm of the hand, will be warmed sufficiently by the hand, if the spirit be well rectified. Ether takes fire most readily.

4 These facts, though related in several accounts, are now doubted; since it has been observed that the parts of a bell-wire which fell on the floor, being

55. Lightning rends some bodies. The electrical spark will strike a hole through a quire of strong paper.

56. If the source of lightning, assigned in this paper be the true one, there should be little thunder heard at sea from land. And accordingly, some old sea-captains, of whom enquiry has been made, do affirm, that the fact agrees perfectly with the hypothesis; for that in crossing the great ocean, they seldom meet with thunder till they come into soundings; and that the islands far from the continent have very little of it. And a curious observer, who lived thirteen years at Bermudas, says, there was less thunder there in that whole time than he has sometimes heard in a month at Carolina.

TO PETER COLLINSON, LONDON.

Introductory Letter to some additional Papers.

Philadelphia, July 29, 1750.

SIR,

AS you first put us on electrical experiments, by sending to our Library Company a tube, with directions how to use it; and as our honorable Proprietary enabled us to carry those experiments to a greater height, by his generous present of a complete electrical apparatus; it is fit that both should know, from time to time, what progress we make. It was in this view I wrote and sent you my former papers on this subject, desiring, that as I had not the honor of a direct correspondence with that bountiful benefactor to our library, they might be communicated to him through your hands. In the same view I write and send you this additional paper. If it happens to bring you nothing new, (which may well be, considering the number of ingenious men in Europe, continually engaged in the same researches) at least it will shew, that the instruments put into our hands

---

broken and partly melted by lightning, did actually burn into the boards. (See Philosophical Transactions, vol. LI. part I.) And Mr. Kinnersley has found that a fine iron wire, melted by Electricity, has had the same effect.

are not neglected; and that if no valuable discoveries are made by us, whatever the cause may be, it is not want of industry and application.

I am, Sir,

Your much obliged humble Servant,
B. FRANKLIN.

Opinions and conjectures, concerning the Properties and Effects of the electrical Matter, and the Means of preserving Buildings, Ships, &c. from Lightning, arising from Experiments and Observations made at Philadelphia, 1749—Golden Fish.—Extraction of effluvial Virtues by Electricity impracticable.

§ 1. THE electrical matter consists of particles extremely subtile since it can permeate common matter, even the densest metals, with such ease and freedom as not to receive any perceptible resistance.

2. If any one should doubt whether the electrical matter passes through the substance of bodies, or only over and along their surfaces, a shock from an electrified large glass jar, taken through his own body, will probably convince him.

3. Electrical matter differs from common matter in this, that the parts of the latter mutually attract, those of the former mutually repel each other. Hence the appearing divergency in a stream of electrified effluvia,

4. But though the particles of electrical matter do repel each other, they are strongly attracted by all other matter[5].

5. From these three things, the extreme subtilty of the electrical matter, the mutual repulsion of its parts, and the strong attraction between them and other matter, arise this effect, that, when a quantity of electrical matter is applied to a mass of common matter, of any bigness or length, within our observation (which hath not already got its quantity) it is immediately and equally diffused through the whole.

---

5 See the ingenious Essays on Electricity, in the Transactions, by Mr. Ellicot.

6. Thus, common matter is a kind of spunge to the electrical fluid. And as a spunge would receive no water, if the parts of water were not smaller than the pores of the spunge ; and even then but slowly, if there were not a mutual attraction between those parts and the parts of the spunge ; and would still imbibe it faster, if the mutual attraction among the parts of the water did not impede, some force being required to separate them : and fastest, if, instead of attraction, there were a mutual repulsion among those parts, which would act in conjunction with the attraction of the spunge : so is the case between the electrical and common matter.

7. But in common matter there is (generally) as much of the electrical as it will contain within its substance. If more is added, it lies without upon the surface, and forms what we call an electrical atmosphere ; and then the body is said to be electrified.

8. It is supposed, that all kinds of common matter do not attract and retain the electrical, with equal strength and force, for reasons to be given hereafter : and that those called electrics *per se*, as glass, &c. attract and retain it strongest, and contain the greatest quantity.

9. We knwo that the electrical fluid is *in* common matter, because we can pump it *out* by the globe or tube. We know that common matter has near as much as it can contain, because, when we add a little more to any portion of it, the additional quantity does not enter, but forms an electrical atmosphere. And we know that common matter has not (generally) more than it can contain, otherwise, all loose portions of it would repel each other, as they constantly do when they have electric atmospheres.

10. The beneficial uses of this electric fluid in the creation we are not yet well acquainted with, though doubtless such there are, and those very considerable ; but we may see some pernicious consequences that would attend a much greater proportion of it. · For, had this globe we live on, as much of it in proportion as we can give to a globe of iron, wood, or the like, the particles of dust and other light

F

ticles rest, and by which they are attracted, one may see, by imagining a line from A to F, and another from E to G, that the portion of the atmosphere included in F, A, E, G, has the line A, E, for its basis. So the portion of atmosphere included in H, A, B, I, has the line A B for its basis. And likewise the portion included in K, B, C, L, has B, C, to rest on; and so on the other side of the figure. Now if you would draw off this atmosphere with any blunt smooth body, and approach the middle of the side A, B, you must come very near, before the force of your attracter exceeds the force or power with which that side holds its atmosphere. But there is a small portion between I, B, K, that has less of the surface to rest on, and to be attracted by, than the neighboring portions, while at the same time there is a mutual repulsion between its particles, and the particles of those portions, therefore here you can get it with more ease, or at a greater distance. Between F, A, H, there is a larger portion that has yet a less surface to rest on, and to attract it ; here, therefore, you can get it away still more easily. But easiest of all between L, C, M, where the quantity is largest, and the surface to attract and keep it back the least. When you have drawn away one of these angular portions of the fluid, another succeeds in its place, from the nature of fluidity, and the mutual repulsion before-mentioned ; and so the atmosphere continues flowing off at such angle, like a stream, till no more is remaining. The extremities of the portions of atmosphere over these angular parts, are likewise at a greater distance from the electrified body, as may be seen by the inspection of the above figure ; the point of the atmosphere of the angle C, being much farther from C, than any other part of the atmosphere over the lines C, B, or B, A: and, besides the distance arising from the nature of the figure, where the attraction is less, the particles will naturally expand to a greater distance by their mutual repulsion. On these accounts we suppose electrified bodies discharge their atmospheres upon unelectrified bodies more easily, and at a greater distance from their angles and points than from their smooth sides.—

Those points will also discharge into the air, when the body has too great an electrical atmosphere, without bringing any non-electric near, to receive what is thrown off: For the air, though an electric *per se*, yet has always more or less water and other non-electric matters mixed with it: and these attract and receive what is so discharged.

17. But points have a property, by which they *draw on*, as well as *throw off* the electrical fluid, at greater distances than blunt bodies can. That is, as the pointed part of an electrified body will discharge the atmosphere of that body, or communicate it farthest to another body, so the point of an unelectrified body will draw off the electrical atmosphere from an electrified body, farther than a blunter part of the same unelectrified body will do. Thus, a pin held by the head, and the point presented to an electrified body, will draw off its atmosphere at a foot distance; where, if the head were presented instead of the point, no such effect would follow. To understand this, we may consider, that if a person standing on the floor would draw off the electrical atmosphere from an electrified body, an iron crow and a blunt knitting-needle held alternately in his hand, and presented for that purpose, do not draw with different forces in proportion to their different masses. For the man, and what he holds in his hand, be it large or small, are connected with the common mass of unelectrified matter; and the force with which he draws is the same in both cases, it consisting in the different proportion of electricity in the electrified body, and that common mass. But the force with which the electrified body retains its atmosphere by attracting it, is proportioned to the surface over which the particles are placed; *i. e.* four square inches of that surface retain their atmosphere with four times the force that one square inch retains its atmosphere. And as in plucking the hairs from the horses tail, a degree of strength not sufficient to pull away a handful at once, could yet easily strip it hair by hair: so a blunt body presented cannot draw off a number of particles at once, but a pointed one, with no greater force, takes them away easily, particle by particle.

18. These explanations of the power and operation of points, when they first occurred to me, and while they first floated in my mind, appeared perfectly satisfactory ; but now I have written them, and considered them more closely, I must own I have some doubts about them; yet, as I have at present nothing better to offer in their stead, I do not cross them out : for, even a bad solution read, and its faults discovered, has often given rise to a good one, in the mind of an ingenious reader.

19. Nor is it of much importance to us to know the manner in which nature executes her laws ; it is enough if we know the laws themselves. It is of real use to know that china left in the air unsupported will fall and break ; but *how* it comes to fall and *why* it breaks are matters of speculation. It is a pleasure indeed to know them, but we can preserve our china without it.

20. Thus in the present case, to know this power of points may possibly be of some use to mankind, though we should never be able to explain it. The following experiments, as well as those in my first paper, show this power. I have a large prime conductor, made of several thin sheets of clothier's pasteboard, formed into a tube, near ten feet long and a foot diameter. It is covered with Dutch embossed-paper, almost totally gilt. This large metallic surface supports a much greater electrical atmosphere than a rod of iron of 50 times the weight would do. It is suspended by silk lines, and when charged will strike, at near two inches distance, a pretty hard stroke, so as to make ones knuckle ache. Let a person standing on the floor present the point of a needle at 12 or more inches distance from it, and while the needle is so presented, the conductor cannot be charged, the point drawing off the fire as fast as it is thrown on by the electrical globe. Let it be charged, and then present the point at the same distance, and it will suddenly be discharged. In the dark you may see the light on the point, when the experiment is made. And if the person holding the point stands upon wax, he will be electrified by receiving the fire at that distance. Attempt to

draw off the electricity with a blunt body, as a bolt of iron round at the end, and smooth (a silversmith's iron punch, inch thick, is what I use) and you must bring it within the distance of three inches before you can do it, and then it is done with a stroke and crack. As the pasteboard tube hangs loose on silk lines, when you approach it with the punch-iron, it likewise will move towards the punch, being attracted while it is charged; but if, at the same instant, a point be presented as before, it retires again, for the point discharges it. Take a pair of large brass scales, of two or more feet beam, the cords of the scales being silk. Suspend the beam by a pack thread from the cieling, so that the bottom of the scales may be about a foot from the floor: the scales will move round in a circle by the untwisting of the pack thread. Set the iron punch on the end upon the floor, in such a place as that the scales may pass over it in making their circle; then electrify one scale, by applying the wire of a charged phial to it. As they move round, you see that scale draw nigher to the floor, and dip more when it comes over the punch; and if that be placed at a proper distance, the scale will snap and discharge its fire into it. But if a needle be stuck on the end of the punch, its point upwards, the scale, instead of drawing nigh to the punch, and snapping, discharges its fire silently through the point, and rises higher from the punch. Nay, even if the needle be placed upon the floor near the punch, its point upwards, the end of the punch, though so much higher than the needle, will not attract the scale and receive its fire, for the needle will get it and convey it away, before it comes nigh enough for the punch to act. And this is constantly observable in these experiments, that the greater quantity of electricity on the pasteboard tube, the farther it strikes or discharges its fire, and the point likewise will draw it off at a still greater distance.

Now if the fire of electricity and that of lightning be the same, as I have endeavored to shew at large, in a former paper, this pasteboard tube and these scales may represent electrified clouds. If a tube of only ten feet long will strike and discharge its fire on the punch at two or three inches distance, an electrified cloud of perhaps 10,000 acres may strike and discharge on the earth at a proportionably greater distance. The horizontal motion of the scales over the floor, may represent the motion of the clouds over the earth; and the erect iron punch, a hill or high building; and then we see how electrified clouds passing over hills or high buildings at too great a height to strike, may be attracted lower till within their striking distance. And lastly, if a needle fixed on the punch with its point upright, or even on the floor below the punch, will draw the fire from the scale silently at a much greater than the striking distance, and so prevent its descending towards the punch; or if in its course it would have come nigh enough to strike, yet being first deprived of its fire it cannot, and the punch is thereby secured from the stroke; I say, if these things are so, may not the knowlege of this power of points be of use to mankind, in preserving houses, churches, ships, &c. from the stroke of lightning, by directing us to fix on the highest parts of those edifices, upright rods of iron made sharp as a needle, and gilt to prevent rusting, and from the foot of those rods a wire down the outside of the building into the ground, or down round one of the shrouds of a ship, and down her side till it reaches the water? Would not these pointed rods probably draw the electral fire silently out of a cloud before it came nigh enough to strike, and thereby secure us from that most sudden and terrible mischief?

21. To determine the question, whether the clouds that contain lightning are electrified or not, I would propose an experiment to be tried where it may be done conveniently. On the top of some high tower or steeple, place a kind of centry-box (as in *Fig.* 9) big enough to contain a man and an electrical stand. From the middle of the stand let an iron rod rise and pass bending out of the door, and then upright 20 or 30 feet, pointed very sharp at the end. If the electrical stand be kept clean and dry, a man standing on it, when such clouds are passing low, might be electrified and

afford sparks, the rod drawing fire to him from a cloud. If any danger to the man should be apprehended (though I think there would be none) let him stand on the floor of his box, and now and then bring near to the rod the loop of a wire that has one end fastened to the leads, he holding it by a wax handle; so the sparks, if the rod is electrified, will strike from the rod to the wire, and not affect him.

22. Before I leave this subject of lightning, I may mention some other similarities between the effects of that, and those of electricity. Lightning has often been known to strike people blind. A pigeon that we struck dead to appearance by the electrical shock, recovering life, drooped about the yard several days, eat nothing, though crumbs were thrown to it, but declined and died. We did not think of its being deprived of sight; but afterwards a pullet, struck dead in like manner, being recovered by repeatedly blowing into its lungs, when set down on the floor, ran headlong against the wall, and on examination appeared perfectly blind. Hence we concluded that the pigeon also had been absolutely blinded by the shock. The biggest animal we have yet killed, or tried to kill, with the electrical stroke, was a well grown pullet.

23. Reading in the ingenious Dr. Miles's account of the thunder storm at Streatham, the effect of the lightning in stripping off all the paint that had covered a gilt moulding of a pannel of wainscot, without hurting the rest of the paint, I had a mind to lay a coat of paint over the filleting of gold on the cover of a book, and try the effects of a strong electrical flash sent through that gold from a charged sheet of glass. But having no paint at hand, I pasted a narrow strip of paper over it; and when dry, sent the flash through the gilding, by which the paper was torn off from end to end, with such force, that it was broke in several places, and in others brought away part of the grain of the Turkey-leather in which it was bound; and convinced me, that had it been painted, the paint would have been stripped off in the same manner with that on the wainscot at Streatham.

G

24. Lightning melts metals, and I hinted in my paper on that subject, that I suspected it to be a cold fusion; I do not mean a fusion by force of cold, but a fusion without heat[7]. We have also melted gold, silver, and copper, in small quantities, by the electrical flash. The manner is this: take leaf-gold, leaf-silver, or leaf-gilt copper, commonly called leaf-brass, or Dutch gold; cut off from the leaf long narrow strips, the breadth of a straw. Place one of these strips between two strips of smooth glass that are about the width of your finger. If one strip of gold, the length of the leaf, be not long enough for the glass, add another to the end of it, so that you may have a little part hanging out loose at each end of the glass. Bind the pieces of glass together from end to end with strong silk thread; then place it so as to be part of an electrical circuit, (the ends of gold hanging out being of use to join with the other parts of the circuit) and send the flash through it, from a large electrified jar or sheet of glass. Then if your strips of glass remain whole, you will see that the gold is missing in several places, and instead of a metallic stain on both the glasses; the stains on the upper and under glass exactly similar in the minutest stroke, as may be seen by holding them to the light; the metal appeared to have been not only melted, but even vitrified, or otherwise so driven into the pores of the glass, as to be protected by it from the action of the strongest *aqua fortis*, or *aqua regia*. I send you enclosed two little pieces of glass with these metallic stains upon them, which cannot be removed without taking part of the glass with them. Sometimes the stain spreads a little wider than the breadth of the leaf, and looks brighter at the edge, as by inspecting closely you may observe in these. Sometimes the glass breaks to pieces; once the upper glass broke into a thousand pieces, looking like coarse salt. The pieces I send you were stained with Dutch gold. True gold makes a darker stain, somewhat reddish; silver, a greenish stain. We once took two

7 See the note in page 38.

pieces of thick looking-glass, as broad as a Gunter's scale, and six inches long; and placing leaf-gold between them, put them between two smoothly-plained pieces of wood, and fixed them tight in a book-binder's small press; yet though they were so closely confined, the force of the electrical shock shivered the glass into many pieces. The gold was melted and stained into the glass, as usual. The circumstances of the breaking of the glass differ much in making the experiment, and sometimes it does not break at all: but this is constant, that the stains in the upper and under pieces are exact counterparts of each other. And though I have taken up the pieces of glass between my fingers immediately after this melting, I never could perceive the least warmth in them.

25. In one of my former papers, I mentioned, that gilding on a book, though at first it communicated the shock perfectly well, yet failed after a few experiments, which we could not account for. We have since found that one strong shock breaks the continuity of the gold in the filletting, and makes it look rather like dust of gold, abundance of its parts being broken and driven off; and it will seldom conduct above one strong shock. Perhaps this may be the reason: when there is not a perfect continuity in the circuit, the fire must leap over the vacancies: there is a certain distance which it is able to leap over according to its strength; if a number of small vacancies, though each be very minute, taken together exceed that distance, it cannot leap over them, and so the shock is prevented.

26. From the before-mentioned law of electricity, that points as they are more or less acute, draw on and throw off the electrical fluid with more or less power, and at greater or less distances, and in larger or smaller quantities in the same time, we may see how to account for the situation of the leaf of gold suspended between two plates, the upper one continually electrified, the under one in a person's hand standing on the floor. When the upper plate is electrified, the leaf is attracted, and raised towards it, and would fly to that plate, were it not for its own points.

The corner that happens to be uppermost when the leaf is
rising, being a sharp point, from the extreme thinness of
the gold, draws and receives at a distance a sufficient quantity of the electric fluid to give itself an electric atmosphere,
by which its progress to the upper plate is stopped, and it
begins to be repelled from that plate, and would be driven
back to the under plate, but that its lowest corner is likewise a point, and throws off or discharges the overplus of
the leaf's atmosphere, as fast as the upper corner draws it
on. Were those two points perfectly equal in acuteness,
the leaf would take place exactly in the middle space, for
its weight is a trifle compared to the power acting on it:
but it is generally nearest the unelectrified plate, because,
when the leaf is offered to the electrified plate, at a distance,
the sharpest point is commonly first affected and raised
towards it; so *that* point, from its greater acuteness, receiving the fluid faster than its opposite can discharge it
at equal distances, it retires from the electrified plate, and
draws nearer to the unelectrified plate, till it comes to a
distance where the discharge can be exactly equal to the
receipt, the latter being lessened, and the former encreased;
and there it remains as long as the globe continues to supply
fresh electrical matter. This will appear plain, when the
difference of acuteness in the corners is made very great.
Cut a piece of Dutch gold, (which is fittest for these experiments on account of its great strength) into the form
of *Fig.* 10, the upper corner a right angle, the two next
obtuse angles, and the lowest a very acute one; and bring
this on your plate under the electrified plate, in such a manner as that the right-angled part may be first raised (which
is done by covering the acute part with the hollow of your
hand) and you will see this leaf take place much nearer to
the upper than the under plate; because without being
nearer, it cannot receive so fast at its right-angled point,
as it can discharge at its acute one. Turn this leaf with
the acute part uppermost, and then it takes place nearest
the unelectrified plate; because, otherwise, it receives faster
at its acute point, than it can discharge at its right-angled

one. Thus the difference of distance is always proportioned to the difference of acuteness. Take care in cutting your leaf, to leave no little ragged particles on the edges, which sometimes form points where you would not have them. You may make this figure so acute below, and blunt above, as to need no under plate, it discharging fast enough into the air. When it is made narrower, as the figure between the pricked lines, we call it the *golden fish*, from its manner of acting. For if you take it by the tail, and hold it at a foot or greater horizontal distance from the prime conductor, it will, when let go, fly to it with a brisk but wavering motion, like that of an eel through the water; it will then take place under the prime conductor, at perhaps a quarter or half an inch distance, and keep a continual shaking of its tail like a fish, so that it seems animated. Turn its tail towards the prime conductor, and then it flies to your finger, and seems to nibble it. And if you hold a plate under it at six or eight inches distance, and cease turning the globe when the electrical atmosphere of the conductor grows small, it will descend to the plate and swim back again several times with the same fish-like motion, greatly to the entertainment of spectators. By a little practice in blunting or sharpening the heads or tails of these figures, you may make them take place as desired, nearer or farther from the electrified plate.

27. It is said in Section 8, of this paper, that all kinds of common matter are supposed not to attract the electrical fluid with equal strength; and that those called electrics *per se*, as glass, &c. attract and retain it strongest, and contain the greatest quantity. This latter position may seem a paradox to some, being contrary to the hitherto received opinion; and therefore I shall now endeavor to explain it.

28. In order to this, let it first be considered, *that we cannot by any means we are yet acquainted with, force the electrical fluid through glass.* I know it is commonly thought that it easily pervades glass; and the experiment of a feather suspended by a thread, in a bottle hermetically sealed, yet moved by bringing a rubbed tube near the out-

side of the bottle, is alleged to prove it.   But, if the electrical fluid so easily pervades glass, how does the phial become *charged* (as we term it) when we hold it in our hands? Would not the fire, thrown in by the wire, pass through to our hands, and so escape into the floor? Would not the bottle in that case be left just as we found it, uncharged, as we know a metal bottle so attempted to be charged would be? Indeed, if there be the least crack, the minutest solution of continuity in the glass, though it remains so tight that nothing else we know of will pass, yet the extremely subtile electric fluid flies through such a crack with the greatest freedom, and such a bottle we know can never be charged: what then makes the difference between such a bottle and one that is sound, but this, that the fluid can pass through the one, and not through the other[8]?

29. It is true, there is an experiment that at first sight would be apt to satisfy a light observer, that the fire, thrown into the bottle by the wire, does really pass through the glass.   It is this: place the bottle on a glass stand, under the prime conductor, suspend a bullet by a chain from the prime conductor, till it comes within a quarter of an inch right over the wire of the bottle; place your knuckle on the glass stand, at just the same distance from the coating of the bottle, as the bullet is from its wire.   Now let the globe be turned, and you see a spark strike from the bullet to the wire of the bottle, and the same instant you see and feel an exactly equal spark striking from the coating on your knuckle, and so on, spark for spark.   This looks as if the whole received by the bottle was again discharged from it.   And yet the bottle by this means is charged[9]! And therefore the fire that thus leaves the bottle, though the same in quantity cannot be the very same fire that entered at the wire, for if it were, the bottle would remain uncharged.

---

8 See the first sixteen Sections of the former paper, called *Farther Experiments*, &c.

9 See Sect. 10, of *Farther Experiments*, &c.

30. If the fire that so leaves the bottle be not the same that is thrown in through the wire, it must be fire that subsisted in the bottle (that is, in the glass of the bottle) before the operation began.

31. If so, there must be a great quantity in glass, because a great quantity is thus discharged, even from very thin glass.

32. That this electrical fluid or fire is strongly attracted by glass, we know from the quickness and violence with which it is resumed by the part that had been deprived of it, when there is an opportunity. And by this, that we cannot from a mass of glass, draw a quantity of electric fire, or electrify the whole mass *minus*, as we can a mass of metal. We cannot lessen or increase its whole quantity, for the quantity it has it holds ; and it has as much as it can hold. Its pores are filled with it as full as the mutual repellency of the particles will admit ; and what is already in, refuses, or strongly repels, any additional quantity. Nor have we any way of moving the electrical fluid in glass, but one ; that is, by covering part of the two surfaces of thin glass with non-electrics, and then throwing an additional quantity of this fluid on one surface, which spreading in the non-electric, and being bound by it to that surface, acts by its repelling force on the particles of the electrical fluid contained in the other surface, and drives them out of the glass into the non-electric on that side from whence they are discharged, and then those added on the charged side can enter. But when this is done, there is no more in the glass, nor less than before, just as much having left it on one side as it received on the other.

33. I feel a want of terms here, and doubt much whether I shall be able to make this part intelligible. By the word *surface*, in this case, I do not mean mere length and breadth without thickness ; but when I speak of the upper or under surface of a piece of glass, the outer or inner surface of the phial, I mean length, breadth, and half the thickness, and beg the favor of being so understood. Now I suppose, that glass in its first principles, and in the furnace, has no

more of this electrical fluid than other common matter:
that when it is blown, as it cools, and the particles of common fire leave it, its pores become a *vacuum:* that the
component parts of glass are extremely small and fine, I
guess from its never shewing a rough face when it breaks,
but always a polish; and from the smallness of its particles I suppose the pores between them must be exceedingly
small, which is the reason that *aqua-fortis*, nor any other
menstruum we have, can enter to separate them and dissolve the substance; nor is any fluid we know of, fine enough
to enter, except common fire, and the electric fluid.   Now
the departing fire, leaving a vacuum, as aforesaid, between
these pores, which air nor water are fine enough to enter
and fill, the electric fluid (which is every where ready in
what we call the non-electrics, and in the non-electric mixtures that are in the air) is attracted in; yet does not become fixed with the substance of the glass, but subsists
there as water in a porous stone, retained only by the attraction of the fixed parts, itself still loose and a fluid.   But
I suppose farther, that in the cooling of the glass, its texture becomes closest in the middle, and forms a kind of
partition, in which the pores are so narrow, that the particles of the electrical fluid, which enter both surfaces at the
same time, cannot go through, or pass and repass from one
surface to the other, and so mix together; yet, though the
particles of electric fluid, imbibed by each surface, cannot
themselves pass through to those of the other, their repellency can, and by this means they act on one another.   The
particles of the electric fluid have a mutual repellency, but
by the power of attraction in the glass they are condensed
or forced nearer to each other.   When the glass has received, and, by its attraction, forced closer together so much
of this electric fluid, as that the power of attracting and
condensing in the one, is equal to the power of expansion
in the other, it can imbibe no more, and that remains its
constant whole quantity; but each surface would receive
more, if the repellency of what is in the opposite surface
did not resist its entrance.   The quantities of this fluid in

each surface being equal, their repelling action on each
other is equal ; and therefore those of one surface cannot
drive out those of the other; but, if a greater quantity is
forced into one surface than the glass would naturally draw
in, this increases the repelling power on that side, and overpowering the attraction on the other, drives out part of the
fluid that had been imbibed by that surface, if there be any
non-electric ready to receive it: such there is in all cases
where glass is electrified to give a shock. The surface that
has been thus emptied, by having its electrical fluid driven
out, resumes again an equal quantity with violence, as soon
as the glass has an opportunity to discharge that over quantity more than it could retain by attraction in its other surface, by the additional repellency of which the *vacuum* had
been occasioned. For experiments favoring (if I may not
say confirming) this hypothesis, I must, to avoid repetition,
beg leave to refer you back to what is said of the electrical
phial in my former pages.

38. Let us now see how it will account for several other
appearances.—Glass, a body extremely elastic, (and perhaps its elasticity may be owing in some degree to the subsisting of so great a quantity of this repelling fluid in its
pores) must, when rubbed, have its rubbed surface somewhat stretched, or its solid parts drawn a little farther
asunder, so that the vacancies in which the electrical fluid
resides, become larger, affording room for more of that fluid,
which is immediately attracted into it from the cushion or
hand rubbing, they being supplied from the common stock.
But the instant the parts of the glass so opened and filled,
have passed the friction, they close again, and force the additional quantity out upon the surface, where it must rest till
that part comes round to the cushion again, unless some
non-electric (as the prime conductor,) first presents to receive it[1]. But if the inside of the globe be lined with a

---

[1] In the dark the electric fluid may be seen on the cushion in two semi-circles
or half-moons, one on the fore part, the other on the back part of the cushions
just where the globe and cushion separate. In the fore crescent the fire is pass-

non-electric, the additional repellency of the electrical fluid, thus collected by friction on the rubbed part of the globe's outer surface, drives an equal quantity out of the inner surface into that non-electric lining, which receiving it, and carrying it away from the rubbed part into the common mass, through the axis of the globe, and frame of the machine, the new collected electrical fluid can enter and remain in the outer surface, and none of it (or a very little) will be received by the prime conductor. As this charged part of the globe comes round to the cushion again, the outer surface delivers its overplus fire into the cushion, the opposite inner surface receiving at the same time an equal quantity from the floor. Every electrician knows that a globe wet within will afford little or no fire, but the reason has not before been attempted to be given, that I know of.

34. So if a tube lined with a non-electric be rubbed[2] little or no fire is obtained from it; what is collected from the hand, in the downward rubbing stroke, entering the pores of the glass, and driving an equal quantity out of the inner surface into the non-electric lining: and the hand in passing up to take a second stroke, takes out again what had been thrown into the outer surface, and then the inner surface receives back again what it had given to the non-electric lining. Thus the particles of electral fluid belonging to the inside surface go in and out of their pores every stroke given to the tube. Put a wire into the tube, the inward end in contact with the non-electric lining, so it will represent the Leyden bottle. Let a second person touch the wire while you rub, and the fire driven out of the inward surface when you give the stroke, will pass through him into the common mass, and return through him when the inner surface resumes its quantity, and therefore this new kind of Leyden bottle cannot be so charged. But thus it may: after every stroke, before you pass your hand up to make

ing out of the cushion into the glass; in the other it is leaving the glass, and returning into the back part of the cushion. When the prime conductor is applied to take it off the glass, the back crescent disappears.

2 Gilt paper, with the gilt face next the glass, does well.

another, let a second person apply his finger to the wire, take the spark, and then withdraw his finger; and so on till he has drawn a number of sparks; thus will the inner surface be exhausted, and the outer surface charged; then wrap a sheet of gilt paper close round the outer surface, and grasping it in your hand you may receive a shock by applying the finger of the other hand to the wire: for now the vacant pores in the inner surface resume their quantity, and the overcharged pores in the outer surface discharge that overplus; the equilibrium being restored through your body, which could not be restored through the glass[3]. If the tube be exhausted of air, a non-electric lining, in contact with the wire, is not necessary; for *in vacuo* the electrical fire will fly freely from the inner surface, without a non-electric conductor; but air resists in motion; for being itself an electric *per se*, it does not attract it, having already its quantity. So the air never draws off an electric atmosphere from any body, but in proportion to the non-electrics mixed with it: it rather keeps such an atmosphere confined, which, from the mutual repulsion of its particles, tends to dissipation, and would immediately dissipate *in vacuo.*— And thus the experiment of the feather inclosed in a glass vessel hermetically sealed, but moving on the approach of the rubbed tube, is explained. When an additional quantity of the electrical fluid is applied to the side of the vessel by the atmosphere of the tube, a quantity is repelled and driven out of the inner surface of that side into the vessel, and there affects the feather, returning again into its pores, when the tube with its atmosphere is withdrawn; not that the particles of that atmosphere did themselves pass through the glass to the feather. And every other appearance I have yet seen, in which glass and electricity are concerned, are, I think, explained with equal ease by the same hypothesis. Yet, perhaps, it may not be a true one, and I shall be obliged to him that affords me a better.

35. Thus I take the difference between non-electrics, and

3 See *Further Experiments*, Sect. 15.

glass, an electric *per se*, to consist in these two particulars. 1st, That a non-electric easily suffers a change in the quantity of the electric fluid it contains. You may lessen its whole quantity, by drawing out a spark, which the whole body will again resume: but of glass you can only lessen the quantity contained in one of its surfaces; and not that, but by supplying an equal quantity at the same time to the other surface: so that the whole glass may always have the same quantity in the two surfaces, their two different quantities being added together. And this can only be done in glass that is thin; beyond a certain thickness we have yet no power that can make this change. And, 2dly, that the electric fire freely removes from place to place, in and through the substance of a non-electric, but not so through the substance of glass. If you offer a quantity to one end of a long rod of metal, it receives it, and when it enters, every particle that was before in the rod pushes its neighbor quite to the further end, where the overplus is discharged; and this instantaneously where the rod is part of the circle in the experiment of the shock. But glass, from the smallness of its pores, or stronger attraction of what it contains, refuses to admit so free a motion: a glass rod will not conduct a shock, nor will the thinnest glass suffer any particle entering one of its surfaces to pass through to the other.

36. Hence we see the impossibility of success in the experiments proposed, to draw out the effluvial virtues of a non-electric, as cinnamon, for instance, and mixing them with the electric fluid, to convey them with that into the body, by including it in the globe, and then applying friction, &c. For though the effluvia of cinnamon, and the electric fluid should mix within the globe, they would never come out together through the pores of the glass, and so go to the prime conductor; for the electric fluid itself cannot come through; and the prime conductor is always supplied from the cushion, and that from the floor. And besides, when the globe is filled with cinnamon, or other non-electric, non-electric fluid can be obtained from its outer

surface, for the reason before-mentioned. I have tried another way, which I thought more likely to obtain a mixture of the electric and other effluvia together, if such a mixture had been possible. I placed a glass plate under my cushion, to cut off the communication between the cushion and floor; then brought a small chain from the cushion into a glass of oil of turpentine, and carried another chain from the oil of turpentine to the floor, taking care that the chain from the cushion to the glass, touched no part of the frame of the machine. Another chain was fixed to the prime conductor, and held in the hand of a person to be electrified. The ends of the two chains in the glass were near an inch distant from each other, the oil of turpentine between.— Now the globe being turned could draw no fire from the floor through the machine, the communication that way being cut off by the thick glass plate under the cushion: it must then draw it through the chains whose ends were dipped in the oil of turpentine. And as the oil of turpentine, being an electric *per se*, would not conduct, what came up from the floor was obliged to jump from the end of one chain to the end of the other, through the substance of that oil, which we could see in large sparks, and so it had a fair opportunity of seizing some of the finest particles of the oil in its passage, and carrying them off with it: but no such effect followed, nor could I perceive the least difference in the smell of the electric effluvia thus collected, from what it has when collected otherwise, nor does it otherwise affect the body of a person electrised. I likewise put into a phial, instead of water, a strong purgative liquid, and then charged the phial, and took repeated shocks from it, in which case every particle of the electrical fluid must, before it went through my body, have first gone through the liquid when the phial is charging, and returned through it when discharging, yet no other effect followed than if it had been charged with water. I have also smelt the electric fire when drawn through gold, silver, copper, lead, iron, wood, and the human body, and could perceive no difference: the odor is always the same, where the spark does not burn what it strikes; and therefore I imagine it does not take that smell from any quality of the bodies it passes through. And indeed, as that smell so readily leaves the electric matter, and adheres to the knuckle receiving the sparks, and to other things; I suspect that it never was connected with it, but arises instantaneously from something in the air acted upon by it. For if it was fine enough to come with the electric fluid through the body of one person, why should it stop on the skin of another?

But I shall never have done, if I tell you all my conjectures, thoughts, and imaginations on the nature and operations of this electric fluid, and relate the variety of little experiments we have tried. I have already made this paper too long, for which I must crave pardon, not having now time to abridge it. I shall only add, that as it has been observed here that spirits will fire by the electric spark in the summer time, without heating them, when Fahrenheit's thermometer is above 70; so when colder, if the operator puts a small flat bottle of spirits in his bosom, or a close pocket, with the spoon, some little time before he uses them, the heat of his body will communicate warmth more than sufficient for the purpose.

ADDITIONAL EXPERIMENTS:

Proving that the Leyden Bottle has no more electrical Fire in it when charged, than before: nor less when discharged: that, in discharging, the Fire does not issue from the Wire and the Coating at the same Time, as some have thought, but that the Coating always receives what is discharged by the Wire, or an equal Quantity; the other Surface being always in a negative State of Electricity, when the inner Surface is in a positive State.

PLACE a thick plate of glass under the rubbing cushion, to cut off the communication of electrical fire from the floor to the cushion; then if there be no fine points or hairy threads sticking out from the cushion, (of which you must be careful) you can get but a few sparks from the prime conductor, which are all the cushion will part with.

Hang a phial then on the prime conductor, and it will not charge though you hold it by the coating.—But,

Form a communication by a chain from the coating to the cushion, and the phial will charge.

For the globe then draws the electric fire out of the outside surface of the phial and forces it through the prime conductor and wire of the phial into the inside surface.

Thus the bottle is charged with its own fire, no other being to be had while the glass plate is under the cushion.

Hang two cork balls by flaxen threads to the prime conductor; then touch the coating of the bottle, and they will be electrified and recede from each other.

For just as much fire as you give the coating, so much is discharged through the wire upon the prime conductor, whence the cork balls receive an electrical atmosphere.—But,

Take a wire bent in the form of a C, with a stick of wax fixed to the outside of the curve, to hold it by; and apply one end of this wire to the coating, and the other at the same time to the prime conductor, the phial will be discharged; and if the balls are not electrified before the discharge, neither will they appear to be so after the discharge, for they will not repel each other.

If the phial really exploded at both ends, and discharged fire from both coating and wire, the balls would be *more* electrified, and recede *farther;* for none of the fire can escape, the wax handle preventing.

But if the fire with which the inside surface is surcharged be so much precisely as is wanted by the outside surface, it will pass round through the wire fixed to the wax handle, restore the equilibrium in the glass, and make no alteration in the state of the prime conductor.

Accordingly we find, that if the prime conductor be electrified, and the cork balls in a state of repellency before the bottle is discharged, they continue so afterwards. If not, they are not electrified by that discharge.

TO PETER COLLINSON, LONDON.

Accumulation of the electrical Fire proved to be in the electrified Glass.—Effect of Lightning on the Needle of Compasses, explained.—Gunpowder fired by the electric Flame.

Philadelphia, July 27, 1750.

Sir,

MR. WATSON, I believe, wrote his Observations on my last paper in haste, without having first well considered the experiments related §. 17[4], which still appear to me decisive in the question,—*Whether the accumulation of the electrical fire be in the electrical glass, or in the non-electric matter connected with the glass?* and to demonstrate that it is really in the glass.

As to the experiment that ingenious gentleman mentions, and which he thinks conclusive on the other side, I persuade myself he will change his opinion of it, when he considers, that as one person applying the wire of the charged bottle to warm spirits, in a spoon held by another person, both standing on the floor, will fire the spirits, and yet such firing will not determine whether the accumulation was in the glass or the non-electric; so the placing another person between them, standing on wax, with a bason in his hand, into which the water from the phial is poured, *while he at the instant of pouring* presents a finger of his other hand to the spirits, does not at all alter the case; the stream from the phial, the side of the bason, with the arms and body of the person on the wax, being all together but as one long wire, reaching from the internal surface of the phial to the spirits.

June 29, 1751. In Capt. Waddell's account of the effects of lightning on his ship, I could not but take notice of the large comazants (as he calls them) that settled on the spintles at the top-mast heads, and burnt like very large torches (before the stroke.) According to my opinion, the electrical fire was then drawing off, as by points,

---

4 See the paper entitled, *Farther Experiments, &c.*

from the cloud ; the largeness of the flame betokening the great quantity of electricity in the cloud: and had there been a good wire communication from the spindle heads to the sea, that could have conducted more freely than tarred ropes, or mats of turpentine wood, I imagine there would either have been no stroke, or, if a stroke, the wire would have conducted it all into the sea without damage to the ship.

His compasses lost the virtue of the load-stone, or the poles were reversed; the north point turning to the south. —By electricity we have *(here* at *Philadelphia)* frequently given polarity to needles, and reversed it at pleasure. Mr. Wilson, at London, tried it on too large masses, and with too small force.

A shock from four large glass jars, sent through a fine sewing-needle, gives it polarity, and it will traverse when laid on water.—If the needle, when struck, lies east and west, the end entered by the electric blast points north.— If it lies north and south, the end that lay towards the north will continue to point north when placed on water, whether the fire entered at that end, or at the contrary end.

The polarity given is strongest when the needle is struck lying north and south, weakest when lying east and west ; perhaps if the force was still greater, the south end, entered by the fire (when the needle lies north and south) might become the north, otherwise it puzzles us to account for the inverting of compasses by lightning; since their needles must always be found in that situation, and by our little experiments, whether the blast entered the north and went out at the south end of the needle, or the contrary, still the end that lay to the north should continue to point north.

In these experiments the ends of the needles are sometimes finely blued like a watch-spring by the electric flame. —This color given by the flash from two jars only, will wipe off, but four jars fix it, and frequently melt the needles. I send you some that have had their heads and points melted off by our mimic lightning; and a pin that

I

had its point melted off, and some part of its head and neck run. Sometimes the surface on the body of the needle is also run, and appears blistered when examined by a magnifying glass : the jars I make use of hold seven or eight gallons, and are coated and lined with tin-foil; each of them takes a thousand turns[5] of a globe nine inches diameter to charge it.

I send you two specimens of tin-foil melted between glass, by the force of two jars only.

I have not heard that any of your European electricians have ever been able to fire gun-powder by the electric flame. We do it here in this manner :—A small cartridge is filled with dry powder, hard rammed, so as to bruise some of the grains; two pointed wires are then thrust in, one at each end, the points approaching each other in the middle of the cartridge, till within the distance of half an inch; then, the cartridge being placed in the circuit, when the four jars are discharged, the electric flame leaping from the point of one wire to the point of the other, within the cartridge amongst the powder, *fires it*, and the explosion of the powder is at the same instant with the crack of the discharge.

Yours, &c.

B. FRANKLIN.

---

5 The cushion being afterwards covered with a long flap of buckskin, which might cling to the globe; and care being taken to keep that flap of a due temperature, between too dry and too moist, we found so much more of the electric fluid was obtained, as that 150 turns were sufficient.   1753.

TO CADWALLADER COLDEN[6], AT NEW YORK: COMMUNICATED TO
MR. COLLINSON.

Unlimited Nature of the electric Force.

Philadelphia, 1751.

SIR,

I ENCLOSE you answers, such as my present hurry
of business will permit me to make, to the principal queries
contained in your's of the 28th instant, and beg leave to
refer you to the latter piece in the printed collection of my
papers, for farther explanation of the difference between
what is called *electrics per se*, and *non-electrics.* When
you have had time to read and consider these papers, I will
endeavor to make any new experiments you shall propose,
that you think may afford farther light or satisfaction to
either of us; and shall be much obliged to you for such
remarks, objections, &c. as may occur to you.—I forget
whether I wrote to you that I have melted brass pins and
steel needles, inverted the poles of the magnetic needle,
given a magnetism and polarity to needles that had none,
and fired dry gunpowder by the electric spark. I have five
bottles that contain eight or nine gallons each, two of which
charged are sufficient for those purposes: but I can charge
and discharge them altogether. There are no bounds (but
what expence and labor give) to the force man may raise
and use in the electrical way: for bottle may be added to
bottle *in infinitum*, and all united and discharged together
as one, the force and effect proportioned to their number
and size. The greatest known effects of common lightning may, I think, without much difficulty, be exceeded in
this way, which a few years since could not have been believed, and even now may seem to many a little extravagant
to suppose.—So we are got beyond the skill of Rabelais's
devils of two years old, who, he humorously says, had only

6 This gentleman was afterwards lieutenant-governor of New York.

learnt to thunder and lighten a little round the head of a cabbage.

I am, with sincere respect,

Your most obliged humble servant,

B. FRANKLIN.

QUERIES AND ANSWERS REFERRED TO IN THE FOREGOING LETTER.

The Terms, electric per se, and non-electric, improper.—New Relation between Metals and Water.—Effects of Air in electrical Experiments.—Experiment for discovering more of the Qualities of the electric Fluid.

Query, WHEREIN consists the difference between an *electric* and a *non-electric* body?

Answer. The terms electric *per se,* and non-electric were first used to distinguish bodies, on a mistaken supposition that those called electrics *per se,* alone contained electric matter in their substance, which was capable of being excited by friction, and of being produced or drawn from them, and communicated to those called non-electrics, supposed to be destitute of it: for the glass, &c. being rubbed, discovered signs of having it, by snapping to the finger, attracting, repelling, &c. and could communicate those signs to metals and water.—Afterwards it was found, that rubbing of glass would not produce the electric matter, unless a communication was preserved between the rubber and the floor; and subsequent experiments proved that the electric matter, was really drawn from those bodies that at first were thought to have none in them. Then it was doubted whether glass, and other bodies called *electrics per se,* had really any electric matter in them, since they apparently afforded none but what they first extracted from those which had been called non-electrics. But some of my experiments show, that glass contains it in great quantity, and I now suspect it to be pretty equally diffused in all the matter of this terraqueous globe. If so, the terms *electric per se*, and *non-electric*, should be laid aside as improper: and (the only difference being this, that some bodies will conduct electric matter, and others will not) the terms *conductor* and *non-conductor* may supply their place. If any portion of electric matter is applied to a piece of conducting matter, it penetrates and flows through it, or spreads equally on its surface; if applied to a piece of non-conducting matter, it will do neither. Perfect conductors of electric matter are only metals and water. Other bodies conducting only as they contain a mixture of those; without more or less of which they will not conduct at all[7]. This (by the way) shews a new relation between metals and water heretofore unknown.

To illustrate this by a comparison, which, however, can only give a faint resemblance. Electric matter passes through conductors as water passes through a porous stone, or spreads on their surfaces as water spreads on a wet stone; but when applied to non-conductors, it is like water dropt on a greasy stone, it neither penetrates, passes through, nor spreads on the surface, but remains in drops where it falls. See farther on this head, in my last printed piece, entitled, *Opinions and Conjectures, &c.* 1749.

Query, What are the effects of air in electrical experiments?

Answer. All I have hitherto observed are these. Moist air receives and conducts the electrical matter in proportion to its moisture, quite dry air not at all: air is therefore to be classed with the non-conductors. Dry air assists in confining the electrical atmosphere to the body it surrounds, and prevents its dissipating: for *in vacuo* it quits easily, and points operate stronger, *i. e.* they throw off or attract the electrical matter more freely, and at greater distances; so that air intervening obstructs its passage from body to body in some degree. A clean electrical phial and wire, containing air instead of water, will not be charged nor give

---

7 This preposition is since found to be too general; Mr. Wilson having discovered that melted wax and rosin will also conduct.

a shock, any more than if it was filled with powder of glass;
but exhausted of air, it operates as well as if filled with
water. Yet an electric atmosphere and air do not seem to
exclude each other, for we breathe freely in such an atmosphere, and dry air will blow through it without displacing
or driving it away. I question whether the strongest dry
north-wester[8] would dissipate it. I once electrified a large
cork-ball at the end of a silk thread three feet long, the
other end of which I held in my fingers, and whirl'd it
round, like a sling one hundred times in the air, with the
swiftest motion I could possibly give it, yet it retained its
electric atmosphere, though it must have passed through
eight hundred yards of air, allowing my arm in giving the
motion to add a foot to the semi-diameter of the circle.—
By quite dry air, I mean the dryest we have : for perhaps
we never have any perfectly free from moisture. An electrical atmosphere raised round a thick wire, inserted in a
phial of air, drives out none of the air, nor on withdrawing that atmosphere will any rush in, as I have found by a
curious experiment[9] accurately made, whence we concluded
that the air's elasticity was not affected thereby.

8 The cold dry wind of North America.

9 The experiment here mentioned was thus made. An empty phial was
stopped with a cork. Through the cork passed a thick wire, as usual in the
Leyden experiment, which wire almost reached the bottom. Through another
part of the cork passed one leg of a small glass syphon, the other leg on the
outside came down almost to the bottom of the phial. This phial was first
held a short time in the hand, which, warming, and of course rarifying the air
within, drove a small part of it out through the syphon. Then a little red ink
in a tea-spoon was applied to the opening of the outer leg of the syphon; so
that as the air within cooled, a little of the ink might rise in that leg. When the
air within the bottle came to be of the same temperature of that without, the
drop of red ink would rest in a certain part of the leg. But the warmth of a
finger applied to the phial would cause that drop to descend, as the least outward coolness applied would make it ascend. When it had found its situation,
and was at rest, the wire was electrified by a communication from the prime
conductor. This was supposed to give an electric atmosphere to the wire
within the bottle, which might likewise rarify the included air, and of course
depress the drop of ink in the syphon. But no such effect followed.

AN EXPERIMENT TOWARDS DISCOVERING MORE OF THE QUALITIES OF THE ELECTRIC FLUID.

FROM the prime conductor, hang a bullet by a wire hook; under the bullet, at half an inch distance, place a bright piece of silver to receive the sparks; then let the wheel be turned, and in a few minutes, (if the repeated sparks continually strike in the same spot) the silver will receive a blue stain, nearly the color of a watch spring.

A bright piece of iron will also be spotted, but not with that color; it rather seems corroded.

On gold, brass, or tin, I have not perceived it makes any impression. But the spots on the silver or iron will be the same, whether the bullet be lead, brass, gold, or silver.

On a silver bullet there will also appear a small spot, as well as on the plate below it.

TO CADWALLADER COLDEN, AT NEW YORK.

Mistake, that only Metals and Waters were Conductors, rectified. —Supposition of a Region of electric Fire above our Atmosphere. —Theorem concerning Light.—Poke-Weed a Cure for Cancers.

Read at the Royal Society, of London, Nov. 11, 1756.

Philadelphia, April 23, 1752.

SIR,

IN considering your favor of the 16th past, I recollected my having wrote you answers to some queries concerning the difference between electrics *per se*, and non-electrics, and the effects of air in electrical experiments, which, I apprehend, you may not have received. The date I have forgotten.

We have been used to call those bodies electrics *per se*, which would not conduct the electric fluid: we once imagined that only such bodies contained that fluid; afterwards that they had none of it, and only educed it from other bodies: but further experiments shewed our mistake. It is to be found in all matter we know of; and the distinctions of electrics *per se*, and non-electrics, should now be dropt as improper, and that of *conductors* and *non-conductors* assumed in its place, as I mentioned in those answers.

I do not remember any experiment by which it appeared that high rectified spirit will not conduct; perhaps you have made such. This I know, that wax, rosin, brimstone, and even glass, commonly reputed electrics *per se*, will, when in a fluid state, conduct pretty well. Glass will do it when only red hot. So that my former position, that only metals and waters were conductors, and other bodies more or less such, as they partook of metal or moisture, was too general.

Your conception of the electric fluid, that it is incomparably more subtle than air, is undoubtedly just. It pervades dense matter with the greatest ease; but it does not seem to mix or incorporate willingly with mere air, as it does with other matter. It will not quit common matter to join with air. Air obstructs, in some degree, its motion. An electric atmosphere cannot be communicated at so great a distance, through intervening air, as through a *vacuum*. Who knows then, but there may be, as the ancients thought, a region of this fire above our atmosphere, prevented by our air, and its own too great distance for attraction, from joining our earth? Perhaps where the atmosphere is rarest, this fluid may be densest, and nearer the earth where the atmosphere grows denser, this fluid may be rarer; yet some of it be low enough to attach itself to our highest clouds, and thence they becoming electrified, may be attracted by, and descend towards the earth, and discharge their watery contents, together with that etherial fire. Perhaps the *auroræ boreales* are currents of this fluid in its own region, above our atmosphere, becoming from their motion visible. There is no end to conjectures. As yet we are but novices in this branch of natural knowlege.

You mention several differences of salts in electrical experiments. Were they all equally dry? Salt is apt to acquire moisture from a moist air, and some sorts more than others. When perfectly dried by lying before a fire, or on a stove, none that I have tried will conduct any better than so much glass.

New flannel, if dry and warm, will draw the electric fluid from non-electrics, as well as that which has been worn.

I wish you had the convenience of trying the experiments you seem to have such expectations from, upon various kinds of spirits, salt, earth, &c. Frequently, in a variety of experiments, though we miss what we expected to find, yet something valuable turns out, something surprizing, and instructing, though unthought of.

I thank you for communicating the illustration of the theorem concerning light. It is very curious. But I must own I am much in the *dark* about *light*. I am not satisfied with the doctrine that supposes particles of matter called light continually driven off from the sun's surface, with a swiftness so prodigious! Must not the smallest particle conceiveable have, with such a motion, a force exceeding that of a twenty-four pounder, discharged from a cannon? Must not the sun diminish exceedingly by such a waste of matter; and the planets, instead of drawing nearer to him as some have feared, recede to greater distances through the lessened attraction. Yet these particles, with this amazing motion, will not drive before them, or remove, the least or lightest dust they meet with: and the sun, for aught we know, continues of his antient dimensions, and his attendants move in their antient orbits.

May not all the phenomena of light be more conveniently solved, by supposing universal space filled with a subtle elastic fluid, which, when at rest, is not visible, but whose vibrations affect that fine sense in the eye, as those of air do the grosser organs of the ear? We do not, in the case of sound, imagine that any sonorous particles are thrown off from a bell, for instance, and fly in strait lines to the ear; why must we believe that luminous particles leave the sun and proceed to the eye? Some diamonds, if rubbed, shine in the dark, without losing any part of their matter. I can

K

make an electrical spark as big as the flame of a candle, much brighter, and, therefore, visible further; yet this is without fuel; and I am persuaded, no part of the electric fluid flies off in such case to distant places, but all goes directly, and is to be found in the place to which I destine it. May not different degrees of the vibration of the above mentioned universal medium, occasion the appearance of different colors? I think the electric fluid is always the same; yet I find that weaker and stronger sparks differ in apparent color, some white, blue, purple, red; the strongest, white; weak ones red. Thus different degrees of vibration given to the air produce the seven different sounds in music, analagous to the seven colors, yet the medium, air, is the same.

If the sun is not wasted by expenditure of light, I can easily conceive that he shall otherwise always retain the same quantity of matter; though we should suppose him made of sulphur constantly flaming. The action of fire only *separates* the particles of matter, it does not *annihilate* them. Water, by heat raised into vapor, returns to the earth in rain; and if we could collect all the particles of burning matter that go off in smoke, perhaps they might, with the ashes, weigh as much as the body before it was fired: and if we could put them into the same position with regard to each other, the mass would be the same as before, and might be burnt over again. The chymists have analysed sulphur, and find it composed, in certain proportions, of oil, salt, and earth; and having, by the analysis, discovered those proportions, they can, of those ingredients, make sulphur. So we have only to suppose, that the parts of the sun's sulphur, separated by fire, rise into his atmosphere, and there being freed from the immediate action of the fire, they collect into cloudy masses, and growing, by degrees too heavy to be longer supported, they descend to the Sun, and are burnt over again. Hence the spots appearing on his face, which are observed to diminish daily in size, their consuming edges being of particular brightness.

It is well we are not as poor Galileo was, subject to the inquisition for *philosophical hersey*. My whispers against the orthodox doctrine, in private letters, would be dangerous ; but your writing and printing would be highly criminal. As it is, you must expect some censure, but one heretic will surely excuse another.

I am heartily glad to hear more instances of the success of the poke-weed, in the cure of that horrible evil to the human body, a cancer. You will deserve highly of mankind for the communication. But I find in Boston they are at a loss to know the right plant, some asserting it is what they call *Mechoachan*, others other things. In one of their late papers it is publicly requested that a perfect description may be given of the plant, its places of growth, &c. I have mislaid the paper, or would send it to you. I thought you had described it pretty fully[1].

I am, Sir, &c,

B. FRANKLIN.

1 As the poke-weed, though out of place, is introduced here, we shall translate and insert two extracts of letters from Dr. Franklin to M. Dubourg, the French translator of a small collection of his works, on the same subject.

LONDON, March 27, 1773.

" I apprehend that our poke-weed is what the botanists term *phytolacca*. This plant bears berries as large as peas; the skin is black, but it contains a crimson juice. It is this juice, thickened by evaporation in the sun, which was employed. It caused great pain, but some persons were said to have been cured   I am not quite certain of the facts ; all that I know is, that Dr. Colden had a good opinion of the remedy.

" LONDON, April 23, 1773.

" You will see by the annexed paper by Dr. Solander, that this herb, poke-weed, in which has been found a specific remedy for cancers, is the most common species of *phtolacca*. (*Phviolacca decandria L.*)"

E. KINNERSLEY, AT BOSTON, TO BENJAMIN FRANKLIN, AT
PHILADELPHIA.

New Experiments.—Paradoxes inferred from them.—Difference in
the Electricity of a Globe of Glass charged, and a Globe of Sul-
phur.—Difficulty of ascertaining which is positive and which ne-
gative.

February 3, 1752.

SIR,

I HAVE the following experiments to communicate: I
held in one hand a wire, which was fastened at the other
end to the handle of a pump, in order to try whether the
stroke from the prime conductor, through my arms, would
be any greater than when conveyed only to the surface of
the earth, but could discover no difference.

I placed the needle of a compass on the point of a long
pin, and holding it in the atmosphere of the prime conductor, at the distance of about three inches, found it to whirl
round like the flyers of a jack, with great rapidity.

I suspended with silk a cork ball, about the bigness of a
pea, and presented to it rubbed amber, sealing-wax, and
sulphur, by each of which it was strongly repelled; then I
tried rubbed glass and china, and found that each of these
would attract it, until it became electrified again, and then
it would be repelled as at first; and while thus repelled by
the rubbed glass or china, either of the others when rubbed
would attract it.   Then I electrified the ball, with the wire
of a charged phial, and presented to it rubbed glass (the
stopper of a decanter) and a china tea-cup, by which it was as
strongly repelled as by the wire; but when I presented either
of the other rubbed electrics, it would be strongly attracted,
and when I electrified it by either of these, till it became
repelled, it would be attracted by the wire of the phial, but
be repelled by its coating.

These experiments surprized me very much, and have
induced me to infer the following paradoxes.

1. If a glass globe be placed at one end of a prime-
conductor, and a sulphur one at the other end, both being
equally in good order, and in equal motion, not a spark of

fire can be obtained from the conductor ; but one globe will draw out, as fast as the other gives in.

2. If a phial be suspended on the conductor, with a chain from its coating to the table, and only one of the globes be made use of at a time, 20 turns of the wheel for instance, will charge it ; after which, so many turns of the other wheel will discharge it ; and as many more will charge it again.

3. The globes being both in motion, each having a separate conductor, with a phial suspended on one of them, and the chain of it fastened to the other, the phial will become charged ; one globe charging positively, the other negatively.

4. The phial being thus charged, hang it in like manner on the other conductor ; set both wheels a going again, and the same number of turns that charged it before, will now discharge it ; and the same number repeated, will charge it again.

5. When each globe communicates with the same prime conductor, having a chain hanging from it to the table, one of them, when in motion (but which I cannot say) will draw fire up through the cushion, and discharge it through the chain ; the other will draw it up through the chain, and discharge it through the cushion.

I should be glad if you would send to my house for my sulphur globe, and the cushion belonging to it, and make the trial ; but must caution you not to use chalk on the cushion, some fine powdered sulphur will do better. If, as I expect, you should find the globes to charge the prime conductor differently, I hope you will be able to discover some method of determining which it is that charges positively.

I am, &c.

E. KINNERSLEY.

B. FRANKLIN, TO E. KINNERSLEY.

*Probable Course of the different Attractions and Repulsions of the
two electrified Globes mentioned in the two preceding Letters.*

Philadelphia, March 2, 1752.

SIR,

I THANK you for the experiments communicated. I
sent immediately for your brimstone globe, in order to
make the trials you desired, but found it wanted centres,
which I have not time now to supply; but the first leisure
I will get it fitted for use, try the experiments, and acquaint you with the result.

In the mean time I suspect, that the different attractions
and repulsions you observed, proceeded rather from the
greater or smaller quantities of the fire you obtained from
different bodies, than from its being of a different *kind*, or
having a different *direction*.   In haste,

I am, &c.

B. FRANKLIN.

B. FRANKLIN, TO E. KINNERSLEY.

*Reasons for supposing, that the glass Globe charges positively, and
the Sulphur negatively.   Hint respecting a leather Globe for Experiments when travelling.*

Philadelphia, March 16, 1752.

SIR,

HAVING brought your brimstone globe to work, I tried
one of the experiments you proposed, and was agreeably
surprized to find, that the glass globe being at one end of
the conductor, and the sulphur globe at the other end, both
globes in motion, no spark could be obtained from the conductor, unless when one globe turned slower, or was not in
so good order as the other; and then the spark was only in
proportion to the difference, so that turning equally, or
turning that slowest which worked best, would again bring
the conductor to afford no spark.

I found also, that the wire of a phial charged by the glass globe, attracted a cork ball that had touched the wire of a phial charged by the brimstone globe, and *vice versa*, so that the cork continued to play between the two phials, just as when one phial was charged through the wire, the other through the coating, by the glass globe alone. And two phials charged, the one by the brimstone globe, the other by the glass globe, would be both discharged by bringing their wires together, and shock the person holding the phials.

From these experiments one may be certain that your 2d, 3d, and 4th proposed experiments, would succeed exactly as you suppose, though I have not tried them, wanting time. I imagine it is the glass globe that charges positively, and the sulphur negatively, for these reasons: 1. Though the sulphur globe seems to work equally well with the glass one, yet it can never occasion so large and distant a spark between my knuckle and the conductor, when the sulphur one is working, as when the glass one is used; which, I suppose, is occasioned by this, that bodies of certain bigness cannot so easily part with a quantity of electrical fluid they have and hold attracted *within* their substance, as they can receive an additional quantity *upon* their surface by way of atmosphere. Therefore so much cannot be drawn *out* of the conductor, as can be thrown *on* it. 2. I observe that the stream or brush of fire, appearing at the end of a wire, connected with the conductor, is long, large, and much diverging, when the glass globe is used, and makes a snapping (or rattling) noise: but when the sulphur one is used, it is short, small, and makes a hissing noise; and just the reverse of both happens, when you hold the same wire in your hand, and the globes are worked alternately: the brush is large, long, diverging, and snapping (or rattling) when the sulphur globe is turned; short, small, and hissing, when the glass globe is turned.—When the brush is long, large, and much diverging, the body to which it joins seems to me to be throwing the fire out; and when the contrary appears, it seems to be drinking in. 3. I observe, that when I hold my knuckle before the sulphur globe, while turning, the stream of fire between my knuckle and the globe seems to spread on its surface, as if it flowed from the finger; on the glass globe it is otherwise. 4. The cool wind (or what was called so) that we used to feel as coming from an electrified point, is, I think, more sensible when the glass globe is used, than when the sulphur one. But these are hasty thoughts. As to your fifth paradox, it must likewise be true, if the globes are alternately worked; but if worked together, the fire will neither come up nor go down by the chain, because one globe will drink it as fast as the other produces it.

I should be glad to know, whether the effects would be contrary if the glass globe is solid, and the sulphur globe is hollow; but I have no means at present of trying.

In your journeys, your glass globes meet with accidents, and sulphur ones are heavy and inconvenient.—*Query.* Would not a thin plane of brimstone, cast on a board, serve on occasion as a cushion, while a globe of leather stuffed (properly mounted) might receive the fire from the sulphur, and charge the conductor positively? Such a globe would be in no danger of breaking[2] I think I can conceive how it may be done; but have not time to add more than that I am,

          Yours, &c.   B. FRANKLIN.

The early LETTERS of Dr. Franklin on Electricity having been translated into French, and printed at Paris; the Abbe Mazeas, in a Letter to Dr. Stephen Hales, dated St. Germain, May 20, 1752, gives the following Account (printed in the Philosophical Transactions) of the Experiment made at Marly, in pursuance of that proposed by Dr. Franklin, pages

     SIR,

THE Philadelphian experiments, that Mr. Collinson, a member of the Royal Society, was so kind as to communi-

---

2 The discoveries of the late ingenious Mr. Symmer, on the positive and negative electricity produced by the mutual friction of white and black silk, &c. afford hints for further improvements to be made with this view.

cate to the public, having been universally admired in France, the king desired to see them performed. Wherefore the duke d'Ayen offered his majesty his country-house at St. Germain, where M. de Lor, professor of experimental philosophy, should put those of Philadelphia in execution. His majesty saw them with great satisfaction, and greatly applauded Messieurs Franklin and Collinson. These applauses of his majesty having excited in Messieurs de Buffon, d'Alibard, and de Lor, a desire of verifying the conjectures of Mr. Franklin, upon the analogy of thunder and electricity, they prepared themselves for making the experiment.

M. d'Alibard chose for this purpose a garden situated at Marly, where he placed upon an electrical body a pointed bar of iron, of forty feet high. On the 10th of May, twenty minutes past two in the afternoon, a stormy cloud having passed over the place where the bar stood, those that were appointed to observe it, drew near, and attracted from it sparks of fire, perceiving the same kind of commotions as in the common electrical experiments.

M. de Lor, sensible of the good success of this experiment, resolved to repeat it at his house in the Estrapade, at Paris. He raised a bar of iron ninety-nine feet high, placed upon a cake of resin, two feet square, and three inches thick. On the 18th of May, between four and five in the afternoon, a stormy cloud having passed over the bar, where it remained half an hour, he drew sparks from the bar, like those from the gun barrel, when in the electrical experiments, the globe is only rubbed by the cushion, and they produced the same noise, the same fire, and the same crackling. They drew the strongest sparks at the distance of nine lines, while the rain, mingled with a little hail, fell from the cloud, without either thunder or lightning; this cloud being, according to all appearance, only the consequence of a storm, which happened elsewhere.

I am, with a profound respect,

Your most humble and obedient servant,

G. MAZEAS.

L

*A more particular Account of the Circumstances and Success of
this extraordinary Experiment was laid before the Royal Academy
of Sciences at Paris, three days afterwards, in a Memorial by M.
d'Alibard, viz.*

EXTRAIT D'UN MEMOIRE

DE M. D'ALIBARD.

Lú à l'Académie Royale des Sciences, le 13 Mai, 1752.

" EN suivant la route que M. Franklin nous a tracée,
j'ai obtenu une satisfaction complette. Voici les préparatifs,
le procédé & le succès.

" 1°. J'ai fait faire à Marly-la-ville, située à six lieües
de Paris au milieu d'une belle plaine dont le sol est fort
élevé, une verge de fer ronde, d'environ un pouce de
diametre, longue de 40 pieds, & fort pointuë par son extrémité supérieure; pour lui ménager une pointe plus fine,
je l'ai fait armer d'acier trempé et ensuite brunir, au défaut
de dorure, pour la préserver de la rouille; outre cela, cette
verge de fer est courbée vers son extrémité inférieure en
deux coudes à angles aigus quoiqu'arrondis; le premier
coude est éloigné de deux pieds du bout inférieur, et le
second est en sens contraire à trois pieds du premier.

" 2°. J'ai fait planter dans un jardin trois grosses perches
de 28 à 29 pieds, disposées en triangle, et éloignées les
unes des autres d'environ huit pieds; deux de ces perches
sont contre un mur, et la troisieme est au-dedans du jardin.
Pour les affermir toutes ensemble, l'on à cloué sur chacune
des entretoises à vingt pieds de hauteur; et comme le grand
vent agitoit encore cette espéce d'édifice, l'on a attaché au
haut de chaque perche de longs cordages, qui tenant lieu
d'aubans, répondent par le bas à de bons piquets fortement
enfoncés en terre à plus de 20 pieds des perches.

" 3°. J'ai fait construire entre les deux perches voisines
du mur, et adosser contre ce mur une petite guérite de bois
capable de contenir un homme et une table.

" 4°. J'ait fait placer au milieu de la guérite une petite table d'environ un demi-pied de hauteur : et sur cette table j'ai fait dresser et affermir un tabouret electrique. Ce tabouret n'est autre chose qu'une petite planche quarrée, portée sur trois bouteilles à vin ; il n'est fait de cette matiere que pour suppléer au defaut d'un gâteau de résine qui me manquoit.

" 5°. Tout étant ainsi préparé, j'ai fait elever perpendiculairement la verge de fer au milieu des trois perches, et je l'ai affermie en l'attachant à chacune des perches avec de forts cordons de soie par deux endroits seulement. Les premiers liens sont au haut des perches, environ trois pouces au-dessous de leurs extrémités supérieures ; les seconds vers la moitié de leur hauteur. Le bout inférieur de la verge de fer est solidement appuyé sur le milieu du tabouret electrique, où j'ai fait creuser un trou propre à le recevoir.

" 6°. Comme il étoit important de garantir de la pluie le tabouret et les cordons de soie, parce qu'ils laisseroient passer la matiéré électrique s'ils étoient mouillés, j'ai pris les précautions nécessaires pour en empêcher. C'est dans cette vuë que j'ai mis mon tabouret sous la guérite, et que j'avois fait courber ma verge de fer à angles aigus ; afin que l'eau qui pourroit couler le long de cette verge, ne pût arriver jusques sur le tabouret. C'est aussi dans le même dessein que j'ai fait clouer sur le haut et au milieu de mes perches, à trois pouces au-dessus des cordons de soie, des especes de boîtes formées de trois petites planches d'environ 15 pouces de long, qui couvrent par-dessus et par les côtés une pareille longueur des cordons de soie, sans les toucher.

" Il s'agissoit de faire, dans le tems de l'orage, deux observations sur cette verge de fer ainsi disposée ; l'une étoit de remarquer à sa pointe une aigrette lumineuse, semblable à celle que l'on apperçoit à la pointe d'une aiguille, quand on l'oppose assez prés d'un corps actuellement électrisé ; l'autre étoit de tirer de la verge de fer des étincelles, comme on en tire du canon de fusil dans les expériences électriques ; et afin de se garantir des piquûres de ces étincelles, j'avois attaché le tenon d'un fil d'archal au cordon d'une longue fiole pour lui servir de manche. . . .

" Le Mécredi 10 Mai, 1752, entre deux et trois heures après midi, le nommé Coiffier, ancien dragon, que j'avois chargé de faire les observations en mon absence, ayant entendu un coup de tonnerre assez fort, vole aussitôt à la machine, prend la fiole avec le fil d'archal, présente le tenon du fil à la verge, en voit sortir une petite étincelle brillante, et en entend le pétillement ; il tire une seconde étincelle plus forte que la première et avec plus de bruit ! il appelle ses voisins, et envoie chercher M. le Prieur. Celuici accourt de toutes ses forces ; les paroissiens voyant la précipitation de leur curé, s'imaginent que le pauvre Coiffier a été tué du tonnerre ; l'allarme se répand dans le village ; la grêle qui survient n'empêche point le troupeau de suivre son pasteur. Cet honnête ecclésiastique arrive près de la machine, et voyant qu'il n'y avoit point de danger, met luimême la main à l'œuvre et tire de fortes étincelles. La nuée d'orage et de grêle ne fut pas plus d'un quart-d'heure à passer au zénith de notre machine, et l'on n'entendit que ce seul coup de tonnerre. Sitôt que le nuage fut passé, et qu'on ne tira plus d'étincelles de la verge de fer, M. le Prieur de Marly fit partir le sieur Coiffier lui-même, pour m'apporter la lettre suivante, qu'il m'écrivit à la hâte.

Je vous annonce, Monsieur, ce que vous attendez : l'expérience est complette. Aujourd' hui à deux heures 20 minutes après midi, le tonnerre a grondé directement sur Marly ; le coup a été assez fort. L'envie de vous obliger, et la curiosité m'ont tiré de mon fauteuil, où j'étois occupé à lire: je suis allé chez Coiffier, qui déja m'avoit dépéché un enfant que j'ai rencontré en chemin, pour me prier de venir ; j'ai doublé le pas à travers un torrent de grêle. Arrivé à l'endroit où est placée la tringle coudée, j'ai présenté le fil d'archal, en avançant successivement vers la tringle, à un pouce et demi, ou environ ; il est sorti de la tringle une petite colonne de fer bleuatre sentant le soufre, qui venoit frapper avec une extrême vivacité le tenon du fil d'archal, et occasionnoit un bruit semblable à celui qu'on feroit en frappant sur la tringle avec une clef. J'ai répété l'expérience au moins six fois dans l'espace d'environ quatre minutes, en présence de plusieurs personnes, et chaque expérience que j'ai faite a duré l'espace d'un pater et d'un ave. J'ai voulu continuer ; l'action du feu s'est ralentie peu à peu ; j'ai approché plus près, et n'ai plus tiré que quelques étincelles, et enfin rien n'a paru.

Le coup de tonnerre qui a occasionné cet événément, n'a été suivi d'aucun autre ; tout s'est terminé par une abondance de grêle. J'étois si occupé dans le moment de l'expérience de ce que voyois, qu'ayant été frappé au bras un peu au-dessus du coude, je ne puis dire si c'est en touchant au fil d'archal ou à la tringle: je ne me suis pas plaint du mal que m'avoit fait le coup dans le moment que je l'ai reçu ; mais comme la douleur continuoit, de retour chez moi, j'ai découvert mon bras en présence de Coiffier, et nous avons apperçu une meurtrissure tournante autour du bras, semblable à celle que feroit un coup de fil d'archal, si j'en avois été frappé à nud. En revenant de chez Coiffier, j'ai rencontré M. le Vicaire, M. de Milly, et le maitre d'école, à qui j'ai rapporté ce qui venoit d'arriver ; ils se sont plaints tous les trois qu'ils sentoient une odeur de soufre qui les frappoit davantage à mesure qu'ils s'approchoient de moi: j'ai porté chez moi la même odeur, et mes domestiques s'en sont apperçus sans que je leur aye rien dit.

Voilà, Monsieur, un récit fait à la hâte, mais naïf et vrai j'atteste, et vous pouvez assurer que je suis prêt à rendre témoignage de cet événement dans toutes les occasions. Coiffier a été le premier qui a fait l'expérience et l'a répétée plusieurs fois ; ce n'est qu'à l'occasion de ce qu'il a vu qu'il m'a envoyé prier de venir. S'il étoit besoin d'autres témoins que de lui et de moi, vous les trouveriez. Coiffier presse pour partir.

Je suis avec une respectueuse considération, Monsieur, votre, et. signè RAULET, Prieur de Marly. 10 Mai, 1752.

" On voit, par le détail de cette lettre, que le fait est assez bien constaté pour ne laisser aucun doute à ce sujet.

Le porteur m'a assuré de vive voix qu'il avoit tiré pendant près d'un quart-d'heure avant que M. le Prieur arrivât, en présence de cinq ou six personnes, des étincelles plus fortes et plus bruyantes que celles dont il est parlé dans la lettre. Ces · premieres personnes arrivant successivement, n'osient approcher qu'à 10 ou 12 pas de la machine ; et à cette distance, malgré le plein soleil, ils voyoient les étincelles et entendoient le brúit. . . . .

" Il résulte de toutes les expériences et observations que j'ai rapportées dans ce mémoire, et surtout de la derniere expérience faite à Marly-la-ville, que la matière du tonnerre est incontestablement la même que celle d'l'électricité. L'idée qu'en a eue M. Franklin cesse d'être une conjecture : la voilà devenue une réalité, et j'ose croire que plus on approfondira tout ce qu'il a publié sur l'électricité, plus on reconnoîtra combien la physique lui est redevable pour cette partie."

===

Letter of Mr. W. Watson, F. R. S. to the Royal Society, concerning the electrical Experiments in England upon Thunder-Clouds.

Read Dec. 1752. Trans. Vol. XLVII.

GENTLEMEN,

AFTER the communications, which we have received from several of our correspondents in different parts of the continent, acquainting us with the success of their experiments last summer, in endeavoring to extract the electricity from the atmosphere during a thunder-storm, in consequence of Mr. Franklin's hypothesis, it may be thought extraordinary, that no accounts have been yet laid before you of our success here from the same experiments. That no want of attention, therefore, may be attributed to those here, who have been hitherto conversant in these enquiries, I thought proper to apprize you, that, though several members of the Royal Society, as well as myself, did, upon the first advices from France, prepare and set up the necessary apparatus for this purpose, we were defeated in our expectations, from the uncommon coolness and dampness of the air here, during the whole summer. We had only at London one thunder-storm; viz. on July 20; and then the thunder was accompanied with rain; so that, by wetting the apparatus, the electricity was dissipated too soon to be perceived upon touching those parts of the apparatus, which served to conduct it. This, I say, in general prevented our verifying Mr. Franklin's hypothesis: but our worthy brother, Mr. Canton, was more fortunate. I take the liberty, therefore, of laying before you an extract of a letter, which I received from that gentleman, dated from Spital-square, July 21, 1752.

" I had yesterday, about five in the afternoon, an opportunity of trying Mr. Franklin's experiment of extracting the electrical fire from the clouds; and succeeded, by means of a tin tube, between three and four feet in length, fixed to the top of a glass, one of about eighteen inches. To the upper end of the tin tube, which was not so high as a stack of chimnies on the same house, I fastened three needles with some wire; and to the lower end was soldered a tin cover, to keep the rain from the glass tube, which was set upright in a block of wood. I attended this apparatus as soon after the thunder began as possible, but did not find it in the least electrified, till between the third and fourth clap; when applying my knuckle to the edge of the cover, I felt and heard an electrical spark; and approaching it a second time, I received the spark at the distance of about half an inch, and saw it distinctly. This I repeated four or five times in the space of a minute, but the sparks grew weaker and weaker; and in less than two minutes the tin tube did not appear to be electrified at all. The rain continued during the thunder, but was considerably abated at the time of making the experiment." Thus far Mr. Canton.

Mr. Wilson likewise of the Society, to whom we are much obliged for the trouble he has taken in these pursuits, had an opportunity of verifying Mr. Franklin's hypothesis. He informed me, by a letter from near Chelmsford, in Essex, dated August 12, 1752, that, on that day about noon, he perceived several electrical snaps, during, or rather at the end of a thunder-storm, from no other apparatus than an iron curtain rod, one end of which he put into the neck of a glass phial, and held this phial in his hand. To the other end of the iron he fastened three needles with some silk. This phial, supporting the rod, he held in one hand, and drew snaps from the rod with a finger of his other. This experiment was not made upon any eminence, but in the garden of a gentleman, at whose house he then was.

Dr. Bevis observed, at Mr. Cave's, at St. John's Gate, nearly the same phenomena as Mr. Canton, of which an account has been already laid before the public.

Trifling as the effects here mentioned are, when compared with those which we have received from Paris and Berlin, they are the only ones, that the last summer here has produced; and as they were made by persons worthy of credit, they tend to establish the authenticity of those transmitted from our correspondents.

I flatter myself, that this short account of these matters will not be disagreeable to you; and am,

With the most profound respect, &c.

W. WATSON [3].

Remarks on the Abbé Nollet's Letters to Benjamin Franklin, of Philadelphia, on Electricity: by David Colden, of New York.

Coldenham, in New York, Dec. 4, 1753.

Sir,

IN considering the Abbé Nollet's Letters to Mr. Franklin, I am obliged to pass by all the experiments which are made with, or in, bottles hermetically sealed, or exhausted of air; because, not being able to repeat the experiments, I could not second any thing which occurs to me thereon, by experimental proof. Wherefore, the first point wherein I can dare to give my opinion, is in the Abbé's 4th letter, p. 66, where he undertakes to prove, that the electric matter passes from one surface to another through the entire thick-

---

3 This is the sometime celebrated Watson, bishop of Landaff.

ness of the glass: he takes Mr. Franklin's experiment of the magical picture, and writes thus of it: " When you electrise a pane of glass coated on both sides with metal, it is evident that whatever is placed on the side opposite to that which receives the electricity from the conductor, receives also an evident electrical virtue." Which Mr. Franklin says, is that equal quantity of electric matter, driven out of this side, by what is received from the conductor on the other side; and which will continue to give an electrical virtue to any thing in contact with it, till it is entirely discharged of its electrical fire. To which the Abbé thus objects: " Tell me (says he), I pray you, how much time is necessary for this pretended discharge? I can assure you, that after having maintained the electrisation for hours, this surface, which ought, as it seems to me, to be entirely discharged of its electrical matter, considering either the vast number of sparks that were drawn from it, or the time that this matter had been exposed to the action of the expulsive cause; this surface, I say, appeared rather better electrised thereby, and more proper to produce all the effects of an actual electric body." *Page* 68.

The Abbé does not tell us what those effects were, *all* the effects I could never observe, and those that *are* to be observed can easily be accounted for, by supposing that side to be entirely destitute of electric matter. The most sensible effect of a body charged with electricity is, that when you present your finger to it, a spark will issue from it to your finger: now when a phial, prepared for the Leyden experiment, is hung to the gun-barrel or prime conductor, and you turn the globe in order to charge it; as soon as the electric matter is excited, you can observe a spark to issue from the external surface of the phial to your finger, which, Mr. Franklin says, is the natural electric matter of the glass driven out by that received by the inner surface from the conductor. If it be only drawn out by sparks, a vast number of them may be drawn; but if you take hold of the external surface with your hand, the phial will soon receive all the electric matter it is capable of,

M

and the outside will then be entirely destitute of its electric matter, and no spark can be drawn from it by the finger: here then is a want of that effect, which all bodies charged with electricity have. Some of the effects of an electric body, which I suppose the Abbé has observed in the exterior surface of a charged phial, are, that all light bodies are attracted by it. This is an effect which I have constantly observed, but do not think that it proceeds from an attractive quality in the exterior surface of the phial, but in those light bodies themselves, which seem to be attracted by the phial. It is a constant observation, that when one body has a greater charge of electric matter in it than another (that is in proportion to the quantity they will hold) this body will attract that which has less: now, I suppose, and it is a part of Mr. Franklin's system, that all those light bodies which appear to be attracted, have more electric matter in them than the external surface of the phial has, wherefore they endeavor to attract the phial to them, which is too heavy to be moved by the small degree of force they exert, and yet being greater than their own weight, moves them to the phial. The following experiment will help the imagination in conceiving this. Suspend a cork ball, or a feather, by a silk thread, and electrise it; then bring this ball nigh to any fixed body, and it will appear to be attracted by that body, for it will fly to it: now, by the consent of electricians, the attractive cause is in the ball itself, and not in the fixed body to which it flies: this is a similar case with the apparent attraction of light bodies, to the external surface of a charged phial.

The Abbé says, *p.* 69, " that he can electrise a hundred men, standing on wax, if they hold hands, and if one of them touch one of these surfaces (the exterior) with the end of his finger:" this I know he can, while the phial is charging, but after the phial is charged I am as certain he cannot: that is, hang a phial, prepared for the Leyden experiment, to the conductor, and let a man, standing on the floor, touch the coating with his finger, while the globe is turned, till the electric matter spews out of the hook of the phial, or some part of the conductor, which I take to be the certainest sign that the phial has received all the electric matter it can: after this appears, let the man, who before stood on the floor, step on a cake of wax, where he may stand for hours, and the globe all that time turned, and yet have no appearance of being electrised. After the electric matter was spewed out as above from the hook of the phial prepared for the Leyden experiment, I hung another phial, in like manner prepared, to a hook fixed in the coating of the first, and held this other phial in my hand; now if there was any electric matter transmitted through the glass of the first phial, the second one would certainly receive and collect it; but having kept the phials in this situation for a considerable time, during which the globe was continually turned, I could not perceive that the second phial was in the least charged, for when I touched the hook with my finger, as in the Leyden experiment, I did not feel the least commotion, nor perceive any spark to issue from the hook.

I likewise made the following experiment: having charged two phials (prepared for the Leyden experiment) through their hooks; two persons took each one of these phials in his hand; one held his phial by the coating, the other by the hook, which he could do by removing the communication from the bottom before he took hold of the hook. These persons placed themselves one on each side of me, while I stood on a cake of wax, and took hold of the hook of that phial which was held by its coating (upon which a spark issued, but the phial was not discharged, as I stood on wax) keeping hold of the hook, I touched the coating of the phial that was held by its hook with my other hand, upon which there was a large spark to be seen between my finger and the coating, and both phials were instantly discharged. If the Abbe's opinion be right, that the exterior surface, communicating with the coating, is charged, as well as the interior, communicating with the hook; how can I, who stand on wax, discharge both these phials, when it is well known I could not discharge one of them singly?

Nay, suppose I have drawn the electric matter from both of them, what becomes of it? For I appear to have no additional quantity in me when the experiment is over, and I have not stirred off the wax: wherefore this experiment fully convinces me, that the exterior surface is not charged; and not only so, but that it wants as much electric matter as the inner has of excess: for by this supposition, which is a part of Mr. Franklin's system, the above experiment is easily accounted for, as follows:

When I stand on wax, my body is not capable of receiving all the electric matter from the hook of one phial, which it is ready to give; neither can it give as much to the coating of the other phial as it is ready to take, when one is only applied to me: but when both are applied, the coating takes from me what the hook gives: thus I receive the fire from the first phial at **B**, the exterior surface of which is supplied from the hand at **A**: I give the fire to the second phial at **C**, whose interior surface is discharged by the hand at **D**. This discharge at **D**, may be made evident by receiving that fire into the hook of a third phial, which is done thus: in place of taking the hook of the second phial in your hand, run the wire of a third phial, prepared as for the Leyden experiment, through it, and hold this third phial in your hand, the second one hanging to it, by the ends of the hooks run through each other: when the experiment is performed, this third phial receives the fire at **D**, and will be charged.

When this experiment is considered, I think, it must fully prove that the exterior surface of a charged phial wants electric matter, while the inner surface has an excess of it. One thing more worthy of notice in this experiment is, that I feel no commotion or shock in my arms, though so great a quantity of electric matter passes them instantaneously: I only feel a pricking in the ends of my fingers. This makes me think the Abbé has mistook, when he says, that there is no difference between the shock felt in performing the Leyden experiment, and the pricking felt on drawing simple sparks, except that of greater to less. In the last experiment, as much electric matter went through my arms, as would have given me a very sensible shock, had there been an immediate communication, by my arms, from the hook to the coating of the same phial; because when it was taken into a third phial, and that phial discharged singly through my arms, it gave me a sensible shock. If these experiments prove that the electric matter does not pass through the entire thickness of the glass, it is a necessary consequence that it must always come out where it entered.

The next thing I meet with is in the Abbé's fifth letter, *p.* 88, where he differs from Mr. Franklin, who thinks that the whole power of giving a shock is in the glass itself, and not in the non-electrics in contact with it. The experiments which Mr. Franklin gave to prove this opinion, in his *Observations on the Leyden Bottle*[4], convinced me that he was in the right; and what the Abbé has asserted, in contradiction thereto, has not made me think otherwise. The Abbé, perceiving as I suppose, that the experiments, as Mr. Franklin had performed them, must prove his assertion, alters them without giving any reason for it, and makes them in a manner that proves nothing. Why will he have the phial, into which the water is to be decanted from a charged phial, held in a man's hand? If the power of giving a shock is in the water contained in the phial, it should remain there though decanted into another phial,

---

4 See page 10 to 16, of this volume.

since no non-electric body touched it to take that power off. The phial being placed on wax is no objection, for it cannot take the power from the water, if it had any, but it is a necessary means to try the fact; whereas, that phial's being charged when held in a man's hand, only proves that water will conduct the electric matter. The Abbé owns, *p.* 94, that he had heard this remarked, but says, why is not a conductor of electricity an electric subject? This is not the question; Mr. Franklin never said that water was not an electric subject; he said, that the power of giving a shock was in the glass, and not in the water; and this, his experiments fully prove; so fully, that it may appear impertinent to offer any more; yet as I do not know that the following has been taken notice of by any body before, my inserting of it in this place may be excused. It is this: hang a phial, prepared for the Leyden experiment, to the conductor, by its hook, and charge it; which done, remove the communication from the bottom of the phial: now the conductor shews evident signs of being electrised; for if a thread be tied round it, and its ends left about two inches long, they will extend themselves out like a pair of horns; but if you touch the conductor, a spark will issue from it, and the threads will fall, nor does the conductor shew the least sign of being electrised after this is done. I think that by this touch, I have taken out all the charge of electric matter that was in the conductor, the hook of the phial, and water or filings of iron contained in it; which is no more than we see all non-electric bodies will receive: yet, the glass of the phial retains its power of giving a shock, as any one will find that pleases to try. This experiment fully evinces, that the water in the phial contains no more electric matter than it would do in an open bason, and has not any of that great quantity which produces the shock and is only retained by the glass. If after the spark is drawn from the conductor, you touch the coating of the phial (which all this while is supposed to hang in the air, free from any non-electric body) the threads on the conductor will instantly start up, and shew that the conductor is electrised. It receives this electrisation from the inner surface of the phial, which, when the outer surface can receive what it wants from the hand applied to it, will give as much as the bodies in contact with it can receive, or if they be large enough, all that it has of excess. It is diverting to see how the threads will rise and fall by touching the coating and conductor of the phial alternately. May it not be that the difference between the charged side of the glass, and the outer or emptied side, being lessened by touching the hook or the conductor; the outer side can receive from the hand which touched it, and by its receiving, the inner side cannot retain so much; and for that reason so much as it cannot contain electrises the water, or filings and conductor; for it seems to be a rule, that the one side must be emptied in the same proportion that the other is filled: though this from experiment appears evident, yet it is still a mystery not to be accounted for.

I am in many places of the Abbé's book surprised to find that experiments have succeeded so differently at Paris, from what they did with Mr. Franklin, and as I have always observed them to do. The Abbé, in making experiments to find the difference between the two surfaces of a charged glass, will not have the phial placed on wax: for, says he, dont you know that being placed on a body originally electric, it quickly loses its virtue? I cannot imagine what should have made the Abbé think so: it certainly is contradictory to the notions commonly received of electrics *per se;* and by experiment I find it entirely otherwise: for having several times left a charged phial, for that purpose, standing on wax for hours, I found it to retain as much of its charge as another that stood at the same time on a table. I left one standing on wax from ten o'clock at night till eight the next morning, when I found it retain a sufficient quantity of its charge, to give me a sensible commotion in my arms, though the room in which the phial stood had been swept in that time, which must have raised much dust to facilitate the discharge of the phial.

I find that a cork-ball suspended between two bottles, the one fully and the other but little charged, will not play between them, but is driven into a situation that makes a triangle with the hook of the phials : though the Abbe has asserted the contrary of this, p. 101, in order to account for the playing of a cork-ball between the wire thrust into the phial, and one that rises up from its coating. The phial which is least charged must have more electric matter given to it, in proportion to its bulk, than the cork ball receives from the hook of the full phial.

The Abbè says, p. 103, "That a piece of metal leaf hung to a silk thread and electrised, will be repelled by the bottom of a charged phial held by its hook in the air :" this I find constantly otherwise, it is with me always first attracted and then repelled : it is necessary, in charging the leaf to be careful, that it does not fly off to some non-electric body, and so discharge itself when you think it is charged ; it is difficult to keep it from flying to your own wrist, or to some part of your body.

The Abbé, p. 108, says, that it is not impossible, as Mr. Franklin says it is, to charge a phial while there is a communication formed between its coating and its hook." I have always found it impossible to charge such a phial so as to give a shock : indeed, if it hang on the conductor without a communication from it, you may draw a spark from it as you may from any body that hangs there, but this is very different from being charged in such a manner as to give a shock. The Abbé, in order to account for the little quantity of electric matter that is to be found in the phial, says, " that it rather follows the metal than the glass, and that it is spewed out into the air from the coating of the phial." I wonder how it comes not to do so too, when it sifts through the glass, and charges the exterior surface, according to the Abbè's system !

The Abbè's objection against Mr. Franklin's two last experiments, I think, have little weight in them : he seems, indeed, much at a loss what to say, wherefore he taxes Mr. Franklin with having concealed a material part of the experiment; a thing too mean for any gentleman to be charged with, who has not shown as great a partiality in relating experiments, as the Abbé has done.

TO DR. PRINGLE, IN LONDON.

Relating a curious Instance of the Effect of Oil on Water.

Philadelphia, Dec. 1, 1762.

SIR,

DURING our passage to Madeira, the weather being warm, and the cabin windows constantly open, for the benefit of the air, the candles at night flared and run very much, which was an inconvenience. At Madeira we got oil to burn, and with a common glass tumbler or breaker, slung in wire, and suspended to the cieling of the cabin, and a little wire hoop for the wick, furnished with corks to float on the oil, I made an Italian lamp, that gave us very good light all over the table.—The glass at bottom contained water to about one third of its height; another third was taken up with oil; the rest was left empty that the sides of the glass might protect the flame from the wind. There is nothing remarkable in all this; but what follows is particular. At supper, looking on the lamp, I remarked, that though the surface of the oil was perfectly tranquil, and duly preserved its position and distance with regard to the brim of the glass, the water under the oil was in great commotion, rising and falling in irregular waves, which continued during the whole evening. The lamp was kept burning as a watch light all night, till the oil was spent, and the water only remained. In the morning I observed, that though the motion of the ship continued the same, the water was now quiet, and its surface as tranquil as that of the oil had been the evening before. At night again, when oil was put upon it, the water resumed its irregular motions, rising in high waves almost to the surface of the oil, but without disturbing the smooth level of that surface. And this was repeated every day during the voyage.

N

Since my arrival in America, I have repeated the experiment frequently thus: I have put a pack-thread round a tumbler, with strings of the same, from each side, meeting above it in a knot at about a foot distance from the top of the tumbler. Then putting in as much water as would fill about one third part of the tumbler, I lifted it up by the knot, and swung it to and fro in the air; when the water appeared to keep its place in the tumbler as steadily as if it had been ice. But pouring gently in upon the water about as much oil, and then again swinging it in the air as before, the tranquillity before possessed by the water, was transferred to the surface of the oil, and the water under it was agitated with the same commotions as at sea.

I have shewn this experiment to a number of ingenious persons. Those who are but slightly acquainted with the principles of hydrostatics, &c. are apt to fancy immediately that they understand it, and readily attempt to explain it; but their explanations have been different, and to me not very intelligible. Others, more deeply skilled in those principles, seem to wonder at it, and promise to consider it. And I think it is worth considering: for a new appearance, if it cannot be explained by our old principles, may afford us new ones, of use perhaps in explaining some other obscure parts of natural knowlege.

I am, &c.

B. FRANKLIN.

Of the Stilling of Waves by means of Oil. Extracted from sundry Letters between Dr. Benjamin Franklin, William Brownrigg, M. D. F. R. S. and the Rev. Mr. Farish.

Read at the Royal Society, June 2, 1774.

Dr. Brownrigg to Dr. Franklin.

Ormathwaite, January 27, 1773.

BY the enclosed from an old friend, a worthy clergyman at Carlisle, whose great learning and extensive knowlege in most sciences would have more distinguished him, had he been placed in a more conspicuous point of view, you will find, that he had heard of your experiment on Derwent Lake, and has thrown together what he could collect on that subject; to which I have subjoined one experiment from the relation of another gentleman.

Extract of a Letter from the Rev. Mr. Farish, to Dr. Brownrigg.

I SOME time ago met with Mr. Dun, who surprised me with an account of an experiment you had tried upon the Derwent water, in company with Sir John Pringle and Dr. Franklin. According to his representation, the water, which had been in great agitation before, was instantly calmed upon pouring in only a very small quantity of oil, and that to so great a distance round the boat as seemed incredible. I have since had the same accounts from others, but I suspect all of a little exaggeration. Pliny mentions this property of oil as known particularly to the divers, who made use of it in his days, in order to have a more steady light at the bottom[4]. The sailors, I have been told, have observed something of the same kind in our days, that the water is always remarkably smoother, in the wake of a ship that has been newly tallowed, than it is in one that is foul. Mr. Pennant also mentions an observation of the like nature made by the seal catchers in Scotland. *Brit. Zool.* Vol. IV. *Article* Seal. When these animals are devouring a very oily fish, which they always do under water, the waves above are observed to be remarkably smooth, and by this mark the fishermen know where to look for them. Old Pliny does not usually meet with all the credit I am inclined to think he deserves. I shall be glad to have an authentic

Note by Dr. Brownrigg.

4 Sir Gilfred Lawson, who served long in the army at Gibraltar, assures me, that the fishermen in that place are accustomed to pour a little oil on the sea, in order to still its motion, that they may be enabled to see the oysters lying at its bottom, which are there very large, and which they take up with a proper instrument. This Sir Gilfred had often seen there performed, and said the same was practised on other parts of the Spanish coast.

account of the Keswick experiment, and if it comes up to the representations that have been made of it, I shall not much hesitate to believe the old gentleman in another more wonderful phenomenon he relates of stilling a tempest only by throwing up a little vinegar into the air.

***

Dr. Franklin to Dr. Brownrigg.

London, Nov. 7, 1773.

DEAR SIR,

I THANK you for the remarks of your learned friend at Carlisle: I had, when a youth, read and smiled at Pliny's account of a practice among the seamen of his time, to still the waves in a storm by pouring oil into the sea; which he mentions, as well as the use made of oil by the divers; but the stilling a tempest by throwing vinegar into the air had escaped me. I think with your friend, that it has been of late too much the mode to slight the learning of the ancients. The learned, too, are apt to slight too much the knowlege of the vulgar. The cooling by evaporation was long an instance of the latter. This art of smoothing the waves by oil is an instance of both.

Perhaps you may not dislike to have an account of all I have heard, and learnt, and done in this way. Take it if you please as follows:

In 1757, being at sea in a fleet of 96 sail bound against Louisbourg, I observed the wakes of two of the ships to be remarkably smooth, while all the others were ruffled by the wind, which blew fresh. Being puzzled with the differing appearance, I at last pointed it out to our captain, and asked him the meaning of it. " The cooks," says he, " have, I suppose, been just emptying their greasy water through the scuppers, which has greased the sides of those ships a little;" and this answer he gave me with an air of some little contempt, as to a person ignorant of what every body else knew. In my own mind I at first slighted his solution, though I was not able to think of another, but recollecting what I had formerly read in Pliny, I resolved to make some experiment of the effect of oil on water, when I should have opportunity.

Afterwards being again at sea in 1762, I first observed the wonderful quietness of oil on agitated water, in the swinging glass lamp I made to hang up in the cabin, as described in my printed paper[5]. This I was continually looking at and considering, as an appearance to me inexplicable. An old sea captain, then a passenger with me, thought little of it, supposing it an effect of the same kind with that of oil put on water to smooth it, which he said was a practice of the Bermudians when they would strike fish, which they could not see if the surface of the water was ruffled by the wind. This practice I had never before heard of, and was obliged to him for the information; though I thought him mistaken as to the sameness of the experiment, the operations being different as well as the effects. In one case, the water is smooth till the oil is put on, and then becomes agitated. In the other it is agitated before the oil is applied, and then becomes smooth. The same gentleman told me, he had heard it was a practice with the fishermen of Lisbon when about to return into the river (if they saw before them too great a surf upon the bar, which they apprehended might fill their boats in passing) to empty a bottle or two of oil, into the sea, which would suppress the breakers, and allow them to pass safely. A confirmation of this I have not since had an opportunity of obtaining: but discoursing of it with another person, who had often been in the Mediterranean, I was informed, that the divers there, who, when under water in their business, need light, which the curling of the surface interrupts by the refractions of so many little waves, let a small quantity of oil now and then out of their mouths, which rising to the surface smooths it, and permits the light to come down to them. All these informations I at times revolved in my mind, and wondered to find no mention of them in our books of experimental philosophy.

---

5 See the preceding paper.

At length being at Clapham, where there is, on the common, a large pond, which I observed one day to be very rough with the wind, I fetched out a cruet of oil, and dropt a little of it on the water. I saw it spread itself with surprising swiftness upon the surface; but the effect of smoothing the waves was not produced: for I had applied it first on the leeward side of the pond, where the waves were largest, and the wind drove my oil back upon the shore. I then went to the windward side where they began to form; and there the oil, though not more than a tea spoonful, produced an instant calm over a space several yards square, which spread amazingly, and extended itself gradually till it reached the lee side, making all that quarter of the pond, perhaps half an acre, as smooth as a looking glass.

After this I contrived to take with me, whenever I went into the country, a little oil in the upper hollow joint of my bamboo cane, with which I might repeat the experiment as opportunity should offer, and I found it constantly to succeed.

In these experiments, one circumstance struck me with particular surprise. This was the sudden, wide, and forcible spreading of a drop of oil on the face of the water, which I do not know that any body has hitherto considered. If a drop of oil is put on a highly polished marble table, or on a looking-glass that lies horizontally, the drop remains in its place, spreading very little. But when put on water, it spreads instantly many feet round, becoming so thin as to produce the prismatic colors, for a considerable space, and beyond them so much thinner as to be invisible, except in its effect of smoothing the waves at a much greater distance. It seems as if a mutual repulsion between its particles took place as soon as it touched the water, and a repulsion so strong as to act on other bodies swimming on the surface, as straw, leaves, chips, &c. forcing them to recede every way from the drop, as from a centre, leaving a large clear space. The quantity of this force, and the distance to which it will operate, I have not yet ascertained; but I think it a curious enquiry, and I wish to understand whence it arises.

'In our journey to the north, when we had the pleasure of seeing you at Ormathwaite, we visited the celebrated Mr. Smeaton, near Leeds. Being about to show him the smoothing experiment on a little pond near his house, an ingenious pupil of his, Mr. Jessop, then present, told us of an odd appearance on that pond, which had lately occurred to him. He was about to clean a little cup in which he kept oil, and he threw upon the water some flies that had been drowned in the oil. These flies presently began to move, and turned round on the water very rapidly, as if they were vigorously alive, though on examination he found they were not so. I immediately concluded that the motion was occasioned by the power of the repulsion above mentioned, and that the oil issuing gradually from the spungy body of the fly continued the motion. He found some more flies drowned in oil, with which the experiment was repeated before us. To show that it was not any effect of life recovered by the flies, I imitated it by little bits of oiled chips and paper cut in the form of a comma, of the size of a common fly; when the stream of repelling particles issuing from the point made the comma turn round the contrary way. This is not a chamber experiment; for it cannot be well repeated in a bowl or dish of water on a table. A considerable surface of water is necessary to give room for the expansion of a small quantity of oil. In a dish of water, if the smallest drop of oil be let fall in the middle, the whole surface is presently covered with a thin greasy film proceeding from the drop; but as soon as that film has reached the sides of the dish, no more will issue from the drop, but it remains in the form of oil, the sides of the dish putting a stop to its dissipation by prohibiting the farther expansion of the film.

Our friend, Sir John Pringle, being soon after in Scotland, learned there, that those employed in the herring fishery could at a distance see where the shoals of herrings were, by the smoothness of the water over them, which might possibly be occasioned, he thought, by some oiliness proceeding from their bodies.

A gentleman from Rhode Island told me, it had been remarked, that the harbor of Newport was ever smooth while any whaling vessels were in it: which probably arose from hence, that the blubber which they sometimes bring loose in the hold, or the leakage of their barr.s, might afford some oil, to mix with that water, which from time to time they pump out to keep their vessel free, and that some oil might spread over the surface of the water in the harbor, and prevent the forming of any waves.

This prevention I would thus endeavor to explain.

There seems to be no natural repulsion between water and air, such as to keep them from coming into contact with each other. Hence we find a quantity of air in water; and if we extract it by means of the air-pump, the same water, again exposed to the air, will soon imbibe an equal quantity.

Therefore air in motion, which is wind, in passing over the smooth surface of water, may rub, as it were, upon that surface, and raise it into wrinkles, which if the wind continues, are the elements of future waves.

The smallest wave once raised does not immediately subside, and leave the neighboring water quiet: but in subsiding raises nearly as much of the water next to it, the friction of the parts making little difference. Thus a stone dropped in a pool raises first a single wave round itself; and leaves it, by sinking to the bottom; but that first wave subsiding raises a second, the second a third, and so on in circles to a great extent.

A small power continually operating will produce a great action. A finger applied to a weighty suspended bell can at first move it but little; if repeatedly applied, though with no greater strength, the motion increases till the bell swings to its utmost height, and with a force that cannot be resisted by the whole strength of the arm and body. Thus the small first-raised waves, being continually acted upon by the wind, are, though the wind does not increase in strength, continually increased in magnitude, rising highly and extending their bases, so as to include a vast mass of water in each wave, which in its motion acts with great violence.

But if there be a mutual repulsion between the particles of oil, and no attraction between oil and water, oil dropped on water will not be held together by adhesion to the spot whereon it falls; it will not be imbibed by the water; it will be at liberty to expand itself; and it will spread on a surface that, besides being smooth to the most perfect degree of polish, prevents, perhaps by repelling the oil, all immediate contact, keeping it at a minute distance from itself: and the expansion will continue till the mutual repulsion between the particles of the oil is weakened and reduced to nothing by their distance.

Now I imagine that the wind, blowing over water thus covered with a film of oil, cannot easily *catch* upon it, so as to raise the first wrinkles, but slides over it, and leaves it smooth as it finds it. It moves a little the oil indeed, which being between it and the water, serves it to slide with, and prevents friction, as oil does between those parts of a machine, that would otherwise rub hard together. Hence the oil dropped on the windward side of a pond proceeds gradually to leeward, as may be seen by the smoothness it carries with it, quite to the opposite side. For the wind being thus prevented from raising the first wrinkles, that I call the elements of waves, cannot produce waves, which are to be made by continually acting upon, and enlarging those elements, and thus the whole pond is calmed.

Totally therefore we might suppress the waves in any required place, if we could come at the windward place where they take their rise. This in the ocean can seldom if ever be done. But perhaps something may be done on particular occasions, to moderate the violence of the waves when we are in the midst of them, and prevent their breaking where that would be inconvenient.

For when the wind blows fresh, there are continually rising on the back of every great wave a number of small ones, which roughen its surface, and give the wind hold, as it were, to push it with greater force. This hold is diminished, by preventing the generation of those small ones. And possibly too, when a wave's surface is oiled, the wind in

O

passing over it, may rather in some degree press it down, and contribute to prevent it rising again, instead of promoting it.

This as mere conjecture would have little weight, if the apparent effects of pouring oil into the midst of waves were not considerable, and as yet not otherwise accounted for.

When the wind blows so fresh, as that the waves are not sufficiently quick in obeying its impulse, their tops being thinner and lighter are pushed forward, broken, and turned over in a white foam. Common waves lift a vessel without entering it; but these when large sometimes break above and pour over it, doing great damage.

That this effect might in any degree be prevented or the height and violence of waves in the sea moderated, we had no certain account; Pliny's authority for the practice of seamen in his time being slighted. But discoursing lately on this subject with his excellency Count Bentinck, of Holland, his son the honorable captain Bentinck, and the learned professor Allemand (to all whom I showed the experiment of smoothing in a windy day the large piece of water at the head of the Green Park) a letter was mentioned, which had been received by the count from Batavia, relative to the saving of a Dutch ship in a storm by pouring oil into the sea. I much desired to see that letter, and a copy of it was promised me, which I afterward received.

Extract of a letter from Mr. Tengnagel to Count Bentinck, dated at Batavia, the 5th of January, 1770.

" NEAR the islands Paul and Amsterdam, we met with a storm, which had nothing particular in it worthy of being communicated to you, except that the captain found himself obliged for greater safety in wearing the ship, to pour oil into the sea, to prevent the waves breaking over her, which had an excellent effect, and succeeded in preserving us. As he poured out but a little at a time, the East India Company owes perhaps its ship to only six demi-ames of olive-oil. I was present upon deck when this was done;

and I should not have mentioned this circumstance to you, but that we have found people here so prejudiced against the experiment, as to make it necessary for the officers on board and myself to give a certificate of the truth on this head, of which we made no difficulty."

On this occasion, I mentioned to captain Bentinck, a thought which had occurred to me in reading the voyages of our late circumnavigators, particularly where accounts are given of pleasant and fertile islands which they much desired to land upon, when sickness made it more necessary, but could not effect a landing through a violent surf breaking on the shore, which rendered it impracticable. My idea was, that possibly by sailing to and fro at some distance from such lee-shore, continually pouring oil into the sea, the waves might be so much depressed, and lessened before they reached the shore, as to abate the height and violence of the surf, and permit a landing; which, in such circumstances, was a point of sufficient importance to justify the expense of the oil that might be requisite for the purpose. That gentleman, who is ever ready to promote what may be of public utility, though his own ingenious inventions have not always met with the countenance they merited, was so obliging as to invite me to Portsmouth, where an opportunity would probably offer, in the course of a few days, of making the experiment on some of the shores about Spithead, in which he kindly proposed to accompany me, and to give assistance with such boats as might be necessary. Accordingly, about the middle of October last, I went with some friends to Portsmouth: and a day of wind happening, which made a lee-shore between Hasler-hospital and the point near Jillkecker, we went from the Centaur with the long-boat and barge towards that shore. Our disposition was this: the long-boat was anchored about a quarter of a mile from the shore; part of the company were landed behind the point (a place more sheltered from the sea) who came round and placed themselves opposite to the long boat, where they might observe the surf, and note if any change occurred in it upon using the oil. Another party, in the barge, plied to windward of the long boat, as far from her as she was from the shore, making trips of about half a mile each, pouring oil continually out of a large stone-bottle, through a whole in the cork, somewhat bigger than a goose-quill. The experiment had not, in the main point, the success we wished, for no material difference was observed in the height or force of the surf upon the shore; but those who were in the long-boat could observe a tract of smoothed water, the whole of the distance in which the barge poured the oil, and gradually spreading in breadth towards the long-boat. I call it smoothed, not that it was laid level; but because, though the swell continued, its surface was not roughened by the wrinkles, or smaller waves, before-mentioned; and none or very few white caps (or waves whose tops turn over in foam) appeared in that whole space, though to windward and leeward of it there were plenty; and a wherry, that came round the point under sail, in her way to Portsmouth, seemed to turn into that tract of choice, and to use it from end to end, as a piece of turnpike-road.

It may be of use to relate the circumstances of an experiment that does not succeed, since they may give hints of amendment in future trials: it is therefore I have been thus particular. I shall only add what I apprehend may have been the reason of our disappointment.

I conceive, that the operation of oil on water is, first, to prevent the raising of new waves by the wind; and, secondly, to prevent its pushing those before raised with such force, and consequently their continuance of the same repeated height, as they would have done, if their surface were not oiled. But oil will not prevent waves being raised by another power, by a stone, for instance, falling into a still pool; for they then rise by the mechanical impulse of the stone, which the greasiness on the surrounding water cannot lessen or prevent, as it can prevent the winds catching the surface and raising it into waves. Now waves once raised, whether by the wind or any other power, have the same mechanical operation, by which they continue to rise and fall, as a *pendulum* will continue to swing, a long time after the force ceases to act by which the motion was first produced: that motion will, however, cease in time; but time is necessary. Therefore, though oil spread on an agitated sea may weaken the push of the wind on those waves whose surfaces are covered by it, and so, by receiving fresh impulse, they may gradually subside; yet a considerable time, or a distance through which they will take time to move, may be necessary to make the effect sensible on any shore in a diminution of the surf: for we know, that when wind ceases suddenly, the waves it has raised do not as suddenly subside, but settle gradually, and are not quite down till after the wind has ceased. So though we should, by oiling them, take off the effect of wind on waves already raised, it is not to be expected that those waves should be instantly levelled. The motion they have received, will for some time, continue; and if the shore is not far distant, they arrive there so soon, that their effect upon it will not be visibly diminished. Possibly therefore, if we had begun our operations at a greater distance, the effect might have been more sensible. And perhaps we did not pour oil in sufficient quantity. Future experiments may determine this.

I was, however, greatly obliged to captain Bentinck, for the chearful and ready aids he gave me: and I ought not to omit mentioning Mr. Banks, Dr. Solander, general Carnac, and Dr. Blagden, who all assisted at the experiment, during that blustering unpleasant day, with a patience and activity that could only be inspired by a zeal for the improvement of knowlege, such especially as might possibly be of use to men in situations of distress.

I would wish you to communicate this to your ingenious friend, Mr. Farish, with my respects: and believe me to be, with sincere esteem,

   Dear, Sir,

     Your most obedient, humble servant,

       B. FRANKLIN.

TO PETER COLLINSON, LONDON.

Electrical Kite.

Philadelphia, Oct. 16, 1752.

SIR,

AS frequent mention is made in public papers from Europe of the success of the Philadelphia experiment for drawing the electric fire from clouds by means of pointed rods of iron erected on high buildings, &c. it may be agreeable to the curious to be informed that the same experiment has succeeded in Philadelphia, though made in a different and more easy manner, which is as follows :

Make a small cross of two light strips of cedar, the arms so long as to reach to the four corners of a large thin silk handkerchief when extended ; tie the corners of the handkerchief to the extremities of the cross, so you have the body of a kite ; which being properly accommodated with a tail, loop, and string, will rise in the air, like those made of paper ; but this being of silk is fitter to bear the wet and wind of a thunder gust without tearing. To the top of the upright stick of the cross is to be fixed a very sharp pointed wire, rising a foot or more above the wood, To the end of the twine, next the hand, is to be tied a silk ribbon, and where the silk and twine join, a key may be fastened. This kite is to be raised when a thunder-gust appears to be coming on, and the person who holds the string must stand within a door or window, or under some cover, so that the silk ribbon may not be wet ; and care must be taken that the twine does not touch the frame of the door or window. As soon as any of the thunder clouds come over the kite, the pointed wire will draw the electric fire from them, and the kite, with all the twine, will be electrified, and the loose filaments of the twine will stand out every way, and be attracted by an approaching finger. And when the rain has wetted the kite and twine, so that it can conduct the electric fire freely, you will find it stream out plentifully from the key on the approach of your knuckle. At this key the phial may be charged; and from electric fire thus obtained, spirits may be kindled, and all the other electric experiments be performed, which are usually done by the help of a rubbed glass globe or tube, and thereby the sameness of the electric matter with that of lightning completely demonstrated.

B. FRANKLIN.

TO PETER COLLINSON, LONDON.

Hypothesis, of the Sea being the grand source of Lightning, retracted. Positive, and sometimes negative, Electricity of the Clouds discovered.—New Experiments and Conjectures in support of this Discovery.—Observations recommended for ascertaining the Direction of the electric Fluid.—Size of Rods for Conductors to Buildings.—Appearance of a Thunder-Cloud described.

Philadelphia, September, 1753.

SIR,

IN my former paper on this subject, written first in 1747, enlarged and sent to England in 1749, I considered the sea as the grand source of lightning, imagining its luminous appearance to be owing to electric fire produced by friction between the particles of water and those of salt. Living far from the sea, I had then no opportunity of making experiments on the sea-water, and so embraced this opinion too hastily.

For in 1750, and 1751, being occasionally on the sea-coast, I found, by experiments, that sea-water in a bottle, though at first it would by agitation appear luminous, yet in a few hours it lost that virtue : *hence and from this,* that I could not by agitating a solution of sea-salt in water produce any light, I first began to doubt of my former hypothesis, and to suspect that the luminous appearance in sea-water must be owing to some other principles.

I then considered whether it were not possible, that the particles of air, being electrics *per se,* might, in hard gales of wind, by their friction against trees, hills, buildings, &c.

as so many minute electric globes, rubbing against non-electric cushions, draw the electric fire from the earth, and that the rising vapors might receive the fire from the air, and by such means the clouds become electrified.

If this were so, I imagined that by forcing a constant violent stream of air against my prime conductor, by bellows, I should electrify it *negatively;* the rubbing particles of air, drawing from it part of its natural quantity of the electric fluid. I accordingly made the experiment, but it did not succeed.

In September 1752, I erected an iron rod to draw the lightning down into my house, in order to make some experiments on it, with two bells to give notice when the rod should be electrified: a contrivance obvious to every electrician.

I found the bells rang sometimes when there was no lightning or thunder, but only a dark cloud over the rod; that sometimes after a flash of lightning they would suddenly stop; and at other times, when they had not rang before, they would, after a flash, suddenly begin to ring; that the electricity was sometimes very faint, so that when a small spark was obtained, another could not be got for some time after; at other times the sparks would follow extremely quick, and once I had a continual stream from bell to bell, the size of a crow quill: even during the same gust there were considerable variations.

In the winter following I conceived an experiment, to try whether the clouds were electrified *positively* or *negatively;* but my pointed rod, with its apparatus, becoming out of order, I did not refit it till towards the spring, when I expected the warm weather would bring on more frequent thunder-clouds.

The experiment was this: to take two phials; charge one of them with lightning from the iron rod, and give the other an equal charge by the electric glass globe, through the prime conductor: when charged, to place them on a table within three or four inches of each other, a small cork ball being suspended by a fine silk thread from the cieling, so as it might play between the wires. If both bottles then were electrified *positively*, the ball being attracted and repelled by one, must be also repelled by the other. If the one *positively*, and the other *negatively;* then the ball would be attracted and repelled alternately by each, and continue to play between them as long as any considerable charge remained.

Being very intent on making this experiment, it was no small mortification to me, that I happened to be abroad during two of the greatest thunder-storms we had early in the spring, and though I had given orders in my family, that if the bells rang when I was from home, they should catch some of the lightning for me in electrical phials, and they did so, yet it was mostly dissipated before my return, and in some of the other gusts, the quantity of lightning I was able to obtain was so small, and the charge so weak, that I could not satisfy myself: yet I sometimes saw what heightened my suspicions, and inflamed my curiosity.

At last, on the 12th of April, 1753, there being a smart gust of some continuance, I charged one phial pretty well with lightning, and the other equally, as near as I could judge, with electricity from my glass globe; and, having placed them properly, I beheld, with great surprise and pleasure, the cork ball play briskly between them; and was convinced that one bottle was electrised *negatively*.

I repeated this experiment several times during the gust, and in eight succeeding gusts, always with the same success; and being of opinion (for reasons I formerly gave in my letter to Mr. Kinnersley, since printed in London) that the glass globe electrises *positively*, I concluded that the clouds are *always* electrised *negatively*, or have always in them less than their natural quantity of the electric fluid.

Yet notwithstanding so many experiments, it seems I concluded too soon; for at last, June the 6th, in a gust which continued from five o'clock, P. M. to seven, I met with one cloud that was electrised positively, though several that passed over my rod before, during the same gust, were in the negative state. This was thus discovered.

P

I had another concurring experiment, which I often repeated, to prove the negative state of the clouds, viz. while
the bells were ringing, I took the phial charged from the
glass globe, and applied its wire to the erected rod, considering, that if the clouds were electrised *positively*, the rod
which received its electricity from them must be so too ; and
then the additional *positive* electricity of the phial would
make the bells ring faster :—but, if the clouds were in a
negative state, they must exhaust the electric fluid from my
rod, and bring that into the same negative state with themselves, and then the wire of a positively charged phial, supplying the rod with what it wanted (which it was obliged
otherwise to draw from the earth by means of the pendulous
brass ball playing between the two bells) the ringing would
cease till the bottle was discharged.

In this manner I quite discharged into the rod several
phials, that were charged from the glass globe, the electric
fluid streaming from the wire to the rod, till the wire would
receive no spark from the finger; and, during this supply to
the rod from the phial, the bells stopped ringing; but by
continuing the application of the phial wire to the rod, I exhausted the natural quantity from the inside surface of the
same phials, or, as I call it, charged them *negatively*.

At length, while I was charging a phial by my glass globe,
to repeat this experiment, my bells, of themselves, stopped
ringing, and, after some pause, began to ring again.—But
now, when I approached the wire of the charged phial to the
rod, instead of the usual stream that I expected from the
wire to the rod, there was no spark ; not even when I brought
the wire and the rod to touch ; yet the bells continued ringing vigorously, which proved to me, that the rod was then
positively electrified, as well as the wire of the phial, and
equally so ; and, consequently, that the particular cloud then
over the rod was in the same positive state.   This was near
the end of the gust.

But this was a single experiment, which, however, destroys my first too general conclusion, and reduces me to
this : *That the clouds of a thunder-gust are most commonly*

in a negative state of electricity, but sometimes in a positive state.

The latter I believe is rare; for though I soon after the last experiment set out on a journey to Boston, and was from home most part of the summer, which prevented my making farther trials and observations; yet Mr. Kinnersley returning from the islands just as I left home, pursued the experiments during my absence, and informs me that he always found the clouds in the *negative* state.

So that, for the most part, in thunder-strokes, *it is the earth that strikes into the clouds, and not the clouds that strike into the earth.*

Those who are versed in electric experiments, will easily conceive, that the effects and appearances must be nearly the same in either case; the same explosion, and the same flash between one cloud and another, and between the clouds and mountains, &c. the same rending of trees, walls, &c. which the electric fluid meets with in its passage, and the same fatal shock to animal bodies; and that pointed rods fixed on buildings, or masts of ships, and communicating with the earth or sea, must be of the same service in restoring the equilibrium silently between the earth and clouds, or in conducting a flash or stroke, if one should be, so as to save harmless the house or vessel: for points have equal power to throw off, as to draw on the electric fire, and rods will conduct up as well as down.

But though the light gained from these experiments makes no alteration in the practice, it makes a considerable one in the theory. And now we as much need an hypothesis to explain by what means the clouds become negatively, as before to shew how they became positively electrified.

I cannot forbear venturing some few conjectures on this occasion: they are what occur to me at present, and though future discoveries should prove them not wholly right, yet they may in the mean time be of some use, by stirring up the curious to make more experiments, and occasion more exact disquisitions.

I conceive then, that this globe of earth and water, with its plants, animals, and buildings, have diffused throughout their substance, a quantity of the electric fluid, just as much as they can contain, which I call the *natural quantity.*

That this natural quantity is not the same in all kinds of common matter under the same dimensions, nor in the same kind of common matter in all circumstances; but a solid foot, for instance, of one kind of common matter, may contain more of the electric fluid than a solid foot of some other kind of common matter; and a pound weight of the same kind of common matter may, when in a rarer state, contain more of the electric fluid than when in a denser state.

For the electric fluid, being attracted by any portion of common matter, the parts of that fluid, (which have among themselves a mutual repulsion) are brought so near to each other by the attraction of the common matter that absorbs them, as that their repulsion is equal to the condensing power of attraction in common matter; and then such portion of common matter will absorb no more.

Bodies of different kinds having thus attracted and absorbed what I call their *natural quantity, i. e.* just as much of the electric fluid as is suited to their circumstances of density, rarity, and power of attracting, do not then show any signs of electricity among each other.

And if more electric fluid be added to one of these bodies, it does not enter, but spreads on the surface, forming an atmosphere; and then such body shews signs of electricity.

I have in a former paper compared common matter to a sponge, and the electric fluid to water: I beg leave once more to make use of the same comparison, to illustrate farther my meaning in this particular.

When a sponge is somewhat condensed by being squeezed between the fingers, it will not receive and retain so much water as when in its more loose and open state.

If *more* squeezed and condensed, some of the water will come out of its inner parts, and flow on the surface.

If the pressure of the fingers be entirely removed, the sponge will not only resume what was lately forced out, but attract an additional quantity.

As the sponge in its rarer state will *naturally* attract and absorb *more* water, and in its denser state will *naturally* attract and absorb *less* water; we may call the quantity it attacks and absorbs in either state, its *natural quantity*, the state being considered.

Now what the sponge is to water, the same is water to the electric fluid.

When a portion of water is in its common dense state, it can hold no more electric fluid than it has: if any be added, it spreads on the surface.

When the same portion of water is rarified into vapor, and forms a cloud, it is then capable of receiving and absorbing a much greater quantity; there is room for each particle to have an electric atmosphere.

Thus water, in its rarified state, or in the form of a cloud, will be in a negative state of electricity; it will have less than its *natural quantity;* that is, less than it is naturally capable of attracting and absorbing in that state.

Such a cloud then, coming so near the earth, as to be within the striking distance; will receive from the earth a flash of the electric fluid; which flash, to supply a great extent of cloud, must sometimes contain a very great quantity of that fluid.

Or such a cloud, passing over woods of tall trees, may from the points and sharp edges of their moist top leaves, receive silently some supply.

A cloud being by any means supplied from the earth, may strike into other clouds that have not been supplied, or not so much supplied; and those to others, till an equilibrium is produced among all the clouds that are within striking distance of each other.

The cloud thus supplied having parted with much of what it first received, may require and receive a fresh supply from the earth, or from some other cloud, which by the wind is brought into such a situation as to receive it more readily from the earth.

Hence repeated and continual strokes and flashes till the clouds have all got nearly their natural quantity as clouds, or till they have descended in showers, and are united again with this terraqueous globe, their original.

Thus, thunder-clouds are generally in a negative state of electricity compared with the earth, agreeable to most of our experiments; yet as by one experiment we found a cloud electrised positively, I conjecture that, in that case, such cloud, after having received what was, in its rare state, only its *natural quantity*, became compressed by the driving winds, or some other means, so that part of what it had absorbed was forced out, and formed an electric atmosphere around it in its denser state. Hence it was capable of communicating positive electricity to my rod.

To show that a body in different circumstances of dilatation and contraction is capable of receiving and retaining more or less of the electric fluid on its surface, I would relate the following experiment: I placed a clean wine glass on the floor, and on it a small silver can. In the can I put about three yards of brass chain; to one end of which I fastened a silk thread, which went right up to the cieling, where it passed over a pulley, and came down again to my hand, that I might at pleasure draw the chain up out of the can, extending it till within a foot of the cieling, and let it gradually sink into the can again.—From the cieling, by another thread of fine raw silk, I suspended a small light lock of cotton, so as that when it hung perpendicularly, it came in contact with the side of the can. Then approaching the wire of a charged phial to the can, I gave it a spark, which flowed round in an electric atmosphere; and the lock of cotton was repelled from the side of the can to the distance of about nine or ten inches. The can would not then receive another spark from the wire of the phial: but as I gradually drew up the chain, the atmosphere of the can diminished by flowing over the rising chain, and the lock of cotton accordingly drew nearer and nearer to the can; and then, if I again brought the phial wire near the can, it would receive another spark, and the cotton fly off again to its first distance; and thus, as the chain was drawn higher, the can would receive more sparks; because the can and extended chain were capable of supporting a greater atmosphere than the can with the chain gathered up into its belly.——And that the atmosphere round the can was diminished by raising the chain, and increased again by lowering it, is not only agreeable to reason, since the atmosphere of the chain must be drawn from that of the can, when it rose, and returned to it again when it fell; but was also evident to the eye, the lock of cotton always approaching the can when the chain was drawn up, and receding when it was let down again.

Thus we see that increase of surface makes a body capable of receiving a greater electric atmosphere : but this experiment does not, I own, fully demonstrate my new hypothesis ; for the brass and silver still continue in their solid state, and are not rarified into vapor, as the water is in clouds. Perhaps some future experiments on vaporised water may set this matter in a clearer light.

One seemingly material objection arises to the new hypothesis, and it is this: If water, in its rarified state, as a cloud, requires, and will absorb more of the electric fluid than when in its dense state as water, why does it not acquire from the earth all it wants at the instant of its leaving the surface, while it is yet near, and but just rising in vapor? To this difficulty I own I cannot at present give a solution satisfactory to myself: I thought, however, that I ought to state it in its full force, as I have done, and submit the whole to examination.

And I would beg leave to recommend it to the curious in this branch of natural philosophy, to repeat with care and accurate observation the experiments I have reported in this and former papers relating to *positive* and *negative* electricity, with such other relative ones as shall occur to them, that it may be certainly known whether the electricity communicated by a glass globe, be *really positive*. And also I would request all who may have an opportunity of observing the recent effects of lightning on buildings, trees,

&c. that they would consider them particularly with a view
to discover the direction.   But in these examinations, this
one thing is always to be understood, viz. that a stream of
the electric fluid passing through wood, brick, metal, &c.
while such fluid passes in *small quantity*, the mutually repulsive power of its parts is confined and overcome by the
cohesion of the parts of the body it passes through, so as
to prevent an explosion; but when the fluid comes in a
quantity too great to be confined by such cohesion, it ex-
plodes, and rends or fuses the body that endeavored to
confine it.   If it be wood, brick, stone, or the like, the
splinters will fly off on that side where there is least resistance.   And thus, when a hole is struck through pasteboard
by the electrified jar, if the surfaces of the pasteboard are
not confined or compressed, there will be a bur raised all
round the hole on both sides the pasteboard; but if one side
be confined, so that the bur cannot be raised on that side,
it will be all raised on the other, which way soever the fluid
was directed.   For the bur round the outside of the hole,
is the effect of the explosion every way from the centre of
the stream, and not an effect of the direction.

In every stroke of lightning, I am of opinion that the
stream of the electric fluid, moving to restore the equili-
brum between the cloud and the earth, does always previously find its passage, and mark out, as I may say, its own
course, taking in its way all the conductors it can find, such
as metals, damp walls, moist wood, &c. and will go considerably out of a direct course, for the sake of the assistance of good conductors; and that, in this course, it is
actually moving, though silently and imperceptibly, before
the explosion, in and among the conductors: which explosion happens only when the conductors cannot discharge it
as fast as they receive it, by reason of their being incom-
plete, disunited, too small, or not of the best materials
for conducting.   Metalline rods, therefore, of sufficient
thickness, and extending from the highest part of an edifice
to the ground, being of the best materials and complete
conductors, will, I think, secure the building from damage,

either by restoring the equilibrium so fast as to prevent a stroke, or by conducting it in the substance of the rod as far as the rod goes, so that there shall be no explosion but what is above its point, between that and the clouds.

If it be asked, what thickness of a metalline rod may be supposed sufficient? In answer, I would remark, that five large glass jars, such as I have described in my former papers, discharge a very great quantity of electricity, which nevertheless will be all conducted round the corner of a book, by the fine filleting of gold on the cover, it following the gold the farthest way about, rather than take the shorter course through the cover, that not being so good a conductor. Now in this line of gold, the metal is so extremely thin as to be little more than the color of gold, and on an octavo book is not in the whole an inch square, and therefore not the thirty-sixth part of a grain, according to M. Reaumur; yet it is sufficient to conduct the charge of five large jars, and how many more I know not. Now, I suppose a wire of a quarter of an inch diameter to contain about five thousand times as much metal as there is in that gold line, and if so, it will conduct the charge of twenty-five thousand such glass jars, which is a quantity, I imagine far beyond what was ever contained in any one stroke of natural lightning. But a rod of half an inch diameter would conduct four times as much as one of a quarter.

And with regard to conducting, though a certain thickness of metal be required to conduct a great quantity of electricity, and, at the same time, keep its own substance firm and unseparated; and a less quantity, as a very small wire for instance, will be destroyed by the explosion; yet such small wire will have answered the end of conducting that stroke, though it becomes incapable of conducting another. And considering the extreme rapidity with which the electric fluid moves without exploding, when it has a free passage, or complete metal communication, I should think a vast quantity would be conducted in a short time, either to or from a cloud, to restore its equilibrium with the earth, by means of a very small wire; and therefore

Q

thick rods should seem not so necessary.—However, as the
quantity of lightning discharged in one stroke, cannot well
be measured, and, in different strokes, is certainly very
various, in some much greater than others; and as iron
(the best metal for the purpose, being least apt to fuse) is
cheap, it may be well enough to provide a larger canal to
guide that impetuous blast than we may imagine necessary:
for, though one middling wire may be sufficient, two or three
can do no harm.   And time, with careful abservations well
compared, will at length point out the proper size to greater
certainty.

Pointed rods erected on edifices may likewise often prevent a stroke, in the following manner: an eye so situated
as to view horizontally the under side of a thunder-cloud,
will see it very ragged, with a number of separate fragments,
or petty clouds, one under another, the lowest sometimes
not far from the earth.   These, as so many stepping stones,
assist in conducting a stroke between the cloud and a building.   To represent these by an experiment, take two or
three locks of fine loose cotton, connect one of them with
the prime conductor by a fine thread of two inches (which
may be spun out of the same lock by the fingers) another
to that, and the third to the second, by like threads.—Turn
the globe and you will see these locks extend themselves
towards the table (as the lower small clouds do towards the
earth) being attracted by it: but on presenting a sharp point
erect under the lowest, it will shrink up to the second, the
second to the first, and all together to the prime conductor,
where they will continue as long as the point continues
under them.   May not, in like manner, the small electrised
clouds, whose equilibrium with the earth is soon restored
by the point, rise up to the main body, and by that means
occasion so large a vacancy, as that the grand cloud cannot
strike in that place?

These thoughts, my dear friend, are many of them crude
and hasty; and if I were merely ambitious of acquiring
some reputation in philosophy, I ought to keep them by me,
till corrected and improved by time, and farther experience.

But since even short hints and imperfect experiments in any new branch of science, being communicated, have oftentimes a good effect, in exciting the attention of the ingenious to the subject, and so become the occasion of more exact disquisition, and more complete discoveries, you are at liberty to communicate this paper to whom you please; it being of more importance that knowlege should increase, than that your friend should be thought an accurate philosopher.

B. FRANKLIN.

TO PETER COLLINSON, LONDON.

Additional Proofs of the positive and negative state of Electricity in the Clouds.—New Method of ascertaining it.

Philadelphia, April 18, 1754.

SIR,

SINCE September last, having been abroad on two long journies, and otherwise much engaged, I have made but few observations on the *positive* and *negative* state of electricity in the clouds. But Mr. Kinnersley kept his rod and bells in good order, and has made many.

Once this winter the bells rang a long time, during a fall of snow, though no thunder was heard, nor lightning seen. Sometimes the flashes and cracks of the electric matter between bell and bell were so large and loud as to be heard all over the house: but by all his observations, the clouds were constantly in a negative state, till about six weeks ago, when he found them once to change in a few minutes from the negative to the positive. About a fortnight after that, he made another observation of the same kind; and last Monday afternoon, the wind blowing hard at S. E. and veering round to N. E. with many thick driving clouds, there were five or six successive changes from negative to positive, and from positive to negative, the bells stopping a minute or two between every change. Besides the methods mentioned in my paper of September last, of discovering the electrical state of the clouds, the following may be used. When your bells are ringing, pass a rubbed tube by the edge of the bell, connected with y.. pointed rod : if the cloud is then in a negative state, the ringing will stop ; if in a positive state, it will continue, and perhaps be quicker. Or, suspend a very small cork-ball by a fine silk thread, so that it may hang close to the edge of the rod-bell: then whenever the bell is electrified, whether positively or negatively, the little ball will be repelled, and continue at some distance from the bell.   Have ready a round-headed glass stopper of a decanter, rub it on your side till it is electrified, then present it to the cork-ball.   If the electricity in the ball is positive, it will be repelled from the glass stopper as well as from the bell. If negative it will fly to the stopper.

B. FRANKLIN.

ELECTRICAL EXPERIMENTS.

With an attempt to account for their several phænomena. Together with some observations on thunder-clouds, in further confirmation of Dr. Franklin's observations on the positive and negative electrical state of the clouds, by John Canton, M. A. and F. R. S.

Dec. 6, 1753.

EXPERIMENT I.

FROM the cieling, or any convenient part of a room, let two cork-balls, each about the bigness of a small pea, be suspended by linen threads of eight or nine inches in length, so as to be in contact with each other.   Bring the excited glass tube under the balls, and they will be separated by it, when held at the distance of three or four feet; let it be brought nearer, and they will stand farther apart; entirely withdraw it, and they will immediately come together. This experiment may be made with very small brass balls hung by silver wire; and will succeed as well with sealing-wax made electrical, as with glass.

EXPERIMENT II.

If two cork-balls be suspended by dry silk threads, the excited tube must be brought within eighteen inches before they will repel each other; which they will continue to do, for some time, after the tube is taken away.

As the balls in the first experiment are not insulated, they cannot properly be said to be electrified: but when they hang within the atmosphere of the excited tube, they may attract and condense the electrical fluid round about them, and be separated by the repulsion of its particles. It is conjectured also, that the balls at this time contain less than their common share of the electrical fluid, on account of the repelling power of that which surrounds them; though some, perhaps, is continually entering and passing through the threads. And if that be the case, the reason is plain why the balls hung by silk, in the second experiment, must be in a much more dense part of the atmosphere of the tube, before they will repel each other. At the approach of an excited stick of wax to the balls, in the first experiment, the electrical fire is supposed to come through the threads into the balls, and be condensed there, in its passage towards the wax; for, according to Mr. Franklin, excited glass *emits* the electrical fluid, but excited wax *receives* it.

EXPERIMENT III.

Let a tin tube, of four or five feet in length, and about two inches in diameter, be insulated by silk; and from one end of it let the cork-balls be suspended by linen threads. Electrify it, by bringing the excited glass tube near the other end, so as that the balls may stand an inch and an half, or two inches apart: then, at the approach of the excited tube, they will by degrees, lose their repelling power, and come into contact; and as the tube is brought still nearer, they will separate again to as great a distance as before: in the return of the tube they will approach each other till they touch, and then repel as at first. If the tin tube be electrified by wax, or the wire of a charged phial, the balls will be affected in the same manner at the approach of excited wax, or the wire of the phial.

EXPERIMENT IV.

Electrify the cork-balls as in the last experiment by glass, and at the approach of an excited stick of wax their repulsion will be increased. The effect will be the same, if the excited glass be brought towards them, when they have been electrified by wax.

The bringing the excited glass to the end, or edge of the tin tube, in the third experiment, is supposed to electrify it positively, or to add to the electrical fire it before contained; and therefore some will be running off through the balls, and they will repel each other. But at the approach of excited glass, which likewise *emits* the electrical fluid, the discharge of it from the balls will be diminished; or part will be driven back, by a force acting in a contrary direction: and they will come nearer together. If the tube be held at such a distance from the balls, that the excess of the density of the fluid round about them, above the common quantity in air, be equal to the excess of the density of that within them, above the common quantity contained in cork; their repulsion will be quite destroyed. But if the tube be brought nearer; the fluid without being more dense than within the balls, it will be attracted by them, and they will recede from each other again.

When the apparatus has lost part of its natural share of this fluid, by the approach of excited wax to one end of it, or is electrified negatively; the electrical fire is attracted and imbibed by the balls to supply the deficiency; and that more plentifully at the approach of excited glass; or a body positively electrified, than before; whence the distance between the balls will be increased, as the fluid surrounding them is augmented. And in general, whether by the approach or recess of any body; if the difference between the density of the internal and external fluid be increased or diminished; the repulsion of the balls will be increased or diminished accordingly.

EXPERIMENT V.

When the insulated tin tube is not electrified, bring the excited glass tube towards the middle of it, so as to be nearly at right angles with it, and the balls at the end will repel each other; and the more so, as the excited tube is brought nearer. When it has been held a few seconds, at the distance of about six inches, withdraw it, and the balls will approach each other till they touch; and then separating again, as the tube is moved farther off, will continue to .repel when it is taken quite away. And this repulsion between the balls will be increased by the approach of excited glass, but diminished by excited wax; just as if the apparatus had been electrified by wax, after the manner described in the third experiment.

EXPERIMENT VI.

Insulate two tin tubes, distinguished by A and B, so as to be in a line with each other, and about half an inch apart; and at the remote end of each, let a pair of cork balls be suspended. Towards the middle of A, bring the excited glass tube, and holding it a short time, at the distance of a few inches, each pair of balls will be observed to separate : withdraw the tube, and the balls of A will come together, and then repel each other again ; but those of B will hardly be affected. By the approach of the excited glass tube, held under the balls of A, their repulsion will be increased: but if the tube be brought, in the same manner, towards the balls of B, their repulsion will be diminished.

In the fifth experiment, the common stock of electrical matter in the tin tube, is supposed to be attenuated about the middle, and to be condensed at the ends, by the repelling power of the atmosphere of the excited glass tube, when held near it. And perhaps the tin tube may lose some of its natural quantity of the electrical fluid, before it receives any from the glass ; as that fluid will more readily run off from the ends and edges of it, than enter at the middle : and accordingly, when the glass tube is withdrawn, and the fluid is again equally diffused through the apparatus, it is found to be electrified negatively: for excited glass brought under the balls will increase their repulsion.

In the sixth experiment, part of the fluid driven out of one tin tube enters the other; which is found to be electrified positively, by the decreasing of the repulsion of its balls, at the approach of excited glass.

EXPERIMENT VII.

Let the tin tube, with a pair of balls at one end, be placed three feet at least from any part of the room, and the air rendered very dry by means of a fire: electrify the apparatus to a considerable degree: then touch the tin tube with a finger, or any other conductor, and the balls will, notwithstanding, continue to repel each other; though not at so great a distance as before.

The air surrounding the apparatus to the distance of two or three feet, is supposed to contain more or less of the electrical fire, than its common share, as the tin tube is electrified positively, or negatively: and when very dry, may not part with its overplus, or have its deficiency supplied so suddenly, as the tin; but may continue to be electrified, after that has been touched for a considerable time.

EXPERIMENT VIII.

Having made the Torricellian vacuum about five feet long, after the manner described in the *Philosophical Transactions*, vol. xlvii. p. 370, if the excited tube be brought within a small distance of it, a light will be seen through more than half its length; which soon vanishes, if the tube be not brought nearer; but will appear again, as that is moved farther off. This may be repeated several times, without exciting the tube afresh.

This experiment may be considered as a kind of occular demonstration of the truth of Mr. Franklin's hypothesis; that when the electrical fluid is condensed on one side of thin glass, it will be repelled from the other, if it meets with no resistance. According to which, at the approach of the excited tube, the fire is supposed to be repelled from the inside of the glass surrounding the vacuum, and to be carried through the columns of mercury; but, as the tube is withdrawn, the fire is supposed to return.

Let an excited stick of wax, of two feet and an half in length, and about an inch in diameter, be held near its middle. Excite the glass tube, and draw it over one half of it; then, turning a little about its axis, let the tube be excited again, and drawn over the same half, and let this operation be repeated several times; then will that half destroy the repelling power of balls electrified by glass, and the other half will increase it.

By this experiment it appears, that wax also may be electrified positively and negatively. And it is probable, that all bodies whatsoever may have the quantity they contain of the electrical fluid increased or diminished. The clouds, I have observed, by a great number of experiments, to be some in a positive, and others in a negative state of electricity. For the cork balls, electrified by them, will sometimes close at the approach of excited glass; and at other times be separated to a greater distance. And this change I have known to happen five or six times in less than half an hour; the balls coming together each time, and remaining in contact a few seconds, before they repel each other again. It may likewise easily be discovered, by a charged phial, whether the electrical fire be drawn out of the apparatus by the negative cloud, or forced into it by a positive one: and by which soever it be electrified, should that cloud either part with its overplus, or have its deficiency supplied suddenly, the apparatus will lose its electricity: which is frequently observed to be the case, immediately after a flash of lightning. Yet when the air is very dry, the apparatus will continue to be electrified for ten minutes, or a quarter of an hour, after the clouds have passed the zenith; and sometimes till they appear more than half-way towards the horizon. Rain, especially when the drops are large, generally brings down the electrical fire: and hail, in summer, I believe never fails. When the apparatus was last electrified, it was by the fall of thawing snow, which happened so lately, as on the 12th of November; that being the twenty-sixth day, and sixty-first time it has been electrified, since it was first set up; which was about the middle of May. And as Fahrenheit's thermometer was but seven degrees above freezing, it is supposed the winter will not entirely put a stop to observations of this sort. At London no more than two thunder storms have happened during the whole summer; and the apparatus was sometimes so strongly electrified in one of them, that the bells, which have been frequently rung by the clouds, so loud as to be heard in every room of the house (the doors being open) were silenced by the almost constant stream of dense electrical fire, between each bell and the brass ball, which would not suffer it to strike.

I shall conclude this paper, already too long, with the following queries:

1. May not air, suddenly rarified, give electrical fire to, and air suddenly condensed, receive electrical fire from, clouds and vapors passing through it?

2. Is not the *aurora borealis*, the flashing of electrical fire from positive, towards negative clouds at a great distance, through the upper part of the atmosphere, where the resistance is least?

EXPERIMENTS

Made in pursuance of those made by Mr. Canton, dated December 6, 1753; with explanations, by Benjamin Franklin.

Read at the Royal Society, Dec 18, 1755.

Philadelphia, March 14, 1755.

PRINCIPLES.

I. ELECTRIC atmospheres, that flow round non-electric bodies, being brought near each other, do not readily mix and unite into one atmosphere, but remain separate, and repel each other.

This is plainly seen in suspended cork balls, and other bodies electrified.

II. An electric atmosphere not only repels another electric atmosphere, but will also repel the electric matter contained in the substance of a body approaching it; and without joining or mixing with it, force it to other parts of the body that contained it.

This is shewn by some of the following experiments.

III. Bodies electrified negatively, or deprived of their natural quantity of electricity, repel each other, (or at least appear to do so, by a mutual receding) as well as those electrified positively, or which have electric atmospheres.

This is shewn by applying the negatively charged wire of a phial to two cork balls, suspended by silk threads, and many other experiments.

PREPARATION.

Fix a tassel of fifteen or twenty threads, three inches long, at one end of a tin prime conductor (mine is about five feet long, and four inches diameter) supported by silk lines.

Let the threads be a little damp, but not wet.

EXPERIMENT I.

Pass an excited glass tube near the other end of the prime conductor, so as to give it some sparks, and the threads will diverge.

Because each thread, as well as the prime conductor, has acquired an electric atmosphere, which repels and is repelled by the atmospheres of the other threads : if those several atmospheres would readily mix, the threads might unite and hang in the middle of one atmosphere, common to them all.

Rub the tube afresh, and approach the prime conductor therewith, crossways, near that end, but not nigh enough to give sparks; and the threads will diverge a little more.

Because the atmosphere of the prime conductor is pressed by the atmosphere of the excited tube, and driven towards the end where the threads are, by which each thread acquires more atmosphere.

Withdraw the tube, and they will close as much.

They close as much, and no more ; because the atmosphere of the glass tube not having mixed with the atmosphere of the prime conductor, is withdrawn intire, having made no addition to, or diminution from it.

Bring the excited tube under the tuft of threads, and they will close a little.

They close, because the atmosphere of the glass tube repels their atmospheres, and drives part of them back on the prime conductor.

Withdraw it, and they will diverge as much.

For the portion of atmosphere which they had lost, returns to them again.

EXPERIMENT II.

Excite the glass tube, and approach the prime conductor with it, holding it across, near the end opposite to that on which the threads hang, at the distance of five or six inches. Keep it there a few seconds, and the threads of the tassels will diverge. Withdraw it, and they will close.

They diverge, because they have received elecrric atmospheres from the electric matter before contained in the substance of the prime conductor ; but which is now repelled and driven away, by the atmosphere of the glass tube, from the parts of the prime conductor opposite and nearest to that atmosphere, and forced out upon the surface of the prime conductor at its other end, and upon the threads hanging thereto. Were it any part of the atmosphere of the glass tube that flowed over and along the prime conductor to the threads, and gave them atmospheres (as is the case when a spark is given to the prime conductor from the glass tube) such part of the tube's atmosphere would have remained, and the threads continue to diverge ; but they close on withdrawing the tube, because the tube takes with it *all its own atmosphere*, and the electric matter, which had been driven out of the substance of the prime conductor, and formed atmospheres round the threads, is thereby permitted to return to its place.

Take a spark from the prime conductor near the threads when they are diverged as before, and they will close.

For by so doing you take away their atmospheres, composed of the electric matter driven out of the substance of the prime conductor, as aforesaid, by the repellency of the atmosphere of the glass tube. By taking this spark you rob the prime conductor of part of its natural quantity of the electric matter : which part so taken is not supplied by the glass tube, for when that is afterwards withdrawn, it takes with it its whole atmosphere, and leaves the prime conductor electrised negatively, as appears by the next operation.

Then withdraw the tube, and they will open again.

For now the electric matter in the prime conductor, returning to its equilibrium, or equal diffusion, in all parts of its substance, and the prime conductor having lost some of its natural quantity, the threads connected with it lose part of theirs, and so are electrised negatively, and therefore repel each other, by *Pr.* III.

Approach the prime conductor with the tube near the same place as at first, and they will close again.

Because the part of their natural quantity of electric fluid, which they had lost, is now restored to them again, by the repulsion of the glass tube forcing that fluid to them from other parts of the prime conductor; so they are now again in their natural state.

Withdraw it, and they will open again.

For what had been restored to them, is now taken from them again, flowing back into the prime conductor and leaving them once more electrised negatively.

Bring the excited tube under the threads, and they will diverge more.

Because more of their natural quantity is driven from them into the prime conductor, and thereby their negative electricity increased.

EXPERIMENT III.

The prime conductor not being electrified, bring the excited tube under the tassel, and the threads will diverge.

Part of their natural quantity is thereby driven out of them into the prime conductor, and they become negatively electrised, and therefore repel each other.

Keeping the tube in the same place with one hand, attempt to touch the threads with the finger of the other hand, and they will recede from the finger.

Because the finger being plunged into the atmosphere of the glass tube, as well as the threads, part of its natural quantity is driven back through the hand and body, by that atmosphere, and the finger becomes, as well as the threads, negatively electrised, and so repels, and is repelled by them. To confirm this, hold a slender light lock of cotton, two or three inches long, near a prime conductor, that is electrified by a glass globe, or tube. You will see the cotton stretch itself out towards the prime conductor. Attempt to touch it with the finger of the other hand, and it will be repelled by the finger. Approach it with a positively charged wire of a bottle, and it will fly to the wire. Bring it near a negatively charged wire of a bottle, it will recede from that wire in the same manner that it did from the finger; which demonstrates the finger to be negatively electrised, as well as the lock of cotton so situated.

Turkey killed by Electricity.—Effect of a shock on the Operator in making the Experiment.

AS Mr. Franklin, in a former letter to Mr. Collinson, mentioned his intending to try the power of a very strong electrical shock upon a turkey, that gentleman accordingly has been so very obliging as to send an account of it, which is to the following purpose.

He made first several experiments on fowls, and found, that two large thin glass jars gilt, holding each about six gallons, were sufficient, when fully charged, to kill common hens outright; but the turkeys, though thrown into violent convulsions, and then lying as dead for some minutes, would recover in less than a quarter of an hour. However, having added three other such to the former two, though not fully charged, he killed a turkey of about ten pounds weight, and believes that they would have killed a much larger. He conceited, as himself says, that the birds killed in this manner eat uncommonly tender.

In making these experiments, he found, that a man could, without great detriment, bear a much greater shock than he had imagined: for he inadvertently received the stroke of two of these jars through his arms and body, when they were very near fully charged. It seemed to him an universal blow throughout the body from head to foot, and was followed by a violent quick trembling in the trunk, which went off gradually, in a few seconds. It was some minutes before he could recollect his thoughts, so as to know what was the matter; for he did not see the flash, though his eye was on the spot of the prime conductor, from whence it struck the back of his hand; nor did he hear the crack, though the by-standers said it was a loud one; nor did he particularly feel the stroke on his hand, though he afterwards found it had raised a swelling there, of the bigness of half a pistol-bullet. His arms and the back of the neck felt somewhat numbed the remainder of the evening, and his breast was sore for a week after, as if it had been bruised. From this experiment may be seen the danger, even under the greatest caution, to the operator, when making these experiments with large jars; for it is not to be doubted, but several of these fully charged would as certainly, by increasing them, in proportion to the size, kill a man, as they before did a turkey.

N. B. The original of this letter, which was read at the Royal Society, has been mislaid.

TO DR. LINING AT CHARLES-TOWN, SOUTH CAROLINA.

Differences in the Qualities of the Glass.—Account of Domien, an Electrician and Traveller.—Conjectures respecting the pores of Glass.—Origin of the author's idea of drawing down Lightning. —No satisfactory Hypothesis respecting the manner in which Clouds become electrified.—Six men knocked down at once by an electrical shock.—Reflections on the spirit of invention.

Philadelphia, March 18, 1755.

SIR,

I SEND you enclosed a paper containing some new experiments I have made, in pursuance of those by Mr. Canton that are printed with my last letters. I hope these, with my explanation of them, will afford you some entertainment[6].

In answer to your several enquiries. The tubes and globes we use here, are chiefly made here. The glass has a greenish cast, but is clear and hard, and, I think, better for electrical experiments than the white glass of London, which is not so hard. There are certainly great differences in glass. A white globe I had made here some years since, would never, by any means, be excited. Two of my friends tried it, as well as myself, without success. At length, putting it on an electric stand, a chain from the prime conductor being in contact with it, I found it had the properties of a non-electric; for I could draw sparks from any part of it, though it was very clean and dry.

All I know of Domien, is, that by his own account he was a native of Transylvania, of Tartar descent, but a priest of the Greek church: he spoke and wrote Latin very readily and correctly. He set out from his own country with an intention of going round the world, as much as possible by land. He travelled through Germany, France, and Holland, to England. Resided some time at Oxford. From England he came to Maryland; thence went to New

---

6 See the preceding article, page 130, for the paper here referred to.

England; returned by land to Philadelphia; and from hence travelled through Maryland, Virginia, and North Carolina to you. He thought it might be of service to him in his travels to know something of electricity. I taught him the use of the tube; how to charge the Leyden phial, and some other experiments. He wrote to me from Charleston, that he had lived eight hundred miles upon electricity, it had been meat, drink, and clothing to him. His last letter to me was, I think, from Jamaica, desiring me to send the tubes you mention, to meet him at the Havanna, from whence he expected to get a passage to La Vera Cruz; designed travelling over land through Mexico to Acapulco; thence to get a passage to Manilla, and so through China, India, Persia, and Turkey, home to his own country; proposing to support himself chiefly by electricity. A strange project! But he was, as you observe, a very singular character. I was sorry the tubes did not get to the Havanna in time for him. If they are still in being, please to send for them, and accept of them. What became of him afterwards I have never heard. He promised to write to me as often as he could on his journey, and as soon as he should get home after finishing his tour. It is now seven years since he was here. If he is still in New Spain, as you imagine from that loose report, i suppose it must be that they confine him there, and prevent his writing: but I think it more likely that he may be dead.

The questions you ask about the pores of glass, I cannot answer otherwise, than that I know nothing of their nature; and suppositions, however ingenious, are often mere mistakes. My hypothesis, that they were smaller near the middle of the glass, too small to admit the passage of electricity, which could pass through the surface till it came near the middle, was certainly wrong: for soon after I had written that letter, I did, in order to *confirm* the hypothesis (which indeed I ought to have done before I wrote it) make an experiment. I ground away five-sixths of the thickness of the glass, from the side of one of my phials, expecting that the supposed denser part being so removed, the electric

S

fluid might come through the remainder of the glass, which
I had imagined more open; but I found myself mistaken.
The bottle charged as well after the grinding as before. I am
now, as much as ever, at a loss to know how or where the
quantity of electric fluid, on the positive side of the glass,
is disposed of.

As to the difference of conductors, there is not only this,
that some will conduct electricity in small quantities, and
yet do not conduct it fast enough to produce the shock; but
even among those that will conduct a shock, there are some
that do it better than others. Mr. Kinnersley has found,
by a very good experiment, that when the charge of a bottle hath an opportunity of passing two ways, *i. e.* straight
through a trough of water ten feet long, and six inches
square; or round about through twenty feet of wire, it
passes through the wire, and not through the water, though
that is the shortest course; the wire being the better conductor. When the wire is taken away, it passes through
the water, as may be felt by a hand plunged in the water;
but it cannot be felt in the water when the wire is used at
the same time. Thus, though a small phial containing
water will give a smart shock, one containing the same
quantity of mercury will give one much stronger, the mercury being the better conductor; while one containing oil
only, will scarce give any shock at all.

Your question, how I came first to think of proposing
the experiment of drawing down the lightning, in order
to ascertain its sameness with the electric fluid, I cannot
answer better than by giving you an extract from the minutes I used to keep of the experiments I made, with
memorandums of such as I purposed to make, the reasons
for making them, and the observations that arose upon them,
from which minutes my letters were afterwards drawn. By
this extract you will see that the thought was not so much
" an out-of-the-way one," but that it might have occurred
to an electrician.

" Nov. 7, 1749. Electrical fluid agrees with lightning in
these particulars: 1. Giving light. 2. Color of the light.

3. Crooked direction. 4. Swift motion. 5. Being conducted by metals. 6. Crack or noise in exploding. 7. Subsisting in water or ice. 8. Rending bodies it passes through. 9. Destroying animals. 10. Melting metals. 11. Firing inflammable substances. 12. Sulphureous smell. —The electric fluid is attracted by points.—We do not know whether this property is in lightning.—But since they agree in all the particulars wherein we can already compare them, is it not probable they agree likewise in this?—Let the experiment be made."

I wish I could give you any satisfaction in the article of clouds. I am still at a loss about the manner in which they become charged with electricity; no hypothesis I have yet formed perfectly satisfying me. Some time since, I heated very hot, a brass plate two feet square, and placed it on an electric stand. From the plate a wire extended horizontally four or five feet, and, at the end of it, hung, by linen threads, a pair of cork balls. I then repeatedly sprinkled water over the plate, that it might be raised from it in vapor, hoping that if the vapor either carried off the electricity of the plate, or left behind it that of the water (one of which I supposed it must do, if, like the clouds, it became electrised itself, either positively or negatively) I should perceive and determine it by the separation of the balls, and by finding whether they were positive or negative; but no alteration was made at all, nor could I perceive that the steam was itself electrised, though I have still some suspicion that the steam was not fully examined, and I think the experiment should be repeated. Whether the first state of electrised clouds is positive or negative, if I could find the cause of that, I should be at no loss about the other, for either is easily deduced from the other, as one state is easily produced by the other. A strongly positive cloud may drive out of a neighboring cloud much of its natural quantity of the electric fluid, and, passing by it, leave it in a negative state. In the same way, a strongly negative cloud may occasion a neighboring cloud to draw into itself from others, an additional quantity, and, passing by it, leave it in a positive state.   How these effects may be produced, you will easily conceive, on perusing and considering the experiments in the enclosed paper: and from them too it appears probable, that every change from positive to negative, and from negative to positive, that, during a thunder-gust, we see in the cork-balls annexed to the apparatus, is not owing to the presence of clouds in the same state, but often to the absence of positive or negative clouds, that, having just passed, leave the rod in the opposite state.

The knocking down of the six men was performed with two of my large jars not fully charged.   I laid one end of my discharging rod upon the head of the first; he laid his hand upon the head of the second; the second his hand on the head of the third, and so to the last, who held, in his hand, the chain that was connected with the outside of the jars.   When they were thus placed, I applied the other end of my rod to the prime conductor, and they all dropped together.   When they got up, they all declared they had not felt any stroke, and wondered how they came to fall; nor did any of them either hear the crack, or see the light of it.   You suppose it a dangerous experiment; but I had once suffered the same myself, receiving, by accident, an equal stroke through my head, that struck me down, without hurting me: and I had seen a young woman who was about to be electrified through the feet (for some indisposition) receive a greater charge through the head, by inadvertently stooping forward to look at the placing of her feet, till her forehead (as she was very tall) came too near my prime conductor: she dropped, but instantly got up again, complaining of nothing.   A person so struck, sinks down doubled, or folded together as it were, the joints losing their strength and stiffness at once, so that he drops on the spot where he stood, instantly, and there is no previous staggering, nor does he ever fall lengthwise.   Too great a charge might, indeed, kill a man, but I have not yet seen any hurt done by it.   It would certainly, as you observe, be the easiest of all deaths.

The experiment you have heard so imperfect an account of, is merely this: I electrified a silver pint can, on an electric stand, and then lowered into it a cork ball, of about an inch diameter, hanging by a silk string, till the cork touched the bottom of the can. The cork was not attracted to the inside of the can as it would have been to the outside, and though it touched the bottom, yet, when drawn out, it was not found to be electrified by that touch, as it would have been by touching the outside. The fact is singular. You require the reason; I do not know it. Perhaps you may discover it, and then you will be so good as to communicate it to me[7]. I find a frank acknowlegment of one's ignorance is not only the easiest way to get rid of a difficulty, but the likeliest way to obtain information, and therefore I practise it: I think it an honest policy. Those who affect to be thought to know every thing, and so undertake to explain every thing, often remain long ignorant of many things that others could and would instruct them in, if they appeared less conceited.

The treatment your friend has met with is so common, that no man who knows what the world is, and ever has been, should expect to escape it. There are every where a number of people, who being totally destitute of any inventive faculty themselves, do not readily conceive that others may possess it: they think of inventions as of miracles; there might be such formerly, but they are ceased. With these, every one who offers a new invention is deemed a pretender: he had it from some other country, or from some book: a man of *their own acquaintance;* one who has no more sense than themselves, could not possibly, in their opinion, have been the inventor of any thing. They are confirmed too, in these sentiments by frequent instances of pretensions to invention, which vanity is daily producing. That vanity too, though an incitement to invention, is, at

---

7 Dr F. afterwards thought, that, possibly, the mutual repulsion of the inner opposite sides of the electrised might prevent the accumulating of an electric atmosphere upon them, and occasion it to stand chiefly on the outside. But recommended it to the farther examination of the curious.

the same time, the pest of inventors. Jealousy and envy deny the merit or the novelty of your invention; but vanity, when the novelty and merit are established, claims it for its own. The smaller your invention is, the more mortification you receive in having the credit of it disputed with you by a rival, whom the jealousy and envy of others are ready to support against you, at least so far as to make the point doubtful. It is not in itself of importance enough for a dispute; no one would think your proofs and reasons worth their attention: and yet, if you do not dispute the point, and demonstrate your right, you not only lose the credit of being in that instance *ingenious*, but you suffer the disgrace of not being *ingenuous;* not only of being a plagiary, but of being a plagiary for trifles. Had the invention been greater it would have disgraced you less; for men have not so contemptible an idea of him that robs for gold on the highway, as of him that can pick pockets for half-pence and farthings. Thus, through envy, jealousy, and the vanity of competitors for fame, the origin of many of the most extraordinary inventions, though produced within but a few centuries past, is involved in doubt and uncertainty. We scarce know to whom we are indebted for the *compass*, and for *spectacles*, nor have even *paper* and *printing*, that record every thing else, been able to preserve with certainty the name and reputation of their inventors. One would not, therefore, of all faculties, or qualities of the mind, wish, for a friend, or a child, that he should have that of invention. For his attempts to benefit mankind in that way, however well imagined, if they do not succeed, expose him, though very unjustly, to general ridicule and contempt; and, if they do succeed, to envy, robbery, and abuse.

I am, &c.

B. FRANKLIN.

TO MONS. DALIBARD, AT PARIS, INCLOSED IN A LETTER TO
MR. PETER COLLINSON.

*Beccaria's work on Electricity——Sentiments of Franklin on pointed
Rods, not fully understood in Europe.——Effect of Lightning on the
Church of Newbury, in New England.——Remarks on the subject.*

Read at the Royal Society, Dec. 18, 1775.

Philadelphia, June 29, 1755.

SIR,

YOU desire my opinion of Père Beccaria's Italian book[8].
I have read it with much pleasure, and think it one of the
best pieces on the subject that I have seen in any language.
Yet as to the article of water-spouts, I am not at present
of his sentiments; though I must own with you, that he
has handled it very ingeniously. Mr. Collinson has my
opinion of whirlwinds and water-spouts at large, written
some time since. I know not whether they will be published; if not, I will get them transcribed for your perusal[9]. It
does not appear to me that Père Beccaria doubts of the
absolute impermeability of glass in the sense I meant it; for
the instances he gives of holes made through glass by the
electric stroke are such as we have all experienced, and
only show that the electric fluid could not pass without
making a hole. In the same manner we say, glass is im-
permeable to water, and yet a stream from a fire-engine will
force through the strongest panes of a window. As to the
effect of points in drawing the electric matter from clouds,
and thereby securing buildings, &c. which, you say, he seems
to doubt, I must own I think he only speaks modestly and
judiciously. I find I have been but partly understood in
that matter. I have mentioned it in several of my letters,
and except once, always in the *alternative, viz.* that pointed

---

8 This work is written conformable to Dr. Franklin's theory, upon artificial
and natural electricity, which compose the two parts of it. It was printed in
Italian, at Turin, in 4to. 1753; between the two parts is a letter to the Abbe
Nollet, in defence of Dr. Franklin's system. A copy of the work in Italian,
with the original MSS. letter of Beccaria to Dr. F. are in the Philadelphia
editor's possession.

9 These papers will be found in a subsequent part of this volume.

rods erected on buildings, and communicating with the moist earth, would either *prevent* a stroke, *or*, if not prevented, would *conduct* it, so as that the building should suffer no damage. Yet whenever my opinion is examined in Europe, nothing is considered but the probability of those rods *preventing* a stroke or explosion, which is only a *part* of the use I proposed for them; and the other part, their conducting a stroke, which they may happen not to prevent, seems to be totally forgotten, though of equal importance and advantage.

I thank you for communicating M. de Buffon's relation of the effect of lightning at Dijon, on the 7th of June last. In return, give me leave to relate an instance I lately saw of the same kind. Being in the town of Newbury, in New England, in November last, I was shewn the effect of lightning on their church, which had been struck a few months before. The steeple was a square tower of wood reaching seventy feet up from the ground to the place where the bell hung, over which rose a taper spire, of wood likewise, reaching seventy feet higher, to the vane of the weather-cock. Near the bell was fixed an iron hammer to strike the hours : and from the tail of the hammer a wire went down through a small gimlet-hole in the floor that the bell stood upon, and through a second floor in like manner; then horizontally under and near the plaistered cieling of that second floor, till it came near a plaistered wall; then down by the side of that wall to a clock, which stood about twenty feet below the bell. The wire was not bigger than a common knitting-needle. The spire was split all to pieces by the lightning, and the parts flung in all directions over the square in which the church stood, so that nothing remained above the bell.

The lightning passed between the hammer and the clock in the above mentioned wire, without hurting either of the floors, or having any effect upon them (except making the gimlet-holes, through which the wire passed, a little bigger,) and without hurting the plaistered wall, or any part of the building, so far as the aforesaid wire and the pendulum wire of the clock extended; which latter wire was about the thickness of a goose-quill. From the end of the pendulum, down quite to the ground, the building was exceedingly rent and damaged, and some stones in the foundation-wall torn out, and thrown to the distance of twenty or thirty feet. No part of the afore mentioned long small wire, between the clock and the hammer, could be found, except about two inches that hung to the tail of the hammer, and about as much that was fastened to the clock; the rest being exploded, and its particles dissipated in smoke and air, as gunpowder is by common fire, and had only left a black smutty track on the plaistering, three or four inches broad, darkest in the middle, and fainter towards the edges, all along the cieling, under which it passed, and down the wall. These were the effects and appearances; on which I would only make the few following remarks, viz.

1. That lightning, in its passage through a building, will leave wood to pass as far as it can in metal, and not enter the wood again till the conductor of metal ceases.

And the same I have observed in other instances, as to walls of brick or stone.

2. The quantity of lightning that passed through this steeple must have been very great, by its effects on the lofty spire above the bell, and on the square tower all below the end of the clock pendulum.

3. Great as this quantity was, it was conducted by a small wire and a clock pendulum, without the least damage to the building so far as they extended.

4. The pendulum rod being of a sufficient thickness, conducted the lightning without damage to itself; but the small wire was utterly destroyed.

5. Though the small wire was itself destroyed, yet it had conducted the lightning with safety to the building.

6. And from the whole it seems probable, that if even such a small wire had been extended from the spindle of the vane to the earth, before the storm, no damage would have been done to the steeple by that stroke of lightning, though the wire itself had been destroyed.

T

TO PETER COLLINSON, LONDON.

Notice of another packet of letters.

Philadelphia, Nov. 23, 1753.

DEAR FRIEND,

IN my last, via Virginia, I promised to send you per next ship, a small philosophical packet: but now having got the materials (old letters and rough drafts) before me, I fear you will find it a great one. Nevertheless, as I am like to have a few days leisure before this ship sails, which I may not have again in a long time, I shall transcribe the whole, and send it; for you will be under no necessity of reading it all at once, but may take it a little at a time, now and then of a winter evening. When you happen to have nothing else to do (if that ever happens) it may afford you some amusement[1].

B. FRANKLIN."

Extract of a letter from a gentleman in Boston, (Mr Bowdoin,) to Benjamin Franklin, concerning the crooked direction and the source of lightning, and the swiftness of the electric fire.

Boston, Dec. 21, 1751.

SIR,

THE experiments Mr. K. has exhibited here, have been greatly pleasing to all sorts of people that have seen them; and I hope, by the time he returns to Philadelphia,

---

[1] These letters and papers are a philosophical correspondence between Dr. Franklin and some of his American Friends *. Mr. Collinson communicated them to the Royal Society, where they were read at different meetings during the year 1756 But Dr. Franklin having particularly requested that they might not be printed, none of them were inserted in the transactions. He had at that time an intention of revising them, and pursuing some of the enquiries farther; but finding that he was not likely to have sufficient leisure, he was at length induced, imperfect as they were, to permit their publication, as some of the hints they contain might possibly be useful to others in their philosophical researches. Note in Mr. Collinson's edition.

* As some of these papers are upon subjects not immediately connected with electricity, we have taken such papers from the order in which they were placed by Mr. Collinson, and transferred them to other parts of this edition.

his tour this way will turn to good account. His experiments are very curious, and I think prove most effectually your doctrine of electricity; that it is a real element, annexed to, and diffused among all bodies we are acquainted with; that it differs in nothing from lightning, the effects of both being similar, and their properties, so far as they are known, the same, &c.

The remarkable effect of lightning on iron, lately discovered, in giving it the magnetic virtue, and the same effect produced on small needles by the electrical fire, is a further and convincing proof that they are both the same element; but, which is very unaccountable, Mr. K. tells me, it is necessary to produce this effect, that the direction of the needle and the electric fire should be north and south; from either to the other, and that just so far as they deviate therefrom, the magnetic power in the needle is less, till their direction being at right angles with the north and south, the effect entirely ceases. We made at Faneuil Hall, where Mr. K—'s apparatus, several experiments, to give some small needles the magnetic virtue; previously examining, by putting them in water, on which they will be supported, whether or not they had any of that virtue; and I think we found all of them to have some small degree of it, their points turning to the north; we had nothing to do then but to invert the poles, which accordingly was done, by sending through them the charge of two large glass jars; the eye of the needle turning to the north, as the point before had done: that end of the needle which the fire is thrown upon, Mr. K. tells me always points to the north.

The electrical fire passing through air has the same crooked direction as lightning[2]. This appearance I endeavor to account for thus: air is an electric *per se*, therefore there must be a mutual repulson betwixt air and the electrical fire. A column or cylinder of air, having the diameter of its base equal to the diameter of the electrical spark, intervenes that part of the body which the spark is taken from,

2 This is most easily observed in large strong sparks taken at some inches distance.

and of the body it aims at. The spark acts upon this column, and is acted upon by it, more strongly than any other neighboring portion of air.

The column, being thus acted upon, becomes more dense, and, being more dense repels the spark more strongly ; its repellency being in proportion to its density: having acquired, by being condensed, a degree of repellency greater than its natural, it turns the spark out of its straight course ; the neighboring air, which must be less dense, and therefore has a smaller degree of repellency, giving it a more ready passage.

The spark, having taken a new direction, must now act on, or most strongly repel the column of air which lies in that direction, and consequently must condense that column in the same manner as the former, when the spark must again change its course, which course will be thus repeatedly changed, till the spark reaches the body that attracted it.

To this account one objection occurs ; that as air is very fluid and elastic, and so endeavors to diffuse itself equally, the supposed accumulated air within the column aforesaid, would be immediately diffused among the contiguous air and circulate to fill the space it was driven from : and consequently that the said column, on the greater density of which the phenomenon is supposed to depend, would not repel the spark more strongly than the neighboring air.

This might be an objection, if the electrical fire was as sluggish and inactive as air. Air takes a sensible time to diffuse itself equally, as is manifest from winds which often blow for a considerable time together from the same point, and with a velocity even in the greatest storms, not exceeding, as it is said, sixty miles an hour : but the electric fire seems propagated instantaneously, taking up no perceptible time in going very great distances. It must then be an inconceivably short time in its progress from an electrified to an unelectrified body, which, in the present case, can be but a few inches apart : but this small portion of time is not sufficient for the elasticity of the air to exert itself, and therefore the column aforesaid must be in a denser state than its neighboring air.

About the velocity of the electric fire more is said below, which perhaps may more fully obviate this objection. But let us have recourse to experiments. Experiments will obviate all objections, or confound the hypothesis, The electric spark, if the foregoing be true, will pass through a vacuum in a right line. To try this, let a wire, be fixed perpendicularly on the plate of an air pump, having a leaden ball on its upper end; let another wire, passing through the top of a receiver, have on each end a leaden ball; let the leaden balls within the receiver, when put on the air pump, be within two or three inches of each other; the receiver being exhausted, the spark given from a charged phial to the upper wire will pass through rarified air, nearly approaching to a vacuum, to the lower wire, and I suppose in a right line, or nearly so; the small portion of air remaining in the receiver, which cannot be entirely exhausted, may possibly cause it to deviate a little, but perhaps not sensibly from a right line. The spark also might be made to pass through air greatly condensed, which perhaps would give a still more crooked direction. I have not had opportunity to make any experiments of this sort, not knowing of an air-pump nearer than Cambridge, but you can easily make them. If these experiments answer, I think the crooked direction of lightning will be also accounted for.

With respect to your letters on electricity; your hypothesis in particular for explaining the phenomena of lightning is very ingenious. That some clouds are highly charged with electrical fire, and that their communicating it to those that have less, to mountains and other eminences, makes it visible and audible, when it is denominated lightning and thunder, is highly probable; but that the sea, which you suppose the grand source of it, can collect it, I think admits of a doubt: for though the sea be composed of salt and water, an electric *per se* and non-electric, and though the friction of electrics *per se* and non-electrics, will collect that fire, yet it is only under certain circumstances,

which water will not admit.   For it seems necessary, that
the electrics *per se* and non-electrics rubbing one another,
should be of such substances as will not adhere to, or
incorporate with each other.   Thus a glass or sulphur
sphere turned in water, and so a friction between them,
will not collect any fire; nor, I suppose, would a sphere of
salt revolving in water: the water adhering to, or incorpo-
rating with those electrics *per se*.   But granting that the
friction between salt and water would collect the electrical
fire ; that fire, being so extremely subtle and active, would
be immediately communicated, either to those lower parts
of the sea from which it was drawn, and so only perform
quick revolutions; or be communicated to the adjacent
islands or continent, and so be diffused instantaneously
through the general mass of the earth.   I say instantaneously, for the greatest distances we can conceive within the
limits of our globe, even that of the two most opposite
points, it will take no sensible time in passing through :
and therefore it seems a little difficult to conceive how there
can be any accumulation of the electrical fire upon the surface of the sea, or how the vapors arising from the sea
should have a greater share of that fire than other vapors.

That the progress of the electrical fire is so amazingly
swift, seems evident from an experiment you yourself (not
out of choice) made, when two or three large glass jars
were discharged through your body.   You neither heard
the crack, was sensible of the stroke, nor, which is more
extraordinary, saw the light; which gave you just reason
to conclude, that it was swifter than sound, than animal
sensation, and even light itself.   Now light (as astronomers
have demonstrated) is about six minutes passing from the
sun to the earth; a distance, they say, of more than eighty
millions of miles.   The greatest rectilinear distance within
the compass of the earth is about eight thousand miles,
equal to its diameter.   Supposing then, that the velocity of
the electric fire be the same as that of light, it will go
through a space equal to the earth's diameter in about $\frac{2}{80}$ of
the second of a minute.   It seems inconceivable then, that

it should be accumulated upon the sea, in its present state, which, as it is a non-electric, must give the fire an instantaneous passage to the neighboring shores, and they convey it to the general mass of the earth. But such accumulation seems still more inconceivable when the electrical fire has but a few feet depth of water to penetrate, to return to the place from whence it is supposed to be collected.

Your thoughts upon these remarks I shall receive with a great deal of pleasure. I take notice that in the printed copies of your letters, several things are wanting which are in the manuscript you sent me. I understand by your son, that you had writ, or was writing, a paper on the effect of the electrical fire on loadstones, needles, &c. which I would ask the favor of a copy of, as well as of any other papers on electricity, written since I had the manuscript, for which I repeat my obligations to you.

I am, &c.

J. BOWDOIN.

TO J. BOWDOIN AT BOSTON.

Observations on the subjects of the preceding letter.—Reasons for supposing the sea to be the grand source of Lightning.—Reasons for doubting this hypothesis.—Improvement in a globe for raising the Electric Fire.

Read at the Royal Society, May 27, 1756.

Philadelphia, Jan. 24, 1752.

SIR,

I AM glad to learn, by your favor of the 21st past, that Mr. Kinnersley's lectures have been acceptable to the gentlemen of Boston, and are like to prove serviceable to himself.

I thank you for the countenance and encouragement you have so kindly afforded my fellow-citizen.

I send you enclosed an extract of a letter containing the substance of what I observed concerning the communication of magnetism to needles by electricity. The minutes

I took at the time of the experiments are mislaid. I am very little acquainted with the nature of magnetism. Dr. Gawin Knight, inventor of the steel magnets, has wrote largely on that subject, but I have not yet had leisure to peruse his writings with the attention necessary to become master of his doctrine.

Your explication of the crooked direction of lightning appears to me both ingenious and solid. When we can account as satisfactorily for the electrification of clouds, I think that branch of natural philosophy will be nearly complete.

The air, undoubtedly, obstructs the motion of the electric fluid. Dry air prevents the dissipation of an electric atmosphere, the denser the more, as in cold weather. I question whether such an atmosphere can be retained by a body *in vacuo*. A common electrical phial requires a non-electric communication from the wire to every part of the charged glass; otherwise, being dry and clean, and filled with air only, it charges slowly, and discharges gradually, by sparks, without a shock: but exhausted of air, the communication is so open and free between the inserted wire and surface of the glass, that it charges as readily, and shocks as smartly as if filled with water: and I doubt not, but that in the experiment you propose, the sparks would not only be near strait *in vacuo*, but strike at a greater distance than in the open air, though perhaps there would not be a loud explosion. As soon as I have a little leisure, I will make the experiment, and send you the result.

My supposition, that the sea might possibly be the grand source of lightning, arose from the common observation of its luminous appearance in the night, on the least motion; an appearance never observed in fresh water. Then I knew that the electric fluid may be pumped up out of the earth, by the friction of a glass globe, on a non-electric cushion; and that, notwithstanding the surprising activity and swiftness of that fluid, and the non-electric communication between all the parts of the cushion and the earth, yet quantities would be snatched up by the revolving surface of the globe, thrown on the prime conductor, and dissipated in air. How this was done, and why that subtle active spirit did not immediately return again from the globe, into some part or other of the cushion, and so into the earth, was difficult to conceive; but whether from its being opposed by a current setting upwards to the cushion, or from whatever other cause, that it did not so return was an evident fact. Then I considered the separate particles of water as so many hard spherules, capable of touching the salt only in points, and imagined a particle of salt could therefore no more be wet by a particle of water, than a globe by a cushion; that there might therefore be such a friction between these originally constituent particles of salt and water, as in a sea of globes and cushions; that each particle of water on the surface might obtain from the common mass, some particles of the universally diffused, much finer, and more subtle electric fluid, and forming to itself an atmosphere of those particles, be repelled from the then generally electrified surface of the sea, and fly away with them into the air. I thought too, that possibly the great mixture of particles electric *per se*, in the ocean water, might, in some degree, impede the swift motion and dissipation of the electric fluid through it to the shores, &c.——But having since found, that salt in the water of an electric phial does not lessen the shock; and having endeavored in vain to produce that luminous appearance from a mixture of salt and water agitated; and observed, that even the sea-water will not produce it after some hours standing in a bottle; I suspect it to proceed from some principle yet unknown to us (which I would gladly make some experiments to discover, if I lived near the sea) and I grow more doubtful of my former supposition, and more ready to allow weight to that objection (drawn from the activity of the electric fluid, and the readiness of water to conduct) which you have indeed stated with great strength and clearness.

In the mean time, before we part with this hypothesis, let us think what to substitute in its place. I have sometimes queried whether the friction of the air, an electric

U

per se, in violent winds, among trees, and against the surface of the earth, might not pump up, as so many glass globes, quantities of the electric fluid, which the rising vapors might receive from the air, and retain in the clouds they form? on which I should be glad to have your sentiments. An ingenious friend of mine supposes the land-clouds more likely to be electrified than the sea-clouds. I send his letter for your perusal, which please to return me.

I have wrote nothing lately on electricity, nor observed any thing new that is material, my time being much taken up with other affairs. Yesterday I discharged four jars through a fine wire, tied up between two strips of glass: the wire was in part melted, and the rest broke into small pieces, from half an inch long, to half a quarter of an inch. My globe raises the electric fire with greater ease, in much greater quantities, by the means of a wire extended from the cushion, to the iron pin of a pump handle behind my house, which communicates by the pump spear with the water in the well.

By this post I send to ****, who is curious in that way, some meteorological observations and conjectures, and desire him to communicate them to you, as they may afford you some amusement, and I know you will look over them with a candid eye. By throwing our occasional thoughts on paper, we more readily discover the defects of our opinions, or we digest them better and find new arguments to support them. This I sometimes practise: but such pieces are fit only to be seen by friends.

I am, &c.

B. FRANKLIN.

J. BOWDOIN, AT BOSTON, TO BENJAMIN FRANKLIN,
PHILADELPHIA.

*Effect of Lightning on Captain Waddel's Compass, and the Dutch
Church at New York.*

Read at the Royal Society, June 3, 1756.

Boston, March, 2, 1752.

SIR,

I HAVE received your favor of the 24th of January
past, inclosing an extract from your letter to Mr. Collinson,
and ****'s letter to yourself, which I have read with a
great deal of pleasure, and am much obliged to you for.
Your extract confirms a correction Mr. Kinnersley made a
few days ago, of a mistake I was under respecting the polarity given to needles by electrical fire, "·that the end
which receives the fire always points north;" and " that
the needle being situated east and west, will not have a
polar direction." You find, however, the polarity strongest
when the needle is shocked lying north and south; weakest
when lying east and west; which makes it probable that
the communicated magnetism is less, as the needle varies
from a north and south situation. As to the needle of
Captain Waddel's compass, if its polarity was reversed by
the lightning, the effect of lightning and electricity, in
regard of that, seems dissimilar; for a magnetic needle in
a north and south situation (as the compass needle was)
instead of having its power reversed, or even diminished,
would have it confirmed or increased by the electric fire.
But perhaps the lightning communicated to some nails in
the binnacle (where the compass is placed) the magnetic
virtue, which might disturb the compass.

This I have heard was the case; if so, the seeming dis-
similarity vanishes: but this remarkable circumstance (if it
took place) I should think would not be omitted in captain
Waddel's account.

I am very much pleased that the explication I sent you,
of the crooked direction of lightning, meets with your
approbation.

As to your supposition about the source of lightning, the luminous appearance of the sea in the night, and the similitude between the friction of the particles of salt and water as you considered them in their original separate state, and the friction of the globe and cushion, very naturally led you to the ocean, as the grand source of lightning: but the activity of lightning, or the electric element, and the fitness of water to conduct it, together with the experiments you mention of salt and water, seem to make against it, and to prepare the way for some other hypothesis. Accordingly you propose a new one, which is very curious, and not so liable, I think, to objections as the former. But there is not as yet, I believe, a sufficient variety of experiments to establish any theory, though this seems the most hopeful of any I have heard of.

The effect which the discharge of your four glass jars had upon a fine wire, tied between two strips of glass, puts me in mind of a very similar one of lightning, that I observed at New York, October, 1750, a few days after I left Philadelphia. In company with a number of gentlemen, I went to take a view of the city from the Dutch church steeple, in which is a clock about twenty or twenty-five feet below the bell. From the clock went a wire through two floors, to the clock-hammer near the bell, the holes in the floor for the wire being perhaps about a quarter of an inch diameter. We were told, that in the spring of 1750, the lightning struck the clock hammer, and descended along the wire to the clock, melting in its way several spots of the wire, from three to nine inches long, through one-third of its substance, till coming within a few feet of the lower end, it melted the wire quite through, in several places, so that it fell down in several pieces; which spots and pieces we saw. When it got to the end of the wire, it flew off to the hinge of a door, shattered the door, and dissipated. In its passage through the holes of the floors it did not do the least damage, which evidences that wire is a good conductor of lightning (as it is of electricity) provided it be substantial enough, and might, in this case, had it been continued to the earth, have conducted it without damaging the building.[3]

Your information about your globe's raising the electric fire in greater quantities, by means of a wire extended from the cushion to the earth, will enable me, I hope, to remedy a great inconvenience I have been under, to collect the fire with the electrifying glass I use, which is fixed in a very dry room, three stories from the ground. When you send your meteorological observations to ****, I hope I shall have the pleasure of seeing them.   I am, &c.

J. BOWDOIN.

Proposal of an Experiment to measure the Time taken up by an Electric Spark, in moving through any given Space. By James Alexander, of New-York.

Read at the Royal Society, Dec. 26, 1756.

IF I remember right, the Royal Society made one experiment to discover the velocity of the electric fire, by a wire of about four miles in length, supported by silk, and by turning it forwards and backwards in a field, so that the beginning and end of the wire were at only the distance of two people, the one holding the Leyden bottle and the beginning of the wire, and the other holding the end of the

---

3 The wire mentioned in this account was re-placed by a small brass chain. In the summer of 1763, the lightning again struck that steeple, and from the clock-hammer near the bell, it pursued the chain as it had before done the wire, went off to the same hinge, and again shattered the same door. In its passage through the same holes of the same floors, it did no damage to the floors, nor to the building during the whole extent of the chain. But the chain itself was destroyed, being partly scattered about in fragments of two or three links melted and stuck together, and partly blown up or reduced to smoke, and dissipated. [See an account of the same effect of lightning on a wire at Newbury, p. 143.] The steeple, when repaired, was guarded by an iron conductor, or rod, extending from the foot of the vane-spindle down the outside of the building, into the earth. The newspapers have mentioned, that in 1765, the lightning fell a third time on the same steeple, and was safely conducted by the rod; but the particulars are not come to hand.

wire and touching the ring of the bottle; but by this experiment no discovery was made, except that the velocity was extremely quick.

As water is a conductor as well as metals, it is to be considered whether the velocity of the electric fire might not be discovered by means of water; whether a river, or lake, or sea, may not be made part of the circuit through which the electric fire passes? instead of the circuit all of wire, as in the above experiment.

Whether in a river, lake, or sea, the electric fire will not dissipate and not return to the bottle? or, will it proceed in strait lines through the water the shortest courses possible back to the bottle?

If the last, then suppose one brook that falls into Delaware doth head very near to a brook that falls into Schuylkill, and let a wire be stretched and supported as before, from the head of the one brook to the head of the other, and let the one end communicate with the water, and let one person stand in the other brook, holding the Leyden bottle, and let another person hold that end of the wire not in the water, and touch the ring of the bottle.——If the electric fire will go as in the last question, then will it go down the one brook to Delaware or Schuylkill, and down one of them to their meeting, and up the other brook; the time of its doing this may possibly be observable, and the further upwards the brooks are chosen, the more observable it would be.

Should this be not observable, then suppose the two brooks falling into Susquehanna and Delaware, and proceeding as before, the electric fire may, by that means, make a circuit round the North Cape of Virginia, and go many hundred miles, and in doing that, it would seem it must take some observable time.

If still no observable time is found in that experiment, then suppose the brooks falling the one into the Ohio, and the other into Susquehanna, or Potowmac, in that the electric fire would have a circuit of some thousands of miles to go down the Ohio to Mississippi, to the Bay of Mexico, round Florida, and round the South Cape of Virginia; which, I think, would give some observable time, and discover exactly the velocity.

But if the electric fire dissipates, or weakens in the water, as I fear it does, these experiments will not answer.

Answer to the foregoing.

Read at the Royal Society, Dec. 25, 1756.

SUPPOSE a tube of any length open at both ends, and containing a moveable wire of just the same length, that fills its bore. If I attempt to introduce the end of another wire into the same tube, it must be done by pushing forward the wire it already contains; and the instant I press and move one end of that wire, the other end is also moved, and introducing one inch of the same wire, I extrude, at the same time, an inch of the first, from the other end of the tube.

If the tube be filled with water, and I inject an additional inch of water at one end, I force out an equal quantity at the other in the very same instant.

·And the water forced out at one end of the tube is not the very same water that was forced in at the other end at the same time, it was only in motion at the same time.

The long wire, made use of in the experiment to discover the velocity of the electric fluid, is itself filled with what we call its natural quantity of that fluid, before the hook of the Leyden bottle is applied to one end of it.

The outside of the bottle being at the time of such application in contact with the other end of the wire, the whole quantity of electric fluid contained in the wire is, probably, put in motion at once.

For at the instant the hook, connected with the inside of the bottle, *gives out;* the coating or outside of the bottle, *draws in* a portion of that fluid.

If such long wire contains precisely the quantity that the outside of the bottle demands, the whole will move out of the wire to the outside of the bottle, and the over quantity which the inside of the bottle contained, being exactly equal, will flow into the wire, and remain there, in the place of the quantity the wire had just parted with to the outside of the bottle.

But if the wire be so long as that one-tenth (suppose) of its natural quantity is sufficient to supply what the outside of the bottle demands, in such case the outside will only receive what is contained in one-tenth of the wire's length, from the end next to it; though the whole will move so as to make room at the other end for an equal quantity issuing, at the same time, from the inside of the bottle.

So that this experiment only shews the extreme facility with which the electric fluid moves in metal; it can never determine the velocity.

And, therefore, the proposed experiment (though well imagined, and very ingenious) of sending the spark round through a vast length of space, by the waters of Susquehanna, or Potowmac, and Ohio, would not afford the satisfaction desired, though we could be sure that the motion of the electric fluid would be in that tract, and not under ground in the wet earth by the shortest way.

B. FRANKLIN.

FROM MR. KINNERSLEY TO B. FRANKLIN.

Experiments on boiling Water, and glass heated by boiling water.—Doctrine of repulsion in electrised bodies doubted.—Electricity of the atmosphere at different heights.—Electrical Horserace.—Electrical thermometer.—In what cases the electrical fire produces heat—Wire lengthened by Electricity.—Good effect of a rod on the house of Mr. West, of Philadelphia.

Philadelphia, March 12, 1761.

Sir,

HAVING lately made the following experiments, I very cheerfully communicate them, in hopes of giving you some degree of pleasure, and exciting you to further explore your favorite, but not quite exhausted subject, *electricity.*

I placed myself on an electric stand, and, being well electrised, threw my hat to an unelectrised person, at a considerable distance, on another stand, and found that the hat-carried some of the electricity with it; for, upon going immediately to the person who received it, and holding a flaxen thread near him, I perceived he was electrised sufficiently to attract the thread.

I then suspended, by silk, a broad plate of metal, and electrised some boiling water under it at about four feet distance, expecting that the vapor, which ascended plentifully to the plate, would, upon the principle of the foregoing experiment, carry up some of the electricity with it ; but was at length fully convinced, by several repeated trials, that it left all its share thereof behind. This I know not how to account for ; but does it not seem to corroborate your hypothesis, that the vapors of which the clouds are formed, leave their share of electricity behind, in the common stock, and ascend in the negative state ?

I put boiling water into a coated Florence flask, and found that the heat so enlarged the pores of the glass, that it could not be charged. The electricity passed through as readily, to all appearance, as through metal; the charge of a three-pint bottle went freely through, without injuring the flask in the least. When it became almost cold, I could charge it as usual. Would not this experiment convince the Abbé Nollet of his egregious mistake? For while the electricity went fairly through the glass, as he contends it always does, the glass could not be charged at all.

I took a slender piece of cedar, about eighteen inches long, fixed a brass cap in the middle, thrust a pin horizontally and at right angles, through each end (the points in contrary directions) and hung it, nicely balanced, like the needle of a compass, on a pin, about six inches long, fixed in the centre of an electric stand. Then electrising the stand, I had the pleasure of seeing what I expected; the wooden needle turned round, carrying the pins with their heads foremost. I then electrised the stand negatively, expecting the needle to turn the contrary way, but was

X

extremely disappointed, for it went still the same way as before. When the stand was electrised positively, I suppose that the natural quantity of electricity in the air being increased on one side, by what issued from the points, the needle was attracted by the lesser quantity on the other side. When electrised negatively, I suppose that the natural quantity of electricity in the air was diminished near the points ; in consequence whereof, the equilibrium being destroyed, the needle was attracted by the greater quantity on the opposite side.

The doctrine of repulsion, in electrised bodies, I begin to be somewhat doubtful of. I think all the phenomena on which it is founded, may be well enough accounted for without it. Will not cork balls, electrised negatively, separate as far as when electrised positively? And may not their separation in both cases be accounted for upon the same principle, namely, the mutual attraction of the natural quantity in the air, and that which is denser or rarer in the cork balls? it being one of the established laws of this fluid, that quantities of different densities shall mutually attract each other, in order to restore the equilibrium.

I can see no reason to conclude that the air has not its share of the common stock of electricity, as well as glass, and perhaps, all other electrics *per se.* For though the air will admit bodies to be electrised in it either positively or negatively, and will not readily carry off the redundancy in the one case, nor supply the deficiency in the other, yet let a person in the negative state, out of doors in the dark, when the air is dry, hold, with his arm extended, a long sharp needle, pointing upwards, and he will soon be convinced that electricity may be drawn out of the air; not very plentifully, for, being a bad conductor, it seems loth to part with it, but yet some will evidently be collected. The air near the person's body having less than its natural quantity, will have none to spare; but, his arm being extended, as above, some will be collected from the remoter air, and will appear luminous, as it converges to the point of the needle.

Let a person electrised negatively present the point of a needle, horizontally, to a cork ball, suspended by silk, and the ball will be attracted towards the point, till it has parted with so much of its natural quantity of electricity as to be in the negative state, in the same degree with the person who holds the needle; then it will recede from the point, being, as I suppose, attracted the contrary way by the electricity of greater density in the air behind it. But, as this opinion seems to deviate from electrical orthodoxy, I should be glad to see these phenomena better accounted for by your superior and more penetrating genius.

Whether the electricity in the air, in clear dry weather, be of the same density at the height of two or three hundred yards, as near the surface of the earth, may be satisfactorily determined by your old experiment of the kite. The twine should have throughout a very small wire in it, and the ends of the wire, where the several lengths are united, ought to be tied down with a waxed thread, to prevent their acting in the manner of points. I have tried the experiment twice, when the air was as dry as we ever have it, and so clear that not a cloud could be seen, and found the twine each time in a small degree electrised positively. The kite had three metalline points fixed to it : one on the top, and one on each side. That the twine was electrised, appeared by the separating of two small cork balls, suspended on the twine by fine flaxen threads, just above where the silk was tied to it, and sheltered from the wind. That the twine was electrised positively, was proved, by applying it to the wire of a charged bottle, which caused the balls to separate further, without first coming nearer together. This experiment showed, that the electricity in the air, at those times, was denser above than below. But that cannot be always the case; for you know we have frequently found the thunder-clouds in the negative state, attracting electricity from the earth; which state, it is probable, they are always in when first formed, and till they have received a sufficient supply. How they come afterwards, towards the latter end of the gust, to be in the positive state, which is sometimes the case, is a subject for further enquiry.

After the above experiments with the wooden needle, I formed a cross, of two pieces of wood, of equal length, intersecting each other at right angles in the middle, hung it horizontally upon a central pin, and set a light horse with his rider, upon each extremity; whereupon, the whole being nicely balanced, and each courser urged on by an electrised point of a pair of spurs, I was entertained with an electrical horse-race.

I have contrived an electrical air thermometer, and made several experiments with it, that have afforded me much satisfaction and pleasure. It is extremely sensible of any alteration in the state of the included air, and fully determines that controverted point, Whether there be any heat in the electric fire? By the enclosed draught, and the following description, you will readily apprehend the construction of it. (See the Plate.)

A B is a glass tube, about eleven inches long, and one inch diameter in the bore. It has a brass ferrule cemented on each end, with a top and bottom part, C and D, to be screwed on, air-tight, and taken off at pleasure. In the centre of the bottom part D, is a male screw, which goes into a brass nut, in the mahogany pedestal E. The wires F and G are for the electric fire to pass through, darting from one to the other. The wire G extends through the pedestal to H, and may be raised and lowered by means of a male screw on it. The wire F may be taken out, and the hook I be screwed into its place. K is a glass tube, with a small bore, open at both ends, cemented in the brass tube L, which screws into the top part C. The lower end of the tube K is immersed in water, colored with cochineal, at the bottom of the tube A B. (I used, at first, colored spirits of wine, but in one experiment I made, it took fire.) On the top of the tube K is cemented, for ornament, a brass ferrule, with a head screwed on it, which has a small air-hole through its side, at *a*. The wire *b*, is a small round spring, that embraces the tube K, so as to stay wherever it

Pl. 4.

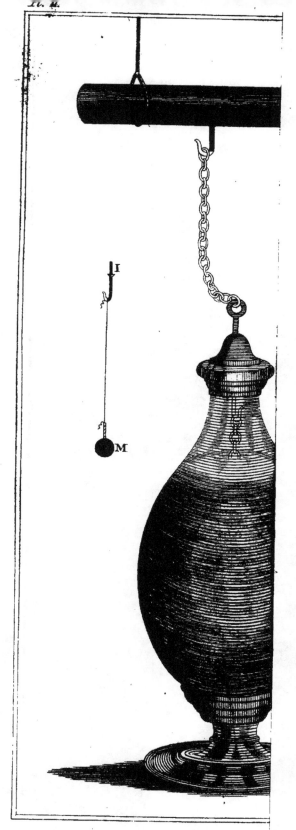

is placed. The weight M is to keep strait whatever may be suspended in the tube A B, on the hook I. Air must be blown through the tube K, into the tube A B, till enough is intruded to raise, by its elastic force, a column of the colored water in the tube K, up to *c*, or thereabouts ; and then, the gage-wire *b*, being slipt down to the top of the column, the thermometer is ready for use.

I set the thermometer on an electric stand, with the chain N fixed to the prime conductor, and kept it well electrised a considerable time; but this produced no sensible effect; which shews, that the electric fire, when in a state of rest, has no more heat than the air, and other matter wherein it resides.

When the wires F and G are in contact, a large charge of electricity sent through them, even that of my case of five and thirty bottles, containing above thirty square feet of coated glass, will produce no rarefaction of the air included in the tube A B; which shows that the wires are not heated by the fire's passing through them.

When the wires are about two inches apart, the charge of a three pint bottle, darting from one to the other, rarefies the air very evidently; which shows, I think, that the electric fire must produce heat in itself, as well as in the air, by its rapid motion.

The charge of one of my glass jars (which will contain about five gallons and a half, wine measure) darting from wire to wire, will, by the disturbance it gives the air, repelling it in all directions, raise the column in the tube K, up to *d*, or thereabouts; and the charge of the above-mentioned case of bottles will raise it to the top of the tube. Upon the air's coalescing, the column, by its gravity, instantly subsides, till it is in equilibrio with the rarefied air; it then gradually descends as the air cools, and settles where it stood before. By carefully observing at what height above the gage-wire *b*, the descending column first stops, the degree of rarefaction is discovered, which, in great explosions, is very considerable.

I hung in the thermometer, successively, a strip of wet writing paper, a wet flaxen and woollen thread, a blade of green grass, a filament of green wood, a fine silver thread, a very small brass wire, and a strip of gilt paper; and found that the charge of the above-mentioned glass jar, passing through each of these, especially the last, produced heat enough to rarefy the air very perceptibly.

I then suspended, out of the thermometer, a piece of small harpsichord wire, about twenty-four inches long, with a pound weight at the lower end, and sent the charge of the case of five and thirty bottles through it, whereby I discovered a new method of wire-drawing. The wire was red hot the whole length, well annealed, and above an inch longer than before. A second charge melted it; it parted near the middle, and measured, when the ends were put together, four inches longer than at first. This experiment, I remember, you proposed to me before you left Philadelphia; but I never tried it till now. That I might have no doubt of the wire's being *hot* as well as red, I repeated the experiment on another piece of the same wire encompassed with a goose-quill, filled with loose grains of gun-powder; which took fire as readily as if it had been touched with a red hot poker. Also tinder, tied to another piece of the wire, kindled by it. I tried a wire about three times as big, but could produce no such effects with that.

Hence it appears that the electric fire, though it has no sensible heat when in a state of rest, will, by its violent motion, and the resistance it meets with, produce heat in other bodies when passing through them, provided they be small enough. A large quantity will pass through a large wire, without producing any sensible heat; when the same quantity passing through a very small one, being there confined to a narrower passage, the particles crowding closer together, and meeting with greater resistance, will make it red hot, and even melt it.

Hence lightning does not melt metal by a cold fusion, as we formerly supposed; but, when it passes through the blade of a sword, if the quantity be not very great, it may heat the point so as to melt it, while the broadest and thick-est part may not be sensibly warmer than before.

And when trees or houses are set on fire by the dreadful quantity which a cloud, or the earth, sometimes discharges, must not the heat, by which the wood is first kindled, be generated by the lightning's violent motion, through the resisting combustible matter?

If lightning, by its rapid motion, produces heat in *itself*; as well as in other bodies (and that it does I think is evi-dent from some of the foregoing experiments made with the thermometer) then its sometimes singeing the hair of animals killed by it, may easily be accounted for. And the reasons of its not always doing so, may, perhaps, be this : the quantity, though sufficient to kill a large animal, may sometimes not be great enough, or not have met with resistance enough, to become, by its motion, burning hot.

We find that dwelling-houses, struck with lightning, are seldom set on fire by it; but when it passes through barns, with hay or straw in them, or store-houses, containing large quantities of hemp, or such like matter, they seldom, if ever, escape a conflagration; which may, perhaps, be owing to such combustibles being apt to kindle with a less degree of heat than is necessary to kindle wood.

We had four houses in this city, and a vessel at one of the wharfs, struck and damaged by lightning last summer. One of the houses was struck twice in the same storm. But I have the pleasure to inform you, that your method of preventing such terrible disasters, has, by a fact which had like to have escaped our knowlege, given a very con-vincing proof of its great utility, and is now in higher repute with us than ever.

Hearing, a few days ago, that Mr. William West, mer-chant in this city, suspected that the lightning in one of the thunder-storms last summer had passed through the iron conductor, which he had provided for the security of his house; I waited on him, to enquire what ground he might have for such suspicion, Mr. West informed me, that his family and neighbors were all stunned with a very terrible explosion, and that the flash and crack were seen and heard at the same instant. Whence he concluded, that the lightning must have been very near, and, as no house in the neighborhood had suffered by it, that it must have passed through his conductor. Mr. White, his clerk, told me that he was sitting, at the time, by a window, about two feet distant from the conductor, leaning against the brick wall with which it was in contact; and that he felt a smart sensation, like an electric shock, in that part of the body which touched the wall. Mr. West further informed me, that a person of undoubted veracity assured him, that, being in the door of an opposite house, on the other side of Water-street (which you know is but narrow) he saw the lightning diffused over the pavement, which was then very wet with rain, to the distance of two or three yards from the foot of the conductor; and that another person of very good credit told him, that he being a few doors off on the other side of the street, saw the lightning above, darting in such direction that it appeared to him to be directly over that pointed rod.

Upon receiving this information, and being desirous of further satisfaction, there being no traces of the lightning to be discovered in the conductor, as far as we could examine it below, I proposed to Mr. West our going to the top of the house, to examine the pointed rod, assuring him, that if the lightning had passed through it, the point must have been melted; and to our great satisfaction, we found it so. This iron rod extended in height about nine feet and a half above a stack of chimnies to which it was fixed (though I suppose three or four feet would have been sufficient.) It was somewhat more than half an inch diameter in the thickest part, and tapering to the upper end. The conductor, from the lower end of it to the earth, consisted of square iron nail rods, not much above a quarter of an inch thick, connected together by interlinking joints. It extended down the cedar roof to the eaves, and from thence down the wall of the house, four story and an half, to the pavement in Water-street, being fastened to the wall in several places, by small iron hooks. The lower end was fixed to a ring, in the top of an iron stake that was drove about four or five feet into the ground.

The above mentioned iron rod had a hole in the top of it, about two inches deep, wherein was inserted a brass wire, about two lines thick, and when first put there, about ten inches long, terminating in a very acute point; but now its whole length was no more than seven inches and a half, and the top very blunt. Some of the metal appears to be missing, the slenderest part of the wire being, as I suspect, consumed into smoke. But some of it, where the wire was a little thicker, being only melted by the lightning, sunk down, while in a fluid state, and formed a rough irregular cap, lower on one side than the other, round the upper end of what remained, and became intimately united therewith.

This was all the damage that Mr. West sustained by a terrible stroke of lightning; a most convincing proof of the great utility of this method of preventing its dreadful effects. Surely it will now be thought as expedient to provide conductors for the lightning, as for the rain.

Mr. West was so good as to make me a present of the melted wire, which I keep as a great curiosity, and long for the pleasure of shewing it to you. In the mean time, I beg your acceptance of the best representation I can give of it, which you will find by the side of the thermometer, drawn in its full dimentions as it now appears. The dotted lines above are intended to shew the form of the wire before the lightning melted it.

And now, Sir, I most heartily congratulate you on the pleasure you must have in finding your great and well grounded expectations so far fulfilled. May this method of security from the destructive violence of one of the most awful powers of nature, meet with such further success, as to induce every good and greatful heart to bless God for the important discovery! May the benefit thereof be diffused over the whole globe! May it extend to the latest

Y

posterity of mankind, and make the name of FRANKLIN, like that of NEWTON, *immortal.*

I am, Sir, with sincere respect,
Your most obedient and humble servant,
EBEN. KINNERSLEY.

TO MR. KINNERSLEY.

Answer to some of the foregoing subjects.—How long the Leyden bottle may be kept charged.—Heated glass rendered permeable by the electric fluid.—Electrical attraction and repulsion.—Reply to other subjects in the preceding paper.—Numerous ways of kindling Fire. Explosion of water.—Knobs and points.

London, February 20, 1762.

SIR,

I RECEIVED your ingenious letter of the 12th of March last, and thank you cordially for the account you give me of the new experiments you have lately made in electricity.—It is a subject that still affords me pleasure, though of late I have not much attended to it.

Your second experiment, in which you attempted, without success, to communicate positive electricity by vapor ascending from the electrised water, reminds me of one I formerly made, to try if negative electricity might be produced by evaporation only. I placed a large heated brass plate, containing four or five square feet on an electric stand: a rod of metal, about four feet long, with a bullet at its end, extended from the plate horizontally. A light lock of cotton, suspended by a fine thread from the cieling, hung opposite to, and within an inch of the bullet. I then sprinkled the heated plate with water, which arose fast from it in vapor. If vapor should be disposed to carry off the electrical, as it does the common fire from bodies, I expected the plate would, by losing some of its natural quantity, become negatively electrised. But I could not perceive, by any motion in the cotton, that it was at all affected: nor by any separation of small cork balls suspended from the plate, could it be observed that the plate was in any manner electrified.

Mr. Canton here has also found, that two tea cups, set on electric stands, and filled one with boiling; the other with cold water, and equally electrified, continued equally so, notwithstanding the plentiful vaporation from the hot water. Your experiment and his agreeing, shews another remarkable difference between electric and common, fire. For the latter quits most readily the body that contains it, where water, or any other fluid, is evaporating from the surface of that body, and escapes with the vapor. Hence the method, long in use in the east, of cooling liquors, by wrapping the bottles round with a wet cloth, and exposing them to the wind. Dr. Cullen, of Edinburgh, has given some experiments of cooling by evaporation ; and I was present at one made by Dr. Hadley, then professor of che- mistry at Cambridge, when, by repeatedly wetting the ball of a thermometer with spirit, and quickening the evapora- tion by the blast of a bellows, the mercury fell from 65, the state of warmth in the common air to 7, which is 22 de- grees below freezing ; and, accordingly, from some water mixed with the spirit, or from the breath of the assistants, or both, ice gathered in small spicula round the ball, to the thickness of near a quarter of an inch. To such a de- gree did the mercury lose the fire it before contained, which, as I imagine, took the opportunity of escaping, in company with the evaporating particles of the spirit, by adhering to those particles.

Your experiments of the Florence flask, and boiling water, is very curious. I have repeated it, and found it to succeed as you describe it, in two flasks out of three. The third would not charge when filled with either hot or cold water. I repeated it, because I remembered I had once attempted to make an electric bottle of a Florence flask, filled with cold water, but could not charge it at all ; which I then imputed to some imperceptible cracks in the small, extremely thin bubbles, of which that glass is full, and I concluded none of that kind would do. But you have shown me my mistake.——Mr. Wilson had formerly acquainted us, that red hot glass would conduct electricity; but that so small a degree of heat, as that communicated by boiling water, would so open the pores of extremely thin glass, as to suffer the electric fluid freely to pass, was not before known. Some experiments similar to yours, have, however, been made here, before the receipt of your letter, of which I shall now give you an account.

I formerly had an opinion that a Leyden bottle, charged and then sealed hermetically, might retain its electricity for ever; but having afterwards some suspicion that possibly that subtle fluid might, by slow imperceptible degrees, soak through the glass, and in time escape, I requested some of my friends, who had conveniences for doing it, to make trial, whether after some months, the charge of a bottle so sealed would be sensibly diminished. Being at Birmingham, in September, 1760, Mr. Bolton of that place opened a bottle that had been charged, and its long tube neck hermetically sealed in January preceding. On breaking off the end of the neck and introducing a wire into it, we found it possessed of a considerable quantity of electricity, which was discharged by a snap and spark. This bottle had lain near seven months on a shelf, in a closet, in contact with bodies that would undoubtedly have carried off all its electricity, if it could have come readily through the glass. Yet as the quantity manifested by the discharge was not apparently so great as might have been expected from a bottle of that size well charged, some doubt remained whether part had escaped while the neck was sealing, or had since, by degrees, soaked through the glass. But an experiment of Mr. Canton's, in which such a bottle was kept under water a week, without having its electricity in the least impaired, seems to show, that when the glass is cold, though extremely thin, the electric fluid is well retained by it. As that ingenious and accurate experimenter made a discovery, like yours, of the effect of heat in rendering thin glass permeable by that fluid, it is but doing him justice to give you his account of it, in his own words, extracted from his letter to me, in which he communicated it, dated October 31, 1760, *viz.*

" Having procured some thin glass balls, of about an inch and an half in diameter, with stems, or tubes, of eight or nine inches in length, I electrified them, some positively on the inside, and others negatively, after the manner of charging the Leyden bottle, and sealed them hermetically. Soon after I applied the naked balls to my electrometer, and could not discover the least sign of their being electrical, but holding them before the fire, at the distance of six or eight inches, they became strongly electrical in a very short time, and more so when they were cooling. These balls will, every time they are heated, give the electrical fluid to, or take it from other bodies, according to the *plus* or *minus* state of it within them. Heating them frequently, I find will sensibly diminish their power; but keeping one of them under water a week did not appear in the least degree to impair it. That which I kept under water, was charged on the 22d of September last, was several times heated before it was kept in water, and has been heated frequently since, and yet it still retains its virtue to a very considerable degree. The breaking two of my balls accidentally gave me an opportunity of measuring their thickness, which I found to be between seven and eight parts in a thousand of an inch.

A down feather, in a thin glass ball, hermetically sealed, will not be affected by the application of an excited tube, or the wire of a charged phial, unless the ball be considerably heated; and if a glass pane be heated till it begins to grow soft, and in that state be held between the wire of a charged phial, and the discharging wire, the course of the electrical fluid will not be through the glass, but on the surface, round by the edge of it."

By this last experiment of Mr. Canton's, it appears, that though by a moderate heat, thin glass becomes, in some degree, a conductor of electricity, yet, when of the thickness of a common pane, it is not, though in a state near melting, so good a conductor as to pass the shock of a discharged bottle. There are other conductors which suffer the electric fluid to pass through them gradually, and yet will not conduct a shock. For instance, a quire of paper will conduct through its whole length, so as to electrify a person, who, standing on wax, presents the paper to an electrified prime conductor; but it will not conduct a shock even through its thickness only; hence the shock either fails, or passes by rendering a hole in the paper. Thus a sieve will pass water gradually, but a stream from a fire engine would either be stopped by it, or tear a hole through it.

It should seem, that to make glass permeable to the electric fluid, the heat should be proportioned to the thickness. You found the heat of boiling water, which is but 210, sufficient to render the extreme thin glass in a Florence flask permeable even to a shock.—Lord Charles Cavendish, by a very ingenious experiment, has found the heat of 400 requisite to render thicker glass permeable to the common current.

" A glass tube, (See the *Plate.*) of which the part C B was solid, had wire thrust in each end, reaching to B and C.

" A small wire was tied on at D, reaching to the floor, in order to carry off any electricity that might run along upon the tube.

" The bent part was placed in an iron pot; filled with iron filings; a thermometer was also put into the filings: a lamp was placed under the pot; and the whole was supported upon glass.

" The wire A being electrified by a machine, before the heat was applied, the corks at E separated, at first upon the principle of the Leyden phial.

" But after the part C B of the tube was heated to 600, the corks continued to separate, though you discharged the electricity by touching the wire at E, the electrical machine continuing in motion.

" Upon letting the whole cool, the effect remained till the thermometer was sunk to 400."

It were to be wished, that this noble philosopher would communicate more of his experiments to the world, as he makes many, and with great accuracy.

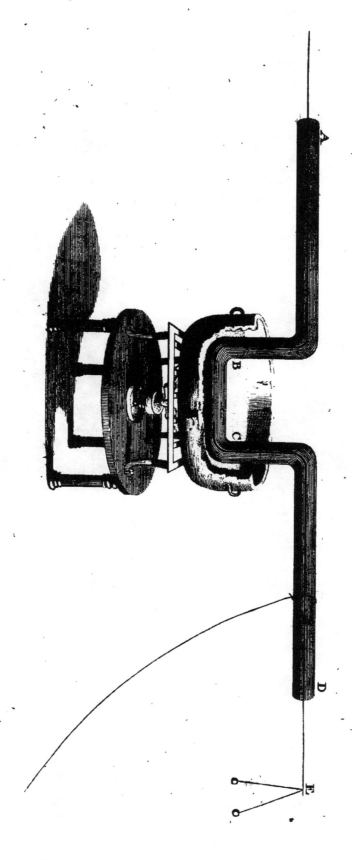

You know I have always looked upon and mentioned the equal repulsion in cases of positive and of negative electricity, as a phenomenon difficult to be explained. I have sometimes, too, been inclined, with you, to resolve all into attraction; but besides that attraction seems in itself as unintelligible as repulsion, there are some appearances of repulsion that I cannot so easily explain by attraction; this for one instance. When the pair of cork balls are suspended by flaxen threads, from the end of the prime conductor, if you bring a rubbed glass tube near the conductor, but without touching it, you see the balls separate, as being electrified positively; and yet you have communicated no electricity to the conductor, for, if you had, it would have remained there, after withdrawing the tube; but the closing of the balls immediately thereupon, shows that the conductor has no more left in it than its natural quantity. Then again approaching the conductor with the rubbed tube, if, while the balls are separated, you touch with a finger that end of the conductor to which they hang, they will come together again, as being, with that part of the conductor, brought to the same state with your finger, *i. e.* the natural state. But the other end of the conductor, near which the tube is held, is not in that state, but in the negative state, as appears on removing the tube; for then part of the natural quantity left at the end near the balls, leaving that end to supply what is wanting at the other, the whole conductor is found to be equally in the negative state. Does not this indicate that the electricity of the rubbed tube had repelled the electric fluid, which was diffused in the conductor while in its natural state, and forced it to quit the end to which the balls were suspended? I own I find it difficult to account for its quitting that end on the approach of the rubbed tube, but on the supposition of repulsion; for, while the conductor was in the same state with the air, *i. e.* the natural state, it does not seem to me easy to suppose, that an attraction should suddenly take place between the air and the natural quantity of the electric fluid in the conductor, so as to draw it to, and accumulate it on the end opposite to that approached by the tube; since bodies, possessing only their natural quantity of that fluid, are not usually seen to attract each other, or to affect mutually the quantities of electricity each contains.

There are likewise appearances of repulsion in other parts of nature. Not to mention the violent force with which the particles of water, heated to a certain degree, separate from each other, or those of gunpowder, when touched with the smallest spark of fire, there is the seeming repulsion between the same poles of the magnet, a body containing a subtle moveable fluid in many respects analogous to the electric fluid. If two magnets are so suspended by strings, as that their poles of the same denomination are opposite to each other, they will separate, and continue so; or if you lay a magnetic steel bar on a smooth table, and approach it with another parallel to it, the poles of both in the same position, the first will recede from the second, so as to avoid the contact, and may thus be pushed (or at least appear to be pushed) off the table. Can this be ascribed to the attraction of any surrounding body or matter drawing them asunder, or drawing the one away from the other? If not, and repulsion exists in nature, and in magnetism, why may it not exist in electricity? We should not, indeed, multiply causes in philosophy without necessity; and the greater simplicity of your hypothesis would recommend it to me, if I could see that all appearances would be solved by it. But I find, or think I find, the two causes more convenient than one of them alone. Thus I might solve the circular motion of your horizontal stick, supported on a pivot, with two pins at their ends, pointing contrary ways, and moving in the same direction when electrified, whether positively or negatively: when positively, the air opposite to the points being electrised positively, repels the points; when negatively, the air opposite the points being also, by their means, electrised negatively, attraction takes place between the electricity in the air behind the heads of the pins, and the negative pins, and so they are, in this case, drawn in the same direction that in the other they were

driven.—You see I am willing to meet you half way, a
complaisance I have not met with in our brother Nollet, or
any other hypothesis-maker, and therefore may value myself a little upon it, especially as they say I have some
ability in defending even the wrong side of a question,
when I think fit to take it in hand.

What you give as an established law of the electric fluid,
" That quantities of different densities mutually attract each
other, in order to restore the equilibrium," is, I think, not
well founded, or else not well expressed. Two large cork
balls, suspended by silk strings, and both well and equally
electrified, separate to a great distance. By bringing into contact with one of them another ball of the same size, suspended
likewise by silk, you will take from it half its electricity. It
will then, indeed, hang at a less distance from the other,
but the full and the half quantities will not appear to attract
each other, that is, the balls will not come together. Indeed, I do not know any proof we have, that one quantity
of electric fluid is attracted by another quantity of that
fluid, whatever difference there may be in their densities.
And, supposing in nature, a mutual attraction between
two parcels of any kind of matter, it would be strange if
this attraction should subsist strongly while those parcels
were unequal, and cease when more matter of the same
kind was added to the smallest parcel, so as to make it equal
to the biggest. By all the laws of attraction in matter, that
we are acquainted with, the attraction is stronger in proportion to the increase of the masses, and never in proportion
to the difference of the masses. I should rather think the
law would be, " That the electric fluid is attracted strongly
by all other matter that we know of, while the parts of that
fluid mutually repel each other." Hence its being equally
diffused (except in particular circumstances) throughout all
other matter. But this you jokingly call " electrical orthodoxy." It is so with some at present, but not with all; and,
perhaps, it may not always be orthodoxy with any body.
Opinions are continually varying, where we cannot have
mathematical evidence of the nature of things: and they

Z

must vary. Nor is that variation without its use, since it occasions a more thorough discussion, whereby error is often dissipated, true knowlege is increased, and its principles become better understood and more firmly established.

Air should have, as you observe, " its share of the common stock of electricity, as well as glass, and, perhaps, all other electrics *per se.*" But I suppose, that, like them, it does not easily part with what it has, or receive more, unless when mixed with some non-electric, as moisture for instance, of which there is some in our driest air. This, however, is only a supposition; and your experiment of restoring electricity to a negatively electrised person, by extending his arm upwards into the air, with a needle between his fingers, on the point of which light may be seen in the night, is, indeed, a curious one. In this town the air is generally moister than with us, and here I have seen Mr. Canton electrify the air in one room positively, and in another, which communicated by a door, he has electrised the air negatively. The difference was easily discovered by his cork balls, as he passed out of one room into another.——Père Beccaria, too, has a pretty experiment, which shows that air may be electrised. Suspending a pair of small light balls, by flaxen threads, to the end of his prime conductor, he turns his globe some time, electrising positively, the balls diverging and continuing separate all the time. Then he presents the point of a needle to his conductor, which gradually drawing off the electric fluid, the balls approach each other, and touch, before all is drawn from the conductor; opening again as more is drawn off, and separating nearly as wide as at first, when the conductor is reduced to the natural state. By this it appears, that when the balls came together, the air surrounding the balls was just as much electrised as the conductor at that time; and more than the conductor, when that was reduced to its natural state. For the balls, though in the natural state, will diverge, when the air that surrounds them is electrised *plus* or *minus*, as well as when that is in its natural state and they are electrised *plus* or *minus* themselves. I foresee that you will apply this experiment to the support of your hypothesis, and I think you may make a good deal of it.

It was a curious inquiry of yours, Whether the electricity of the air, in clear dry weather, be of the same density at the height of two or three hundred yards, as near the surface of the earth?....and I am glad you made the experiment. Upon reflection, it should seem probable, that whether the general state of the atmosphere at any time be positive or negative, that part of it which is next the earth will be nearer the natural state, by having given to the earth in one case, or having received from it in the other. In electrising the air of a room, that which is nearest the walls, or floor, is least altered. There is only one small ambiguity in the experiment, which may be cleared by more trials; it arises from the supposition that bodies may be electrised positively by the friction of air blowing strongly on them, as it does on the kite and its string. If at some times the electricity appears to be negative, as that friction is the same, the effect must be as from a negative state of the upper air.

I am much pleased with your electrical thermometer, and the experiments you have made with it. I formerly satisfied myself by an experiment with my phial and syphon, that the elasticity of the air was not increased by the mere existence of an electric atmosphere within the phial; but I did not know, till you now inform me, that heat may be given to it by an electric explosion. The continuance of its rarefaction, for some time after the discharge of your glass jar and of your case of bottles, seem to make this clear. The other experiments on wet paper, wet thread, green grass, and green wood, are not so satisfactory; as possibly the reducing part of the moisture to vapor, by the electric fluid passing through it, might occasion some expansion which would be gradually reduced by the condensation of such vapor. The fine silver thread, the very small brass wire, and the strip of gilt paper, are also subject to a similar objection, as even metals, in such circumstances are often partly reduced to smoke, particularly the gilding on paper.

But your subsequent beautiful experiment on the wire, which you made hot by the electric explosion, and in that state fired gunpowder with it, puts it out of all question, that heat is produced by our artificial electricity, and that the melting of metals in that way, is not by what I formerly called a cold fusion. A late instance here, of the melting a bell-wire, in a house struck by lightning, and parts of the wire burning holes in the floor on which they fell, has proved the same with regard to the electricity of nature. I was too easily led into that error by accounts given, even in philosophical books, and from remote ages downwards, of melting money in purses, swords in scabbards, &c. without burning the inflammable matters that were so near those melted metals. But men are, in general, such careless observers that a philosopher cannot be too much on his guard in crediting their relations of things extraordinary, and should never build an hypothesis on any thing but clear facts and experiments, or it will be in danger of soon falling, as this does, like a house of cards.

How many ways there are of kindling fire, or producing heat in bodies! By the sun's rays, by collision, by friction, by hammering, by putrefaction, by fermentation, by mixtures of fluids, by mixtures of solids with fluids, and by electricity. And yet the fire when produced, though in different bodies it may differ in circumstances, as in color, vehemence, &c. yet in the same bodies it is generally the same. Does not this seem to indicate that the fire existed in the body, though in a quiescent state, before it was by any of these means excited, disengaged, and brought forth to action and to view? May it not constitute a part, and even a principal part, of the solid substance of bodies? If this should be the case, kindling fire in a body would be nothing more than developing this inflammable principle, and setting it at liberty to act in separating the parts of that body, which then exhibits the appearances of scorching, melting, burning, &c. When a man lights an hundred candles from the flame of one, without diminishing that flame, can it be properly said to have *communicated* all that fire?

When a single spark from a flint, applied to a magazine of gunpowder, is immediately attended with this consequence, that the whole is in flame, exploding with immense violence, could all this fire exist first in the spark? We cannot conceive it. And thus we seem led to this supposition, that there is fire enough in all bodies to singe, melt, or burn them, whenever it is, by any means, set at liberty, so that it may exert itself upon them, or be disengaged from them. This liberty seems to be afforded it by the passage of electricity through them, which we know can and does, of itself, separate the parts even of water; and perhaps the immediate appearances of fire are only the effects of such separations? If so, there would be no need of supposing that the electric fluid *heats itself* by the swiftness of its motion, or heats bodies by the resistance it meets with in passing through them. They would only be heated in proportion as such separation could be more easily made. Thus a melting heat cannot be given to a large wire in the flame of a candle, though it may to a small one; and this not because the large wire resists *less* that action of the flame which tends to separate its parts, but because it resists it *more* than the smaller wire; or because the force being divided among more parts acts weaker on each.

This reminds me, however, of a little experiment I have frequently made, that shows, at one operation, the different effects of the same quantity of electric fluid passing through different quantities of metal. A strip of tinfoil, three inches long, a quarter of an inch wide at one end, and tapering all the way to a sharp point at the other, fixed between two pieces of glass, and having the electricity of a large glass jar sent through it, will not be discomposed in the broadest part; towards the middle will appear melted in spots; where narrower, it will be quite melted; and about half an inch of it next the point will be reduced to smoke.

You were not mistaken in supposing that your account of the effect of the pointed rod, in securing Mr. West's house from damage by a stroke of lightning, would give me great pleasure. I thank you for it most heartily, and for the pains you have taken in giving me so complete a description of its situation, form, and substance, with the draft of the melted point. There is one circumstance, *viz.* that the lightning was seen to diffuse itself from the foot of the rod over the wet pavement, which seems, I think, to indicate that the earth under the pavement was very dry, and that the rod should have been sunk deeper, till it came to earth moister, and therefore apter to receive and dissipate the electric fluid. And although, in this instance, a conductor formed of nail rods, not much above a quarter of an inch thick, served well to convey the lightning, yet some accounts I have seen from Carolina, give reason to think that larger may be sometimes necessary, at least for the security of the conductor itself, which when too small, may be destroyed in executing its office, though it does, at the same time, preserve the house. Indeed, in the construction of an instrument so new, and of which we could have so little experience, it is rather lucky that we should at first be so near the truth as we seem to be, and commit so few errors.

There is another reason for sinking deeper the lower end of the rod, and also for turning it outwards under ground to some distance from the foundation; it is this, that water dripping from the eaves falls near the foundation, and sometimes soaks down there in greater quantities, so as to come near the end of the rod, though the ground about it be drier. In such case, this water may be exploded, that is, blown into vapor, whereby a force is generated, that may damage the foundation. Water reduced to vapor, is said to occupy 14,000 times its former space. I have sent a charge through a small glass tube, that has borne it well while empty, but when filled first with water, was shattered to pieces and driven all about the room:—finding no part of the water on the table, I suspected it to have been reduced to vapor; and was confirmed in that suspicion afterwards, when I had filled a like piece of tube with ink, and laid it on a sheet of clean paper, whereon, after the explosion, I could find neither any moisture nor any sully from the ink. This experiment of the explosion of water, which I believe was first made by that most ingenious electrician, father Beccaria, may account for what we sometimes see in a tree struck by lightning, when part of it is reduced to fine splinters like a broom; the sap vessels being so many tubes containing a watery fluid, which, when reduced to vapor, rends every tube lengthways. And perhaps it is this rarefaction of the fluids in animal bodies killed by lightning or electricity, that, by separating its fibres, renders the flesh so tender, and apt so much sooner to putrify. I think too, that much of the damage done by lightning to stone and brick walls may sometimes be owing to the explosion of water, found, during showers, running or lodging in the joints or small cavities or cracks that happen to be in the walls.

Here are some electricians that recommend knobs instead of points on the upper end of the rods, from a supposition that the points invite the stroke. It is true that points draw electricity at greater distances in the gradual silent way; but knobs will draw at the greatest distance a stroke. There is an experiment that will settle this. Take a crooked wire of the thickness of a quill, and of such a length as that one end of it being applied to the lower part of a charged bottle, the upper may be brought near the ball on the top of the wire that is in the bottle. Let one end of this wire be furnished with a knob, and the other may be gradually tapered to a fine point. When the point is presented to discharge the bottle, it must be brought much nearer before it will receive the stroke, then the knob requires to be. Points besides tend to repel the fragments of an electrised cloud, knobs draw them nearer. An experiment, which I believe I have shewn you, of cotton fleece hanging from an electrised body, shows this clearly when a point or a knob is presented under it.

You seem to think highly of the importance of this discovery, as do many others on our side of the water. Here it is very little regarded; so little, that though it is now seven or eight years since it was made public, I have not heard of a single house as yet attempted to be secured by it. It is true the mischiefs done by lightning are not so frequent here as with us, and those who calculate chances may perhaps find that not one death (or the destruction of one house) in an hundred thousand happens from that cause, and that therefore it is scarce worth while to be at any expence to guard against it.——But in all countries there are particular situations of buildings more exposed than others to such accidents, and there are minds so strongly impressed with the apprehension of them, as to be very unhappy every time a little thunder is within their hearing; it may therefore be well to render this little piece of new knowlege as general and as well understood as possible, since to make us *safe* is not all its advantage, it is some to make us *easy*. And as the stroke it secures us from might have chanced perhaps but once in our lives, while it may relieve us a hundred times from those painful apprehensions, the latter may possibly on the whole contribute more to the happiness of mankind than the former.

Your kind wishes and congratulations are very obliging. I return them cordially;—being, with great regard and esteem,

My dear Sir,
Your affectionate friend,
And most obedient humble servant,
B. FRANKLIN."

EFFECTS OF LIGHTNING IN CAROLINA,
Referred to in the preceding Letter—of the Effects of Lightning on two of the Rods commonly affixed to Houses there, for securing them against Lightning.

Charleston, Nov. 1, 1760.

" ——— It is some years since Mr. Raven's rod was struck by lightning. I hear an account of it was published at the time, but I cannot find it. According to the best information I can now get, he had fixed to the outside of his chimney a large iron rod, several feet in length, reaching above the chimney; and to the top of this rod the points were fixed. From the lower end of this rod, a small brass wire was continued down to the top of another iron rod driven into the earth. On the ground-floor in the chimney stood a gun, leaning against the back wall, nearly opposite to where the brass wire came down on the outside. The lightning fell upon the points, did no damage to the rod they were fixed to; but the brass wire, all down till it came opposite to the top of the gun-barrel, was destroyed[4]. There the lightning made a hole through the wall or back of the chimney, to get to the gun-barrel[5], down which it seems to have passed, as, although it did not hurt the barrel, it damaged the butt of the stock, and blew up some bricks of the hearth. The brass wire below the hole in the wall remained good. No other damage, as I can learn, was done to the house. I am told the same house had formerly been struck by lightning, and much damaged, before these rods were invented."

Mr. William Maine's Account of the Effects of the Lightning on his Rod, dated at Indian Land, in South Carolina, August 28, 1760.

.... " I had a set of electrical points, consisting of three prongs, of large brass wire tipt with silver, and perfectly sharp, each about seven inches long; these were rivetted at equal distances into an iron nut about three quarters of an inch square, and opened at top equally to the distance of six or seven inches from point to point, in a regular triangle. This nut was screwed very tight on the top of an iron rod of above half an inch diameter, or the thickness of a common curtain-rod, composed of several joints, annexed by hooks turned at the ends of each joint,

---

4 A proof that it was not of sufficient substance to conduct with safety to itself (though with safety *so far* to the wall) so large a quantity of the electric fluid.

5 A more substantial conductor.

and the whole fixed to the chimney of my house by iron staples. The points were elevated *(a)* six or seven inches above the top of the chimney; and the lower joint sunk three feet in the earth, in a perpendicular direction.

Thus stood the points on Tuesday last about five in the evening, when the lightning broke with a violent explosion on the chimney, eut the rod square off just under the nut, and I am persuaded, melted the points, nut, and top of the rod, entirely up; as after the most diligent search, nothing of either was found *(b)*, and the top of the remaining rod was cased over with a congealed solder. The lightning ran down the rod, starting almost all the staples *(c)*, and unhooking the joints without affecting the rod *(d)*, except on the inside of each hook where the joints were coupled, the surface of which was melted *(e)*, and left as cased over with solder.——No part of the chimney was damaged *(f)*, only at the foundation *(g)*, where it was shattered almost quite round, and several bricks were torn out *(h)*, Considerable cavities were made in the earth quite round the foundation, but most within eight or nine inches of the rod. It also shattered the bottom weather-board *(i)*, at one corner of the house, and made a large hole in the earth by the corner post. On the other side of the chimney, it ploughed up several furrows in the earth, some yards in length. It ran down the inside of the chimney *(k)*, carrying only soot with it; and filled the whole house with its flash *(l)*, smoke, and dust. It tore up the hearth in several places *(m)*, and broke some pieces of china in the bœufet *(n)*. A copper tea-kettle standing in the chimney was beat together, as if some great weight had fallen upon it *(o)*; and three holes, each about half an inch diameter, melted through the bottom *(p)*. What seems to me the most surprising is, that the hearth under the kettle was not hurt, yet the bottom of the kettle was drove inward, as if the lightning proceeded from under it upwards *(q)*, and the cover was thrown to the middle of the floor *(r)*. The fire dogs, an iron logger-head, an Indian pot, an earthen cup, and a cat, were all in the chimney at the time unhurt,

though a great part of the hearth was torn up *(s)*. My
wife's sister, two children, and a negro wench, were all who
happened to be in the house at the time: the first, and one
child sat within five feet of the chimney; and were so stunned, that they never saw the lightning nor heard the explosion; the wench, with the other child in her arms, sitting
at a greater distance, was sensible of both; though every
one was so stunned that they did not recover for some time;
however it pleased God that no farther mischief ensued.
The kitchen, at 90 feet distance, was full of negroes, who
were all sensible of the shock; and some of them tell me,
that they felt the rod about a minute after, when it was so
hot that they could not bear it in hand.

REMARKS BY DR. FRANKLIN.

THE foregoing very sensible and distinct account may
afford a good deal of instruction relating to the nature and
effects of lightning, and to the construction and use of this
instrument for averting the mischiefs of it. Like other
new instruments, this appears to have been at first in some
respects imperfect; and we find that we are, in this as in
others, to expect improvement from experience chiefly:
but there seems to be nothing in the account, that should
discourage us in the use of it; since at the same time
that its imperfections are discovered, the means of removing them are pretty easily to be learnt from the circumstances of the account itself; and its utility upon the whole
is manifest.

One intention of the pointed rod, is, to *prevent* a stroke
of lightning. *(See pages* 123, 143.*)* But to have a better chance of obtaining this end, the points should not be
too near to the top of the chimney or highest parts of the
building to which they are affixed, but should be extended
five or six feet above it; otherwise their operation in silently drawing off the fire (from such fragments of cloud
float in the air between the great body of cloud and the
earth) will be prevented. For the experiment with the
lock of cotton hanging below the electrified prime conduc-

tor shows, that a finger under it, being a blunt body, extends the cotton, drawing its lower part downwards ; when
a needle, with its point presented to the cotton, makes it
fly up again to the prime conductor; and that this effect is
strongest when as much of the needle as possible appears
above the end of the finger ; grows weaker as the needle is
shortened between the finger and thumb; and is reduced to nothing when only a short part below the point
appears above the finger.   Now it seems the points of Mr.
Maine's rod were elevated only *(a) six or seven inches
above the top of the chimney ;* which, considering the bulk
of the chimney and the house, was too small an elevation.
For the great body of the matter near them would hinder
their being easily brought into a negative state by the repulsive power of the electrised cloud, in which negative state
it is that they attract most strongly and copiously the electric fluid from other bodies, and convey it into the earth.

(b) Nothing of the points, &c. could be found.   This is
a common effect.   *(See page* 145.)   Where the quantity
of the electric fluid passing is too great for the conductor
through which it passes, the metal is either melted, or reduced to smoke and dissipated ; but where the conductor is
sufficiently large, the fluid passes in it without hurting it.
Thus these three wires were destroyed, while the rod to
which they were fixed, being of greater substance, remained
unhurt ; its end only, to which they were joined, being a
little melted, some of the melted part of the lower ends of
those wires uniting with it, and appearing on it like solder.

(c) (d) (e) As the several parts of the rod were connected only by the ends being bent round into hooks, the
contact between hook and hook was much smaller than the
rod ; therefore the current through the metal being confined in those narrow passages, melted part of the metal, as
appeared on examining the inside of each hook.   Where
metal is melted by lightning, some part of it is generally
exploded ; and these explosions in the joints appear to have
been the cause of unhooking them ; and, by that violent
action, of starting also most of the staples.   We learn from

hence, that a rod in one continued piece is preferable to one composed of links or parts hooked together.

(f) No part of the chimney was damaged: because the lightning passed in the rod. And this instance agrees with others in showing, that the second and principal intention of the rods is obtainable, viz. that of *conducting* the lightning. In all the instances yet known of the lightning's falling on any house guarded by rods, it has pitched down upon the point of the rod, and has not fallen upon any other part of the house. Had the lightning fallen on this chimney, un-furnished with a rod, it would probably have rent it from top to bottom, as we see, by the effects of the lightning on the points and rod, that its quantity was very great ; and we know that many chimneys have been so demolished. But *no part of this was damaged, only (f) (g) (h) at the foundation, where it was shattered and several bricks torn out.* Here we learn the principal defect in fixing this rod. The lower joint being sunk but three feet into the earth, did not it seems go low enough to come at water, or a large body of earth so moist as to receive readily from its end the quantity it conducted. The electric fluid therefore, thus accumulated near the lower end of the rod, quitted it at the surface of the earth, dividing in search of other passages. Part of it tore up the surface in furrows, and made holes in it : part entered the bricks of the foundation, which being near the earth are generally moist, and, in exploding that moisture, shattered them. *(See page 182.)* Part went through or under the foundation, and got under the hearth, blowing up great part of the bricks *(m) (s)*, and producing the other effects *(o) (p) (q) (r)*. The iron dogs, loggerhead, and iron pot were not hurt, being of sufficient substance, and they probably protected the cat. The copper tea-kettle being thin suffered some damage. Perhaps, though found on a sound part of the hearth, it might at the time of the stroke have stood on the part blown up, which will account both for the bruising and melting.

That *it ran down the inside of the chimney (k)* I apprehend must be a mistake. Had it done so, I imagine it would have brought something more than soot with it ; it would probably have ripped off the pargetting, and brought down fragments of plaster and bricks.   The shake, from the explosion on the rod, was sufficient to shake down a good deal of loose soot.   Lightning does not usually enter houses by the doors, windows, or chimneys, as open passages, in the manner that air enters them : its nature is, to be attracted by substances, that are conductors of electricity ; it penetrates and passes *in* them, and, if they are not good conductors as are neither wood, brick, stone nor plaster, it is apt to rend them in its passage.   It would not easily pass through the air from a cloud to a building were it not for the aid afforded it in its passage by intervening fragments of clouds below the main body, or or by the falling rain.

It is said that *the house was filled with its flash (l)*. Expressions like this are common in accounts of the effects of lightning, from which we are apt to understand that the lightning filled the house.   Our language indeed seems to want a word to express the *light* of lightning as distinct from the lightning itself.   When a tree on a hill is struck by it.   the lightning of that stroke exists only in a narrow vein between the cloud and tree, but its light fills a vast space many miles round ; and people at the greatest distance from it are apt to say, "The lightning came into our rooms through our windows."   As it is in itself extremely bright, it cannot, when so near as to strike a house, fail illuminating highly every room in it through the windows ; and this I suppose to have been the case at Mr. Maine's ; and that, except in and near the hearth, from the causes above-mentioned, it was not in any other part of the house ; *the flash* meaning no more than *the light* of the lightning.   It is for want of considering this difference, that people suppose there is a kind of lightning not attended with thunder.   In fact there is probably a loud explosion accompanying every flash of lightning, and at the same instant ;—but as sound travels slower than light, we often hear the sound some seconds of time after having seen the light ; and as sound does not travel so far as light, we sometimes see the light at a distance too great to hear the sound.

(n). The *breaking some pieces of china in the bœufet,* may nevertheless seem to indicate that the lightning was there: but as there is no mention of its having hurt any part of the bœufet, or of the walls of the house, I should rather ascribe that effect to the concussion of the air, or shake of the house by the explosion.

Thus, to me it appears, that the house and its inhabitants were saved by the rod, though the rod itself was unjointed by the stroke ; and that, if it had been made of one piece, and sunk deeper in the earth, or had entered the earth at a greater distance from the foundation, the mentioned small damages (except the melting of the points) would not have happened.

TO DR. HEBERDEN, LONDON.

On the Electricity of the Tourmalin.

Craven-street, June 7, 1759.

Sir,

I NOW return the smallest of your tourmalins, with hearty thanks for the kind present of the other, which though I value highly for its rare and wonderful properties, I shall ever esteem it more for the friendship I am honored with by the giver.

I hear that the negative electricity of one side of the tourmalin, when heated, is absolutely denied (and all that has been related of it ascribed to prejudice in favor of a system) by some ingenious gentlemen abroad, who profess to have made the experiments on the stone with care and exactness. The experiments have succeeded differently with me ; yet I would not call the accuracy of those gentlemen in question. Possibly the tourmalins they have tried were not properly cut ; so that the positive and negative powers were obliquely placed, or in some manner whereby their effects were confused, or the negative parts more easily supplied by the positive. Perhaps the lapidaries who have hitherto cut these stones, had no regard to the situation of the two powers, but chose to make the faces of the stone where they could obtain the greatest breadth, or some other advantage in the form. If any of these stones, in their natural state, can be procured here, I think it would be right to endeavor finding, before they are cut, the two sides that contain the opposite powers, and make the faces there. Possibly, in that case, the effects might be stronger, and more distinct; for though both these stones that I have examined have evidently the two properties, yet, without the full heat given by boiling water, they are somewhat confused; the virtue seems strongest towards one end of the face; and in the middle, or near the other end, scarce discernible; and the negative, I think, always weaker than the positive.

I have had the large one new cut, so as to make both sides alike, and find the change of form has made no change of power, but the properties of each side remain the same as I found them before. It is now set in a ring in such a manner as to turn on an axis, that I may conveniently, in making experiments, come at both sides of the stone. The little rim of gold it is set in, has made no alteration in its effects. The warmth of my finger, when I wear it, is sufficient to give it some degree of electricity, so that it is always ready to attract light bodies.

The following experiments have satisfied me that M. Æpinus's account of the positive and negative states of the opposite sides of the heated tourmalin is well founded.

I heated the large stone in boiling water.

As soon as it was dry, I brought it near a very small cork ball, that was suspended by a silk thread.

The ball was attracted by one face of the stone, which I call A, and then repelled.

The ball in that state was also repelled by the positively charged wire of a phial, and attracted by the other side of the stone, B.

The stone being heated afresh, and the side B brought near the ball, it was first attracted, and presently after repelled by that side.

In this second state it was repelled by the negatively charged wire of a phial.

Therefore, if the principles now generally received, relating to positive and negative electricity, are true, the side A of the large stone, when the stone is heated in water, is in a positive state of electricity; and the side B, in a negative state.

The same experiments being made with the small stone stuck by one edge on the end of a small glass tube, with sealing-wax, the same effects are produced. The flat side of the small stone gives the signs of positive electricity; the high side gives the signs of negative electricity.

Again:

I suspended the small stone by a silk thread.

I heated it as it hung, in boiling water.

I heated the large one in boiling water.

Then I brought the large stone near to the suspended small one,

Which immediately turned its flat side to the side B of the large stone, and would cling to it.

I turned the ring, so as to present the side A of the large stone, to the flat side of the small one.

The flat side was repelled, and the small stone, turning quick, applied its high side to the side A of the large one.

This was precisely what ought to happen, on the supposition that the flat side of the small stone, when heated in water, is positive, and the high side negative; the side A of the large stone positive, and the side B negative.

The effect was apparently the same as would have been produced, if one magnet had been suspended by a thread, and the different poles of another brought alternately near it.

I find that the face A, of the large stone, being coated with leaf-gold (attached by the white of an egg, which will bear dipping in hot water) becomes quicker and stronger in its effect on the cork ball, repelling it the instant it comes in contact; which I suppose to be occasioned by the united force of the different parts of the face, collected and acting together through the metal.

I am, &c.

B. FRANKLIN.

PROFESSOR WINTHROP, TO B. FRANKLIN.

New Observation relating to Electricity in the Atmosphere.

Cambridge, (Massachusetts,) Sept. 29, 1762.

SIR,

THERE is an observation relating to electricity in the atmosphere, which seemed new to me, though perhaps it will not to you: however, I will venture to mention it. I have some points on the top of my house, and the wire where it passes within-side the house is furnished with bells, according to your method, to give notice of the passage of the electric fluid. In summer, these bells, generally ring at the approach of a thunder-cloud; but cease soon after it begins to rain. In winter, they sometimes though not very often, ring while it is snowing; but never, that I remember, when it rains. But what was unexpected to me was, that, though the bells had not rung while it was snowing, yet, the next day, after it had done snowing, and the weather was cleared up, while the snow was driven about by a high wind at W. or N. W. the bells rung for several hours (though with little intermissions) as briskly as ever I knew them, and I drew considerable sparks from the wire. The phenomenon I never observed but twice, viz. on the 31st of January, 1760, and the 3d of March, 1762.

I am, Sir, &c.

ALEXANDER SMALL, (OF LONDON,) TO DR. FRANKLIN.

Flash of Lightning that struck St. Bride's Steeple.

I HAVE just recollected that in one of our great storms of lightning, I saw an appearance, which I never observed before, nor ever heard described. I am persuaded that I saw *the* flash which struck St. Bride's steeple. Sitting at my window, and looking to the north, I saw what appeared to me a solid strait rod of fire, moving at a very sharp angle with the horizon. It appeared to my eye as about two inches diameter, and had nothing of the zig-zag lightning motion. I instantly told a person sitting with me, that some place must be struck at that instant. I was so much surprised at the vivid distinct appearance of the fire, that I did not hear the clap of thunder, which stunned every one besides. Considering how low it moved, I could not have thought it had gone so far, having St. Martin's, the New Church, and St. Clement's steeples in its way. It struck the steeple a good way fromthe top, and the first impression it made in the side is in the same direction I saw it move in. It was succeeded by two flashes, almost united, moving in a pointed direction. There were two distinct houses struck in Essex-street. I should have thought the rod would have fallen in Covent-Garden, it was so low. Perhaps the appearance is frequent, though never before seen by

Your's,

ALEXANDER SMALL.

TO PETER FRANKLIN, NEWPORT.

Best Method of securing a Powder Magazine from Lightning.

.... YOU may acquaint the gentleman that desired you to inquire my opinion of the best method of securing a powder magazine from lightning, that I think they cannot do better than to erect a mast not far from it, which may reach fifteen or twenty feet above the top of it, with a thick iron rod in one piece fastened to it, pointed at the highest end, and reaching down through the earth till it comes to water. Iron is a cheap metal; but if it were dearer, as this is a public thing the expence is insignificant; therefore I would have the rod at least an inch thick, to allow for its gradually wasting by rust; it will last as long as the mast, and may be renewed with it. The sharp point for five or six inches should be gilt.

But there is another circumstance of importance to the strength, goodness, and usefulness of the powder, which does not seem to have been enough attended to: I mean the keeping it perfectly dry. For want of a method of doing this, much is spoiled in damp magazines, and much so damaged as to become of little value.—If, instead of barrels it were kept in cases of bottles well corked; or in large tin canisters, with small covers shutting close by means of oiled paper between, or covering the joining on the canister; or if in barrels, then the barrels lined with thin sheet lead; no moisture in either of these methods could possibly enter the powder, since glass and metals are both impervious to water.

By the latter of these means you see tea is brought dry and crisp from China to Europe, and thence to America, though it comes all the way by sea in the damp hold of a ship. And by this method, grain, meal, &c. if well dried before it is put up, may be kept for ages sound and good.

There is another thing very proper to line small barrels with; it is what they call tin-foil, or leaf-tin, being tin milled between rollers till it becomes as thin as paper, and more pliant, at the same time that its texture is extremely close. It may be applied to wood with common paste, made with boiling-water thickened with flour; and, so laid on; will lie very close and stick well: but I should prefer a hard sticky varnish for that purpose, made of linseed oil much boiled. The heads might be lined separately, the tin wrapping a little round their edges. The barrel, while the lining is laid on, should have the end hoops slack, so that the staves standing at a little distance from each other, may admit the head into its groove. The tin-foil should be plyed into the groove. Then, one head being put in, and that end hooped tight, the barrel would be fit to receive the powder, and when the other head is put in and the hoops drove up, the powder would be safe from moisture even if the barrel were kept under water. This tin-foil is but about eighteen pence sterling a pound, and is so extremely thin, that I imagine a pound of it would line three or four powder-barrels.

I am, &c.

B. FRANKLIN.

OF LIGHTNING,
And the Methods now used in America for securing Buildings and Persons from its mischievous Effects.

EXPERIMENTS made in electricity first gave philosophers a suspicion, that the matter of lightning was the same with the electric matter. Experiments afterwards made on lightning obtained from the clouds by pointed rods, received into bottles, and subjected to every trial, have since proved this suspicion to be perfectly well founded; and that whatever properties we find in electricity, are also the properties of lightning.

This matter of lightning, or of electricity, is an extreme subtle fluid, penetrating other bodies, and subsisting in them, equally diffused.

When by any operation of art or nature, there happens to be a greater proportion of this fluid in one body than in another, the body which has most will communicate to that which has least, till the proportion becomes equal; provided the distance between them be not too great; or, if it is too great, till there be proper conductors to convey it from one to the other.

If the communication be through the air without any conductor, a bright light is seen between the bodies, and a sound is heard. In our small experiments, we call this light and sound the electric spark and snap; but in the great operations of nature, the light is what we call *lightning*, and the sound (produced at the same time, though generally arriving later at our ears than the light does to our eyes) is, with its echoes, called *thunder*.

If the communication of this fluid is by a conductor, it may be without either light or sound, the subtle fluid passing in the substance of the conductor.

If the conductor be good and of sufficient bigness, the fluid passes through it without hurting it. If otherwise, it is damaged or destroyed.

All metals, and water, are good conductors.—Other bodies may become conductors by having some quantity of water in them, as wood, and other materials used in building, but not having much water in them, they are not good conductors, and therefore are often damaged in the operation.

Glass, wax, silk, wool, hair, feathers, and even wood, perfectly dry are non-conductors: that is, they resist instead of facilitating the passage of this subtle fluid.

When this fluid has an opportunity of passing through two conductors, one good and sufficient, as of metal, the other not so good, it passes in the best, and will follow it in any direction.

The distance at which a body charged with this fluid will discharge itself suddenly, striking through the air into another body that is not charged, or not so highly charged, is different according to the quantity of the fluid, the dimensions and form of the bodies themselves, and the state of the air between them.—This distance, whatever it happens to be, between any two bodies, is called their *striking distance*, as, till they come within that distance of each other, no stroke will be made.

The clouds have often more of this fluid in proportion than the earth; in which case, as soon as they come near enough (that is, within the striking distance) or meet with a conductor, the fluid quits them and strikes into the earth. A cloud fully charged with this fluid, if so high as to be beyond the striking distance from the earth, passes quietly without making noise or giving light; unless it meets with other clouds that have less.

Tall trees and lofty buildings, as the towers and spires of churches, become sometimes conductors between the clouds and the earth; but not being good ones, that is, not conveying the fluid freely, they are often damaged.

Buildings that have their roofs covered with lead, or other metal, the spouts of metal continued from the roof into the ground to carry of the water, are never hurt by lightning, as, whenever it falls on such a building, it passes in the metals and not in the walls.

When other buildings happen to be within the striking distance from such clouds, the fluid passes in the walls whether of wood, brick, or stone, quitting the walls only when it can find better conductors near them, as metal rods, bolts, and hinges of windows or doors, gilding on wainscot or frames of pictures, the silvering on the backs of looking glasses, the wires for bells, and the bodies of animals, as containing watery fluids. And in passing through the house, it follows the direction of these conductors, taking as many in its way as can assist it in its passage, whether in a strait, or crooked line, leaping from one to the other, if not far distant from each other, only rending the wall in the spaces where these partial good conductors are too distant from each other.

An iron rod being placed on the ouside of a building, from the highest part continued down into the moist earth, in any direction strait or crooked, following the form of the roof or parts of the building, will receive the lightning at its upper end, attracting it so as to prevent its striking any other part; and affording it a good conveyance into the earth, will prevent its damaging any part of the building.

A small quantity of metal is found able to conduct a great quantity of this fluid. A wire no bigger than a goose quill has been known to conduct (with safety to the building as far as the wire was continued) a quantity of lightning that did prodigious damage both above and below it; and probably larger rods are not necessary, though it is common in America, to make them of half an inch, some of three quarters, or an inch diameter.

The rod may be fastened to the wall, chimney, &c. with staples of iron.—The lightning will not leave the rod (a good conductor) to pass into the wall (a bad conductor) through those staples.—It would rather, if any were in the walls, pass out of it into the rod to get more readily by that conductor into the earth.

If the building be very large and extensive, two or more rods may be placed at different parts, for greater security.

Small ragged parts of clouds, suspended in the air between the great body of clouds and the earth (like leaf gold in electrical experiments) often serve as partial conductors for the lightning, which proceeds from one of them to another, and by their help comes within the striking distance to the earth or a building. It therefore strikes through those conductors a building that would otherwise be out of the striking distance.

Long sharp points communicating with the earth, and presented to such parts of clouds, drawing silently from them the fluid they are charged with, they are then attracted to the cloud, and may leave the distance so great as to be beyond the reach of striking.

It is therefore that we elevate the upper end of the rod six or eight feet above the highest part of the building, tapering it gradually to a fine sharp point, which is gilt to prevent its rusting.

Thus the pointed rod either prevents a stroke from the cloud, or, if a stroke is made, conducts it to the earth with safety to the building.

The lower end of the rod should enter the earth so deep as to come at the moist part, perhaps two or three feet; and if bent when under the surface so as to go in a horizontal line six or eight feet from the wall, and then bent again downwards three or four feet, it will prevent damage to any of the stones of the foundation.

A person apprehensive of danger from lightning, happening during the time of thunder to be in a house not so secured, will do well to avoid sitting near the chimney, near a looking glass, or any gilt pictures or wainscot; the safest place is the middle of the room (so it be not under a metal lustre suspended by a chain) sitting in one chair and laying the feet up in another. It is still safer to bring two or three mattrasses or beds into the middle of the room, and, folding them up double, place the chair upon them; for they not being so good conductors as the walls, the lightning will not chuse an interrupted course through the air of the room and the bedding, when it can go through a continued better conductor, the wall. But where it can be had, a hammoc or swinging bed, suspended by silk cords equally distant from the walls on every side, and from the cieling and floor above and below, affords the safest situation a person can have in any room whatever; and what indeed may be deemed quite free from danger of any stroke by lightning.

B. FRANKLIN.

Paris, *Sep.* 1767.

J. WINTHROP, PROFESSER OF NATURAL PHILOSOPHY AT CAM-
BRIDGE (MASSACHUSETTS) TO DR. FRANKLIN

St. Bride's Steeple.—Utility of Electrical Conductors to Steeples, —Singular kind of Glass Tube.

January 6, 1768.

" ...... I have read in the Philosophical Transactions the account of the effects of lightning on St. Bride's steeple. It is amazing to me, that after the full demonstration you had given, of the identity of lightning and of electricity, and the power of metalline conductors, they should ever think of repairing that steeple without such conductors. How astonishing is the force of prejudice even in an age of so much knowlege and free enquiry!"

ANSWER TO THE ABOVE.

...... It is perhaps not so extraordinary that unlearned men, such as commonly compose our church vestries, should not yet be acquainted with, and sensible of the benefits of metal conductors in averting the stroke of lightning, and preserving our houses from its violent effects, or that they should be still prejudiced against the use of such conductors, when we see how long even philosophers, men of extensive science and great ingenuity, can hold out against the evidence of new knowlege, that does not square with

C c

their preconceptions; and how long men can retain a practice that is conformable to their prejudices, and expect a benefit from such practice, though constant experience shows its inutility. A late piece of the Abbé Nollet, printed last year in the memoirs of the French Academy of Sciences, affords strong instances of this : for though the very relations he gives of the effects of lightning in several churches and other buildings, show clearly, that it was conducted from one part to another by wires, gildings, and other pieces of metal that were *within*, or connected with the building, yet in the same paper he objects to the providing metalline conductors *without* the building, as useless or dangerous[6]. He cautions people not to ring the church bells during a thunder storm, lest the lightning, in its way to the earth, should be conducted down to them by the bell ropes[7], which are but bad conductors ; and yet is against fixing metal rods on the outside of the steeple, which are known to be much better conductors, and which it would certainly chuse to pass in rather than dry hemp. And though for a thousand years past bells have been solemnly

---

6 Notre curiosité pourroit peut-être s'applaudir des recherches qu'elle nous a fait faire sur la nature du tonnèrre, et sur la mécanisme de ses principaux effets, mais ce n'est point ce qu'il y a de plus important ; il vaudroit bien mieux que nous puissions trouver quelque moyen de nous en garantir ; on y a pensé ; on s'est même flatté d'avoir fait cette grande découverte ; mais malheureusement douze années d'épreuves et un peu de réflexion, nous apprennent qu'il ne faut pas compter sur les promesses qu'on nous a faites. Je l'ai dit, il y a long temps, et avec regret, toutes ces pointes de fer qu'on dresse en l'air, soit comme *électroscopes*, soit comme préservatifs,...... sont plus propre à nous attirer le feu du tonnerre qu' à nous en préserver ; ...... et je persiste à dire que le projet d'épuiser une nuée orageuse du feu dont elle est chargée, n'est pas celui d'un physicien. *Memoire sur les Effets du Tonnerre.*

7 Les cloches, en virtu de leur bénédiction, doivent écarter les orages et nous préserver des coups de foudre ; mais l'église permet à la prudence humaine le choix des momens où il convient d'user de ce préservatif. Je ne sais si le son, considéré physiquement, est capable ou non de faire créver une nuée et de causer l'épanchement de son feu vers les objets terrèstres, mais il est certain et prouvé par l'expérience, que la tonnèrre peut tomber sur un clocher, soit que l'on y sonne ou que l'on n'y sonne point ; et si cela arrive dans le premier cas, les sonneurs sont en grand danger, parcequ'ils tiennent des cordes par lesquelles la commotion de la foudre peut se communiquer jusqà eux : il est donc plus sage de laisser les cloches en repos quand l'orage est arrivé au-dessus de l'église. Ibid.

consecrated by the Romish church[8], in expectation that the
sound of such blessed bells would drive away those storms
and secure our buildings from the stroke of lightning; and
during so long a period, it has not been found by experience, that places within the reach of such blessed sound,
are safer than others where it is never heard; but that on
the contrary, the lightning seems to strike steeples of choice,
and that at the very time the bells are ringing[9]; yet still
they continue to bless the new bells, and jangle the old ones
whenever it thunders.—One would think it was now time
to try some other trick;—and ours is recommended (whatever this able philosopher may have been told to the contrary) by more than twelve years experience, wherein,
among the great number of houses furnished with iron rods
in North America, not one so guarded has been materially
hurt with lightning, and several have been evidently preserved by their means; while a number of houses, churches,
barns, ships, &c. in different places, unprovided with rods,
have been struck and greatly damaged, demolished or burnt.
Probably the vestries of our English churches are not generally well acquainted with these facts; otherwise, since as
good protestants they have no faith in the blessing of bells,
they would be less excusable in not providing this other

---

8 Suivant le rituel de Paris, lorsqu'on bénit des cloches, on recite les oraisons
suivantes:

*Benedic, Domine . . . . . quotiescumque sonuerit, procul recedat virtus in-
sidiantium, umbra phantasmatis, incursio turbinum, percussio fulminum,
læsio tonitruum, calamitas tempestatum, omnisque spiritus procellarum, &c.*

*Deus, qui per beatum Moisen, &c. . . . . . . procul pellentur insidiæ inimici,
fragor grandinum, procella turbinum, impetus tempestatum, temperentur in-
festa tonitrua, &c.*

*Omnipotens sempiterne Deus, &c. . . . . . . ut ante sonitum ejus effugentur
ignita jacula inimici, percussio fulminum, impetus lapidum, læsio tempestatum, &c.*

9. En 1718. M. Deslandes fit savoir à l'Academie Royale des sciences, que
la nuit du 14 ou 15 d'Avril de la même année, le tonnerre étoit tombé sur vingt-
quatre églises, dequis Landernau jusqu'à Saint Pol-de-Leon en Bretagne;
que ces églises étoient précisément celles où l'on sonnoit, et que la foudre avoit
épargné celles ou l'on ne sonnoit pas: que dans celle de Gouisnon, qui fut
entièrement ruinée, le tonnerre tua deux personnes de quatre qui sonnoient,
&c. *Hist. de l'Ac. R. des Sci.* 1719.

security for their respective churches, and for the good
people that may happen to be assembled in them during a
tempest, especially as those buildings, from their greater
height, are more exposed to the stroke of lightning than
our common dwellings.

I have nothing new in the philosophical way to communicate to you, except what follows.   When I was last year
in Germany, I met with a singular kind of glass, being a
tube about eight inches long, half an inch in diameter, with
a hollow ball of near an inch diameter at one end, and one
of an inch and half at the other, hermetically sealed, and
half filled with water.—If one end is held in the hand, and
the other a little elevated above the level, a constant succession of large bubbles proceeds from the end in the hand to
the other end, making an appearance that puzzled me
much, till I found that the space not filled with water was
also free from air, and either filled with a subtle invisible
vapor continually rising from the water, and extremely
rarefiable by the least heat at one end, and condensable
again by the least coolness at the other ; or it is the very
fluid of fire itself, which parting from the hand pervades
the glass, and by its expansive force depresses the water till
it can pass between it and the glass, and escape to the other
end, where it gets through the glass again into the air.   I
am rather inclined to the first opinion, but doubtful between
the two.   An ingenious artist here, Mr. Nairne, mathematical instrument-maker, has made a number of them from
mine, and improved them, for his are much more sensible
than those I brought from Germany.—I bored a very small
hole through the wainscot in the seat of my window,
through which a little cold air constantly entered, while the
air in the room was kept warmer by fires daily made in it,
being winter time.   I placed one of his glasses, with the
elevated end against this hole ; and the bubbles from the
other end, which was in a warmer situation, were continually passing day and night, to the no small surprise of even
philosophical spectators.   Each bubble discharged is larger
than that from which it proceeds, and yet that is not dimi-

nished; and by adding itself to the bubble at the other end, that bubble is not increased, which seems very paradoxical. When the balls at each end are made large, and the connecting tube very small and bent at right angles, so that the balls, instead of being at the ends, are brought on the side of the tube, and the tube is held so as that the balls are above it, the water will be depressed in that which is held in the hand, and rise in the other as a jet or fountain; when it is all in the other, it begins to boil, as it were, by the vapor passing up through it; and the instant it begins to boil, a sudden coldness is felt in the ball held; a curious experiment, this, first observed and shown me by Mr. Nairne. There is something in it similar to the old observation, I think mentioned by Aristotle, that the bottom of a boiling pot is not warm; and perhaps it may help to explain that fact;—if indeed it be a fact.—When the water stands at an equal height in both these balls, and all at rest; if you wet one of the balls by means of a feather dipt in spirit, though that spirit is of the same temperament as to heat and cold with the water in the glasses, yet the cold occasioned by the evaporation of the spirit from the wetted ball will so condense the vapor over the water contained in that ball, as that the water of the other ball will be pressed up into it, followed by a succession of bubbles, till the spirit is all dried away. Perhaps the observations on these little instruments may suggest and be applied to some beneficial uses. It has been thought, that water reduced to vapor by heat was rarefied only fourteen thousand times, and on this principle our engines for raising water by fire are said to be constructed: but if the vapor so much rarefied from water, is capable of being itself still farther rarefied to a boundless degree by the application of heat to the vessels or parts of vessels containing the vapor (as at first it is applied to those containing the water) perhaps a much greater power may be obtained, with little additional expence. Possibly too, the power of easily moving water from one end to the other of a moveable beam (suspended in the middle like a

scale-beam) by a small degree of heat, may be applied ad-
vantageously to some other mechanical purposes.

I am, &c.

B. FRANKLIN.

*Experiments, Observations, and Facts, tending to support the Opi-
nion of the Utility of long pointed Rods, for securing Buildings
from Damage by Strokes of Lightning.*

Read at the committee appointed to consider the erection of conductors
to secure the magazines at Purfleet, Aug. 27, 1772.

EXPERIMENT I.

THE prime conductor of an electric machine, A. B.
(*See the plate*) being supported about 10 inches and a half
above the table by a wax-stand, and under it erected a *pointed wire* 7 inches and a half high, and one-fifth of an inch
thick, and tapering to a sharp point, and communicating
with the table ; when the *point* (being uppermost) is *covered*
by the end of a finger, the conductor may be full charged,
and the electrometer, c, (Mr. Henley's) will rise to the
height indicating a full charge : but the moment the point is
uncovered, the ball of the electrometer drops, showing the
prime conductor to be instantly discharged and nearly emptied of its electricity.   Turn the wire its *blunt* end upwards
(which represents an unpointed bar) and no such effect follows, the electrometer remaining at its usual height when
the prime conductor is charged.

OBSERVATION.

What quantity of lightning, a high pointed rod well communicating with the earth may be expected to discharge
from the clouds silently in a short time, is yet unknown ;
but I have reason from a particular fact to think it may at
some times be very great.   In Philadelphia I had such a
rod fixed to the top of my chimney, and extending about
nine feet above it.   From the foot of this rod, a wire (the
thickness of a goose-quill) came through a covered glass
tube in the roof, and down through the well of the stair-

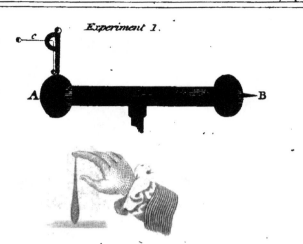

Experiment 1.

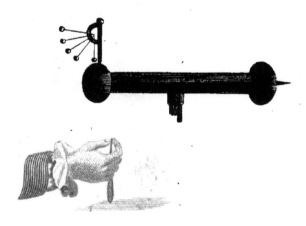

Exp. 2.

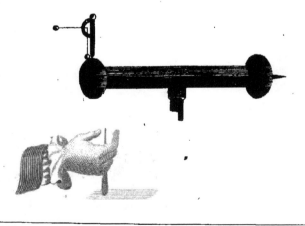

Exp. 3.

Philad. Pub. by W. Duane 1809.

Pl. V.   Vol. III.   page 22.

Exp. 4.

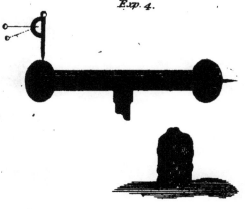

Exp. 5.

Exp. 6.

Philad. Pub. by W. Duane 1809.

case; the lower end connected with the iron spear of a pump. On the stair-case opposite to my chamber door, the wire was divided; the ends separated about six inches, a little bell on each end; and between the bells a little brass ball suspended by a silk thread, to play between and strike the bells when clouds passed with electricity in them. After having frequently drawn sparks and charged bottles from the bell of the upper wire, I was one night awaked by loud cracks on the stair-case. Starting up and opening the door, I perceived that the brass ball instead of vibrating as usual between the bells, was repelled and kept at a distance from both; while the fire passed sometimes in very large quick cracks from bell to bell; and sometimes in a continued dense white stream, seemingly as large as my finger, whereby the whole stair-case was enlighted as with sunshine, so that one might see to pick up a pin[1]. And from the apparent quantity thus discharged, I cannot but conceive that a *number*[2] of such conductors must considerably lessen that of any approaching cloud, before it comes so near as to deliver its contents in a general stroke :—An effect not to be expected from bars *unpointed;* if the above experiment with the blunt end of the wire is deemed pertinent to the case.

EXPERIMENT II.

The pointed wire under the prime conductor continuing of the same height, *pinch* it between the thumb and finger near the top, so as *just to conceal* the point; then turning the globe, the electrometer will rise and mark the full charge. Slip the fingers down so as to discover about half

---

1 Mr. de Romas saw still greater quantities of lightning brought down by the wire of his kite. He had "explosions from it, the noise of which greatly resembled that of thunder, and were heard (from without) into the heart of the city, notwithstanding the various noises there The fire seen at the instant of the explosion had the shape of a spindle eight inches long and five lines in diameter. Yet from the time of the explosion to the end of the experiment, no lightning was seen above, nor any thunder heard. At another time the streams of fire issuing from it were observed to be an inch thick and ten feet long."—*See Dr. Priestley's History of Electricity*, pages 134—6, *first edition.*

2 Twelve were proposed on and near the magazines at Purfleet.

an inch of the wire, then another half inch, and then another; at every one of these motions *discovering more and
more* of the pointed wire; you will see the electrometer fall
quick and proportionably, stopping when you stop.   If you
slip down the *whole distance* at once, the ball falls instantly
down to the stem.

OBSERVATION.

From this experiment it seems that a greater effect in
drawing off the lightning from the clouds may be expected
from *long* pointed rods, than from *short* ones; I mean from
such as show the greatest length, *above the building* they
are fixed on.

EXPERIMENT III.

Instead of pinching the point between the thumb and
finger, as in the last experiment, keep the thumb and finger
each at *near an inch distance* from it, but at the *same height*,
the point between them.   In this situation, though the point
is fairly exposed to the prime conductor, it has little or no
effect; the electrometer rises to the height of a full charge.
—But the moment the fingers are *taken away*, the ball falls
quick to the stem.

OBSERVATION.

To explain this, it is supposed, that one reason of the
sudden effect produced by a long naked pointed wire is,
that (by the repulsive power of the positive charge in the
prime conductor) the natural quantity of electricity contained in the pointed wire is driven down into the earth,
and the point of the wire made strongly *negative;* whence
it attracts the electricity of the prime conductor more
strongly than bodies in their natural state would do; the
small quantity of common matter in the point, not being able
by its attractive force to retain its *natural quantity of the
electric fluid*, against the force of that repulsion.—But the
finger and thumb being substantial and blunt bodies, though
as near the prime conductor, hold up better their *own*
natural quantity against the force of that repulsion; and
so, continuing nearly in their natural state, they jointly ope-

'rate on the electric fluid in the point, opposing its descent and *aiding the point* to retain it; contrary to the repelling power of the prime conductor, which would drive it down. —And this may also serve to explain the different powers of the point in the preceding experiment, on the slipping down the finger and thumb to different distances.

Hence is collected, that a pointed rod erected *between two tall chimnies*, and very little higher (an instance of which I have seen) cannot have so good an effect, as if it had been erected on one of the chimneys, its whole length above it.

EXPERIMENT IV.

If, *instead* of a long pointed wire, a *large solid body* (to represent a building without a point) be brought under and as near the prime conductor, when charged; the ball of the electrometer will *fall* a little; and on taking away the large body, will *rise again*.

OBSERVATION.

Its *rising again* shows that the prime conductor lost little or none of its electric charge, as it had done through the point: the *falling* of the ball while the large body was under the conductor therefore shows, that a quantity of its atmosphere was drawn from the end where the electrometer is placed to the part immediately over the large body, and there accumulated *ready* to strike into it with its whole undiminished force, as soon as within the striking distance; and, were the prime conductor moveable like a *cloud*, it would approach the body by attraction till within that distance. The swift motion of clouds, as driven by the winds, probably prevents this happening so often as otherwise it might do: for, though parts of the cloud may stoop towards a building as they pass, in consequence of such attraction, yet they are carried forward beyond the striking distance, before they could by their descending come within it.

EXPERIMENT V.

Attach a small light *lock of cotton* to the underside of the prime conductor, so that it may hang down towards the pointed wire mentioned in the first experiment. *Cover the* point with your finger, and the globe being turned, the cotton will extend itself, stretching down towards the finger, as at *a*; but on *uncovering* the point, it instantly flies up to the prime conductor, as at *b*, and continues there as long as the point is uncovered. The moment you cover it again, the cotton flies down again, extending itself towards the finger; and the same happens in degree, if (instead of the finger) you use, uncovered, the *blunt* end of the wire uppermost.

OBSERVATION.

To explain this, it is supposed that the cotton, by its connection with the prime conductor, receives from it a quantity of its electricity; which occasions its being attracted by the *finger* that remains still in nearly its natural state. But when a *point* is opposed to the cotton, its electricity is thereby taken from it, faster than it can at a distance be supplied with a fresh quantity from the conductor. Therefore being reduced *nearer* to the natural state, it is attracted *up* to the electrified prime conductor; *rather than down*, as before, to the finger.

Supposing farther that the prime conductor represents a cloud charged with the electric fluid; the cotton, a ragged fragment of cloud (of which the underside of great thunderclouds are seen to have many) the finger, a chimney or highest part of a building.——We then may conceive that when such a cloud passes over a *building*, some one of its ragged under-hanging fragments may be drawn down by the chimney or other high part of the edifice; creating thereby a *more easy communication* between it and the great cloud.——But a *long pointed rod* being presented to this fragment, may occasion its receding, like the cotton, up to the great cloud; and thereby *increase*, instead *of lessening* the distance, so as often to make it *greater* than the striking distance Turning the *blunt end of a wire* uppermost (which represents the unpointed bar) it appears that the same good effect is not from that to be expected. A long pointed rod it is therefore imagined, may *prevent* some strokes; as well as *conduct* others that fall upon it, when a great body of cloud comes on so heavily that the above repelling operation on fragments cannot take place.

EXPERIMENT VI.

Opposite the side of the prime conductor, place *separately* isolated by wax stems, Mr. Canton's two boxes with pith balls suspended by fine linen threads. On each box, lay a wire six inches long and one-fifth of an inch thick, tapering to a sharp point; but so laid as that four inches of the *pointed* end of *one* wire, and an equal length of the *blunt* end of the *other*, may project beyond the ends of the boxes; and both at eighteen inches distance from the prime conductor. Then charging the prime conductor by a turn or two of the globe, the balls of each pair will separate; those of the box, whence the point projects most, *considerably*; the others *less*. Touch the prime conductor, and those of the box with the *blunt* point will *collapse*, and join. Those connected with the *point* will at the same time approach each other, *till* within about an inch, and there *remain.*

OBSERVATION.

This seems a proof, that though the small sharpened part of the wire must have had a *less natural* quantity in it, before the operation, than the thick blunt part; yet a greater quantity was *driven down from it* to the balls. Thence it is again inferred, that the pointed rod is rendered *more negative:* and farther, that if a *stroke must fall* from the cloud over a building, furnished with such a rod, it is more likely to be drawn to that pointed rod, than to a blunt one; as being more strongly negative, and of course its attraction stronger. And it seems more eligible, that the lightning should fall on the point of the conductor (provided to convey it into the earth) than on any other part of the building, *thence* to proceed to such conductor: which end is also more likely to be obtained by the length and loftiness of the rod; as protecting more extensively the building under it.

It has been *objected*, that erecting pointed rods upon *edifices*, is to *invite* and draw the lightning into *them;* and therefore dangerous. Were such rods to be erected on buildings, *without continuing the communication* quite down into the moist earth, this objection might then have weight; but when such complete conductors are made, the lightning is invited not into the building, but into the *earth*, the situation it aims at, and which it always seizes every help to obtain, even from broken partial metalline conductors.

It has also been suggested, that from such electric experiments *nothing certain can be concluded as to the great operations of nature;* since it is often seen, that experiments, which have succeeded in small, in large have failed. It is true that in mechanics this has sometimes happened. But when it is considered that we owe our first knowlege of the nature and operations of lightning, to observations on such small experiments; and that on carefully comparing the most accurate accounts of former facts, and the exactest relations of those that have occurred since, the effects have surprisingly agreed with the theory; it is humbly conceived that in natural philosophy, in this branch of it at least, the suggestion has not so much weight; and that the farther new experiments now adduced in recommendation of *long* sharp-pointed rods, may have some claim to credit and consideration.

It has been urged too, that though points may have considerable effects on a *small* prime conductor at *small distances;* yet on *great* clouds and at *great distances*, nothing is to be expected from them. To this it is answered, that in those *small* experiments it is evident the points act at a greater than the *striking* distance; and in the large way, their service is *only expected* where there is *such* nearness of the cloud, as to *endanger a stroke;* and there, it cannot be doubted the points must have some effect. And if the quantity discharged by a single pointed rod may be so considerable as I have shown it; the quantity discharged by a number will be proportionably greater.

But this part of the theory does not depend alone on *small* experiments. Since the practice of erecting pointed rods in America (now near twenty years) five of them have been struck by lightning, viz. Mr. Raven's and Mr. Maine's, in South Carolina ; Mr. Tucker's, in Virginia ; Mr. West's and Mr. Moulder's, in Philadelphia. Possibly there may have been more that have not come to my knowlege. But in every one of these, the lightning did *not* fall upon the *body of the house*, but precisely on the several *points* of the rods ; and, though the conductors were sometimes *not suf-ficiently large and complete*, was conveyed into the earth, without any material damage to the buildings. Facts then *in great*, as far as we have them authenticated, justify the opinion that is drawn from the experiments *in small* as above related.

It has also been objected, that unless we knew the quan-tity that might *possibly* be discharged at one stroke from the clouds, we cannot be sure we have provided *sufficient* con-ductors ; and therefore cannot depend on their conveying away *all* that may fall on their points. Indeed we have no-thing to form a judgment by in this but past facts ; and we know of no instance where a *complete* conductor to the moist earth *has* been insufficient, if half an inch diameter. It is probable that many strokes of lightning have been convey-ed through the common leaden pipes affixed to houses to carry down the water from the roof to the ground : and there is no account of such pipes being melted and destroy-ed, as must sometimes have happened if they had been insufficient. We can then only judge of the dimensions proper for a conductor of lightning, as we do of those pro-per for a *conductor of rain*, by past observation. And as we think a pipe of three inches bore sufficient to carry off the rain that falls on a square of 20 feet, because we never saw such a pipe glutted by any shower ; so we may judge a conductor of an inch diameter, more than sufficient for any stroke of lightning that will fall on its point. It is true that if another deluge should happen wherein the windows of heaven are to be opened, such pipes may be unequal to the falling quantity ; and if God for our sins should think fit to rain fire upon us, as upon some cities of old, it is not expected that our conductors of whatever size, should secure our houses against a miracle. Probably as water drawn up into the air and there forming clouds, is disposed to fall again in *rain* by its natural gravity, as soon as a number of particles sufficient to make a drop can get together ; so when the clouds are (by whatever means) over or undercharged with the *electric fluid*, to a degree sufficient to attract them towards the earth, the equilibrium is restored, before the difference becomes great beyond that degree. Mr. Lane's *electrometer*, for limiting precisely the quantity of a shock that is to be administered in a medical view, may serve to make this more easily intelligible. The discharging knob does by a screw approach the conductor to the distance intended, but there remains fixed. Whatever power there may be in the glass globe to collect the fulminating fluid, and whatever capacity of receiving and accumulating it there may be in the bottle or glass jar; yet neither the accumulation nor the discharge ever exceeds the destined quantity. Thus, were the *clouds* always at a certain fixed distance from the earth, all discharges would be made when the quantity accumulated was equal to the distance : but there is a circumstance which by occasionally lessening the distance, lessens the discharge ; to wit, the moveableness of the clouds, and their being drawn nearer to the earth by attraction when electrified; so that discharges are thereby rendered more frequent and of course less violent. Hence whatever the quantity may be in nature, and whatever the power in the clouds of collecting it ; yet an accumulation and force beyond what mankind has hitherto been acquainted with is scarce to be expected[3].

B. F,

August 27, 1772.

3 It may be fit to mention here, that the immediate occasion of the dispute concerning the preference between pointed and blunt conductors of lightning, arose as follows :—A powder-mill having blown up at Brescia, in consequence of its being struck with lightning, the English board of ordnance applied to their painter, Mr. Wilson, then of some note as an electrician, for a method to prevent the like accident to their magazines at Purfleet. Mr. Wilson having

TO PROFESSER LANDRIANI, OF ITALY.

On the Utility of Electrical Conductors.

Philadelphia, Oct. 14, 1787,

SIR,

I HAVE received the excellent work, *Upon the Utility of Electrical Conductors*, which you had the goodness to send me. I read it with great pleasure, and beg you to accept my sincere thanks for it.

Upon my return to this country, I found the number of conductors much increased, many proofs of their efficacy in preserving buildings from lightning having demonstrated their utility. Among other instances, my own house was one day attacked by lightning, which occasioned the neighbors to run in to give assistance, in case of its being on fire. But no damage was done, and my family was only found a good deal frightened with the violence of the explosion.

Last year, my house being enlarged, the conductor was obliged to be taken down. I found, upon examination, that the pointed termination of copper, which, was originally nine inches long, and about one third of an inch in diameter in its thickest part, had been almost entirely melted ; and that its connection with the rod of iron below was very slight. Thus, in the course of time, this invention has proved of use to the author of it, and has added this personal advantage to the pleasure he before received, from having been useful to others.

---

advised a blunt conductor, and it being understood that Dr. Franklin's opinion formed upon the spot, was for a pointed one ; the matter was referred in 1772, to the Royal Society, and by them as usual, to a committee, who, after consultation, prescribed a method conformable to Dr. Franklin's theory. But a harmless stroke of lightning, having under particular circumstances, fallen upon one of the buildings and its apparatus in May 1777 ; the subject came again into violent agitation, and was again referred to the society, and by the society again referred to a new committee, which committee confirmed the decision of the first committee; and it produced an acrimonious controversy in the Royal Society, and in a series of pamphlets ; which, however, ended in the triumph of the Franklinian theory. The pamphlets are all in the possession of the Philadelphia editor.

Mr. Rittenhouse, our astronomer, has informed me, that having observed with his excellent telescope, many conductors that are within the field of his view, he has remarked in various instances, that the points were melted in like manner. There is no example of a house, provided with a perfect conductor, which has suffered any considerable damage; and even those which are without them have suffered little, since conductors have become common in this city.

B. FRANKLIN.

TO JOHN PRINGLE, M.D.

On the Effects of Electricity in Paralytic Cases.

Craven-street, Dec. 21, 1757.

SIR,

IN compliance with your request, I send you the following account of what I can at present recollect relating to the effects of electricity in paralytic cases, which have fallen under my observation.

Some years since, when the newspapers made mention of great cures performed in Italy and Germany, by means of electricity, a number of paralytics were brought to me from different parts of Pennsylvania, and the neighboring provinces, to be electrised, which I did for them at their request. My method was, to place the patient first in a chair, on an electric stool, and draw a number of large strong sparks from all parts of the affected limb or side. Then I fully charged two six-gallon glass jars, each of which had about three square feet of surface coated; and sent the united shock of these through the affected limb or limbs, repeating the stroke commonly three times each day. The first thing observed, was an immediate greater sensible warmth in the lame limbs that had received the stroke than in the others; and the next morning the patients usually related, that they had in the night felt a pricking sensation in the flesh of the paralytic limbs; and would sometimes show a number of small red spots, which they supposed were occasioned by those prickings. The limbs, too, were found more capable of voluntary motion, and seemed to receive strength. A man, for instance, who could not the first day lift the lame hand from off his knee, would the next day raise it four or five inches, the third day higher; and on the fifth day was able, but with a feeble languid motion, to take off his hat. These appearances gave great spirits to the patients, and made them hope a perfect cure; but I do not remember that I ever saw any amendment after the fifth day; which the patients perceiving, and finding the shocks pretty severe, they became discouraged, went home, and in a short time relapsed; so that I never knew any advantage from electricity in palsies that was permanent. And how far the apparent temporary advantage might arise from the exercise in the patients' journey, and coming daily to my house, or from the spirits given by the hope of success, enabling them to exert more strength in moving their limbs, I will not pretend to say.

Perhaps some permanent advantage might have been obtained, if the electric shocks had been accompanied with proper medicine and regimen, under the direction of a skilful physician. It may be, too, that a few great strokes, as given in my method, may not be so proper as many small ones; since by the account from Scotland of a case, in which two hundred shocks from a phial were given daily, it seems, that a perfect cure has been made. As to any uncommon strength supposed to be in the machine used in that case, I imagine it could have no share in the effect produced; since the strength of the shock from charged glass, is in proportion to the quantity of surface of the glass coated; so that my shock from those large jars, must have been much greater than any that could be received from a phial held in the hand.

I am, with great respect, Sir,

Your most obedient servant,

B. FRANKLIN.

E e

Electrical Experiments on Amber.

Saturday, July 3, 1762.

TO try, at the request of a friend, whether amber finely powdered might be melted and run together again by means of the electric fluid, I took a piece of small glass tube, about two inches and a half long, the bore about one-twelfth of an inch diameter, the glass itself about the same thickness; I introduced into this tube some powder of amber, and with two pieces of wire nearly fitting the bore, one inserted at one end, the other at the other, I rammed the powder hard between them in the middle of the tube, where it stuck fast, and was in length about half an inch. Then leaving the wires in the tube, I made them part of the electric circuit, and discharged through them three rows of my case of bottles. The event was, that the glass was broke into very small pieces, and those dispersed with violence in all directions. As I did not expect this, I had not, as in other experiments, laid thick paper over the glass to save my eyes, so several of the pieces struck my face smartly, and one of them cut my lip a little so as to make it bleed. I could find no part of the amber; but the table where the tube lay was stained very black in spots, such as might be made by a thick smoke forced on it by a blast, and the air was filled with a strong smell, somewhat like that from burnt gunpowder. Whence I imagined, that the amber was burnt, and had exploded as gunpowder would have done in the same circumstances.

That I might better see the effect on the amber, I made the next experiment in a tube formed of a card rolled up and bound strongly with packthread. Its bore was about one-eighth of an inch diameter. I rammed powder of amber into this as I had done in the other, and as the quantity of amber was greater, I increased the quantity of electric fluid, by discharging through it at once five rows of my bottles. On opening the tube, I found that some of the powder had exploded, an impression was made on the tube, though it was not hurt, and most of the powder remaining was turned black, which I suppose might be by the smoke forced through it from the burned part : some of it was hard ; but as it powdered again when pressed by the fingers, I suppose that hardness not to arise from melting any parts in it, but merely from my ramming the powder when I charged the tube.

B. FRANKLIN.

TO THOMAS RONAYNE, ESQ. AT CORKE[4], IRELAND.

On the Electricity of the Fogs in Ireland.

London, April 20, 1766.

SIR,

I HAVE received your very obliging and very ingenious letter by Captain Kearney. Your observations upon the electricity of fogs, and the 'air in Ireland, and upon different circumstances of storms, appear to me very curious, and I thank you for them. There is not, in my opinion, any part of the earth whatever which is, or can be, naturally in a state of negative electricity : and though different circumstances may occasion an inequality in the distribution of the fluid, the equilibrium is immediately restored by means of its extreme subtlety, and of the excellent conductors with which the humid earth is amply provided. I am of opinion, however, that when a cloud, well charged positively, passes near the earth, it repels and forces down into the earth that natural portion of electricity, which exists near its surface, and in buildings, trees, &c. so as actually to reduce them to a negative state before it strikes them. I am of opinion too, that the negative state in which you have frequently found the balls, which are suspended from your apparatus, is not always occasioned by clouds in a negative state ; but more commonly by clouds positively electrified, which have passed over them, and which in

4 This letter is translated from the French edition of Dr. Franklin's works.

their passage have repelled and driven off a part of the electrical matter, which naturally existed in the apparatus ; so that what remained after the passing of the clouds, diffusing itself uniformly through the apparatus, the whole became reduced to a negative state.

If you have read my experiments made in continuation of those of Mr. Canton, you will readily understand this ; but you may easily make a few experiments, which will clearly demonstrate it.   Let a common glass be warmed before the fire that it may continue very dry for some time ; set it upon a table, and place upon it the small box made use of by Mr. Canton, so that the balls may hang a little beyond the edge of the table.   Rub another glass, which has previously been warmed in a similar manner, with a piece of black silk or a silk handkerchief, in order to electrify it.   Hold then the glass above the little box, at about the distance of three or four inches from that part, which is most distant from the balls ; and you will see the balls separate from each other ; being positively electrified by the natural portion of electricity, which was in the box, and which is driven to the further part of it by the repulsive power of the atmosphere in the excited glass.   Touch the box near the little balls (the excited glass continuing in the same state) and the balls will again unite ; the quantity of electricity which had been driven to this part being drawn off by your finger.   Withdraw then both your finger and the glass at the same instant, and the quantity of electricity which remained in the box, uniformly diffusing itself, the balls will again be separated ; being now in a negative state. While things are in this situation, begin once more to excite your glass, and hold it above the box, but not too near, and you will find, that when brought within a certain distance, the balls will at first approach each other, being then in a natural state.   In proportion as the glass is brought nearer, they will again separate, being positive.   When the glass is moved beyond them, and at some little farther distance, they will unite again, being in a natural state. When it is entirely removed, they will separate again, being then made negative. The excited glass in this experiment may represent a cloud positively charged, which you see is capable of producing in this manner all the different changes in the apparatus, without the least necessity for supposing any negative cloud.

I am nevertheless fully convinced, that there are negative clouds; because they sometimes absorb, through the medium of the apparatus, the positive electricity of a large jar, the hundredth part of which the apparatus itself would have not been able to receive or contain at once. In fact, it is not difficult to conceive, that a large cloud, highly charged positively, may reduce smaller clouds to a negative state, when it passes above or near them, by forcing a part of their natural portion of the fluid either to their inferior surfaces, whence it may strike into the earth, or to the opposite side, whence it may strike into the adjacent clouds; so that when the large cloud has passed off to a distance, the small clouds shall remain in a negative state, exactly like the apparatus; the former (like the latter) being frequently insulated bodies, having communication neither with the earth nor with other clouds. Upon the same principle it may easily be conceived, in what manner a large negative cloud may render others positive.

The experiment which you mention, of filling your glass, is analogous to one which I made in 1751 or 1752. I had supposed in my preceding letters, that the pores of glass were smaller in the interior parts than near the surface, and that on this account they prevented the passage of the electrical fluid. To prove whether this was actually the case or not, I ground one of my phials in a part where it was extremely thin, grinding it considerably beyond the middle, and very near to the opposite superfices, as I found, upon breaking it after the experiment. It was charged nevertheless after being ground, equally well as before, which convinced me, that my hypothesis on this subject was erroneous It is difficult to conceive where the immense superfluous quantity of electricity on the charged side of a glass is deposited.

I send you my paper concerning meteors, which was lately published here in the Philosophical Transactions, immediately after a paper by Mr. Hamilton on the same subject.

I am, Sir, &c.

B. FRANKLIN.

Mode of ascertaining, whether the Power, giving a Shock to those who touch either the Surinam Eel, or the Torpedo, be electrical.

1. TOUCH the fish with a stick of dry sealing-wax, or a glass rod, and observe if the shock be communicated by means of those bodies.

Touch the same fish with an iron, or other metalline rod.

If the shock be communicated by the latter body, and not by the others, it is probably not the mechanical effect, as has been supposed, of some muscular action in the fish, but of a subtle fluid, in this respect analogous at least to the electric fluid.

2. Observe farther, whether the shock can be conveyed without the metal being actually in contact with the fish, and if it can, whether, in the space between, any light appear, and a slight noise or crackling be heard.

If so, these also are properties common to the electric fluid.

3. Lastly, touch the fish with the wire of a small Leyden bottle, and if the shock can be received across, observe whether the wire will attract and repel light bodies, and you feel a shock, while holding the bottle in one hand, and touching the wire with the other.

If so, the fluid, capable of producing such effects seems to have all the known properties of the electric fluid.

ADDITION, 12th *August,* 1772,

In Consequence of the Experiments and Discoveries made in France by Mr. Walsh, and communicated by him to Dr. Franklin.

Let several persons, standing on the floor, hold hands, and let one of them touch the fish, so as to receive a shock.

If the shock be felt by all, place the fish, flat on a plate of metal, and let one of the persons holding hands touch this plate, while the person farthest from the plate touches the upper part of the fish, with a metal rod: then observe, if the force of the shock be the same as to all the persons forming the circle, or is stronger than before.

Repeat this experiment with this difference: let two or three of the persons forming the circle, instead of holding by the hand, hold each an uncharged electrical bottle, so that the little balls at the end of the wires may touch, and observe, after the shock, if these wires will attract and repel light bodies, and if a ball of cork, suspended by a long silk string between the wires, a little distance from the bottles, will be alternately attracted and repelled by them.

TO M. DUBOURG

On the Analogy between Magnetism and Electricity.

London, March 10, 1773.

Sir,

AS to the magnetism, which seems produced by electricity, my real opinion is, that these two powers of nature have no affinity with each other, and that the apparent production of magnetism is purely accidental. The matter may be explained thus:

1st, The earth is a great magnet.

2dly, There is a subtle fluid, called the magnetic fluid, which exists in all ferruginous bodies, equally attracted by all their parts, and equally diffused through their whole substance; at least where the equilibrium is not disturbed by a power superior to the attraction of the iron,

3dly, This natural quantity of the magnetic fluid, which is contained in a given piece of iron, may be put in motion so as to be more rarefied in one part and more condensed in another; but it cannot be withdrawn by any force that we are yet made acquainted with, so as to leave the whole in a negative state, at least relatively to its natural quantity;

neither can it be introduced so as to put the iron into a positive state, or render it *plus*. In this respect, therefore magnetism differs from electricity.

4thly, A piece of soft iron allows the magnetic fluid which it contains to be put in motion by a moderate force, so that being placed in a line with the magnetic pole of the earth, it immediately acquires the properties of a magnet; its magnetic fluid being drawn or forced from one extremity to the other; and this effect continues as long as it remains in the same position, one of its extremities becoming positively magnetised, and the other negatively. This temporary magnetism ceases as soon as the iron is turned east and west, the fluid immediately diffusing itself equally through the whole iron, as in its natural state.

5thly, The magnetic fluid in hard iron, or steel, is put in motion with more difficulty, requiring a force greater than the earth to excite it; and when once it has been forced from one extremity of the steel to the other, it is not easy for it to return; and thus a bar of steel is converted into a permanent magnet.

6thly, A great heat, by expanding the substance of this steel, and increasing the distance between its particles, affords a passage to the electric fluid, which is thus again restored to its proper equilibrium; the bar appearing no longer to possess magnetic virtue.

7thly, A bar of steel which is not magnetic, being placed in the same position, relatively to the pole of the earth, which the magnetic needle assumes, and in this position being heated and suddenly cooled, becomes a permanent magnet. The reason is, that while the bar was hot, the magnetic fluid which it naturally contained was easily forced from one extremity to the other by the magnetic virtue of the earth; and that the hardness and condensation, produced by the sudden cooling of the bar, retained it in this state without permitting it to resume its original situation.

8thly, The violent vibrations of the particles of a steel bar, when forcibly struck in the same position, separate the particles in such a manner during their vibration, that they permit a portion of the magnetic fluid to pass, influenced by the natural magnetism of the earth; and it is afterwards so forcibly retained by the re-approach of the particles when the vibration ceases, that the bar becomes a permanent magnet.

9thly, An electric shock passing through a needle in a like position, and dilating it for an instant, renders it, for the same reason, a permanent magnet: that is, not by imparting magnetism to it, but by allowing its proper magnetic fluid to put itself in motion.

10thly, Thus, there is not in reality more magnetism in a given piece of steel after it is become magnetic, than existed in it before. The natural quantity is only displaced or repelled. Hence it follows, that a strong apparatus of magnets may charge millions of bars of steel, without communicating to them any part of its proper magnetism; only putting in motion the magnetism which already existed in these bars.

I am chiefly indebted to that excellent philosopher of Petersburgh, Mr. Æpinus, for this hypothesis, which appears to me equally ingenious and solid. I say *chiefly*, because, as it is many years since I read his book, which I have left in America, it may happen, that I may have added to or altered it in some respect; and if I have misrepresented any thing, the error ought to be charged to my account.

If this hypothesis appears admissible, it will serve as an answer to the greater part of your questions. I have only one remark to add, which is, that however great the force is of magnetism employed, you can only convert a given portion of steel into a magnet of a force proportioned to its capacity of retaining its magnetic fluid in the new position in which it is placed, without letting it return. Now this power is different in different kinds of steel, but limited in all kinds whatever.

B. FRANKLIN.

F f

TO MESSRS. DUBOURG AND D'ALIBARD.[5]

Concerning the Mode of rendering Meat tender by Electricity.

MY DEAR FRIENDS,

MY answer to your questions concerning the mode of rendering meat tender by electricity, can only be founded upon conjecture; for I have not experiments enough to warrant the facts. All that I can say at present is, that I think electricity might be employed for this purpose, and I shall state what follows as the observations or reasons, which make me presume so.

It has been observed, that lightning, by rarefying and reducing into vapor the moisture contained in solid wood, in an oak, for instance, has forcibly separated its fibres, and broken it into small splinters; that by penetrating intimately the hardest metals, as iron, it has separated the parts in an instant, so as to convert a perfect solid into a state of fluidity: it is not then improbable, that the same subtle, matter, passing through the bodies of animals with rapidity, should possess sufficient force to produce an effect nearly similar.

The flesh of animals, fresh killed in the usual manner, is firm, hard, and not in a very eatable state, because the particles adhere too forcibly too each other. At a certain period, the cohesion is weakened and in its progress towards putrefaction, which tends to produce a total separation, the flesh becomes what we call tender, or is in that state most proper to be used as our food.

It has frequently been remarked, that animals killed by lightning putrify immediately. This cannot be invariably the case, since a quantity of lightning sufficient to kill, may not be sufficient to tear and divide the fibres and particles of flesh, and reduce them to that tender state, which is the

---

5 This letter has no date, but the one to which it is an answer is dated May 1, 1773.

prelude to putrefaction. Hence it is, that some animals killed in this manner will keep longer than others. But the putrefaction sometimes proceeds with surprising celerity. A respectable person assured me, that he once knew a remarkable instance of this : A whole flock of sheep in Scotland, being closely assembled under a tree, were killed by a flash of lightning; and it being rather late in the evening, the proprietor, desirous of saving something, sent persons early the next morning to flay them : but the putrefaction was such, and the stench so abominable, that they had not the courage to execute their orders, and the bodies were accordingly buried in their skins. It is not unreasonable to presume, that between the period of their death and that of their putrefaction, a time intervened in which the flesh might be only tender, and only sufficiently so to be served at table. · Add to this, that persons, who have eaten of fowls killed by our feeble imitation of lightning (electricity) and dressed immediately, have asserted, that the flesh was remarkably tender.

The little utility of this practice has perhaps prevented its being much adopted. For though it sometimes happens, that a company unexpectedly arriving at a country-house, or an unusual conflux of travellers to an inn, may render it necessary, to kill a number of animals for immediate use ; yet as travellers have commonly a good appetite, little attention has been paid to the trifling inconvenience of having their meat a little tough. As this kind of death is nevertheless more sudden, and consequently less severe, than any other, if this should operate as a motive with compassionate persons to employ it for animals sacrificed for their use, they may conduct the process thus :

Having prepared a battery of six large glass jars (each from 20 to 24 pints) as for the Leyden experiment, and having established a communication, as usual, from the interior surface of each with the prime conductor, and having given them a full charge (which with a good machine may be executed in a few minutes, and may be estimated by an electrometer) a chain which communicates with the exte-

rior of the jars must be wrapped round the thighs of the
fowl; after which the operator, holding it by the wings,
turned back and made to touch behind, must raise it so
high that the head may receive the first shock from the
prime conductor.   The animal dies instantly. Let the head
be immediately cut off to make it bleed, when it may be
plucked and dressed immediately.   This quantity of electricity is supposed sufficient for a turkey of ten pounds
weight, and perhaps for a lamb.   Experience alone will
inform us of the requisite proportions for animals of different forms and ages.   Probably not less will be required to
render a small bird, which is very old, tender, than for a
larger one, which is young.   It is easy to furnish the requisite quantity of electricity, by employing a greater or
less number of jars.   As six jars, however, discharged at
once, are capable of giving a very violent shock, the operator must be very circumspect, lest he should happen to
make the experiment on his own flesh, instead of that of
the fowl.

B. FRANKLIN.

TO M. DUBOURG

*In Answer to some Queries concerning the Choice of Glass for the
Leyden Experiment.*

London, June 1, 1773.

Sir,

I WISH, with you, that some chemist (who should, if
possible, be at the same time an electrician) would, in pursuance of the excellent hints contained in your letter, undertake to work upon glass with the view you have recommended.   By means of a perfect knowlege of this substance, with respect to its electrical qualities, we might
proceed with more certainty, as well in making our own
experiments, as in repeating those, which have been made
by others in different countries, which I believe have frequently been attended with different success on account of

differences in the glass employed, thence occasioning frequent misunderstandings and contrariety of opinions.

There is another circumstance much to be desired with respect to glass, and that is, that it should not be subject to break when highly charged in the Leyden experiment. I have known eight jars broken out of twenty, and at another time, twelve out of thirty-five. A similar loss would greatly discourage electricians desirous of accumulating a great power for certain experiments.—We have never been able hitherto to account for the cause of such misfortunes. The first idea which occurs is, that the positive electricity, being accumulated on one side of the glass, rushes violently through it, in order to supply the deficiency on the other side and to restore the equilibrium. This however I cannot conceive to be the true reason, when I consider, that a great number of jars being united, so as to be charged and discharged at the same time, the breaking of a single jar will discharge the whole; for, if the accident proceeded from the weakness of the glass, it is not probable, that eight of them should be precisely of the same degree of weakness, as to break every one at the same instant, it being more likely, that the weakest should break first, and, by breaking, secure the rest; and again, when it is necessary to produce a certain effect, by means of the whole charge passing through a determined circle (as, for instance, to melt a small wire) if the charge, instead of passing in this circle, rushed through the sides of the jars, the intended effect would not be produced; which, however, is contrary to fact. For these reasons, I suspect, that there is, in the substance of the glass, either some little globules of air, or some portions of unvitrified sand or salt, into which a quantity of the electric fluid may be forced during the charge, and there retained till the general discharge: and that the force being suddenly withdrawn, the elasticity of the fluid acts upon the glass in which it is inclosed, not being able to escape hastily without breaking the glass. I offer this only as a conjecture, which I leave to others to examine.

The globe which I had that could not be excited, though it was from the same glass-house which furnished the other excellent globes in my possession, was not of the same frit. The glass which was usually manufactured there, was rather of the green kind, and chiefly intended for drinking-glasses and bottles; but the proprietors being desirous of attempting a trial of white glass, the globe in question was of this frit. The glass not being of a perfect white, the proprietors were dissatisfied with it, and abandoned their project. I suspected that too great a quantity of salt was admitted into the composition; but I am no judge of these matters.

B. FRANKLIN.

TO MISS STEPHENSON.

Concerning the Leyden Bottle.

London, March 22, 1762.

I MUST retract the charge of idleness in your studies, when I find you have gone through the doubly difficult task of reading so big a book, on an abstruse subject, and in a foreign language.

In answer to your question concerning the Leyden phial. —The hand that holds the bottle receives and conducts away the electric fluid that is driven out of the outside by the repulsive power of that which is forced into the inside of the bottle. As long as that power remains in the same situation, it must prevent the return of what it had expelled; though the hand would readily supply the quantity if it could be received.

Your affectionate friend,
B. FRANKLIN.

Physical and Meteorological Observations, Conjectures, and Suppositions.

Read at the Royal Society, June 3, 1756.

THE particles of air are kept at a distance from each other by their mutual repulsion.

Every three particles, mutually and equally repelling each other, must form an equilateral triangle.

All the particles of air gravitate towards the earth, which gravitation compresses them, and shortens the sides of the triangles, otherwise their mutual repellency would force them to greater distances from each other.

Whatever particles of other matter (not endued with that repellency) are supported in air, must adhere to the particles of air, and be supported by them ; for in the vacancies there is nothing they can rest on.

Air and water mutually attract each other. Hence water will dissolve in air, as salt in water.

The specific gravity of matter is not altered by dividing the matter, though the superfices be increased. Sixteen leaden bullets, of an ounce each, weigh as much in water as one of a pound, whose superfices is less.

Therefore the supporting of salt in water is not owing to its superfices being increased.

A lump of salt, though laid at rest at the bottom of a vessel of water, will dissolve therein, and its parts move every way, till equally diffused in the water, therefore there is a mutual attraction between water and salt. Every particle of water assumes as many of salt as can adhere to it ; when more is added, it precipitates, and will not remain suspended.

Water, in the same manner, will dissolve in air, every particle of air assuming one or more particles of water. When too much is added, it precipitates in rain.

But there not being the same contiguity between the particles of air as of water, the solution of water in air is not carried on without a motion of the air, so as to cause a fresh accession of dry particles.

Part of a fluid, having more of what it dissolves, will communicate to other parts that have less. Thus very salt water, coming in contact with fresh, communicates its saltness till all is equal, and the sooner if there is a little motion of the water.

Even earth will dissolve, or mix with air. A stroke of a horse's hoof on the ground, in a hot dusty road, will raise a cloud of dust, that shall, if there be a light breeze, expand every way, till perhaps near as big as a common house. It is not by mechanical motion communicated to the particles of dust by the hoof, that they fly so far, not by the wind, that they spread so wide; but the air near the ground, more heated by the hot dust struck into it, is rarefied and rises, and in rising mixes with the cooler air, and communicates of its dust to it, and it is at length so diffused as to become invisible. Quantities of dust are thus carried up in dry seasons: showers wash it from the air, and bring it down again. For water attracting it stronger, it quits the air, and adheres to the water.

Air, suffering continual changes in the degrees of its heat, from various causes and circumstances, and consequently, changes in its specific gravity, must therefore be in continual motion.

A small quantity of fire mixed with water (or degree of heat therein) so weakens the cohesion of its particles, that those on the surface easily quit it, and adhere to the particles of air.

Air moderately heated will support a greater quantity of water invisibly than cold air; for its particles being by heat repelled to a greater distance from each other, thereby more easily keep the particles of water that are annexed to them from running into cohesions that would obstruct, refract, or reflect the light.

Hence when we breathe in warm air, though the same quantity of moisture may be taken up from the lungs, as when we breathe in cold air, yet that moisture is not so visible.

Water being extremely heated, *i. e.* to the degree of boiling, its particles in quitting it so repel each other, as to take up vastly more space than before, and by that repellency support themselves, expelling the air from the space they occupy. That degree of heat being lessened, they again mutually attract, and having no air particles mixed to adhere to, by which they might be supported and kept at a distance, they instantly fall, coalesce, and become water again.

The water commonly diffused in our atmosphere never receives such a degree of heat from the sun, or other cause as water has when boiling; it is not, therefore, supported by such heat, but by adhering to air.

Water being dissolved in, and adhering to air, that air will not readily take up oil, because of the mutual repellency between water and oil.

Hence cold oils evaporate but slowly, the air having generally a quantity of dissolved water.

Oil being heated extremely, the air that approaches its surface will be also heated extremely; the water then quitting it, it will attract and carry off the oil, which can now adhere to it. Hence the quick evaporation of oil heated to a great degree.

Oil being dissolved in air, the particles to which it adheres will not take up water.

Hence the suffocating nature of air impregnated with burnt grease, as from snuffs of candles and the like. A certain quantity of moisture should be every moment discharged and taken away from the lungs; air that has been frequently breathed, is already overloaded, and, for that reason, can take no more, so will not answer the end. Greasy air refuses to touch it. In both cases suffocation for want of the discharge.

Air will attract and support many other substances.

A particle of air loaded with adhering water, or any other matter, is heavier than before and would descend.

The atmosphere supposed at rest, a loaded descending particle must act with a force on the particles it passes be-

G g

tween, or meets with, sufficient to overcome, in some degree, their mutual repellency, and push them nearer to
each other.

Thus, supposing the particles A
B C D, and the other near them
to be at the distance caused by
their mutual repellency (confined
by their common gravity) if A
would descend to E, it must pass
between B and C ; when it comes
between B and C, it will be nearer
to them than before, and must ei-
ther have pushed them nearer to F and G, contrary to their
mutual repellency or pass through by a force exceeding its
repellency with them.   It then approaches D, and, to move
it out of the way, must act on it with a force sufficient to
overcome its repellency with the two next lower particles,
by which it is kept in its present situation.

Every particle of air, therefore, will bear any load inferior to the force of these repulsions.

Hence the support of fogs, mists, clouds.

Very warm air, clear, though supporting a very great
quantity of moisture, will grow turbid and cloudy on the
mixture of colder air, as foggy turbid air will grow clear
by warming.

Thus the sun shining on a morning fog, dissipates it ;
clouds are seen to waste in a sun-shiny day.

But cold condenses and renders visible the vapor ; a
tankard or decanter filled with cold water will condense the
moisture of warm clear air on its outside, where it becomes
visible as dew, coalesces into drops, descends in little
streams.

The sun heats the air of our atmosphere most near the
surface of the earth ; for there, besides the direct rays,
there are many reflections.   Moreover, the earth itself being heated, communicates of its heat to the neighboring air.

· The higher regions, having only the direct rays of the
sun passing through them, are comparatively very cold

Hence the cold air on the tops of mountains, and snow on some of them all the year, even in the torrid zone. Hence hail in summer.

If the atmosphere were, all of it (both above and below) always of the same temper as to cold or heat, then the upper air would always be *rarer* than the lower, because the pressure on it is less; consequently lighter, and therefore would keep its place.

But the upper air may be more condensed by cold, than the lower air by pressure; the lower more expanded by heat, than the upper for want of pressure. In such case the upper air will become the heavier, the lower the lighter.

The lower region of air being heated and expanded heaves up, and supports for some time the colder heavier air above, and will continue to support it while the equilibrium is kept. Thus water is supported in an inverted open glass, while the equilibrium is maintained by the equal pressure upwards of the air below; but the equilibrium by any means breaking, the water descends on the heavier side, and the air rises into its place.

The lifted heavy cold air over a heated country, becoming by any means unequally supported, or unequal in its weight the heaviest part descends first, and the rest follows impetuously. Hence gusts after heats, and hurricanes in hot climates. Hence the air of gusts and hurricanes is cold, though in hot climates and seasons; it coming from above.

The cold air descending from above, as it penetrates our warm region full of watry particles, condenses them, renders them visible, forms a cloud thick and dark, overcasting sometimes, at once, large and extensive; sometimes, when seen at a distance, small at first, gradually increasing; the cold edge, or surface of the cloud, condensing the vapors next it, which form smaller clouds that join it, increase its bulk, it descends with the wind and its acquired weight, draws nearer the earth, grows denser with continual additions of water, and discharges heavy showers.

Small black clouds thus appearing in a clear sky, in hot climates, portend storms, and warn seamen to hand their sails.

The earth, turning on its axis in about twenty-four hours, the equatorial parts must move about fifteen miles in each minute; in northern and southern latitudes this motion is gradually less to the poles, and there nothing.

If there was a general calm over the face of the globe, it must be by the air's moving in every part as fast as the earth or sea it covers.

He that sails, or rides, has insensibly the same degree of motion as the ship or coach with which he is connected. If the ship strikes the shore, or the coach stops suddenly, the motion continuing in the man, he is thrown forward. If a man were to jump from the land into a swift sailing ship, he would be thrown backward (or towards the stern) not having at first the motion of the ship.

He that travels by sea or land, towards the equinoctial, gradually acquires motion; from it, loses.

But if a man were taken up from latitude 40 (where suppose the earth's surface to move twelve miles per minute) and immediately set down at the equinoctial, without changing the motion he had, his heels would be struck up, he would fall westward. If taken up from the equinoctial, and set down in latitude 40, he would fall eastward.

The air under the equator, and between the tropics, being constantly heated and rarefied by the sun, rises. Its place is supplied by air from northern and southern latitudes, which coming from parts wherein the earth and air had less motion, and not suddenly acquiring the quicker motion of the equatorial earth, appears an east wind blowing westward; the earth moving from west to east, and slipping under the air[6].

Thus, when we ride in a calm, it seems a wind against us: if we ride with the wind, and faster, even that will seem a small wind against us.

The air rarefied between the tropics, and rising, must flow in the higher region north and south. Before it rose,

6 See a paper on this subject, by the late ingenious Mr. Hadley, in the Philosophical Transactions, wherein this hypothesis for explaining the trade-winds first appeared.

it had acquired the greatest motion the earth's rotation could give it. It retains some degree of this motion, and descending in higher latitudes, where the earth's motion is less, will appear a westerly wind, yet tending towards the equatorial parts, to supply the vacancy occasioned by the air of the lower regions flowing thitherwards.

Hence our general cold winds are about north west, our summer cold gusts the same.

The air in sultry weather, though not cloudy, has a kind of haziness in it, which makes objects at a distance appear dull and indistinct. This haziness is occasioned by the great quantity of moisture equally diffused in that air. When, by the cold wind blowing down among it, it is condensed into clouds, and falls in rain, the air becomes purer and clearer. Hence, after gusts, distant objects appear distinct, their figures sharply terminated.

Extreme cold winds congeal the surface of the earth, by carrying off its fire. Warm winds afterwards blowing over that frozen surface will be chilled by it. Could that frozen surface be turned under, and warmer turned up from beneath it, those warm winds would not be chilled so much.

The surface of the earth is also sometimes much heated by the sun: and such heated surface not being changed heats the air that moves over it.

Seas, lakes, and great bodies of water, agitated by the winds, continually change surfaces; the cold surface in winter is turned under by the rolling of the waves, and a warmer turned up; in summer, the warm is turned under, and colder turned up. Hence the more equal temper of sea-water, and the air over it. Hence, in winter, winds from the sea seem warm, winds from the land cold. In summer the contrary.

Therefore the lakes north-west of us[7], as they are not so much frozen, nor so apt to freeze as the earth, rather moderate than increase the coldness of our winter winds.

7 In Pennsylvania.

The air over the sea being warmer, and therefore lighter in winter than the air over the frozen land, may be another cause of our general N. W. winds, which blow off to sea at right angles from our North-American coast. The warm light sea air rising, the heavy cold land air pressing into its place.

Heavy fluids descending, frequently form eddies, or whirlpools, as is seen in a funnel, where the water acquires a circular motion, receding every way from a centre, and leaving a vacancy in the middle, greatest above, and lessening downwards, like a speaking trumpet, its big end upwards.

Air descending, or ascending, may form the same kind of eddies, or whirlings, the parts of air acquiring a circular motion, and receding from the middle of the circle by a centrifugal force, and leaving there a vacancy; if descending, greatest above, and lessening downwards; if ascending, greatest below, and lessening upwards; like a speaking trumpet, standing its big end on the ground.

When the air descends with violence in some places, it may rise with equal violence in others, and form both kinds of whirlwinds.

The air in its whirling motion receding every way from the centre or axis of the trumpet leaves there a *vacuum*, which cannot be filled through the sides, the whirling air, as an arch, preventing; it must then press in at the open ends.

The greatest pressure inwards must be at the lower end, the greatest weight of the surrounding atmosphere being there. The air entering rises within, and carries up dust, leaves, and even heavier bodies that happen in its way, as the eddy, or whirl, passes over land.

If it passes over water, the weight of the surrounding atmosphere forces up the water into the vacuity, part of which, by degrees, joins with the whirling air, and adding weight, and receiving accelerated motion, recedes still farther from the center or axis of the trump, as the pressure lessens; and at last, as the trump widens, is broken into small particles, and so united with air as to be supported by it, and become black clouds at the top of the trump.

Thus these eddies may be whirlwinds at land, waterspouts at sea. A body of water so raised, may be suddenly let fall, when the motion, &c. has not strength to support it, or the whirling arch is broken so as to admit the air: falling in the sea, it is harmless, unless ships happen under it; but if in the progressive motion of the whirl it has moved from the sea, over the land, and then breaks, sudden, violent, and mischievous torrents are the consequences.

DR. PERKINS OF BOSTON, TO DR. FRANKLIN, AT PHILADELPHIA.

On Water-Spouts.

Read at the Royal Society, June 3, 1756.

Boston, October 16, 1752.

SIR,

I FIND by a word or two in your last[8], that you are willing to be found fault with; which authorises me to let you know what I am at a loss about in your papers, which is only in the article of the water-spout. I am in doubt, whether water in bulk, or even broken into drops, ever ascends into the region of the clouds *per vorticem;* i. e. whether there be, in reality, what I call a direct waterspout. I make no doubt of direct and inverted whirlwinds; your description of them, and the reason of the thing, are sufficient. I am sensible too, that they are very strong, and often move considerable weights. But I have not met with any historical accounts that seem exact enough to remove my scruples concerning the ascent abovesaid.

Descending spouts (as I take them to be) are many times seen, as I take it, in the calms, between the sea and land

---

8 A Letter on Inoculation, which is transferred to a subsequent part of this volume, that the papers on meteorological subjects may not be interrupted.

trade-winds on the coast of Africa. These contrary winds, or diverging, I can conceive may occasion them, as it were by suction, making a breach in a large cloud. But I imagine they have, at the same time, a tendency to hinder any direct or rising spout, by carrying off the lower part of the atmosphere as fast as it begins to rarefy; and yet spouts are frequent here, which strengthens my opinion, that all of them descend.

But however this be, I cannot conceive a force producible by the rarefication and condensation of our atmosphere, in the circumstances of our globe, capable of carrying water, in large portions, into the region of the clouds. Supposing it to be raised, it would be too heavy to continue the ascent beyond a considerable height, unless parted into small drops; and even then, by its centrifugal force, from the manner of conveyance, it would be flung out of the circle, and fall scattered, like rain.

But I need not expatiate on these matters to you. I have mentioned my objections, and, as truth is my pursuit, shall be glad to be informed. I have seen few accounts of these whirl or eddy winds, and as little of the spouts; and these, especially, lame and poor things to obtain any certainty by. If you know any thing determinate that has been observed, I shall hope to hear from you; as also of any mistake in my thoughts. I have nothing to object to any other part of your suppositions: and as to that of the trade-winds, I believe nobody can.

I am, &c.

P. S. The figures in the *Philosophical Transactions* show, by several circumstances, that they all descended, though the relators seemed to think they took up water.[9]

---

9 Two engraved representations of water-spouts, from the Philosophical Transactions, are given in this edition, the better to illustrate the plate on the same subject, by Dr. Franklin.

DR. PERKINS OF BOSTON, TO DR. FRANKLIN AT PHILADEL-
PHIA.

The same subject continued.

Read at the Royal Society, June 24, 1756.

Boston, October 23, 1752.

SIR,

IN the inclosed, you have all I have to say of that matter. It proved longer than I expected, so that I was forced
to add a cover to it. I confess it looks like a dispute; but
that is quite contrary to my intentions. The sincerity of
friendship and esteem were my motives; nor do I doubt
your scrupling the goodness of the intention. However, I
must confess I cannot tell exactly how far I was actuated by
hopes of better information, in discovering the whole foundation of my opinion, which, indeed, is but an opinion, as
I am very much at a loss about the validity of the reasons.
I have not been able to differ from you in sentiment concerning any thing else in your *Suppositions.* In the present
case I lie open to conviction, and shall be the gainer when
informed. If I am right, you will know that, without my
adding any more. Too much said on a merely speculative
matter, is but a robbery committed on practical knowlege.
Perhaps I am too much pleased with these dry notions:
however, by this you will see that I think it unreasonable
to give you more trouble about them, than your leisure
and inclination may prompt you to.

I am, &c.

SINCE my last I considered, that, as I had begun with
the reasons of my dissatisfaction about the ascent of water
in spouts, you would not be unwilling to hear the whole I
have to say, and then you will know what I rely upon.

What occasioned my thinking all spouts descend, is, that
I found some did certainly do so. A difficulty appeared
concerning the ascent of so heavy a body as water, by any
force I was apprised of, as probably sufficient. And, above

H h

all, a view of Mr. Stuart's portraits of spouts, in the *Philosophical Transactions.*

Some observations on these last will include the chief part of my difficulties.

Mr. Stuart has given us the figures of a number observed by him in the Mediterranean; all with some particulars which make for my opinion, if well drawn.

The great spattering, which relators mention in the water where the spout descends, and which appears in all his draughts, I conceive to be occasioned by drops descending very thick and large into the place.

On the place of this spattering, arises the appearance of a bush, into the centre of which the spout comes down. This bush I take to be formed by a spray, made by the force of these drops, which being uncommonly large, and descending with unusual force by a stream of wind descending from the cloud with them, increases the height of the spray : which wind being repulsed by the surface of the waters rebounds and spreads ; by the first rising the spray higher than it otherwise would go ; and by the last making the top of the bush appear to bend outwards *(i. e.)* the cloud of spray is forced off from the trunk of the spout, and falls backward.

The bush does the same where there is no appearance of a spout reaching it ; and is depressed in the middle, where the spout is expected. This, I imagine, to be from numerous drops of the spout falling into it, together with the wind I mentioned, by their descent, which beat back the rising spray in the centre.

This circumstance, of the bush bending outwards at the top, seems not to agree with what I call a direct whirlwind, but consistent with the reversed ; for a direct one would sweep the bush inwards ; if, in that case, any thing of a bush would appear.

The pillar of water, as they call it, from its likeness, I suppose to be only the end of the spout immersed in the bush, a little blackened by the additional cloud, and perhaps, appears to the eye beyond its real bigness, by a refraction in the bush, and which refraction may be the cause of the appearance of separation, betwixt the part in the bush, and that above it. The part in the bush is cylindrical, as it is above (*i. e.*) the bigness the same from the top of the bush to the water. Instead of this shape, in case of a whirlwind, it must have been pyramidical.

Another thing remarkable, is, the curve in some of them : this is easy to conceive, in case of descending parcels of drops through various winds, at least till the cloud condenses so fast as to come down, as it were, *uno rivo.* But it is harder to me to conceive it in the ascent of water, that it should be conveyed along, secure of not leaking or often dropping through the under side, in the prone part : and, should the water be conveyed so swiftly, and with such force, up into the cloud, as to prevent this, it would, by a natural disposition to move on in a present direction, presently straiten the curve, raising the shoulder very swiftly, till lost in the cloud.

Over every one of Stuart's figures, I see a cloud : I suppose his clouds were first, and then the spout; I do not know whether it be so with all spouts, but suppose it is. Now, if whirlwinds carried up the water, I should expect them in fair weather, but not under a cloud ; as is observable of whirlwinds ; they come in fair weather, not under the shade of a cloud, nor in the night: since shade cools the air : but, on the contrary, violent winds often descend from the clouds ; strong gusts which occupy small spaces ; and from the higher regions, extensive hurricanes, &c.

Another thing is the appearance of the spout *coming from* the cloud. This I cannot account for on the notion of a direct spout, but in the real descending one, it is easy. I take it, that the cloud begins first of all to pour out drops at that particular spot, or *foramen;* and, when that current of drops increases, so as to force down wind and vapor, the spout becomes so far as that goes opaque. I take it, that no clouds drop spouts, but such as make very fast, and happen to condense in a particular spot, which perhaps is coldest, and gives a determination downwards, so as to make a passage through the subjacent atmosphere.

If spouts ascend, it is to carry up the warm rarefied air below, to let down all and any that is colder above; and, if so, they must carry it through the cloud they go into (for that is cold and dense, I imagine) perhaps far into the higher region, making a wonderful appearance at a convenient distance to observe it, by the swift rise of a body of vapor, above the region of the clouds. But as this has never been observed in any age, if it be supposable that is all.

I cannot learn by mariners, that any wind blows towards a spout more than any other way; but it blows towards a whirlwind, for a large distance round.

I suppose there has been no instance of the water of a spout being salt, when coming across any vessel at sea. I suppose too, that there have been no salt rains; these would make the case clear.

I suppose it is from some unhappy effects of these dangerous creatures of nature, that sailors have an universal dread on them, of breaking in their decks, should they come across them.

I imagine spouts, in cold seasons, as Gordon's in the Downs, prove the descent.

Query. Whether there is not always more or less cloud, first, where a spout appears?

Whether they are not, generally, on the borders of trade-winds; and whether this is for, or against me?

Whether there be any credible account of a whirlwind's carrying up all the water in a pool, or small pond: as when shoal, and the banks low, a strong gust might be supposed to blow it all out?

Whether a violent tornado, of a small extent, and other sudden and strong gusts, be not winds from above, descending nearly perpendicular; and, whether many that are called whirlwinds at sea, are any other than these; and so might be called air-spouts, if they were objects of sight?

I overlooked, in its proper place, Stuart's No. 11, which is curious for its inequalities, and, in particular, the approach to breaking, which, if it would not be too tedious, I would have observed a little upon, in my own way, as, I think, this would argue against the ascent, &c. but I must pass it, not only for the reason mentioned, but want of room besides.

As to Mr. Stuart's occular demonstration of the ascent in his great perpendicular spout, the only one it appears, in, I say, as to this, what I have written supposes him mistaken, which, yet, I am far from asserting.

The force of an airy vortex, having less influence on the solid drops of water, than on the interspersed cloudy vapors, makes the last whirl round swifter, though it descend slower: and this might easily deceive, without great care, the most unprejudiced person.

TO DR. PERKINS, BOSTON.

Water-Spouts and Whirlwinds compared.

Read at the Royal Society, June 24, 1753.

Philadelphia, Feb. 4, 1753.

SIR,

I OUGHT to have written to you, long since, in answer to yours of October 16, concerning the water-spout; but business partly, and partly a desire of procuring further information, by enquiry among my seafaring acquaintance, induced me to postpone writing, from time to time, till I am now almost ashamed to resume the subject, not knowing but you may have forgot what has been said upon it.

Nothing certainly, can be more improving to a searcher into nature, than objections judiciously made to his opinion, taken up, perhaps, too hastily: for such objections oblige him to re-study the point, consider every circumstance carefully, compare facts, make experiments, weigh arguments, and be slow in drawing conclusions. And hence a sure advantage results; for he either confirms a truth, before too slightly supported; or discovers an error, and receives instruction from the objector.

In this view I consider the objections and remarks you
sent me, and thank you for them sincerely: but, how much
soever my inclinations lead me to philosophical enquiries,
I am so engaged in business, public and private, that those
more pleasing pursuits are frequently interrupted, and the
chain of thought, necessary to be closely continued in such
disquisitions, is so broken and disjointed, that it is with
difficulty I satisfy myself in any of them: and I am now
not much nearer a conclusion, in this matter of the spout,
than when I first read your letter.

Yet, hoping we may, in time, sift out the truth between
us, I will send you my present thoughts, with some observations on your reasons on the accounts in the *Transactions*,
and on other relations I have met with. Perhaps, while I
I am writing, some new light may strike me, for I shall
now be obliged to consider the subject with a little more attention.

I agree with you, that, by means of a vacuum in a whirlwind, water cannot be supposed to rise in large masses to
the region of the clouds; for the pressure of the surrounding atmosphere could not force it up in a continued body,
or column, to a much greater height, than thirty feet. But,
if there really is a vacuum in the centre, or near the axis of
whirlwinds, then, I think, water may rise in such vacuum to
that height, or to a less height, as the vacuum may be less
perfect.

I had not read Stuart's account, in the *Transactions*, for
many years, before the receipt of your letter, and had quite
forgot it; but now, on viewing his draughts, and considering his descriptions, I think they seem to favor *my hypothesis;* for he describes and draws columns of water, of
various heights, terminating abruptly at the top, exactly as
water would do, when forced up by the pressure of the atmosphere into an exhausted tube.

I must, however, no longer call it *my hypothesis*, since I
find Stuart had the same thought, though somewhat ob-
scurely expressed, where he says, " he imagines this phenomenon may be solved by suction (improperly so called)

or rather pulsion, as in the application of a cupping glass to the flesh, the air being first voided by the kindled flax."

In my paper, I supposed a whirlwind and a spout to be the same thing, and to proceed from the same cause; the only difference between them being, that the one passes over land, the other over water. I find, also, in the *Transactions*, that M. de la Pryme was of the same opinion; for he there describes two spouts, as he calls them, which were seen at different times, at Hatfield, in Yorkshire, whose appearances in the air were the same with those of the spouts at sea, and effects the same with those of real whirlwinds.

Whirlwinds have generally a progressive, as well as a circular motion; so had what is called the spout, at Topsham, as described in the Philosophical Transactions, which also appears, by its effects described, to have been a real whirlwind. Water-spouts have, also, a progressive motion; this is sometimes greater, and sometimes less; in some violent, in others barely perceivable. The whirlwind at Warrington continued long in Acrement-Close.

Whirlwinds generally arise after calms and great heats: the same is observed of water-spouts, which are, therefore, most frequent in the warm latitudes. The spout that happened in cold weather, in the Downs, described by Mr. Gordon, in the *Transactions*, was, for that reason, thought extraordinary; but he remarks withal, that the weather, though cold when the spout appeared, was soon after much colder; as we find it, commonly, less warm after a whirlwind.

You agree, that the wind blows every way towards a whirlwind, from a large space round. An intelligent whaleman of Nantucket, informed me that three of their vessels, which were out in search of whales, happening to be becalmed, lay in sight of each other, at about a league distance, if I remember right, nearly forming a triangle: after some time, a water-spout appeared near the middle of the triangle, when a brisk breeze of wind sprung up, and every vessel made sail; and then it appeared to them all, by the

setting of the sails, and the course each vessel stood, that
the spout was to the leeward of every one of them; and
they all declared it to have been so, when they happened afterwards in company, and came to confer about it. So
that in this particular likewise, whirlwinds and water-spouts
agree.

But, if that which appears a water-spout at sea, does
sometimes, in its progressive motion, meet with and pass
over land, and there produce all the phenomena and effects
of a whirlwind, it should thence seem still more evident,
that a whirlwind and a spout are the same. I send you,
herewith, a letter from an ingenious physician of my acquaintance, which gives one instance of this, that fell within
his observation.

A fluid, moving from all points horizontally, towards a
centre, must, at that centre, either ascend or descend.
Water being in a tub, if a hole be opened in the middle of
the bottom, will flow from all sides to the centre, and there
descend in a whirl. But, air flowing on and near the surface of land or water, from all sides, towards a centre,
must, at that centre ascend; the land or water hindering its
descent.

If these concentring currents of air be in the upper
region, thay may, indeed, descend in the spout or whirlwind; but then, when the united current reached the earth
or water, it would spread, and, probably, blow every way
from the centre. There may be whirlwinds of both kinds,
but from the commonly observed effects, I suspect the rising
one to be the most common: when the upper air descends,
it is, perhaps, in a greater body, extending wider, as in our
thunder-gusts, and without much whirling; and, when air
descends in a spout, or whirlwind, I should rather expect
it would press the roof of a house *inwards*, or force *in* the
tiles, shingles, or thatch, force a boat down into the water,
or a piece of timber into the earth, than that it would lift
them up, and carry them away.

It has so happened, that I have not met with any accounts of spouts, that certainly descended; I suspect they are not frequent. Please to communicate those you mention. The apparent dropping of a pipe from the clouds towards the earth or sea, I will endeavor to explain hereafter.

The augmentation of the cloud, which, as I am informed, is generally, if not always the case, during a spout, seems to shew an ascent, rather than a descent of the matter of which such cloud is composed; for a descending spout, one would expect, should diminish a cloud. I own, however, that cold air descending, may, by condensing the vapors in a lower region, form and increase clouds ; which, I think, is generally the case in our common thunder-gusts, and, therefore, do not lay great stress on this argument.

Whirlwinds and spouts, are not always, though most commonly, in the day time. The terrible whirlwind, which damaged a great part of Rome, June 11, 1749, happened in the night of that day. The same was supposed to have been first a spout, for it is said to be beyond doubt, that it gathered in the neighboring sea, as it could be tracked from Ostia to Rome. I find this is in Père Boschovich's account of it, as abridged in the Monthly Review for December, 1750.

In that account, the whirlwind is said to have appeared as a very black, long, and lofty cloud, discoverable, notwithstanding the darkness of the night, by its continually lightning or emitting flashes on all sides, pushing along with a surprising swiftness, and within three or four feet of the ground. Its general effects on houses, were stripping off the roofs, blowing away chimneys, breaking doors and windows, *forcing up the floors, and unpaving the rooms* (some of these effects seem to agree well with a supposed vacuum in the centre of the whirlwind) and the very rafters of the houses were broken and dispersed, and even hurled against houses at a considerable distance, &c.

It seems, by an expression of Père Boschovich's, as if the wind blew from all sides towards the whirlwind; for, having carefully observed its effects, he concludes of all

I i

whirlwinds, " that their motion is circular, and their action attractive."

He observes, on a number of histories of whirlwinds, &c. " that a common effect of them is, to carry up into the air, tiles, stones, and animals themselves, which happen to be in their course, and all kinds of bodies unexceptionably, throwing them to a considerable distance, with great impetuosity."

Such effects seem to shew a rising current of air.

I will endeavor to explain my conceptions of this matter by figures, representing a plan and an elevation of a spout or whirlwind.

I would only first beg to be allowed two or three positions, mentioned in my former paper.

1. That the lower region of air is often more heated, and so more rarefied, than the upper; consequently, specifically lighter. The coldness of the upper region is manifested by the hail which sometimes falls from it in a hot day.

2. That heated air may be very moist, and yet the moisture so equally diffused and rarefied, as not to be visible, till colder air mixes with it, when it condenses, and becomes visible. Thus our breath, invisible in summer, becomes visible in winter.

Now let us suppose a tract of land, or sea, of perhaps sixty miles square, unscreened by clouds, and unfanned by winds, during great part of a summer's day, or, it may be, for several days successively, till it is violently heated, together with the lower region of air in contact with it, so that the said lower air becomes specifically lighter than the superincumbent higher region of the atmosphere, in which the clouds commonly float: let us suppose, also, that the air surrounding this tract has not been so much heated during those days, and therefore remains heavier. The consequence of this should be, as I conceive, that the heated lighter air, being pressed on all sides, must ascend, and the heavier descend; and, as this rising cannot be in all parts, or the whole area of the tract at once, for that would leave too extensive a vacuum, the rising will begin precisely in

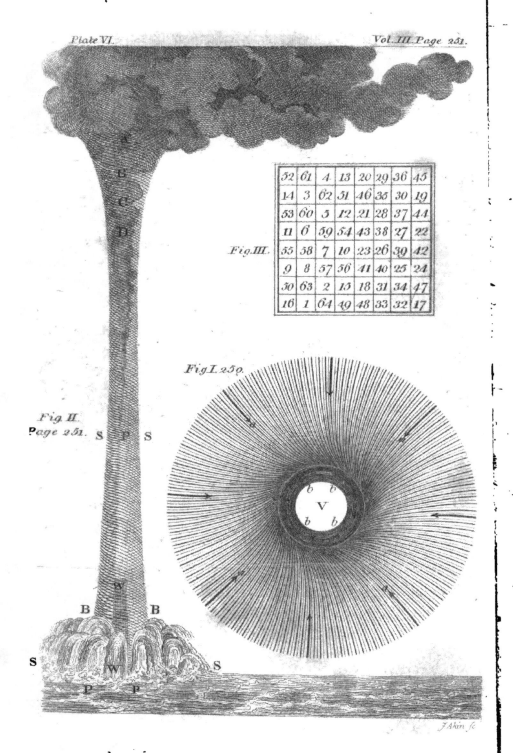

Plate VI.

Vol. III. Page 251.

Fig. III.

52	61	4	13	20	29	36	45
14	3	62	51	46	35	30	19
53	60	5	12	21	28	37	44
11	6	59	54	43	38	27	22
55	58	7	10	23	26	39	42
9	8	57	56	41	40	25	24
50	63	2	15	18	31	34	47
16	1	64	49	48	33	32	17

Fig. I. 250.

Fig. II.
Page 251.

J. Aken sc.

that column that happens to be the lightest, or most rarefied; and the warm air will flow horizontally from all points to this column, where the several currents meeting, and joining to rise, a whirl is naturally formed, in the same manner as a whirl is formed in the tub of water, by the descending fluid flowing from all sides of the tub, to the hole in the centre.

And, as the several currents arrive at this central rising column, with a considerable degree of horizontal motion, they cannot suddenly change it to a vertical motion; therefore as they gradually, in approaching the whirl, decline from right to curved or circular lines; so, having joined the whirl, they *ascend* by a spiral motion, in the same manner as the water *descends* spirally through the hole in the tub before-mentioned.

Lastly, as the lower air, and nearest the surface, is most rarefied by the heat of the sun, that air is most acted on by the pressure of the surrounding cold and heavy air, which is to take its place; consequently, its motion towards the whirl is swiftest, and so the force of the lower part of the whirl, or trump, strongest, and the centrifugal force of its particles greatest; and hence the vacuum round the axis of the whirl should be greatest near the earth or sea, and be gradually diminished as it approaches the region of the clouds, till it ends in a point, as at P, *Fig.* II. *in the plate*, forming a long and sharp cone.

In Fig. I. which is a plan or ground-plat of a whirlwind, the circle V. represents the central vacuum.

Between *a a a a* and *b b b b* I suppose a body of air, condensed strongly by the pressure of the currents moving towards it, from all sides without, and by its centrifugal force from within, moving round with prodigious swiftness, (having, as it were, the entire momenta of all the currents ———> ———> ———> ———> united in itself) and with a power equal to its swiftness and density.

It is this whirling body of air between *a a a a* and *b b b b* that rises spirally; by its force it tears buildings to pieces, twists up great trees by the roots, &c. and, by its spiral motion, raises the fragments so high, till the pressure of the surrounding and approaching currents diminishing, can no longer confine them to the circle, or their own centrifugal force encreasing, grows too strong for such pressure, when they fly off in tangent lines, as stones out of a sling, and fall on all sides, and at great distances.

If it happens at sea, the water under and between *a a a* and *b b b b* will be violently agitated and driven about, and parts of it raised with the spiral current, and thrown about so as to form a bush-like appearance.

This circle is of various diameters, sometimes very large.

If the vacuum passes over water, the water may rise in it in a body, or column, to near the height of thirty-two feet.

If it passes over houses, it may burst their windows or walls outwards, pluck off the roofs, and pluck up the floors, by the sudden rarefaction of the air contained within such buildings; the outward pressure of the atmosphere being suddenly taken off: so the stopped bottle of air bursts under the exhausted receiver of the air pump.

Fig. II. is to represent the elevation of a water-spout, wherein I suppose P P P to be the cone, at first a vacuum, till W W, the rising column of water, has filled so much of it. S S S S, the spiral whirl of air, surrounding the vacuum, and continued higher in a close column after the vacuum ends in the point P, till it reaches the cool region of the air. B B, the bush described by Stuart, surrounding the foot of the column of water.

Now, I suppose this whirl of air will, at first be as invisible as the air itself, though reaching, in reality, from the water, to the region of cool air, in which our low summer thunder-clouds commonly float: but presently it will become visible at its extremities. *At its lower end,* by the agitation of the water, under the whirling part of the circle, between P and S forming Stuart's bush, and by the swelling and rising of the water, in the beginning vacuum, which is, at first, a small, low, broad cone, whose top gradually rises and sharpens, as the force of the whirl en-

creases. *At its upper end* it becomes visible, by the warm air
brought up to the cooler region, where its moisture begins
to be condensed into thick vapor, by the cold, and is seen
first at A, the highest part, which being now cooled, condenses what rises next at B, which condenses that at C,
and that condenses what is rising at D, the cold operating
by the contact of the vapors faster in a right line downwards
than the vapors can climb in a spiral line upwards; they
climb, however, and as by continual addition they grow
denser, and, consequently, their centrifugal force greater,
and being risen above the concentrating currents that compose the whirl, fly off, spread, and form a cloud.

It seems easy to conceive, how, by this successive condensation from above, the spout appears to drop or descend
from the cloud, though the materials of which it is composed are all the while ascending.

The condensation of the moisture, contained in so great
a quantity of warm air as may be supposed to rise in a
short time in this prodigiously rapid whirl, is perhaps, sufficient to form a great extent of cloud, though the spout
should be over land, as those at Hatfield; and if the land
happens not to be very dusty, perhaps the lower part of the
spout will scarce become visible at all; though the upper,
or what is commonly called the descending part, be very
distinctly seen.

The same may happen at sea, in case the whirl is not violent enough to make a high vacuum, and raise the column,
&c. In such case, the upper part A B C D only will be
visible, and the bush, perhaps, below.

But if the whirl be strong, and there be much dust on
the land, and the column W W be raised from the water,
then the lower part becomes visible, and sometimes even
united to the upper part. For the dust may be carried up in
the spiral whirl, till it reach the region where the vapor is
condensed, and rise with that even to the clouds: and the
friction of the whirling air, on the sides of the column W
W, may detach great quantities of its water, break it into
drops, and carry them up in the spiral whirl mixed with

the air; the heavier drops may, indeed, fly off, and fall, in
a shower, round the spout; but much of it will be broken
into vapor, yet visible; and thus, in both cases, by dust at
land, and by water at sea, the whole tube may be darkened
and rendered visible.

As the whirl weakens, the tube may (in appearance) separate in the middle; the column of water subsiding, and
the superior condensed part drawing up to the cloud.   Yet
still the tube, or whirl of air, may remain entire, the middle only becoming invisible, as not containing visible matter.

Dr. Stuart says, " It was observable of all the spouts he
saw, but more perceptible of the great one; that, towards
the end, it began to appear like a hollow canal, only black
in the borders, but white in the middle; and though at first
it was altogether black and opaque, yet, now, one could
very distinctly perceive the sea water to fly up along the
middle of this canal, as smoke up a chimney."

And Dr. Mather, describing a whirlwind, says, " a thick
dark small cloud arose, with a pillar of light in it, of about
eight or ten feet diameter, and passed along the ground
in a tract not wider than a street, horribly tearing up trees
by the roots, blowing them up in the air like feathers, and
throwing up stones of great weight to a considerable height
in the air, &c."

These accounts, the one of water-spouts, the other of a
whirlwind, seem, in this particular, to agree; what one gentleman describes as a tube, black in the borders, and white
in the middle, the other calls a black cloud, with a pillar of
light in it; the latter expression has only a little more of
the *marvellous*, but the thing is the same; and it seems not
very difficult to understand.   When Dr. Stuart's spouts
were full charged, that is, when the whirling pipe of air
was filled between *a a a a* and *b b b b*, Fig. I. with quantities of drops, and vapor torn off from the column W W

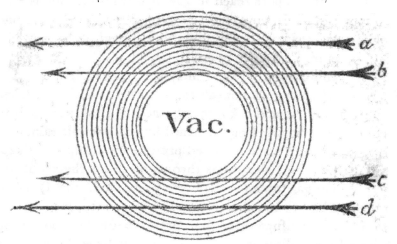

Fig. II, the whole was rendered so dark, as that it could not be seen through, nor the spiral ascending motion disco- vered; but when the quantity ascending lessened, the pipe became more transparent, and the ascending motion visible. For by inspection of the figure given in this page, repre- senting a section of our spout, with the vacuum in the mid- dle, it is plain that if we look at such a hollow pipe in the direction of the arrows, and suppose opaque particles to be equally mixed in the space between the two circular lines, both the part between the arrows *a* and *b*, and that between the arrows *c* and *d*, will appear much darker than that be- tween *b* and *c*, as there must be many more of those opaque particles in the line of vision across the sides, than across the middle. It is thus that a hair in a microscope evidently appears to be a pipe, the sides shewing darker than the middle. Dr. Mather's whirl was probably filled with dust, the sides were very dark, but the vacuum within rendering the middle more transparent, he calls it a pillar of light.

It was in this more transparent part, between *b* and *c*, that Stuart could see the spiral motion of the vapors, whose lines on the nearest and farthest side of the transparent part crossing each other, represented smoke ascending in a chim- ney; for the quantity being still too great in the line of sight through the sides of the tube, the motion could not be dis- covered there, and so they represented the solid sides of the chimney.

When the vapors reach in the pipe from the clouds near to the earth, it is no wonder now to those who understand electricity, that flashes of lightning should descend by the spout, as in that of Rome.

But you object, if water may be thus carried into the clouds, why have we not salt rains? The objection is strong and reasonable, and I know not whether I can answer it to your satisfaction. I never heard but of one salt rain, and that was where a spout passed pretty near a ship, so I suppose it to be only the drops thrown off from the spout, by the centrifugal force (as the birds were at Hatfield) when they had been carried so high as to be above, or to be too strongly centrifugal, for the pressure of the concurring winds surrounding it: and, indeed, I believe there can be no other kind of salt rain; for it has pleased the goodness of God so to order it, that the particles of air will not attract the particles of salt, though they strongly attract water.

Hence, though all metals, even gold, may be united with air, and rendered volatile, salt remains fixt in the fire, and no heat can force it up to any considerable height, or oblige the air to hold it. Hence, when salt rises, as it will a little way, into air with water, there is instantly a separation made; the particles of water adhere to the air, and the particles of salt fall down again, as if repelled and forced off from the water by some power in the air; or, as some metals, dissolved in a proper *menstruum*, will quit the solvent when other matter approaches, and adhere to that, so the water quits the salt, and embraces the air; but air will not embrace the salt, and quit the water, otherwise our rains would indeed be salt, and every tree and plant on the face of the earth be destroyed, with all the animals that depend on them for subsistence.....He who hath proportioned and given proper qualities to all things, was not unmindful of this. Let us adore HIM with praise and thanksgiving.

By some accounts of seamen, it seems the column of water W W, sometimes falls suddenly; and if it be, as some say, fifteen or twenty yards diameter, it must fall with great force, and they may well fear for their ships. By one account, in the *Transactions*, of a spout that fell at Colne, in Lancashire, one would think the column is sometimes lifted off from the water, and carried over land, and there let fall in a body; but this, I suppose, happens rarely.

Stuart describes his spouts as appearing no bigger than a mast, and sometimes less; but they were seen at a league and a half distance.

I think I formerly read in Dampier, or some other voyager, that a spout, in its progressive motion, went over a ship becalmed, on the coast of Guinea, and first threw her down on one side, carrying away her foremast, then suddenly whipped her up, and threw her down on the other side, carrying away her mizen-mast, and the whole was over in an instant. I suppose the first mischief was done by the fore-side of the whirl, the latter by the hinder-side, their motion being contrary.

I suppose a whirlwind, or spout, may be stationary, when the concurring winds are equal; but if unequal, the whirl acquires a progressive motion, in the direction of the strongest pressure.

When the wind that gives the progressive motion becomes stronger below than above, or above than below, the spout will be bent, and, the cause ceasing, straiten again.

Your queries, towards the end of your paper, appear judicious, and worth considering. At present I am not furnished with facts sufficient to make any pertinent answer to them; and this paper has already a sufficient quantity of conjecture,

Your manner of accommodating the accounts to your hypothesis of descending spouts, is, I own, ingenious, and perhaps that hypothesis may be true. I will consider it farther, but, as yet, I am not satisfied with it, though hereafter I may be.

Here you have my method of accounting for the principal phenomena, which I submit to your candid examination.

And as I now seem to have almost written a book, instead of a letter, you will think it high time I should conclude; which I beg leave to do, with assuring you, that

I am, Sir, &c.

B. FRANKLIN.

DR. MERCER, TO DR. FRANKLIN, AT PHILADELPHIA.

Description of a Water-Spout at Antigua.

Read at the Royal Society, June 24, 1756.

New-Brunswick, November 11, 1752.

SIR,

I AM favored with your letter of the 2d instant, and shall, with pleasure, comply with your request, in describing (as well as my memory serves me) the water-spout I saw at Antigua; and shall think this, or any other service I can do, well repaid, if it contributes to your satisfaction in so curious a disquisition.

I had often seen water-spouts at a distance, and heard many strange stories of them, but never knew any thing satisfactory of their nature or cause, until that which I saw at Antigua; which convinced me that a water-spout is a whirlwind, which becomes visible in all its dimensions by the water it carries up with it.

There appeared, not far from the mouth of the harbor of St. John's, two or three water-spouts, one of which took its course up the harbor. Its progressive motion was slow and unequal, not in a strait line, but, as it were, by jerks or starts. When just by the wharf, I stood about one hundred yards from it. There appeared in the water a circle of about twenty yards diameter, which, to me, had a dreadful, though pleasing appearance. The water in this circle was violently agitated, being whisked about, and carried up into the air with great rapidity and noise, and reflected a lustre, as if the sun shined bright on that spot, which was more conspicuous, as there appeared a dark circle around it. When it made the shore, it carried up with the same violence shingles, staves', large pieces of the roofs of houses, &c. and one small wooden house it lifted entire from the foundation on which it stood, and carried it to the distance of fourteen feet, where it settled without breaking or oversetting; and, what is remarkable, though the whirlwind moved from west to east, the house moved from east to west. Two or three negroes and a white woman, were killed by the fall of timber, which it carried up into the air and dropped again. After passing through the town, I believe it was soon dissipated; for, except tearing a large limb from a tree, and part of the cover of a sugar-work near the town, I do not remember any farther damage done by it. I conclude, wishing you success in your enquiry,

And am, &c.

W. MERCER.

DR. PERKINS, OF BOSTON, TO DR. FRANKLIN, AT PHILA-DELPHIA.

Shooting Stars.

Read at the Royal Society, July 8, 1756.

Boston, May 14, 1753.

Sir,

I RECEIVED your letter of April last, and thank you for it. Several things in it make me at a loss which side the truth lies on, and determine me to wait for farther evidence.

As to shooting-stars, as they are called, I know very little, and hardly know what to say. I imagine them to be passes of electric fire from place to place in the atmosphere, perhaps occasioned by accidental pressures of a non-electric circumambient fluid, and so by propulsion, or elicited by the circumstance of a distant quantity *minus* electrified, which it shoots to supply, and becomes apparent by its

---

1 I suppose shingles, staves, timber, and other lumber, might be lying in quantities on the wharf, for sale, as brought from the northern colonies. B. F.

contracted passage through a non-electric medium. Electric
fire in our globe is always in action, sometimes ascending,
descending, or passing from region to region. I suppose
it avoids too dry air, and therefore we never see these
shoots ascend. It always has freedom enough to pass down
unobserved, but, I imagine, not always so, to pass to distant climes and meridians less stored with it.

The shoots are sometimes all one way, which, in the last
case, they should be.

Possibly there may be collections of particles in our atmosphere, which gradually form, by attraction, either similar ones *per se*, or dissimilar particles, by the intervention
of others. But then, whether they shoot or explode of
themselves, or by the approach of some suitable foreign
collection, accidentally brought near by the usual commotions and interchanges of our atmosphere, especially when
the higher and lower regions intermix, before change of
winds and weather, I leave.

I believe I have now said enough of what I know nothing
about. If it should serve for your amusement, or any
way oblige you, it is all I aim at, and shall, at your desire,
be always ready to say what I think, as I am sure of your
candor.

I am, &c.

DR. PERKINS TO DR. FRANKLIN.

Water-Spouts and Whirlwinds.

Read at the Royal Society, July 8, 1756.

SPOUTS have been generally believed ascents of water
from below, to the region of the clouds, and whirlwinds
the means of conveyance. The world has been very well
satisfied with these opinions, and prejudiced with respect
to any observations about them. Men of learning and capacity have had many opportunities in passing those regions
where these phenomena were most frequent, but seem in-
dustriously to have declined any notice of them, unless to

escape danger, as a matter of mere impertinence in a case so clear and certain as their nature and manner of operation are taken to be. Hence it has been very difficult to get any tolerable accounts of them. None but those they fell near can inform us any thing to be depended on; three or four such instances follow, where the vessels were so near, that their crews could not avoid knowing something remarkable with respect to the matters in question.

Captain John Wakefield, junior, passing the Straits of Gibraltar, had one fall by the side of his ship; it came down of a sudden, as they think, and all agree the descent was certain.

Captain Langstaff, on a voyage to the West Indies, had one come across the stern of his vessel, and passed away from him. The water came down in such quantity that the present capt. Melling, who was then a common sailor at the helm, says it almost drowned him, running into his mouth, nose, ears, &c. and adds, that it tasted perfectly fresh.

One passed by the side of Captain Howland's ship, so near that it appeared pretty plain that the water descended from first to last.

Mr. Robert Spring was so near one in the Straits of Malacca, that he could perceive it to be a small very thick rain.

All these assure me, that there was no wind drawing towards them, nor have I found any others that have observed such a wind.

It seems plain, by these few instances, that whirlwinds do not always attend spouts; and that the water really descends in some of them. But the following consideration, in confirmation of this opinion, may, perhaps, render it probable that all the spouts are descents.

It seems unlikely that there should be two sorts of spouts, one ascending and the other descending.

It has not yet been proved that any one spout ever ascended. A specious appearance is all that can be produced in favor of this; and those who have been most positive about it, were at more than a league's distance when they observed, as Stuart and others, if I am not mistaken. However, I believe it impossible to be certain whether water ascends or descends at half the distance.

It may not be amiss to consider the places where they happen most. These are such as are liable to calms from departing winds on both sides, as on the borders of the equinoctial trade winds, calms on the coast of Guinea, in the Straits of Malacca, &c. places where the under region of the atmosphere is drawn off horizontally. I think they do not come where the calms are without departing winds; and I take the reason to be, that such places and places where winds blow towards one another, are liable to whirlwinds, or other ascents of the lower region, which I suppose contrary to spouts. But the former are liable to descents, which I take to be necessary to their production. Agreeable to this, it seems reasonable to believe, that any Mediterranean sea should be more subject to spouts than others. The sea usually so called is so. The Straits of Malacca is. Some large gulphs may probably be so, in suitable latitudes; so the Red Sea, &c. and all for this reason, that the heated lands on each side draw off the under region of the air, and make the upper descend, whence sudden and wonderful condensations may take place, and make these descents.

It seems to me, that the manner of their appearance and procedure, favor the notion of a descent.

More or less of a cloud, as I am informed, always appears over the place first; then a spattering on the surface of the water below; and when this is advanced to a considerable degree, the spout emerges from the cloud, and descends, and that, if the causes are sufficient, down to the places of spattering, with a roaring in proportion to the quantity of the discharge; then it abates, or stops, sometimes more gradually, sometimes more suddenly.

I must observe a few things on these particulars, to shew how I think they agree with my hypothesis.

The preceding cloud over the place shews condensation, and, consequently, tendency downwards, which therefore must naturally prevent any ascent. Besides that, so far as

I can learn, a whirlwind never comes under a cloud, but in a clear sky.

The spattering may be easily conceived to be caused by a stream of drops, falling with great force on the place, imagining the spout to begin so, when a sudden and great condensation happens in a contracted space, as the Ox-Eye on the coast of Guinea.

The spout appearing to descend from the cloud seems to be, by the stream of nearly contiguous drops bringing the air into consent, so as to carry down a quantity of the vapor of the cloud; and the pointed appearance it makes may be from the descending course being swiftest in the middle, or centre of the spout: this naturally drawing the outer parts inward, and the centre to a point; and that will appear foremost that moves swiftest. The phenomenon of retiring and advancing, I think may be accounted for, by supposing the progressive motion to exceed or not equal the consumption of the vapor by condensation. Or more plainly thus: the descending vapor which forms the apparent spout, if it be slow in its progress downwards, is condensed as fast as it advances, and so appears at a stand; when it is condensed faster than it advances, it appears to retire; and *vice versa.*

Its duration, and manner of ending, are as the causes, and may vary by several accidents.

The cloud itself may be so circumstanced as to stop it; as when, extending wide, it weighs down at a distance round about, while a small circle at the spout being exonerated by the discharge ascends and shuts up the passage. A new determination of wind may, perhaps, stop it too. Places liable to these appearances are very liable to frequent and sudden alterations of it.

Such accidents as a clap of thunder, firing cannon, &c. may stop them, and the reason may be, that any shock of this kind may occasion the particles that are near cohering, immediately to do so; and then the whole, thus condensed falls at once (which is what I suppose is vulgarly called the breaking of the spout) and in the interval, between this period and that of the next set of particles being ready to unite, the spout shuts up. So that if this reasoning is just, these phenomena agree with my hypothesis.

The usual temper of the air, at the time of their appearance, if I have a right information, is for me too; it being then pretty cool for the season and climate; and this is worth remark, because cool air is weighty, and will not ascend; besides, when the air grows cool, it shews that the upper region descends, and conveys this temper down; and when the tempers are equal, no whirlwind can take place. But spouts have been known, when the lower region has been really cold. Gordon's spout in the downs is an instance of this—(*vide Philosophical Transactions*)—where the upper region was probably not at all cooler, if so cold as the lower: it was a cold day in the month of March, hail followed, but not snow, and it is observable, that not so much as hail follows or accompanies them in moderate seasons or climes, when and where they are most frequent. However, it is not improbable, that just about the place of descent may be cooler than the neighboring parts, and so favor the wonderful celerity of condensation. But, after all, should we allow the under region to be ever so much the hottest, and a whirlwind to take place in it: suppose then the sea-water to ascend, it would certainly cool the spout, and then, query, whether it would not very much, if not wholly, obstruct its progress.

It commonly rains when spouts disappear, if it did not before, which it frequently does not, by the best accounts I have had; but the cloud encreases much faster after they disappear, and it soon rains. The first shews the spout to be a contracted rain, instead of the diffused one that follows; and the latter that the cloud was not formed by ascending water, for then it would have ceased growing when the spout vanished.

However it seems that spouts have sometimes appeared after it began to rain; but this is one way a proof of my hypothesis, viz. as whirlwinds do not come under a cloud.

I forgot to mention, that the increase of cloud, while the spout subsists, is no argument of an ascent of water, by the spout. Since thunder-clouds sometimes encrease greatly while it rains very hard.

Divers effects of spouts seem not so well accounted for any other way as by descent.

The bush round the feet of them seems to be a great spray of water made by the violence of descent, like that in great falls of water from high precipices.

The great roar, like some vast inland falls, is so different from the roar of whirlwinds, by all accounts, as to be no ways compatible.

The throwing things from it with great force, instead of carrying them up into the air, is another difference.

There seems some probability that the sailors traditionary belief, that spouts may break in their decks, and so destroy vessels, might originate from some facts of that sort in former times. This danger is apparent on my hypothesis, but it seems not so on the other: and my reason for it is, that the whole column of a spout from the sea to the clouds cannot, in a natural way, even upon the largest supposition, support more than about three feet water, and from truly supposable causes, not above one foot, as may appear more plainly by and bye. Supposing now the largest of these quantities to rise, it must be disseminated into drops, from the surface of the sea to the region of the clouds, or higher; for this reason it is quite unlikely to be collected into masses, or a body, upon its falling; but would descend in progression according to the several degrees of altitude the different portions had arrived at when it received this new determination.

Now that there cannot more rise upon the common hypothesis than I have mentioned, may appear probable, if we attend to the only efficient cause in supposed ascending spouts, viz. whirlwinds.

We know that the rarefaction of the lower, and the condensation of the upper region of air, are the only natural causes of whirlwinds. Let us then suppose the former as hot as their greatest summer heat in England, and the latter as cold as the extent of their winter.   These extremes have been found there to alter the weight of the air one-tenth, which is equal to a little more than three feet water.   Were this case possible, and a whirlwind take place in it, it might act with a force equal to the mentioned difference.   But as this is the whole strength, so much water could not rise ; therefore to allow it due motion upwards, we must abate, at least, one-fourth part, perhaps more, to give it such a swift ascension as some think usual.   But here several difficulties occur, at least they are so to me.   As, whether this quantity would render the spout opaque ? since it is plain that in drops it could not do so.   How, or by what means it may be reduced small enough ? or, if the water be not reduced into vapor, what will suspend it in the region of the clouds when exonerated there ? And, if vaporized while ascending, how can it be dangerous by what they call the breaking? For it is difficult to conceive how a condensative power should instantaneously take place of a rarefying and disseminating one.

The sudden fall of the spout, or rather, the sudden ceasing of it, I accounted for, in my way, before.   But it seems necessary to mention something I then forgot.   Should it be said to do so (i. e.) to fall, because all the lower rarefied air is ascended, whence the whirlwind must cease, and its burden drop ; I cannot agree to this, unless the air be observed on a sudden to have grown much colder, which I cannot learn has been the case.   Or should it be supposed that the spout was, on a sudden, obstructed at the top, and this the cause of the fall, however plausible this might appear, yet no more water would fall than what was at the same time contained in the column, which is often, by many and satisfactory accounts to me, again far from being the case.

We are, I think, sufficiently assured, that not only tons, but scores or hundreds of tons descend in one spout. Scores of tons more than can be contained in the trunk of it, should we suppose water to ascend.

But, after all, it does not appear that the above-mentioned different degrees of heat and cold concur in any region where spouts usually happen, nor, indeed, in any other.

Observations on the Meteorological Paper; by a Gentleman in Connecticut.

Read at the Royal Society, Nov. 4, 1756.

" AIR and water mutually attract each other, (saith Mr. F.) hence water will dissolve in air, as salt in water." I think that he hath demonstrated, that the supporting of salt in water is not owing to its superfices being increased, because " the specific gravity of salt is not altered by dividing of it, any more than that of lead, sixteen bullets of which, of an ounce each, weigh as much in water as one of a pound." But yet, when this came to be applied to the supporting of water in air, I found an objection rising in my mind.

In the first place, I have always been loth to seek for any new hypothesis, or particular law of nature, to account for any thing that may be accounted for from the known general, and universal law of nature; it being an argument of the infinite wisdom of the author of the world, to effect so many things by one general law. Now I had thought that the rising and support of water in air, might be accounted for from the general law of gravitation, by only supposing the spaces occupied by the same quantity of water increased.

And, with respect to the lead, I queried thus in my own mind: whether if the superfices of a bullet of lead should be increased four or five fold by an internal vacuity, it would weigh the same in water as before. I mean, if a pound of lead should be formed into a hollow globe, empty within, whose superfices should be four or five times as big as that of the same lead when a solid lump, it would weigh as much in water as before. I supposed it would not. If this concavity was filled with water, perhaps it might; if with air, it would weigh at least as much less, as this difference between the weight of that included air, and that of water.

Now although this would do nothing to account for the dissolution of salt in water, the smallest lumps of salt being no more hollow spheres, or any thing of the like nature, than the greatest; yet, perhaps, it might account for water's rising and being supported in air. For you know that such hollow globules, or bubbles, abound upon the surface of the water, which even by the breath of our mouths, we can cause to quit the water, and rise in the air.

These bubbles I used to suppose to be the coats of water, containing within them air rarefied and expanded with fire, and that, therefore, the more friction and dashing there is upon the surface of the waters, and the more heat and fire, the more they abound.

And I used to think, that although water be specifically heavier than air, yet such a bubble, filled only with fire and very rarefied air, may be lighter than a quantity of common air, of the same cubical dimensions, and, therefore, ascend; for the rarefied air inclosed, may more fall short of the same bulk of common air, in weight, than the watery coat exceeds a like bulk of common air in gravity.

This was the objection in my mind, though, I must confess, I know not how to account for the watery coat's encompassing the air, as above-mentioned, without allowing the attraction between air and water, which the gentleman supposes; so that I do not know but that this objection, examined by that sagacious genius, will be an additional confirmation of the hypothesis.

The gentleman observes, " that a certain quantity of moisture should be every moment discharged and taken away from the lungs; and hence accounts for the suffocating nature of snuffs of candles, as impregnating the air with grease, between which and water there is a natural repellency; and of air that hath been frequently breathed in, which is overloaded with water, and, for that reason, can take no more air. Perhaps the same observation will account for the suffocating nature of damps in wells.

But then if the air can support and take off but such a proportion of water, and it is necessary that water be so taken off from the lungs, I queried with myself how it is we can breathe in an air full of vapors, so full as that they continually precipitated. Do not we see the air overloaded, and casting forth water plentifully, when there is no suffocation?

The gentleman again observes, " That the air under the equator, and between the tropics, being constantly heated and rarefied by the sun, rises; its place is supplied by air from northern and southern latitudes, which, coming from parts where the air and earth had less motion, and not suddenly acquiring the quicker motion of the equatorial earth, appears an east wind blowing westward; the earth moving from west to east, and slipping under the air."

In reading this, two objections occurred to my mind:

First, that it is said, the trade-wind doth not blow in the forenoon, but only in the afternoon.

Secondly, that either the motion of the northern and southern air towards the equator is so slow, as to acquire almost the same motion as the equatorial air when it arrives there, so that there will be no sensible difference; or else the motion of the northern and southern air towards the equator, is quicker, and must be sensible; and then the trade-wind must appear either as a south-east or north-east wind: south of the equator, a south-east wind; north of the equator, a north-east. For the apparent wind must be compounded of this motion from north to south, or *vice versa;* and of the difference between its motion from west to east, and that of the equatorial air.

Observations in Answer to the foregoing, by B. Franklin.

Read at the Royal Society, Nov. 4, 1756.

1st. THE supposing a mutual attraction between the particles of water and air, is not introducing a new law of nature; such attractions taking place in many other known instances.

2dly. Water is specifically 850 times heavier than air. To render a bubble of water, then, specifically lighter than air, it seems to me that it must take up more than 850 times the space it did before it formed the bubble; and within the bubble should be either a vacuum or air rarefied more than 850 times. If a vacuum, would not the bubble be immediately crushed by the weight of the atmosphere? And no heat, we know of, will rarefy air any thing near so much; much less the common heat of the sun, or that of friction by the dashing on the surface of the water: besides, water agitated ever so violently produces no heat, as has been found by accurate experiments.

3dly. A hollow sphere of lead has a firmness and consistency in it, that a hollow sphere or bubble of fluid unfrozen water cannot be supposed to have. The lead may support the pressure of the water it is immerged in, but the bubble could not support the pressure of the air, if empty within.

4thly. Was ever a visible bubble seen to rise in air? I have made many, when a boy, with soap-suds and a tobacco-pipe; but they all descended when loose from the pipe, though slowly, the air impeding their motion: they may, indeed, be forced up by a wind from below, but do not rise of themselves, though filled with warm breath.

5thly. The objection relating to our breathing moist air seems weighty, and must be farther considered. The air that has been breathed has, doubtless, acquired an addition of the perspirable matter which nature intends to free the body from, and which would be pernicious if retained and returned into the blood: such air then may become unfit for respiration, as well for that reason, as on account of its moisture. Yet I should be glad to learn, by some accurate experiment, whether a draft of air, two or three times inspired, and expired, perhaps in a bladder, has, or has not, acquired more moisture than our common air in the dampest weather. As to the precipitation of water in the air we breathe, perhaps it is not always a mark of that air's being overloaded. In the region of the clouds, indeed, the air must be overloaded if it lets fall its water in drops, which we call rain; but those drops may fall through a drier air near the earth; and accordingly we find that the hygroscope sometimes shews a less degree of moisture, during a shower, than at other times when it does not rain at all. The dewy dampness, that settles on the insides of our walls and wainscots, seems more certainly to denote an air overloaded with moisture; and yet this is no sure sign: for, after a long continued cold season, if the air grows suddenly warm, the walls, &c. continuing longer their coldness, will, for some time, condense the moisture of such air, till they grow equally warm, and then they condense no more, though the air is not become drier. And, on the other hand, after a warm season, if the air grows cold, though moister than before, the dew is not so apt to gather on the walls. A tankard of cold water will, in a hot and dry summer's day, collect a dew on its outside; a tankard of hot water will collect none in the moistest weather.

6thly. It is, I think, a mistake that the trade-winds blow only in the afternoon. They blow all day and all night, and all the year round, except in some particular places. The southerly sea-breezes on your coasts, indeed, blow chiefly in the afternoon. In the very long run from the west side of America to Guam, among the Philippine Islands, ships seldom have occasion to hand their sails, so equal and steady is the gale, and yet they make it in about 60 days, which could not be if the wind blew only in the afternoon.

7thly. That really is, which the gentleman justly supposes ought to be, on my hypothesis. In sailing southward, when you first enter the trade-wind, you find it north-east, or thereabouts, and it gradually grows more east as you approach the line. The same observation is made of its changing from south-east to east gradually, as you come from the southern latitudes to the equator.

Observations on the Meteorological Paper; sent by Cadwallader Colden, of New York to B. Franklin.

Read at the Royal Society, Nov. 4, 1756.

THAT power by which the air expands itself, you attribute to a mutual repelling power in the particles which compose the air, by which they are separated from each other with some degree of force ; now this force, on this supposition, must not only act when the particles are in mutual contact, but likewise when they are at some distance from each other. How can two bodies, whether they be great or small, act at any distance, whether that distance be small or great, without something intermediate on which they act? For if any body act on another, at any distance from it, however small that distance be, without some medium to continue the action, it must act where it is not, which to me seems absurd.

It seems to me, for the same reason, equally absurd to give a mutual attractive power between any other particles supposed to be at a distance from each other, without any thing intermediate to continue their mutual action. I can neither attract nor repel any thing at a distance, without something between my hand and that thing, like a string, or a stick ; nor can I conceive any mutual action without some middle thing, when the action is continued to some distance.

The encrease of the surface of any body lessens its weight, both in air, and water, or any other fluid, as appears by the slow descent of leaf-gold in the air.

The observation of the different density of the upper and lower air, from heat and cold, is good, and I do not remember it is taken notice of by others ; the consequences also are well drawn ; but as to winds, they seem principally to arise from some other cause. Winds generally blow from some large tracts of land, and from mountains. Where I live, on the north side of the mountains, we frequently have a strong southerly wind, when they have as strong a northerly wind, or calm, on the other side of these mountains. The continual passing of vessels on Hudson's River, through these mountains, give frequent opportunities of observing this.

In the spring of the year the sea-wind (by a piercing cold) is always more uneasy to me, accustomed to winds which pass over a tract of land, than the north-west wind.

You have received the common notion of water-spouts, which, from my own occular observation, I am persuaded is a false conception. In a voyage to the West Indies, I had an opportunity of observing many water-spouts. One of them passed nearer than thirty or forty yards to the vessel I was in, which I viewed with a good deal of attention; and though it be now forty years since I saw it, it made so strong an impression on me, that I very distinctly remember it. These water-spouts were in the calm latitudes, that is, between the trade and the variable winds, in the month of July. That spout which passed so near us was an inverted cone, with the *tip* or *apex* towards the sea, and reached within about eight feet of the surface of the sea, its basis in a large black cloud. We were entirely becalmed. It passed slowly by the vessel. I could plainly observe, that a violent stream of wind issued from the spout, which made a hollow of about six feet diameter in the surface of the water, and raised the water in a circular uneven ring round the hollow, in the same manner that a strong blast from a pair of bellows would do when the pipe is placed perpendicular to the surface of the water; and we plainly heard the same hissing noise which such a blast of wind must produce on the water. I am very sure there was nothing like the sucking of water from the sea into the spout, unless the spray, which was raised in a ring to a small height, could be mistaken for a raising of water. I could plainly distinguish a distance of about eight feet between the sea and the tip of the cone, in which nothing interrupted the sight, which must have been, had the water been raised from the sea.

M m

In the same voyage I saw several other spouts at a greater distance, but none of them whose tip of the cone came so near the surface of the water. In some of them the axis of the cone was considerably inclined from the perpendicular, but in none of them was there the least appearance of sucking up of water. Others of them were bent or arched. I believe that a stream of wind issued from all of them, and it is from this stream of wind that vessels are often everset, or founder at sea suddenly. I have heard of vessels being overset when it was perfectly calm, the instant before the stream of wind struck them, and immediately after they were overset; which could not otherwise be but by such a stream of wind from a cloud.

That wind is generated in clouds will not admit of a dispute. Now if such wind be generated within the body of the cloud, and issue in one particular place, while it finds no passage in the other parts of the cloud, I think it may not be difficult to account for all the appearances in waterspouts: and from hence the reason of breaking those spouts, by firing a cannon-ball through them, as thereby a horizontal vent is given to the wind. When the wind is spent, which dilated the cloud, or the fermentation ceases, which generates the air and wind, the clouds may descend in a prodigious fall of water or rain. A remarkable intestine motion, like a violent fermentation, is very observable in the cloud from whence the spout issues. No salt-water, I am persuaded, was ever observed to fall from the clouds, which must certainly have happened if sea-water had been raised by a spout.

Answer to the foregoing Observations, by B. Franklin.

Read at the Royal Society, Nov. 4, 1756.

I AGREE with you, that it seems absurd to suppose that a body can act where it is not. I have no idea of bodies at a distance attracting or repelling one another without the assistance of some medium, though I know not

what that medium is, or how it operates. When I speak
of attraction or repulsion, I make use of those words for
want of others more proper, and intend only to express
effects which I see, and not *causes* of which I am ignorant.
When I press a blown bladder between my knees, and
find I cannot bring its sides together, but my knees feel a
springy matter, pushing them back to a greater distance, or
repelling them, I conclude that the air it contains is the
cause. And when I operate on the air, and find I cannot
by pressure force its particles into contact, but they still
spring back against the pressure, I conceive there must be
some medium between its particles that prevents their closing, though I cannot tell what it is. And if I were acquainted with that medium, and found its particles to
approach and recede from each other, according to the
pressure they suffered, I should imagine there must be
some finer medium between them, by which these operations were performed.

I allow that increase of the surface of a body may occasion it to descend slower in air, water, or any other fluid:
but do not conceive, therefore, that it lessens its weight.
Where the increased surface is so disposed as that in its falling a greater quantity of the fluid it sinks in must be moved
out of its way, a greater time is required for such removal.
Four square feet of sheet lead sinking in water *broadways*,
cannot descend near so fast as it would *edgeways*, yet its
weight in the hydrostatic balance would, I imagine, be the
same, whether suspended by the middle or by the corner.

I make no doubt but that ridges of high mountains do
often interrupt, stop, reverberate, or turn the winds that
blow against them, according to the different degrees of
strength of the winds, and angles of incidence. I suppose
too, that the cold upper parts of mountains may condense
the warmer air that comes near them, and so by making it
specifically heavier, cause it to descend on one or both sides
of the ridge into the warmer valleys. which will seem a
wind blowing from the mountains.

Damp winds, though not colder by the thermometer, give a more easy sensation of cold than dry ones, because (to speak like an electrician) they *conduct* better; that is, are better fitted to convey away the heat from our bodies. The body cannot feel *without* itself; our sensation of cold is not in the air *without* the body, but in those parts of the body which have been deprived of their heat by the air. My desk, and its lock, are, I suppose, of the same temperament when they have been long exposed to the same air; but now if I lay my hand on the wood, it does not seem as cold to me as the lock; because (as I imagine) wood is not so good a conductor, to receive and convey away the heat from my skin, and the adjacent flesh, as metal is. Take a piece of wood, of the size and shape of a dollar, between the thumb and finger of one hand, and a dollar, in like manner, with the other hand: place the edges of both, at the same time, in the flame of a candle: and though the edge of the wooden piece takes flame, and the metal piece does not, yet you will be obliged to drop the latter before the former, it conducting the heat more suddenly to your fingers. Thus we can, without pain, handle glass and china cups filled with hot liquors, as tea, &c. but not silver ones. A silver tea-pot must have a wooden handle. Perhaps it is for the same reason that woollen garments keeping the body warmer than linen ones equally thick; woollen keeping the natural heat in, or, in other words, not conducting it out to air.

In regard to water-spouts, having, in a long letter to a gentleman of the same sentiment with you as to their direction, said all that I have to say in support of my opinion; I need not repeat the arguments therein contained, as I intend to send you a copy of it by some other opportunity, for your perusal. I imagine you will find all the appearances you saw, accounted for by my hypothesis. I thank you for communicating the account of them. At present I would only say, that the opinion of winds being generated in clouds by fermentation, is new to me, and I am unacquainted with the facts on which it is founded. I likewise find it difficult to conceive of winds confined in the body of clouds, which I imagine have little more solidity than the fogs on the earth's surface. The objection from the freshness of rain-water is a strong one, but I think I have answered it in the letter above mentioned, to which I must beg leave, at present, to refer you.

Extracts from Dampier's Voyages.

Read at the Royal Society, December 16, 1756.

A SPOUT is a small ragged piece, or part of a cloud, hanging down about a yard seemingly, from the blackest part thereof. Commonly it hangs down sloping from thence, or sometimes appearing with a small bending, or elbow, in the middle. I never saw any hang perpendicularly down. It is small at the lower end, seeming no bigger than one's arm, but still fuller towards the cloud from whence it proceeds.

When the surface of the sea begins to work, you shall see the water for about one hundred paces in circumference foam and move gently round, till the whirling motion increases; and then it flies upwards in a pillar, about one hundred paces in compass at the bottom, but gradually lessening upwards, to the smallness of the spout itself, through which the rising sea-water seems to be conveyed into the clouds. This visibly appears by the clouds increasing in bulk and blackness. Then you shall presently see the cloud drive along, though before it seemed to be without any motion. The spout also keeping the same course with the cloud, and still sucking up the water as it goes along, and they make a wind as they go. Thus it continues for half an hour, more or less, until the sucking is spent, and then breaking off, all the water which was below the spout, or pendulous piece of cloud, falls down again into the sea, making a great noise with its falling and clashing motion in the sea.

It is very dangerous for a ship to be under a spout when it breaks; therefore we always endeavor to shun it, by keeping at a distance, if possibly we can. But for want of wind to carry us away, we are often in great fear and danger, for it is usually calm when spouts are at work, except only just where they are. Therefore men at sea, when they see a spout coming, and know not how to avoid it, do sometimes fire shot out of their great guns into it, to give it air or vent, that so it may break; but I did never hear that it proved to be of any benefit.

And now we are on this subject, I think it not amiss to give you an account of an accident that happened to a ship once on the coast of Guinea, some time in or about the year 1674. One capt. Records of London, bound for the coast of Guinea, in a ship of three hundred tons, and sixteen guns, called the Blessing, when he came into latitude seven or eight degrees north, he saw several spouts, one of which came directly towards the ship, and he having no wind to get out of the way of the spout, made ready to receive it by furling the sails. It came on very swift, and broke a little before it reached the ship, making a great noise, and raising the sea round it, as if a great house, or some such thing, had been cast into the sea. The fury of the wind still lasted, and took the ship on the starboard-bow with such violence, that it snapt off the boltsprit and foremast both at once, and blew the ship all along, ready to overset it; but the ship did presently right again, and the wind whirling round, took the ship a second time with the like fury as before, but on the contrary side, and was again like to overset her the other way: the mizen-mast felt the fury of this second blast, and was snapt short off, as the foremast and boltsprit had been before. The mainmast and main-top-mast received no damage, for the fury of the wind (which was presently over) did not reach them. Three men were in the foretop when the foremast broke, and one on the boltsprit, and fell with them into the sea, but all of them were saved. I had this relation from Mr. John Canby, who was then quarter-master and steward of her; one Abraham Wise was chief-mate, and Leonard Jefferies second-mate.

We are usually much afraid of them, yet this was the only damage that I ever heard done by them. They seem terrible enough, the rather because they come upon you while you lie becalmed, like a log in the sea, and cannot get out of their way. But though I have seen and been beset by them often, yet the fright was always the greatest of the harm."—*Dampier*, vol. I. page 451.

Account of a Spout on the Coast of New Guinea—from the same.

" WE had fair clear weather, and a fine moderate gale from south-east to east by north; but at day-break the clouds began to fly, and it lightened very much in the east north-east. At sun rising the sky looked very red in the east near the horizon; and there were many black clouds both to the south and north of it. About a quarter of an hour after the sun was up, there was a squall to the windward of us, when, on a sudden, one of our men on the forecastle, called out that he saw something astern, but could not tell what. I looked out for it, and immediately saw a spout beginning to work within a quarter of a mile of us, exactly in the wind: we presently put right before it. It came very swiftly, whirling the water up in a pillar, about six or seven yards high. As yet I could not see any pendulous cloud from whence it might come; and was in hopes it would soon lose its force. In four or five minutes time it came within a cable's length of us, and passed away to leeward; and then I saw a long pale stream coming down to the whirling water. This stream was about the bigness of a rainbow. The upper end seemed vastly high, not descending from any dark cloud, and, therefore, the more strange to me, I never having seen the like before. It past about a mile to the leeward of us, and then broke. This was but a small spout, and not strong nor[2] lasting; yet

---

2 Probably if it had been lasting, a cloud would have been formed above it. These extracts from Dampier, seem, in different instances, to favor both opinions, and, therefore, are inserted entire, for the reader's consideration.

I perceived much wind in it as it passed by." Vol. III. page 223.

Account of another Spout—from the same.

" WE saw a spout but a small distance from us; it fell down out of a black cloud that yielded great store of rain, thunder, and lightning. This cloud hovered to the south-ward of us for the space of three hours, and then drew to the westward a great pace, at which time it was that we saw the spout, which hung fast to the cloud till it broke, and then the cloud whirled about to the south-east, then to the north-east, where meeting with an island, it spent itself, and so dispersed; and immediately we had a little of the tail of it, having had none before." Vol. III. page 182.

C. COLDEN OF NEW YORK, TO DR. FRANKLIN.

Read at the Royal Society, December 6, 1756.

April 2, 1754.

ANY knowlege I have of the winds, and other changes which happen in the atmosphere, is so very defective, that it does not deserve the name; neither have I received any satisfaction from the attempts of others on this subject. It deserves then your thoughts, as a subject in which you may distinguish yourself, and be useful.

Your notion of some things conducting heat or cold better than others pleases me, and I wish you may pursue the scent. If I remember right, Dr. Boerhaave, in his chemistry, thinks that heat is propagated by the vibration of a subtle elastic fluid, dispersed through the atmosphere and through all bodies. Sir Isaac Newton says, there are many phenomena to prove the existence of such a fluid; and this opinion has my assent to it. I shall only observe that it is essentially different from that which I call ether; for ether, properly speaking, is neither a fluid nor elastic;

its power consists in re-acting any action communicated to it, with the same force it receives the action.

I long to see your explication of water-spouts, but I must tell you before hand, that it will not be easy for you to convince me that the principal phenomena were not occasioned by a stream of wind issuing with great force, my eyes and ears both concurring to give me this sentiment, I could have no more evidence than to feel the effects, which I had no inclination to do.

It surprises me a little, that wind, generated by fermentation is new to you, since it may be every day observed in fermenting liquor. You know with what force fermenting liquors will burst the vessels which contain them, if the generated wind have not vent; and with what force it issues on giving it a small vent, or by drawing the cork of a bottle. Dr. Boerhaave says, that the steam issuing from fermenting liquors received through a very small vent-hole, into the nose, will kill as suddenly and certainly as lightning. That air is generated by fermentation, I think you will find fully proved in Dr. Hales's Analysis of the Air, in his Vegetable Statics. If you have not read the book, you have a new pleasure to come.

The solution you give to the objection I made from the contrary winds blowing from the opposite sides of the mountains, from their being eddies, does not please me, because the extent of these winds is by far too large to be occasioned by any eddy. It is forty miles from New York to our mountains, through which Hudson's River passes. The river runs twelve miles in the mountains, and from the north side of the mountains it is about ninety miles to Albany. I have myself been on board a vessel more than once, when we have had a strong northerly wind against us, all the way from New-York, for two or three days. We have met vessels from Albany, who assured us, that, on the other side of the mountains, they had, at the same time, a strong continued southerly wind against them; and this frequently happens.

N n

I have frequently seen, both on the river, in places where there could be no eddy-winds, and on the open sea, two vessels sailing with contrary winds, within half a mile of each other; but this happens only in easy winds, and generally calm in other places near these winds.

You have, no doubt, frequently observed a single cloud pass, from which a violent gust of wind issues, but of no great extent. I have observed such a gust make a lane through the woods, of some miles in length, by laying the trees flat to the ground, and not above eight or ten chains in breadth. Though the violence of the wind be in the same direction in which the cloud moves and precedes it, yet wind issues from all sides of it; so that supposing the cloud moves south-easterly, those on the north-east side of it feel a south-west wind, and others on the south-west side, a north-east. And where the cloud passes over, we frequently have a south-east wind from the hinder part of it, but none violent, except the wind in the direction in which the cloud moves. To shew what it is which prevents the wind from issuing out equally on all sides, is not an easy problem to me, and I shall not attempt to solve it; but when you shall show what it is which restrains the electrical fluid from spreading itself into the air surrounding it, when it rushes with great violence through the air along, or in the conductor, for a great extent in length, then I may hope to explain the other problem, and remove the difficulty we have in conceiving it.

TO PETER COLLINSON, LONDON.

Account of a Whirlwind in Maryland.

Philadelphia, Aug. 25, 1755.

DEAR SIR,

AS you have my former papers on whirlwinds, &c. I now send you an account of one which I had lately an opportunity of seeing and examining myself.

Being in Maryland, riding with colonel Tasker, and some other gentlemen, to his country seat, where I and my son were entertained by that amiable and worthy man with great hospitality and kindness, we saw, in the vale below us, a small whirlwind beginning in the road, and showing itself by the dust it raised and contained. It appeared in the form of a sugar-loaf, spinning on its point, moving up the hill towards us, and enlarging as it came forward. When it passed by us, its smaller part near the ground appeared no bigger than a common barrel, widening upwards, it seemed, at forty or fifty feet high, to be twenty or thirty feet in diameter. The rest of the company stood looking after it, but my curiosity being stronger, I followed it, riding close by its side, and observed its licking up, in its progress, all the dust that was under its smaller part. As it is a common opinion that a shot, fired through a water-spout, will break it, I tried to break this little whirlwind, by striking my whip frequently through it, but without any effect. Soon after, it quitted the road and took into the woods, growing every moment larger and stronger, raising, instead of dust, the old dry leaves with which the ground was thick covered, and making a great noise with them and the branches of the trees, bending some tall trees round in a circle swiftly and very surprisingly, though the progressive motion of the whirl was not so swift but that a man on foot might have kept pace with it, but the circular motion was amazingly rapid. By the leaves it was now filled with, I could plainly perceive that the current of air they were driven by moved upwards in a spiral line; and when I saw the passing whirl continue entire, after leaving the trunks and bodies of large trees which it had enveloped, I no longer wondered that my whip had no effect on it in its smaller state. I accompanied it about three quarters of a mile, till some limbs of dead trees, broken off by the whirl, flying about, and falling near me, made me more apprehensive of danger: and then I stopped, looking at the top of it as it went on, which was visible, by means of the leaves contained in it, for a very great height above the trees. Many of the leaves, as they got loose from the upper and widest part, were scattered in the wind; but so great was their height in the air, that they appeared no bigger than flies. My son, who was, by this time, come up with me, followed the whirlwind till it left the woods, and crossed an old tobacco-field, where, finding neither dust nor leaves to take up, it gradually became invisible below, as it went away over that field. The course of the general wind then blowing was along with us as we travelled, and the progressive motion of the whirlwind was in a direction nearly opposite, though it did not keep a strait line, nor was its progressive motion uniform, it making little sallies on either hand as it went, proceeding sometimes faster, and sometimes slower, and seeming sometimes for a few seconds almost stationary, then starting forwards pretty fast again. When we rejoined the company, they were admiring the vast height of the leaves now brought by the common wind, over our heads. These leaves accompanied us as we travelled, some falling now and then round about us, and some not reaching the ground till we had gone near three miles from the place where we first saw the whirlwind begin. Upon my asking colonel Tasker if such whirlwinds were common in Maryland, he answered pleasantly, No, not at all common, but we got this on purpose to treat Mr. Franklin. ....And a very high treat it was to,

Dear Sir,

Your affectionate friend and humble servant,

B. FRANKLIN.

TO ALEXANDER SMALL, LONDON.

On the North-East Storms in North America.

May 12, 1760.

DEAR SIR,

AGREEABLE to your request, I send you my reasons for thinking that our north-east storms in North America begin first, in point of time, in the south-west parts: that is to say, the air in Georgia, the farthest of our colonies to the south-west, begins to move south-westerly before the air of Carolina, which is the next colony north-eastward; the air of Carolina, has the same motion before the air of Virginia, which lies still more north-eastward; and so on, north-easterly through Pennsylvania, New York, New England, &c. quite to Newfoundland.

These north-east storms are generally very violent, continue sometimes two or three days, and often do considerable damage in the harbors along the coast. They are attended with thick clouds and rain.

What first gave me this idea, was the following circumstance. About twenty years ago, a few more or less, I cannot from my memory be certain, we were to have an eclipse of the moon at Philadelphia, on a Friday evening, about nine o'clock. I intended to observe it, but was prevented by a north-east storm, which came on about seven, with thick clouds as usual, that quite obscured the whole hemisphere. Yet when the post brought us the Boston newspaper, giving an account of the effects of the same storm in those parts, I found the beginning of the eclipse had been well observed there, though Boston lies N. E. of Philadelphia about four hundred miles. This puzzled me, because the storm began with us so soon as to prevent any observation, and being a north-east storm, I imagined it must have begun rather sooner in places farther to the north-easward than it did at Philadelphia. I therefore mentioned it in a letter to my brother, who lived at Boston; and he informed me the storm did not begin with them till near eleven o'clock, so that they had a good observation of the eclipse: and upon comparing all the other accounts I received from the several colonies, of the time of beginning of the same storm, and since that of other storms of the same kind, I found the beginning to be always later the farther north-eastward. I have not my notes with me here in England, and cannot, from memory, say the proportion of time to distance, but I think it is about an hour to every hundred miles.

From thence I formed an idea of the cause of these storms, which I would explain by a familiar instance or two.— Suppose a long canal of water stopped at the end by a gate. The water is quite at rest till the gate is open, then it begins to move out through the gate ; the water next the gate is first in motion, and moves towards the gate ; the water next to that first water moves next, and so on successively, till the water at the head of the canal is in motion, which is last of all. In this case all the water moves indeed towards the gate, but the successive times of beginning motion are the contrary way, viz. from the gate backwards to the head of the canal. Again, suppose the air in a chamber at rest, no current through the room till you make a fire in the chimney. Immediately the air in the chimney being rarefied by the fire rises ; the air next the chimney flows in to supply its place, moving towards the chimney ; and, in consequence, the rest of the air successively, quite back to the door. Thus to produce our north-east storms, I suppose some great heat and rarefaction of the air in or about the Gulph of Mexico ; the air thence rising has its place supplied by the next more northern, cooler, and therefore denser and heavier, air ; that, being in motion, is followed by the next more northern air, &c. in a successive current, to which current our coast and inland ridge of mountains give the direction of north-east, as they lie N. E. and S. W.

This I offer only as an hypothesis to account for this particular fact ; and perhaps, on farther examination, a better and truer may be found. I do not suppose all storms generated in the same manner. Our north-west thunder-gusts in America, I know are not ; but of them I have written my opinion fully in a paper which you have seen.

I am, &c.

B. FRANKLIN.

TO DR. PERCIVAL, MANCHESTER, ENGLAND.

Meteorological Imaginations and Conjectures.[3]

THERE seems to be a region higher, in the air over all countries, where it is always winter, where frost exists continually, since in the midst of summer, on the surface of the earth, ice falls often from above in the form of hail.

Hailstones, of the great weight we sometimes find them, did not probably acquire their magnitude before they began to descend. The air, being eight hundred times rarer than water, is unable to support it but in the shape of vapor, a state in which its particles are separated. As soon as they are condensed by the cold of the upper region, so as to form a drop, that drop begins to fall. If it freezes into a grain of ice, that ice descends. In descending, both the drop of water and the grain of ice are augmented by particles of the vapor they pass through in falling, and which they condense by coldness, and attach to themselves.

It is possible that, in summer, much of what is rain, when it arrives at the surface of the earth, might have been snow when it began its descent; but being thawed, in passing through the warm air near the surface, it is changed from snow into rain.

How immensely cold must be the original particle of hail, which forms the centre of the future hailstone, since it is capable of communicating sufficient cold, if I may so speak, to freeze all the mass of vapor condensed round it, and form a lump of perhaps six or eight ounces in weight !

When, in summer time, the sun is high, and continues long every day above the horizon, his rays strike the earth more directly, and with longer continuance, than in the winter ; hence the surface is more heated, and to a greater depth, by the effect of those rays.

When rain falls on the heated earth, and soaks down into it, it carries down with it a great part of the heat, which by that means descends still deeper.

---

3 This paper was inserted in the Memoirs of the Literary and Philosophical Society of Manchester, Vol. II. page 378. It was communicated by Dr. Percival, and read December 22, 1784.

The mass of earth, to the depth of perhaps thirty feet, being thus heated to a certain degree, continues to retain its heat for some time. Thus the first snows that fall in the beginning of winter, seldom lie long on the surface, but are soon melted, and soon absorbed. After which, the winds that blow over the country on which the snows had fallen, are not rendered so cold as they would have been, by those snows, if they had remained, and thus the approach of the severity of winter is retarded ; and the extreme degree of its cold is not always at the time we might expect it, viz. when the sun is at its greatest distance, and the day shortest, but some time after that period, according to the English proverb, which says, " as the day lengthens, the cold strengthens ;" the causes of refrigeration continuing to operate, while the sun returns too slowly, and his force continues too weak to counteract them.

During several of the summer months of the year 1783, when the effects of the sun's rays to heat the earth in these northern regions should have been the greatest, there existed a constant fog over all Europe, and great part of North America. This fog was of a permanent nature: it was dry, and the rays of the sun seemed to have little effect towards dissipating it, as they easily do a moist fog, arising from water. They were indeed rendered so faint in passing through it, that when collected in the focus of a burning glass, they would scarce kindle brown paper. Of course, their summer effect in heating the earth was exceedingly diminished.

Hence the surface was early frozen.

Hence the first snows remained on it unmelted, and received continual additions.

Hence perhaps the winter of 1783-4, was more severe than any that had happened for many years.

The cause of this universal fog is not yet ascertained. Whether it was adventitious to this earth, and merely a smoke proceeding from the consumption by fire of some of those great burning balls or globes which we happen to meet with in our rapid course round the sun, and which are sometimes seen to kindle and be destroyed in passing our atmosphere, and whose smoke might be attracted and retained by our earth; or whether it was the vast quantity of smoke, long continuing to issue during the summer from Hecla, in Iceland, and that other volcano which arose out of the sea near that island, which smoke might be spread by various winds over the northern part of the world, is yet uncertain.

It seems however worth the enquiry, whether other hard winters, recorded in history, were preceded by similar permanent and widely extended summer fogs: Because, if found to be so, men might from such fogs conjecture the probability of a succeeding hard winter, and of the damage to be expected by the breaking up of frozen rivers in the spring; and take such measures as are possible and practicable, to secure themselves and effects from the mischiefs that attended the last.

Passy, May, 1784.

***

ON THE AURORA BOREALIS.

Read before the Royal Academy of Sciences of Paris, April, 1779.

Suppositions and Conjectures towards forming an Hypothesis, for the Explanation of the Aurora Borealis.

1. AIR heated by any means, becomes rarefied, and specifically lighter than other air in the same situation not heated.

2. Air being made thus lighter rises, and the neighboring cooler heavier air takes its place.

3. If in the middle of a room you heat the air by a stove, or pot of burning coals near the floor, the heated air will rise to the ceiling, and spread over the cooler air till it comes to the cold walls; there, being condensed and made heavier, it descends to supply the place of that cool air, which had moved towards the stove or fire, in order to supply the

O o

place of the heated air, which had ascended from the space around the stove or fire.

4. Thus there will be a continual circulation of air in the room ; which may be rendered visible by making a little smoke, for that smoke will rise and circulate with the air.

5. A similar operation is performed by nature on the air of this globe. Our atmosphere is of a certain height, perhaps at a medium [   ] miles : above that height it is so rare as to be almost a vacuum. The air heated between the tropics is continually rising ; its place is supplied by northerly and southerly winds, which come from the cooler regions.

6. The light heated air, floating above the cooler and denser, must spread northward and southward ; and descend near the two poles, to supply the place of the cool air, which had moved towards the equator.

7. Thus a circulation of air is kept up in our atmosphere, as in the room above-mentioned.

8. That heavier and lighter air may move in currents of different and even opposite direction, appears sometimes by the clouds that happen to be in those currents, as plainly as by the smoke in the experiment above-mentioned. Also in opening a *door* between two chambers, one of which has been warmed, by holding a candle near the top, near the bottom, and near the middle, you will find a strong current of warm air passing out of the warmed room above, and another of cool air entering below ; while in the middle there is little or no motion.

9. The great quantity of vapor rising between the tropics forms clouds, which contain much electricity.

Some of them fall in rain, before they come to the polar regions.

10. If the rain be received in an isolated vessel, the vessel will be electrified ; for every drop brings down some electricity with it.

11. The same is done by snow or hail.

12. The electricity so descending, in temperate climates, is received and imbibed by the earth.

13. If the clouds are not sufficiently discharged by this gradual operation, they sometimes discharge themselves suddenly by striking into the earth, where the earth is fit to receive their electricity.

14. The earth in temperate and warm climates is generally fit to receive it, being a good conductor.

15. A certain quantity of heat will make some bodies good conductors, that will not otherwise conduct.

16. Thus wax rendered fluid, and glass softened by heat, will both of them conduct.

17. And water, though naturally a good conductor, will not conduct well, when frozen into ice by a common degree of cold; not at all, where the cold is extreme.

18. Snow falling upon frozen ground has been found to retain its electricity; and to communicate it to an isolated body, when after falling, it has been driven about by the wind.

19. The humidity, contained in all the equatorial clouds that reach the polar regions, must there be condensed and fall in snow.

20. The great cake of ice that eternally covers those regions may be too hard frozen to permit the electricity, descending with that snow, to enter the earth.

21. It may therefore be *accumulated upon that ice.*

22. The atmosphere being heavier in the polar regions than in the equatorial, will there be lower; as well from that cause, as from the smaller effect of the centrifugal force: consequently the distance of the vacuum above the atmosphere will be less at the poles, than elsewhere; and probably much less than the distance (upon the surface of the globe) extending from the pole to those latitudes in which the earth is so thawed as to receive and imbibe electricity; (the frost continuing to lat. 80, which is ten degrees, or six hundred miles from the pole; while the height of the atmosphere there of such density as to obstruct the motion of the electric fluid, can scarce be esteemed above [   ] miles).

23. The *vacuum* above is a good conductor,

24. May not then the great quantity of electricity, brought into the polar regions by the clouds, which are condensed there, and fall in snow, which electricity would enter the earth, but cannot penetrate the ice; may it not, I say, *(as a bottle overcharged)* break through that low atmosphere, and run along in the vacuum over the air towards the equator; diverging as the degrees of longitude enlarge; strongly visible where densest, and becoming less visible as it more diverges; till it finds a passage to the earth in more temperate climates, or is mingled with their upper air?

25. If such an operation of nature were really performed, would it not give all the appearances of an aurora borealis?

26. And would not the auroras become more frequent *after the approach of winter:* not only because more visible in longer nights; but also because in summer the long presence of the sun may soften the surface of the great ice cake, and render it a conductor, by which the accumulation of electricity in the polar regions will be prevented?

27. The *atmosphere of the polar regions* being made more dense by the extreme cold, and all the moisture in that air being frozen; may not any great light arising therein, and passing through it, render its density in some degree visible, during the night time, to those who live in the rarer air of more southern latitudes; and would it not in that case, although in itself a complete and full circle, extending perhaps ten degrees from the pole, appear to spectators so placed (who could see only a part of it) *in the form of a segment;* its chord resting on the horizon, and its arch elevated more or less above it as seen from latitudes more or less distant, *darkish in color,* but yet *sufficiently transparent* to permit some stars to be seen through it.

28. The *rays* of electric matter issuing out of a body diverge by mutually repelling each other, unless there be some conducting body near, to receive them: and if that conducting body be at a greater distance, they will *first diverge,* and then *converge* in order to enter it. May not this account for some of the varieties of figure seen at times in the *motions* of the luminous matter of the auroras: since it is

possible, that in passing over the atmosphere, from the north in all directions or meridians, towards the equator, the rays of that matter may find, in many places, portions of cloudy region, or moist atmosphere under them, which (being in the natural or negative state) may be fit to receive them, and towards which they may therefore converge : and when one of those receiving bodies is more than saturated, they may *again* diverge from it, towards other surrounding masses of such humid atmosphere, and thus form the *crowns*, as they are called, and other figures mentioned in the histories of this meteor ?

29. If it be true that the clouds which go to the polar regions and carry thither the vapors of the equatorial and temperate regions, have their vapors condensed by the extreme cold of the polar regions, and fall in snow or hail ; the winds which come from those regions ought to be generally dry, unless they gain some humidity by sweeping the ocean in their way. And if I mistake not, the winds between the north-east and the north-west, are for the most part dry, when they have continued for some time.

[In the Philosophical Transactions for 1774, p. 122, is a letter from Mr. I. S. Winn, to Dr. Franklin, stating, that since he had first made the observation concerning the south or south-west winds succeeding an aurora, he had found it invariably obtaining in twenty-three instances ; and he adds in a note a fresh confirming instance. In reply, Dr. Franklin makes the following conjecture.]

THE *Auroræ Boreales*, though visible almost every night of clear weather in the more northern regions and very high in the atmosphere, can scarce be visible in England, but when the atmosphere is pretty clear of clouds for the whole space between us and those regions ; and therefore are seldom visible there. This extensive clearness may have been produced by a long continuance of northerly winds. When the winds have long continued in one quarter the return is often violent. Allowing the fact so repeatedly observed by Mr. Winn, perhaps this may account for the violence of the southerly winds, that soon follow the appearance of the aurora on our coasts.

TO DR. LINING, AT CHARLESTON, SOUTH CAROLINA.

On Cold produced by Evaporation.

New-York, April 14, 1757.

SIR,

IT is a long time since I had the pleasure of a line from you ; and, indeed, the troubles of our country, with the hurry of business I have been engaged in on that account, have made me so bad a correspondent, that I ought not to expect punctuality in others.

But being about to embark for England, I could not quit the continent without paying my respects to you, and, at the same time, taking leave to introduce to your acquaintance a gentleman of learning and merit, colonel Henry Bouquet, who does me the favor to present you this letter, and with whom I am sure you will be much pleased.

Professer Simpson, of Glasgow, lately communicated to me some curious experiments of a physician of his acquaintance, by which it appeared, that an extraordinary degree of cold, even to freezing, might be produced by evaporation. I have not had leisure to repeat and examine more than the first and easiest of them, *viz.*—Wet the ball of a thermometer by a feather dipt in spirit of wine, which has been kept in the same room, and has, of course, the same degree of heat or cold. The mercury sinks presently three or four degrees, and the quicker, if during the evaporation you blow on the ball with bellows ; a second wetting and blowing, when the mercury is down, carries it yet lower. I think I did not get it lower than five or six degrees from where it naturally stood, which was at that time sixty. But it is said, that a vessel of water being placed in another somewhat larger, containing spirit, in such a manner that the vessel of water is surrounded with the spirit, and both placed under the receiver of an air pump ; on exhausting the air, the spirit, evaporating, leaves such a degree of cold as to freeze the water, though the thermometer, in the open air, stands many degrees above the freezing point.

I know not how this phenomenon is to be accounted for, but it gives me occasion to mention some loose notions relating to heat and cold, which I have for some time entertained, but not yet reduced into any form. Allowing common fire, as well as electrical, to be a fluid capable of permeating other bodies, and seeking an equilibrium, I imagine some bodies are better fitted by nature to be conductors of that fluid than others ; and, that, generally, those which are the best conductors of the electric fluid, are also the best conductors of this ; and è contra.

Thus a body which is a good conductor of fire readily receives it into its substance, and conducts it through the whole to all the parts, as metals and water do ; and if two bodies, both good conductors, one heated, the other in its common state, are brought into contact with each other, the body which has most fire readily communicates of it to that which had least, and that which had least readily receives it, till an equilibrium is produced. Thus, if you take a dollar between your fingers with one hand, and a piece of wood, of the same dimensions, with the other, and bring both at the same time to the flame of a candle, you will find yourself obliged to drop the dollar before you drop the wood, because it conducts the heat of the candle sooner to your flesh. Thus, if a silver tea-pot had a handle of the same metal, it would conduct the heat from the water to the hand, and become too hot to be used ; we therefore give to a metal tea-pot a handle of wood, which is not so good a conductor as metal. But a china or stone tea-pot being in some degree of the nature of glass, which is not a good conductor of heat, may have a handle of the same stuff. Thus, also, a damp moist air shall make a man more sensible of cold, or chill him more, than a dry air that is colder, because a moist air is fitter to receive and conduct away the heat of his body. This fluid, entering bodies in great quantity, first expands them, by separating their parts, a little, afterwards, by farther separating their parts, it renders solids' fluid, and at length dissipates their parts in air. Take this fluid from melted lead, or from water, the parts cohere again, the first grows solid, the latter becomes ice: and this is sooner done by the means of good conductors. Thus, if you take, as I have done, a square bar of lead, four inches long, and one inch thick, together with three pieces of wood planed to the same dimensions, and lay them

 as in the margin, on a smooth board, fixt so as not to be easily separated or moved, and pour into the cavity they form, as much melted lead as will fill it, you will see the melted lead chill, and become firm, on the side next the leaden bar, some time before it chills on the other three sides in contact with the wooden bars, though before the lead was poured in, they might all be supposed to have the same degree of heat or coldness, as they had been exposed in the same room to the same air. You will likewise observe, that the leaden bar, as it has cooled the melted lead more than the wooden bars have done, so it is itself more heated by the melted lead. There is a certain quantity of this fluid called fire, in every living human body, which fluid, being in due proportion, keeps the parts of the flesh and blood at such a just distance from each other, as that the flesh and nerves are supple, and the blood fit for circulation. If part of this due proportion of fire be conducted away, by means of a contact with other bodies, as air, water, or metals, the parts of our skin and flesh that come into such contact first, draw more near together than is agreeable, and give that sensation which we call cold; and if too much be conveyed away, the body stiffens, the blood ceases to flow, and death ensues. On the other hand, if too much of this fluid be communicated to the flesh, the parts are separated too far, and pain ensues, as when they are separated by a pin or lancet. The sensation that the separation by fire occasions, we call heat or burning. My desk on which I now write, and the lock

of my desk, are both exposed to the same temperature of the air, and have therefore the same degree of heat or cold : yet if I lay my hand successively on the wood and on the metal, the latter feels much the coldest, not that it is really so, but being a better conductor, it more readily than the wood takes away and draws into itself the fire that was in my skin. Accordingly if I lay one hand, part on the lock, and part on the wood, and after it had laid on some time, I feel both parts with my other hand, I find the part that has been in contact with the lock, very sensibly colder to the touch, than the part that lay on the wood. How a living animal obtains its quantity of this fluid called fire, is a curious question. I have shown, that some bodies (as metals) have a power of attracting it stronger than others ; and I have some times suspected, that a living body had some power of attracting out of the air, or other bodies, the heat it wanted. Thus metals hammered, or repeatedly bent, grow hot in the beat or hammered part. But when I consider that air, in contact with the body, cools it ; that the surrounding air is rather heated by its contact with the body ; that every breath of cooler air drawn in, carries off part of the body's heat when it passes out again ; that therefore there must be in the body a fund for producing it, or otherwise the animal would soon grow cold : I have been rather inclined to think, that the fluid *fire*, as well as the fluid *air*, is attracted by plants in their growth, and becomes consolidated with the other materials of which they are formed, and makes a great part of their substance : that when they come to be digested, and to suffer in the vessels a kind of fermentation, part of the fire, as well as part of the air, recovers its fluid active state again, and diffuses itself in the body digesting and separating it : that the fire so reproduced, by digestion and separation continually leaving the body, its place is supplied by fresh quantities, arising from the continual separation. That whatever quickens the motion of the fluids in an animal quickens the separation, and reproduces more of the fire ; as exercise. That all the fire emitted by wood, and other combustibles, when burning

existed in them before, in a solid state, being only discovered when separating. That some fossils, as sulphur, sea
coal, &c. contain a great deal of solid fire; and that, in
short, what escapes and is dissipated in the burning of
bodies, besides water and earth, is generally the air and
fire that before made parts of the solid. Thus I imagine
that animal heat arises by or from a kind of fermentation in
the juices of the body, in the same manner as heat arises in
the liquors preparing for distillation, wherein there is a separation of the spirituous, from the watery and earthy parts.
And it is remarkable, that the liquor in a distiller's vat,
when in its highest and best state of fermentation, as I
have been informed, has the same degree of heat with the
human body : that is, about 94 or 96.

Thus, as by a constant supply of fuel in a chimney, you
keep a warm room, so, by a constant supply of food in the
stomach, you keep a warm body; only where little exercise
is used, the heat may possibly be conducted away too fast;
in which case such materials are to be used for cloathing.
and bedding, against the effects of an immediate contact of
the air, as are, in themselves, bad conductors of heat, and
consequently, prevent its being communicated through their
substance to the air. Hence, what is called *warmth* in wool
and its preference on that account, to linen; wool not being
so good a conductor : and hence all the natural coverings
of animals, to keep them warm, are such as retain and confine the natural heat in the body, by being bad conductors,
such as wool, hair, feathers, and the silk by which the silkworm, in its tender embrio state, is first cloathed, Cloathing, thus considered, does not make a man warm by *giving*
warmth, but by *preventing* the too quick dissipation of the
heat produced in his body, and so occasioning an accumulation.

There is another curious question I will just venture to
touch upon, viz. Whence arises the sudden extraordinary
degree of cold, perceptible on mixing some chemical liquors, and even on mixing salt and snow, where the composition appears colder than the coldest of the ingredients?
I have never seen the chemical mixtures made, but salt and

snow I have often mixed myself, and am fully satisfied that the composition feels much colder to the touch, and lowers the mercury in the thermometer more than either ingredient would do separately. I suppose, with others, that cold is nothing more than the absence of heat or fire. Now if the quantity of fire before contained or diffused in the snow and salt was expelled in the uniting of the two matters, it must be driven away either through the air or the vessel containing them. If it is driven off through the air, it must warm the air, and a thermometer held over the mixture, without touching it, would discover the heat, by the rising of the mercury, as it must, and always does in warm air.

This, indeed, I have not tried, but I should guess it would rather be driven off through the vessel, especially if the vessel be metal, as being a better conductor than air; and so one should find the bason warmer after such mixture. But, on the contrary, the vessel grows cold, and even water, in which the vessel is sometimes placed for the experiment, freezes into hard ice on the bason. Now I know not how to account for this, otherwise than by supposing, that the composition is a better conductor of fire than the ingredients separately, and, like the lock compared with the wood, has a stronger power of attracting fire, and does accordingly attract it suddenly from the fingers, or a thermometer put into it, from the bason that contains it, and from the water in contact with the outside of the bason; so that the fingers have the sensation of extreme cold, by being deprived of much of their natural fire; the thermometer sinks, by having part of its fire drawn out of the mercury; the bason grows colder to the touch, as, by having its fire drawn into the mixture, it is become more capable of drawing and receiving it from the hand; and through the bason, the water loses its fire that kept it fluid; so it becomes ice. One would expect, that from all this attracted acquisition of fire to the composition, it should become warmer; and, in fact, the snow and salt dissolve at the same time into water, without freezing.

I am, Sir, &c.   B. FRANKLIN.

TO THE SAME.

On the Production of Cold by Evaporation.

London, June 17, 1758.

DEAR SIR,

IN a former letter I mentioned the experiment for cooling bodies by evaporation, and that I had, by repeatedly wetting the thermometer with common spirits, brought the mercury down five or six degrees. Being lately at Cambridge, and mentioning this in conversation with Dr. Hadley, professor of chemistry there, he proposed repeating the experiments with ether, instead of common spirits, as the ether is much quicker in evaporation. We accordingly went to his chamber, where he had both ether and a thermometer. By dipping first the ball of the thermometer into the ether, it appeared that the ether was precisely of the same temperament with the thermometer, which stood then at 65 ; for it made no alteration in the height of the little column of mercury. But when the thermometer was taken out of the ether, and the ether, with which the ball was wet, began to evaporate, the mercury sunk several degrees. The wetting was then repeated by a feather that had been dipped into the ether, when the mercury sunk still lower. We continued this operation, one of us wetting the ball, and another of the company blowing on it with the bellows, to quicken the evaporation, the mercury sinking all the time, till it came down to 7, which is 25 degrees below the freezing point, when we left off. Soon after it passed the freezing point, a thin coat of ice began to cover the ball. Whether this was water collected and condensed by the coldness of the ball, from the moisture in the air, or from our breath ; or whether the feather, when dipped into the ether, might not sometimes go through it, and bring up some of the water that was under it, I am not certain ; perhaps all might contribute. The ice continued increasing till we ended the experiment, when it appeared near a quarter of an inch thick all over the ball, with a number of small spicula, pointing outwards. From this experiment one may see the possibility of freezing a man to death on a

warm summer's day, if he were to stand in a passage
through which the wind blew briskly, and to be wet frequently with ether, a spirit that is more inflammable than
brandy or common spirits of wine.

It is but within these few years, that the European philosophers seem to have known this power in nature, of cooling bodies by evaporation. But in the east they have long
been acquainted with it. A friend tells me, there is a passage in Bernier's Travels through Hindustan, written near
one hundred years ago, that mentions it as a practice (in
travelling over dry desarts in that hot climate) to carry water in flasks wrapt in wet woollen cloths, and hung on the
shady side of the camel, or carriage, but in the free air;
whereby, as the cloths gradually grow drier, the water contained in the flasks is made cool. They have likewise a
kind of earthen pots, unglazed, which let the water gradually and slowly ooze through their pores, so as to keep the
outside a little wet, notwithstanding the continual evaporation, which gives great coldness to the vessel, and the water contained in it. Even our common sailors seem to have
had some notion of this property; for I remember, that being at sea, when I was a youth, I observed one of the
sailors, during a calm in the night, often wetting his finger in
his mouth, and then holding it up in the air, to discover, as
he said, if the air had any motion, and from which side it
came; and this he expected to do, by finding one side of
his finger grow suddenly cold, and from that side he should
look for the next wind; which I then laughed at as a fancy.

May not several phenomena, hitherto unconsidered, or
unaccounted for, be explained by this property? During
the hot Sunday at Philadelphia, in June, 1750, when the
thermometer was up at 100 in the shade, I sat in my chamber without exercise, only reading or writing, with no other
clothes on than a shirt, and a pair of long linen drawers, the
windows all open, and a brisk wind blowing through the
house, the sweat ran off the backs of my hands, and my
shirt was often so wet, as to induce me to call for dry ones
to put on; in this situation, one might have expected, that

the natural heat of the body 96, added to the heat of the air 100, should jointly have created or produced a much greater degree of heat in the body; but the fact was, that my body never grew so hot as the air that surrounded it, or the inanimate bodies immersed in the same air. For I remember well, that the desk, when I laid my arm upon it; a chair, when I sat down in it; and a dry shirt out of the drawer, when I put it on, all felt exceeding warm to me, as if they had been warmed before a fire. And I suppose a dead body would have acquired the temperature of the air, though a living one, by continual sweating, and by the evaporation of that sweat, was kept cold. May not this be a reason why our reapers in Pennsylvania, working in the open field, in the clear hot sun-shine common in our harvest-time, find themselves well able to go through that labor, without being much incommoded by the heat, while they continue to sweat, and while they supply matter for keeping up that sweat, by drinking frequently of a thin evaporable liquor, water mixed with rum; but if the sweat stops, they drop, and sometimes die suddenly, if a sweating is not again brought on by drinking that liquor, or, as some rather chuse in that case, a kind of hot punch, made with water, mixed with honey, and a considerable proportion of vinegar? May there not be in negroes a quicker evaporation of the perspirable matter from their skins and lungs, which, by cooling them more, enables them to bear the sun's heat better than whites do? (if that is a fact, as it is said to be; for the alleged necessity of having negroes rather than whites, to work in the West-India fields, is founded upon it) though the color of their skins would otherwise make them more sensible of the sun's heat, since black cloth heats much sooner, and more, in the sun, than white cloth. I am persuaded, from several instances happening within my knowlege, that they do not bear cold weather so well as the whites; they will perish when exposed to a less degree of it, and are more apt to have their limbs frost-bitten; and may not this be from the same cause? Would not the earth grow much hotter under the summer-sun, if a constant evaporation from its surface, greater as the sun shines stronger, did not, by tending to cool it, balance, in some degree the warmer effects of the sun's rays? Is it not owing to the constant evaporation from the surface of every leaf, that trees, though shone on by the sun, are always, even the leaves themselves, cool to our sense? at least much cooler than they would otherwise be? May it not be owing to this, that fanning ourselves when warm, does really cool us, though the air is itself warm that we drive with the fan upon our faces; for the atmosphere round, and next to our bodies, having imbibed as much of the perspired vapor as it can well contain, receives no more, and the evaporation is therefore checked and retarded, till we drive away that atmosphere, and bring drier air in its place, that will receive the vapor, and thereby facilitate and increase the evaporation? Certain it is, that mere blowing of air on a dry body does not cool it, as any one may satisfy himself, by blowing with a bellows on the dry ball of a thermometer; the mercury will not fall; if it moves at all, it rather rises, as being warmed by the friction of the air on its surface? To these queries of imagination, I will only add one practical observation; that wherever it is thought proper to give ease, in cases of painful inflammation in the flesh (as from burnings, or the like) by cooling the part; linen cloths, wet with spirit, and applied to the part inflamed, will produce the coolness required, better than if wet with water, and will continue it longer. For water, though cold when first applied, will soon acquire warmth from the flesh, as it does not evaporate fast enough; but the cloths wet with spirit, will continue cold as long as any spirit is left to keep up the evaporation, the parts warmed escaping as soon as they are warmed, and carrying off the heat with them.

I am, Sir, &c.

B. FRANKLIN.

J. BOWDOIN, IN BOSTON, TO DR. FRANKLIN.

Concerning the Light in Sea-Water.

Read at the Royal Society, December 6, 1756.

November 12, 1753.

.............WHEN I was at the eastward, I had an opportunity of observing the luminous appearance of the sea when disturbed: at the head and stern of the vessel, when under way, it appeared very bright.   The best opportunity I had to observe it was in a boat, in company with several gentlemen going from Portsmouth, about three miles, to our vessel lying at the mouth of Piscataqua river.   Soon after we set off (it being in the evening) we observed a luminous appearance, where the oars dashed the water.   Sometimes it was very bright, and afterwards, as we rowed along, gradually lessened, till almost imperceptible, and then re-illumined.   This we took notice of several times in the passage.   When I got on board the vessel, I ordered a pail to be dipped up, full of sea-water, in which, on the water's being moved a sparkling light appeared.   I took a linen cloth, and strained some of the water through it, and there was a like appearance on the cloth, which soon went off; but on rubbing the cloth with my finger, it was renewed.   I then carried the cloth to the light, but could not perceive any thing upon it which should cause that appearance.

Several gentlemen were of opinion, that the separated particles of putrid, animal, and other bodies, floating on the surface of the sea, might cause that appearance; for putrid fish, &c. they said, will cause it: and the sea-animals which have died, and other bodies putrified therein since the creation, might afford a sufficient quantity of these particles to cover a considerable portion of the surface of the sea; which particles being differently dispersed, might account for the different degrees of light in the appearance above-mentioned.   But this account seems liable to this obvious objection, that as putrid fish, &c. make a luminous appearance without being moved or disturbed, it might be expected that the supposed putrid particles on the surface of the sea, should always appear luminous, where there is not a greater light; and, consequently, that the whole surface of the sea, covered with those particles, should always, in dark nights, appear luminous, without being disturbed. But this is not the fact.

Among the rest, I threw out my conjecture, that the said appearance might be caused by a great number of little animals, floating on the surface of the sea, which, on being disturbed, might, by expanding their fins, or otherwise moving themselves, expose such a part of their bodies as exhibits a luminous appearance, somewhat in the manner of a glow-worm, or fire-fly: that these animals may be more numerous in some places than others; and, therefore, that the appearance above-mentioned being fainter and stronger in different places, might be owing to that: that certain circumstances of weather, &c. might invite them to the surface, on which, in a calm, they might sport themselves and glow; or in storms, being forced up, make the same appearance.

There is no difficulty in conceiving that the sea may be stocked with animalcula for this purpose, as we find all nature crowded with life. But it seems difficult to conceive that such small portions of matter, even if they were wholly luminous, should affect our sight; much more so, when it is supposed that only a part of them is luminous. But, if we consider some other appearances, we may find the same difficulty to conceive of them; and yet we know they take place. For instance, the flame of a candle, which, it is said, may be seen four miles round. The light which fills this circle of eight miles diameter, was contained, when it first left the candle, within a circle of half an inch diameter. If the density of light, in these circumstances, be as those circles to each other, that is, as the squares of their diameters, the candle-light, when come to the eye, will be 1,027,709,337,600 times rarer than when it quitted the half inch circle. Now the aperture of the eye, through which the light passes, does not exceed one-tenth of an inch diameter, and the portion of the lesser circle, which corresponds to this small portion of the greater circle, must be proportionably, that is, 1,027,709,337,600 times less than one-tenth of an inch; and yet this infinitely small point (if you will allow the expression) affords light enough to make it visible four miles; or, rather, affords light sufficient to affect the sight at that distance.

The smallness of the animalcula is no objection then to this conjecture; for supposing them to be ten thousand times less than the *minimum visible*, they may, notwithstanding, emit light enough to affect the eyes, and so to cause the luminous appearance aforesaid. This conjecture I send you for want of something better * * *.

TO PETER FRANKLIN, IN NEWPORT.

On the Saltness of Sea-Water.

London, May 7, 1760.

.... IT has, indeed, as you observe, been the opinion of some very great naturalists, that the sea is salt only from the dissolution of mineral or rock-salt, which its waters happened to meet with. But this opinion takes it for granted that all water was originally fresh, of which we can have no proof. I own I am inclined to a different opinion, and rather think all the water on this globe was originally salt, and that the fresh water we find in springs and rivers, is the produce of distillation. The sun raises the vapors from the sea, which form clouds, and fall in rain upon the land, and springs and rivers are formed of that rain. As to the rock-salt found in mines, I conceive, that instead of communicating its saltness to the sea, it is itself drawn from the sea, and that of course the sea is now fresher than it was originally. This is only another effect of nature's distillery, and might be performed various ways.

It is evident from the quantities of sea-shells, and the bones and teeth of fishes found in high lands, that the sea has formerly covered them.   Then, either the sea has been higher than it now is, and has fallen away from those high lands, or they have been lower than they are, and were lifted up out of the water to their present height, by some internal mighty force, such as we still feel some remains of, when whole continents are moved by earthquakes.   In either case it may be supposed that large hollows, or valleys among hills, might be left filled with sea-water, which evaporating, and the fluid part drying away in a course of years, would leave the salt covering the bottom; and that salt coming afterwards to be covered with earth, from the neighboring hills, could only be found by digging through that earth.   Or, as we know from their effects, that there are deep fiery caverns under the earth, and even under the sea, if at any time the sea leaks into any of them, the fluid parts of the water must evaporate from that heat, and pass off through some volcano, while the salt remains, and by degrees, and continual acretion, becomes a great mass. Thus the cavern may at length be filled, and the volcano connected with it cease burning, as many it is said have done; and future miners, penetrating such cavern, find what we call a salt-mine.   This is a fancy I had on visiting the salt-mines at Northwich, with my son.   I send you a piece of the rock-salt which he brought up with him out of the mine.

I am, Sir, &c.

B. FRANKLIN.

TO MISS STEPHENSON, WANSTEAD.

On the Bristol Waters, and the Tide in Rivers,

London, Sept. 13, 1760.

MY DEAR FRIEND,

I HAVE your agreeable letter from Bristol, which I take this first leisure hour to answer, having for some time been much engaged in business.

Your first question, *What is the reason the water at this place, though cold at the spring, becomes warm by pumping?* It will be most prudent in me to forbear attempting to answer, til', by a more circumstantial account, you assure me of the fact. I own I should expect that operation to warm, n t so much the water pumped, as the person pumping.——The rubbing of dry solids together has been long observed to produce heat; but the like effect has never yet, that I have heard, been produced by the mere agitation of fluids, or friction of fluids with solids. Water in a bottle shook for hours by a mill-hopper, it is said, discovered no sensible addition of heat. The production of animal heat by exercise is therefore to be accounted for in another manner, which I may hereafter endeavor to make you acquainted with.

This prudence of not attempting to give reasons before one is sure of facts, I learnt from one of your sex, who, as Selden tells us, being in company with some gentlemen that were viewing, and considering something which they called a Chinese shoe, and disputing earnestly about the manner of wearing it, and how it could possibly be put on; put in her word, and said modestly, *Gentlemen, are you sure it is a shoe?——Should not that be settled first?*

But I shall now endeavor to explain what I said to you about the tide in rivers, and to that end shall make a figure, which though not very like a river, may serve to convey my meaning.——Suppose a canal one hundred and forty miles long, communicating at one end with the sea, and filled therefore with sea water. I chuse a canal at first, rather than a river, to throw out of consideration the effects produced by the streams of fresh water from the land, the inequality in breadth, and the crookedness of courses.

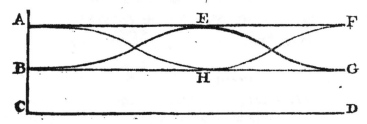

Let A, C, be the head of the canal; C, D, the bottom of it; D, F, the open mouth of it next the sea. Let the strait pricked line, B, G, represent low water mark the whole length of the canal, A, F, high water mark :—Now if a person standing at E, and observing at the time of high water there, that the canal is quite full at that place up to the line E, should conclude that the canal is equally full to the same height from end to end, and therefore there was as much more water come into the canal since it was down at low water mark, as would be included in the oblong space A, B, G, F, he would be greatly mistaken. For the tide is *a wave*, and the top of the wave, which makes high water, as well as every other lower part, is progressive ; and it is high water successively, but not at the same time, in all the several points between G, F, and A, B.—And in such a length as I have mentioned it is low water at F, G, and also at A, B, at or near the same time with its being high water at E ; so that the surface of the water in the canal, during that situation, is properly represented by the curve pricked line B, E, G. And on the other hand, when it is low water at E, H, it is high water both at F, G, and at A, B, at or near the same time : and the surface would then be described by the inverted curve line. A, H, F.

In this view of the case, you will easily see, that there must be very little more water in the canal at what we call high water, that there is at low water, those terms not relating to the whole canal at the same time, but successively to its parts. And if you suppose the canal six times as long, the case would not vary as to the quantity of water at different times of the tide ; there would only be six waves in the canal at the same time, instead of one, and the hollows in the water would be equal to the hills.

That this is not mere theory, but comformable to fact, we know by our long rivers in America. The Delaware, on which Philadelphia stands, is in this particular similar to the canal I have supposed of one wave: for when it is high water at the Capes or mouth of the river, it is also high water at Philadelphia, which stands about one hundred and forty miles from the sea ; and there is at the same time a low water in the middle between the two high waters ;

where, when it comes to be high water, it is at the same time low water at the Capes and at Philadelphia. And the longer rivers have some a wave and half, some two, three, or four waves, according to their length. In the shorter rivers of this island, one may see the same thing in part: for instance, it is high water at Gravesend an hour before it is high water at London Bridge ; and twenty miles below Gravesend an hour before it is high water at Gravesend. Therefore at the time of high water at Gravesend the top of the wave is there, and the water is then not so high by some feet where the top of the wave was an hour before, or where it will be an hour after, as it is just then at Gravesend.

Now we are not to suppose, that because the swell or top of the wave runs at the rate of twenty miles an hour, that therefore the current, or water itself of which the wave is composed runs at that rate. Far from it. To conceive this motion of a wave, make a small experiment or two. Fasten one end of a cord in a window near the top of a house, and let the other end come down to the ground ; take this end in your hand, and you may, by a sudden motion, occasion a wave in the cord that will run quite up to the window ; but though the wave is progressive from your hand to the window, the parts of the rope do not proceed with the wave, but remain where they were, except only that kind of motion that produces the wave. So if you throw a stone into a pond of water when the surface is still and smooth, you will see a circular wave proceed from the stone at its centre, quite to the sides of the pond ; but the water does not proceed with the wave, it only rises and falls to form it in the different parts of its course ; and the waves that follow the first, all make use of the same water with their predecessors.

But a wave in water is not indeed in all circumstances exactly like that in a cord ; for water being a fluid, and gravitating to the earth, it naturally runs from a higher place to a lower ; therefore the parts of the wave in water do actually run a little both ways from its top towards its lower sides, which the parts of the wave in the cord cannot do. Thus, when it is high and standing water at Gravesend, the water twenty miles below has been running ebb, or towards the sea for an hour, or ever since it was high water there; but the water at London Bridge will run flood, or from the sea yet another hour, till it is high water, or the top of the wave arrives at that bridge, and then it will have run ebb an hour at Gravesend, &c. Now this motion of the water, occasioned only by its gravity, or tendency to run from a higher place to a lower, is by no means so swift as the motion of the wave. It scarce exceeds perhaps two miles in an hour.

If it went as the wave does twenty miles an hour, no ships could ride at anchor in such a stream, nor boats row against it.

In common speech, indeed, this current of the water both ways from the top of the wave is called *the tide;* thus we say, *the tide runs strong, the tide runs at the rate of one, two, or three miles an hour,* &c. and when we are at a part of the river behind the top of the wave, and find the water lower than high-water mark, and running towards the sea, we say, *the tide runs ebb;* and we are before the top of the wave, and find the water higher than low-water mark, and running from the sea, we say, *the tide runs flood;* but these expressions are only locally proper; for a tide strictly speaking, is *one whole wave,* including all its parts higher and lower, and these waves succeed one another about twice in twenty-four hours.

This motion of the water, occasioned by its gravity, will explain to you why the water near the mouths of rivers may be salter at high water than at low. Some of the salt-water, as the tide wave enters the river, runs from its top and fore side, and mixes with the fresh, and also pushes it back up the river.

Supposing that the water commonly runs during the flood at the rate of two miles in an hour, and that the flood runs five hours, you see that it can bring at most into our canal only a quantity of water equal to the space included in the

breadth of the canal, ten miles of its length, and the depth
between low and high-water mark; which is but a fourteenth
part of what would be necessary to fill all the space between
low and high-water mark, for one hundred and forty miles,
the whole length of the canal.

And indeed such a quantity of water as would fill that
whole space, to run in and out every tide, must create so
outrageous a current, as would do infinite damage to the
shores, shipping, &c. and make the navigation of a river
almost impracticable.

I have made this letter longer than I intended, and
therefore reserve for another what I have further to say on
the subject of tides and rivers.   I shall now only add, that
I have not been exact in the numbers, because I would
avoid perplexing you with minute calculations, my design
at present being chiefly to give you distinct and clear ideas
of the first principles.

After writing six folio pages of philosophy to a young
girl, is it necessary to finish such a letter with a compliment?—Is not such a letter of itself a compliment?—Does
it not say, she has a mind thirsty after knowlege, and capable of receiving it; and that the most agreeable things
one can write to her are those that tend to the improvement
of her understanding?—It does indeed say this, but then
it is still no compliment; it is no more than plain honest
truth, which is not the character of a compliment. So if
I would finish my letter in the *mode*, I should yet add some
thing that means nothing, and is *merely* civil and polite.
But being naturally aukward at every circumstance of cere-
mony, I shall not attempt it.   I had rather conclude abruptly with what pleases me more than any compliment can
please you, that I am allowed to subscribe myself.

Your affectionate friend,

B. FRANKLIN.

TO THE SAME.

On the same Subject.

Craven-street, Monday, March 30, 1761.

MY DEAR FRIEND,

SUPPOSING the fact, that the water of the well at Bristol is warmer after some time pumping, I think your manner of accounting for that increased warmth very ingenious and probable. It did not occur to me, and therefore I doubted of the fact.

You are, I think quite right in your opinion, that the rising of the tides in rivers is not owing to the immediate influence of the moon on the rivers. It is rather a subsequent effect of the influence of the moon on the sea, and does not make its appearance in some rivers till the moon has long passed by. I have not expressed myself clearly if you have understood me to mean otherwise. You know I have mentioned it as a fact, that there are in some rivers several tides all existing at the same time; that is, two, three, or more, high-waters, and as many low-waters, in different parts of the same river, which cannot possibly be all effects of the moon's immediate action on that river; but they may be subsequent effects of her action on the sea.

In the enclosed paper you will find my sentiments on several points relating to the air, and the evaporation of water. It is Mr. Collinson's copy, who took it from one I sent through his hands to a correspondent in France some years since; I have, as he desired me, corrected the mistakes he made in transcribing, and must return it to him; but if you think it worth while, you may take a copy of it: I would have saved you any trouble of that kind, but had not time.

Some day in the next or the following week, I purpose to have the pleasure of seeing you at Wanstead; I shall accompany your good mamma thither, and stay till the next morning, if it may be done without incommoding your family too much—We may then discourse any points in that paper that do not seem clear to you; and taking a walk to lord Tilney's ponds, make a few experiments there

R r

to explain the nature of the tides more fully. In the mean time believe me to be, with the highest esteem and regard, your sincerely affectionate friend,

B. FRANKLIN.

TO THE SAME.

Salt-Water rendered fresh by Distillation.—Method of relieving Thirst by Sea-Water.

Craven-street, August 10, 1761.

WE are to set out this week for Holland, where we may possibly spend a month, but purpose to be at home again before the coronation. I could not go without taking leave of you by a line at least, when I am so many letters in your debt.

In yours of May 19, which I have before me, you speak of the ease with which salt water may be made fresh by distillation, supposing it to be, as I had said, that in evaporation the air would take up water but not the salt that was mixed with it. It is true that distilled sea water will not be salt, but there are other disagreeable qualities that rise with the water in distillation; which indeed several besides Dr. Hales have endeavored by some means to prevent; but as yet their methods have not been brought much into use.

I have a singular opinion on this subject, which I will venture to communicate to you, though I doubt you will rank it among my whims. It is certain that the skin has *imbibing* as well as *discharging* pores; witness the effects of a blistering plaister, &c. I have read that a man, hired by a physician to stand by way of experiment in the open air naked during a moist night, weighed near three pounds heavier in the morning. I have often observed myself, that however thirsty I may have been before going into the water to swim, I am never long so in the water. These imbibing pores, however, are very fine, perhaps fine enough in filtering to separate salt from water; for though I have soaked (by swimming, when a boy) several hours in the day for several days successively in salt water, I never found my blood and juices salted by that means, so as to make me thirsty or feel a salt taste in my mouth: and it is remarkable, that the flesh of sea fish, though bred in salt-water, is not salt. Hence I imagine, that if people at sea, distressed by thirst, when their fresh water is unfortunately spent, would make bathing-tubs of their empty water-casks, and, filling them with sea-water, sit in them an hour or two each day, they might be greatly relieved. Perhaps keeping their clothes constantly wet might have an almost equal effect; and this without danger of catching cold. Men do not catch cold by wet clothes at sea. Damp, but not wet linen may possibly give colds; but no one catches cold by bathing, and no clothes can be wetter than water itself. Why damp clothes should then occasion colds, is a curious question, the discussion of which I reserve for a future letter, or some future conversation.

Adieu, my little philosopher. Present my respectful compliments to the good ladies your aunts, and to miss Pitt; and believe me ever

Your affectionate friend,

And humble servant,

B. FRANKLIN,

TO THE SAME.

Tendency of Rivers to the Sea—Effects of the Sun's Rays on Cloths of different Colors.

September 20, 1761.

MY DEAR FRIEND,

IT is, as you observed in our late conversation, a very general opinion, that *all rivers run into the sea,* or deposit their waters there. 'Tis a kind of audacity to call such general opinions in question, and may subject one to censure. But we must hazard something in what we think the cause of truth: and if we propose our objections modestly, we shall, though mistaken, deserve a censure less severe, than when we are both mistaken and insolent.

That some rivers run into the sea is beyond a doubt : such, for instance, are the Amazons, and I think the Oronoko and the Mississippi. The proof is, that their waters are fresh quite to the sea, and out to some distance from the land. Our question is, whether the fresh waters of those rivers whose beds are filled with salt water to a considerable distance up from the sea (as the Thames, the Delaware, and the rivers that communicate with Chesapeake-bay in Virginia) do ever arrive at the sea? And as I suspect they do not, I am now to acquaint you with my reasons ; or, if they are not allowed to be reasons, my conceptions at least, of this matter.

The common supply of rivers is from springs, which draw their origin from rain that has soaked into the earth. The union of a number of springs forms a river. The waters as they run exposed to the sun, air, and wind, are continually evaporating. Hence in travelling one may often see where a river runs, by a long bluish mist over it, though we are at such a distance as not to see the river itself. The quantity of this evaporation is greater or less, in proportion to the surface exposed by the same quantity of water to those causes of evaporation. While the rivers runs in a narrow confined channel in the upper hilly country, only a small surface is exposed ; a greater as the river widens. Now if a river ends in a lake, as some do, whereby its waters are spread so wide as that the evaporation is equal to the sum of all its springs, that lake will never overflow :— and if instead of ending in a lake, it was drawn into greater length as a river, so as to expose a surface equal in the whole to that lake, the evaporation would be equal, and such river would end as a canal ; when the ignorant might suppose, as they actually do in such cases, that the river loses itself by running under ground, whereas in truth it has run up into the air.

Now, how many rivers that are open to the sea widen much before they arrive at it, not merely by the additional waters they receive, but by having their course stopped by the opposing flood-tide ; by being turned back twice in twenty-four hours and by finding broader beds in the low flat countries to dilate themselves in; hence the evaporation of the fresh water is proportionably increased; so that in some rivers it may equal the springs of supply. In such cases, the salt water comes up the river, and meets the fresh in that part where, if there were a wall or bank of earth across, from side to side, the river would form a lake, fuller indeed at some times than at others, according to the seasons, but whose evaporation would, one time with another, be equal to its supply.

When the communication between the two kinds of water is open, this supposed wall of separation may be conceived as a moveable one, which is not only pushed some miles higher up the river by every flood tide from the sea, and carried down again as far by every tide of ebb, but which has even this space of vibration removed nearer to the sea in wet seasons, when the springs and brooks in the upper country are augmented by the falling rains, so as to swell the river, and farther from the sea in dry seasons.

Within a few miles above and below this moveable line of separation, the different waters mix a little, partly by their motion to and fro, and partly from the greater specific gravity of the salt water, which inclines it to run under the fresh, while the fresh water, being lighter, runs over the salt.

Cast your eye on the map of North America, and observe the bay of Chesapeake in Virginia, mentioned above; you will see, communicating with it by their mouths, the great rivers Susquehanna, Potowmac, Rappahannoc, York, and James, besides a number of smaller streams, each as big as the Thames. It has been proposed by philosophical writers, that to compute how much water any river discharges into the sea in a given time, we should measure its depth and swiftness at any part above the tide; as, for the Thames, at Kingston or Windsor. But can one imagine, that if all the water of those vast rivers went to the sea, it would not first have pushed the salt water out of that narrow-mouthed bay, and filled it with fresh?—The

Susquehana alone would seem to be sufficient for this, if it were not for the loss by evaporation.   And yet that bay is salt quite up to Annapolis.

As to our other subject, the different degrees of heat imbibed from the sun's rays by cloths of different colors, since I cannot find the notes of my experiment to send you, I must give it as well as I can from memory.

But first let me mention an experiment you may easily make yourself.   Walk but a quarter of an hour in your garden when the sun shines, with a part of your dress white, and a part black ; then apply your hand to them alternately, and you will find a very great difference in their warmth. The black will be quite hot to the touch, the white still cool.

Another. Try to fire the paper with a burning glass.   If it is white, you will not easily burn it ;—but if you bring the focus to a black spot, or upon letters, written or printed, the paper will immediately be on fire under the letters.

Thus fullers and dyers find black cloths, of equal thickness with white ones, and hung out equally wet, dry in the sun much sooner than the white, being more readily heated by the sun's rays.   It is the same before a fire ; the heat of which sooner penetrates black stockings than white ones, and so is apt sooner to burn a man's shins.   Also beer much sooner warms in a black mug set before the fire, than in a white one, or in a bright silver tankard.

My experiment was this.   I took a number of little square pieces of broad cloth from a taylor's pattern-card, of various colors.   There were black, deep blue, lighter blue, green, purple, red, yellow, white, and other colors, or shades of colors.   I laid them all out upon the snow in a bright sun-shiney morning.   In a few hours (I cannot now be exact as to the time) the black being warmed most by the sun, was sunk so low as to be below the stroke of the sun's rays ; the dark blue almost as low, the lighter blue not quite so much as the dark, the other colors less as they were lighter ; and the quite white remained on the surface of the snow, not having entered it at all.

What signifies philosophy that does not apply to some use ?—May we not learn from hence, that black clothes are not so fit to wear in a hot sunny climate or season, as white ones ; because in such clothes the body is more heated by the sun when we walk abroad, and are at the same time heated by the exercise, which double heat is apt to bring on putrid dangerous fevers ? That soldiers and seamen, who must march and labor in the sun, should in the East or West Indies have an uniform of white ? That summer hats, for men or women, should be white, as repelling that heat which gives head-aches to many, and to some the fatal stroke that the French call the *coup de soleil ?* That the ladies summer hats, however, should be lined with black, as not reverberating on their faces those rays which are reflected upwards from the earth or water ? That the putting a white cap of paper or linen *within* the crown of a black hat, as some do, will not keep out the heat, though it would if placed *without.*   That fruit-walls being blacked may receive so much heat from the sun in the day-time, as to continue warm in some degree through the night, and thereby preserve the fruit from frosts, or forward its growth ?—with sundry other particulars of less or greater importance, that will occur from time to time to attentive minds ?

I am yours, affectionately,

B. FRANKLIN.

TO THE SAME.

On the Effect of Air on the Barometer, and the Benefits derived from the Study of Insects.

Craven Street, June 11, 1760.

'TIS a very sensible question you ask, how the air can affect the barometer, when its opening appears covered with wood ?   If indeed it was so closely covered as to admit of no communication of the outward air to the surface of the mercury, the change of weight in the air could not possibly affect it. But the least crevice is sufficient for the purpose ;

a pinhole will do the business.   And if you could look behind the frame to which your barometer is fixed, you would
certainly find some small opening.

There are indeed some barometers in which the body of
mercury at the lower end is contained in a close leather bag,
and so the air cannot come into immediate contact with the
mercury ; yet the same effect is produced.   For the leather
being flexible, when the bag is pressed by any additional
weight of air it contracts, and the mercury is forced up into
the tube ; when the air becomes lighter, and it pressure less,
the weight of the mercury prevails, and it descends again
into the bag.

Your observation on what you have lately read concerning insects is very just and solid.   Superficial minds are
apt to despise those who make that part of the creation
their study, as mere triflers; but certainly the world has
been much obliged to them.   Under the care and management of man, the labors of the little silkworm afford employment and subsistence to thousands of families, and become
an immense article of commerce.   The bee, too, yields us
its delicious honey, and its wax useful to a multitude of
purposes.   Another insect, it is said, produces the cochineal, from whence we have our rich scarlet dye.   The usefulness of the cantharides or Spanish flies, in medicine, is
known to all, and thousands owe their lives to that knowlege.   By human industry and observation, other properties of other insects may possibly be hereafter discovered,
and of equal utility.   A thorough acquaintance with the
nature of these little creatures may also enable mankind to
prevent the increase of such as are noxious, or secure us
against the mischiefs they occasion.   These things doubtless your books make mention of: I can only add a particular late instance which I had from a Swedish gentleman
of good credit.   In the green timber, intended for ship-
building at the king's yard in that country, a kind of worms
were found, which every year became more numerous and
more pernicious, so that the ships were greatly damaged
before they came into use.   The king sent Linnæus, the

great naturalist, from Stockholm, to enquire into the affair, and see if the mischief was capable of any remedy. He found, on examination, that the worm was produced from a small egg, deposited in the little roughnesses on the surface of the wood, by a particular kind of fly or beetle; from whence the worm, as soon as it was hatched, began to eat into the substance of the wood, and after some time came out again a fly of the parent kind, and so the species increased. The season in which the fly laid its eggs, Linnæus knew to be about a fortnight (I think) in the month of May, and at no other time in the year. He therefore advised, that some days before that season, all the green timber should be thrown into the water, and kept under water till the season was over. Which being done by the king's order, the flies missing the usual nests, could not increase; and the species was either destroyed or went elsewhere: and the wood was effectually preserved; for after the first year, it became too dry and hard for their purpose.

There is, however, a prudent moderation to be used in studies of this kind. The knowlege of nature may be ornamental, and it may be useful, but if to attain an eminence in that, we neglect the knowlege and practice of essential duties, we deserve reprehension. For there is no rank in natural knowlege of equal dignity and importance with that of being a good parent, a good child, a good husband or wife, a good neighbor or friend, a good subject or citizen, that is, in short, a good christian. Nicholas Gimcrack, therefore, who neglected the care of his family, to pursue butterfles, was a just object of ridicule, and we must give him up as fair game to the satyrist.

Adieu, my dear friend, and believe me ever

Yours affectionately,

B. FRANKLIN.

TO DR. JOSEPH PRIESTLEY.[4]
Effect of Vegetation on Noxious Air.

.... THAT the vegetable creation should restore the air which is spoiled by the animal part of it, looks like a rational system, and seems to be of a piece with the rest. Thus fire purifies water all the world over. It purifies it by distillation, when it raises it in vapors, and lets it fall in rain ; and farther still by filtration, when, keeping it fluid, it suffers that rain to percolate the earth. We knew before, that putrid animal substances were converted into sweet vegetables, when mixed with the earth, and applied as manure ; and now, it seems, that the same putrid substances, mixed with the air, have a similar effect. The strong thriving state of your mint, in putrid air, seems to shew, that the air is mended by taking something from it, and not by adding to it. I hope this will give some check to the rage of destroying trees that grow near houses, which has accompanied our late improvements in gardening, from an opinion of their being unwholesome. I am certain, from long observation, that there is nothing unhealthy in the air of woods ; for we Americans have every where our country habitations in the midst of woods, and no people on earth enjoy better health, or are more prolific.

B. FRANKLIN.

TO THE SAME.[5]

On the Inflammability of the Surface of certain Rivers in America.

Craven-street, April 10, 1774.

DEAR SIR,

IN compliance with your request, I have endeavored to recollect the circumstances of the American experiments I formerly mentioned to you, of raising a flame on the surface of some waters there.

---

4 This extract is taken from Dr. Priestley's Experiments on Air, Vol. I. page 94. It was written in answer to a note from Dr. Priestley, informing Dr. Franklin of the result of certain experiments on some plants which he had seen at Dr. Priestley's house in a very flourishing state, in jars of highly noxious air.

5. From Priestley's Experiments on Air, Vol. I. page 321.

When I passed through New Jersey in 1764, I heard it several times mentioned, that by applying a lighted candle near the surface of some of their rivers, a sudden flame would catch and spread on the water, continuing to burn for near half a minute. But the accounts I received were so imperfect, that I could form no guess at the cause of such an effect, and rather doubted the truth of it. I had no opportunity of seeing the experiment; but calling to see a friend who happened to be just returning home from making it himself, I learned from him the manner of it; which was to chuse a shallow place, where the bottom could be reached by a walking-stick, and was muddy; the mud was first to be stirred with the stick, and when a number of small bubbles began to arise from it, the candle was applied. The flame was so sudden and so strong, that it catched his ruffle and spoiled it, as I saw. New Jersey having many pine-trees in many parts of it, I then imagined that something like a volatile oil of turpentine might be mixed with the waters from a pine-swamp, but this supposition did not quite satisfy me. I mentioned the fact to some philosophical friends on my return to England, but it was not much attended to. I suppose I was thought a little too credulous.

In 1765, the Reverend Dr. Chandler received a letter from Dr. Finley, President of the College in that province, relating the same experiment. It was read at the Royal Society, November 21, of that year, but not printed in the Transactions; perhaps because it was thought too strange to be true, and some ridicule might be apprehended, if any member should attempt to repeat it, in order to ascertain, or refute it. The following is a copy of that account.

" A worthy gentleman, who lives at a few miles distance, informed me, that in a certain small cove of a mill-pond, near his house, he was surprised to see the surface of the water blaze like inflamed spirits. I soon after went to the place, and made the experiment with the same success. The bottom of the creek was muddy, and when stirred up, so as to cause a considerable curl on the surface, and a lighted candle held within two or three inches of it, the whole surface was in a blaze, as instantly as the vapor of warm inflammable spirits, and continued when strongly agitated, for the space of several seconds. It was at first imagined to be peculiar to that place ; but upon trial it was soon found, that such a bottom in other places exhibited the same phenomenon. The discovery was accidentally made by one belonging to the mill."

I have tried the experiment twice here in England, but without success. The first was in a slow running water with a muddy bottom. The second in a stagnant water at the bottom of a deep ditch. Being some time employed in stirring this water, I ascribed an intermitting fever, which seized me a few days after, to my breathing too much of that foul air, which I stirred up from the bottom, and which I could not avoid while I stooped, endeavoring to kindle it. The discoveries you have lately made, of the manner in which inflammable air is in some cases produced, may throw light on this experiment, and explain its succeeding in some cases, and not in others. With the highest esteem and respect,

I am, dear Sir, your most obedient humble servant,

B. FRANKLIN.

TO DR. PERCIVAL[6].

On the different Quantities of Rain which fall at different Heights over the same Ground.

Read in the Philosophical Society of Manchester, January 21, 1784.

ON my return to London I found your favor of the 16th of May (1771). I wish I could, as you desire, give you a better explanation of the phenomenon in question, since you seem not quite satisfied with your own ; but I think we want more and a greater variety of experiments in different circumstances, to enable us to form a thoroughly satisfactory hypothesis. Not that I make the least doubt of the facts already related, as I know both lord Charles Cavendish, and Dr. Heberden to be very accurate experimenters :

---

6 This letter was published in the Memoirs of the Literary and Philosophical Society of Manchester, Vol. II. page 126.

but I wish to know the event of the trials proposed in your six queries; and also, whether in the same place where the lower vessel receives nearly twice the quantity of water that is received by the upper, a third vessel placed at half the height will receive a quantity proportionable. I will however endeavor to explain to you what occurred to me, when I first heard of the fact.

I suppose it will be generally allowed, on a little consideration of the subject, that scarce any drop of water was, when it began to fall from the clouds, of a magnitude equal to that it has acquired, when it arrives at the earth; the same of the several pieces of hail; because they are often so large and so weighty, that we cannot conceive a possibility of their being suspended in the air, and remaining at rest there, for any time, how small soever; nor do we conceive any means of forming them so large, before they set out to fall. It seems then, that each beginning drop, and particle of hail, receives continual addition in its progress downwards. This may be several ways: by the union of numbers in their course, so that what was at first only descending mist, becomes a shower; or by each particle, in its descent through air that contains a great quantity of dissolved water, striking against, attaching to itself, and carrying down with it such particles of that dissolved water, as happen to be in its way; or attracting to itself such as do not lie directly in its course by its different state, with regard either to common or electric fire; or by all these causes united.

In the first case, by the uniting of numbers, larger drops might be made, but the quantity falling in the same place would be the same at all heights; unless, as you mention, the whole should be contracted in falling, the lines described by all the drops converging, so that what set out to fall from a cloud of many thousand acres, should reach the earth in perhaps a third of that extent, of which I somewhat doubt. In the other cases we have two experiments.

1. A dry glass bottle filled with very cold water, in a warm day, will presently collect from the seemingly dry

air that surrounds it a quantity of water, that shall cover
its surface and run down its sides, which perhaps is done by
the power wherewith the cold water attracts the fluid, common fire that had been united with the dissolved water in
the air, and drawing the fire through the glass into itself,
leaves the water on the outside.

2. An electrified body left in a room for some time, will
be more covered with dust than other bodies in the same
room not electrified, which dust seems to be attracted from
the circumambient air.

Now we know that the rain, even in our hottest days,
comes from a very cold region. Its falling sometimes in the
form of ice, shows this clearly; and perhaps even the rain
is snow or ice, when it first moves downwards, though
thawed in falling: and we know that the drops of rain are
often electrified: but those causes of addition to each drop
of water, or piece of hail, one would think could not long
continue to produce the same effect; since the air, through
which the drops fall, must soon be stripped of its previously dissolved water, so as to be no longer capable of augmenting them. Indeed very heavy showers, of either, are
never of long continuance; but moderate rains often continue
so long as to puzzle this hypothesis: so that upon the whole
I think, as I intimated before, that we are yet hardly ripe
for making one.

B. FRANKLIN.

<hr>

TO NAIRNE, OF LONDON.

On the properties of an Hygrometer.

Read in the Transactions of the American Philosophical Society,
January 26, 1780.

Passy, near Paris, Nov. 13, 1780.

SIR,

THE qualities hitherto sought in a hygrometer, or instrument to discover the degrees of moisture and dryness
in the air, seem to have been, an aptitude to receive humidity readily from a moist air, and to part with it as
readily to a dry air. Different substances have been found

to possess more or less of this quality; but when we shall have found the substance that has it in the greatest perfection, there will still remain some uncertainty in the conclusions to be drawn from the degree shown by the instrument, arising from the actual state of the instrument itself as to heat and cold. Thus, if two bottles or vessels of glass or metal being filled, the one with cold and the other with hot water, are brought into a room, the moisture of the air in the room will attach itself in quantities to the surface of the cold vessel, while if you actually wet the surface of the hot vessel, the moisture will immediately quit it, and be absorbed by the same air. And thus, in a sudden change of the air from cold to warm, the instrument remaining longer cold may condense and absorb more moisture, and mark the air as having become more humid than it is in reality, and the contrary in a change from warm to cold.

But if such a suddenly changing instrument could be freed from these imperfections, yet when the design is to discover the different degrees of humidity in the air of different countries, I apprehend the quick sensibity of the instrument to be rather a disadvantage; since to draw the desired conclusions from it, a constant and frequent observation day and night in each country will be necessary for a year or years, and the mean of each different set of observations is to be found and determined. After all which some uncertainty will remain respecting the different degrees of exactitude with which different persons may have made and taken notes of their observations.

For these reasons, I apprehend that a substance which, though capable of being distended by moisture and contracted by dryness, is so slow in receiving and parting with its humidity, that the frequent changes in the atmosphere have not time to affect it sensibly, and which therefore should gradually take nearly the medium of all those changes and preserve it constantly, would be the most proper substance of which to make such an hygrometer.

Such an instrument, you, my dear sir, though without intending it, have made for me; and I, without desiring or expecting it, have received from you. It is therefore with propriety that I address to you the following account of it; and the more, as you have both a head to contrive and a hand to execute the means of perfecting it. And I do this with greater pleasure, as it affords me the opportunity of renewing that ancient correspondence and acquaintance with you, which to me was always so pleasing and so instructive.

You may possibly remember, that in or about the year 1758, you made for me a set of artificial magnets, six in number, each five and a half inches long, half an inch broad, and one eighth of an inch thick. These, with two pieces of soft iron, which together equalled one of the magnets, were inclosed in a little box of mahogany wood, the grain of which ran with, and not across, the length of the box: and the box was closed by a little shutter of the same wood, the grain of which ran across the box; and the ends of this shutting piece were bevelled so as to fit and slide in a kind of dove-tail groove when the box was to be shut or opened.

I had been of opinion, that good mahogany wood was not affected by moisture so as to change its dimensions, and that it was always to be found as the tools of the workman left it. Indeed the difference at different times in the same country is so small as to be scarcely in a common way observable. Hence the box, which was made so as to allow sufficient room for the magnets to slide out and in freely, and, when in, afforded them so much play that by shaking the box one could make them strike the opposite sides alternately, continued in the same state all the time I remained in England, which was four years, without any apparent alteration. I left England in August 1762, and arrived at Philadelphia in October the same year. In a few weeks after my arrival, being desirous of showing your magnets to a philosophical friend, I found them so tight in the box, that it was with difficulty I got them out; and constantly during the two years I remained there, viz. till November 1764, this difficulty of getting them out and in continued.

This little shutter too, as wood does not shrink lengthways of the grain, was found too long to enter its grooves, and, not being used, was mislaid and lost; and afterwards I had another made that fitted.

In December, 1764, I returned to England, and after some time I observed that my box was become full big enough for my magnets, and too wide for my new shutter; which was so much too short for its grooves, that it was apt to fall out; and to make it keep in I lengthened it by adding to each end a little coat of sealing-wax.

I continued in England more than ten years, and during all that time, after the first change, I perceived no alteration. The magnets had the same freedom in their box, and the little shutter continued with the added sealing-wax to fit its grooves, till some weeks after my second return to America.

As I could not imagine any other cause for this change of dimensions in the box, when in the different countries, I concluded, first generally that the air of England was moister than that of America. And this I supposed an effect of its being an island, where every wind that blew must necessarily pass over some sea before it arrived, and of course lick up some vapor. I afterwards indeed doubted whether it might be just only so far as related to the city of London, where I resided; because there are many causes of moisture in the city air, which do not exist to the same degree in the country; such as the brewers and dyers boiling caldrons, and the great number of pots and tea-kettles continually on the fire, sending forth abundance of vapor; and also the number of animals who by their breath continually increase it; to which may be added, that even the vast quantity of sea coals burnt there, do in kindling, discharge a great deal of moisture.

When I was in England the last time, you also made for me a little achromatic pocket telescope, the body was brass, and it had a round case (I think of thin wood) covered with shagreen. All the while I remained in England, though possibly there might be some small changes in the dimensions of this case, I neither perceived nor suspected any. There was always comfortable room for the telescope to slip in and out. But soon after I arrived in America, which was in May 1775, the case became too small for the instrument, it was with much difficulty and various contrivances that I got it out, and I could never after get it in again, during my stay there, which was eighteen months. I brought it with me to Europe, but left the case as useless, imagining I should find the continental air of France as dry as that of Pennsylvania, where my magnet box had also returned a second time to its narrowness, and pinched the pieces, as heretofore, obliging me too, to scrape the sealing-wax off the ends of the shutter.

I had not been long in France, before I was surprised to find, that my box was become as large as it had always been in England, the magnets entered and came out with the same freedom, and when in, I could rattle them against its sides ; this has continued to be the case without sensible variation. My habitation is out of Paris distant almost a league, so that the moist air of the city cannot be supposed to have much effect upon the box. I am on a high dry hill, in a free air, as likely to be dry as any air in France. Whence it seems probable that the air of England in general may, as well as that of London, be moister than the air of America, since that of France is so, and in a part so distant from the sea.

The greater dryness of the air in America appears from some other observations. The cabinet work formerly sent us from London, which consisted in thin plates of fine wood glued upon fir, never would stand with us ; the veneering, as those plates are called, would get loose and come off ; both woods shrinking, and their grains often crossing, they were for ever cracking and flying. And in my electrical experiments there, it was remarkable, that a mahogany table, on which my jars stood under the prime conductor to be charged, would often be so dry, particularly when the wind had been some time at north-west, which with us is a very drying wind, as to isolate the jars, and prevent their being charged till I had formed a communication between their coatings and the earth. I had a like table in London, which I used for the same purpose all the while I resided there ; but it was never so dry as to refuse conducting the electricity.

Now what I would beg leave to recommend to you, is, that you would recollect, if you can, the species of mahogany of which you made my box, for you know there is a good deal of difference in woods that go under that name ; or if that cannot be, that you would take a number of pieces of the closest and finest grained mahogany that you can meet with, plane them to the thinness of about a line, and the width of about two inches across the grain, and fix each of the pieces in some instrument that you can contrive, which will permit them to contract and dilate, and will show, in sensible degrees, by a moveable hand upon a marked scale, the otherwise less sensible quantities of such contraction and dilation. If these instruments are all kept in the same place while making, and are graduated together while subject to the same degrees of moisture or dryness, I apprehend you will have so many comparable hygrometers, which, being sent into different countries, and continued there for some time, will find and show there the mean of the different dryness and moisture of the air of those countries, and that with much less trouble than by any hygrometer hitherto in use.

B. FRANKLIN.

TO DR. JOHN PRINGLE[7], LONDON.

On the Difference of Navigation in shoal and deep Water,

Craven-street, May 10, 1768.

SIR,

YOU may remember, that when we were travelling together in Holland, you remarked, that the trackschuyt in

---

7 Afterwards called sir John Pringle.

one of the stages went slower than usual, and enquired of
the boatman, what might be the reason; who answered, that
it had been a dry season, and the water in the canal was
low.   On being again asked if it was so low as that the boat
touched the muddy bottom; he said, no, not so low as that,
but so low as to make it harder for the horse to draw the
boat.   We neither of us at first could conceive that if there
was water enough for the boat to swim clear of the bottom,
its being deeper would make any difference; but as the man
affirmed it seriously, as a thing well known among them;
and as the punctuality required in their stages was likely to
make such difference, if any there were, more readily observed by them than by other watermen who did not pass
so regularly and constantly backwards and forwards in the
same track; I began to apprehend there might be something in it, and attempted to account for it from this consideration, that the boat in proceeding along the canal, must
in every boat's length of her course, move out of her way
a body of water, equal in bulk to the room her bottom took
up in the water; that the water so moved must pass on each
side of her and under her bottom to get behind her; that if
the passage under her bottom was straitened by the shal-
lows, more of that water must pass by her sides, and with
a swifter motion, which would retard her, as moving the
contrary way; or that the water becoming lower behind the
boat than before, she was pressed back by the weight of its
difference in height, and her motion retarded by having that
weight constantly to overcome.   But as it is often lost time
to attempt accounting for uncertain facts, I determined to
make an experiment of this when I should have convenient
time and opportunity.

   After our return to England, as often as I happened to be
on the Thames, I enquired of our watermen whether they
were sensible of any difference in rowing over shallow or
deep water.   I found them all agreeing in the fact, that
there was a very great difference, but they differed widely
in expressing the quantity of the difference; some supposing it was equal to a mile in six, others to a mile in

three, &c. As I did not recollect to have met with any mention of this matter in our philosophical books, and conceiving that if the difference should really be great, it might be an object of consideration in the many projects now on foot for digging new navigable canals in this island, I lately put my design of making the experiment in execution, in the following manner.

I provided a trough of plained boards fourteen feet long, six inches wide and six inches deep, in the clear, filled with water within half an inch of the edge, to represent a canal. I had a loose board of nearly the same length and breadth, that, being put into the water, might be sunk to any depth, and fixed by little wedges where I would chuse to have it stay, in order to make different depths of water, leaving the surface at the same height with regard to the sides of the trough. I had a little boat in form of a lighter or boat of burthen, six inches long, two inches and a quarter wide, and one inch and a quarter deep. When swimming, it drew one inch water. To give motion to the boat, I fixed one end of a long silk thread to its bow, just even with the water's edge, the other end passed over a well-made brass pully, of about an inch diameter, turning freely on a small axis ; and a shilling was the weight. Then placing the boat at one end of the trough, the weight would draw it through the water to the other.

Not having a watch that shows seconds, in order to measure the time taken up by the boat in passing from end to end, I counted as fast as I could count to ten repeatedly, keeping an account of the number of tens on my fingers. And as much as possible to correct any little inequalities in my counting, I repeated the experiment a number of times at each depth of water, that I might take the medium. And the following are the results.

	Water 1½ inches deep.	2 inches.	4½ inches,
1st exp.	100	94	79
2	104	93	78
3	104	91	77
4	106	87	79
5	100	88	79
6	99	86	80
7	100	90	79
8	100	88	81
	813	717	632

Medium 101   Medium 89   Medium 79

I made many other experiments, but the above are those in which I was most exact ; and they serve sufficiently to show that the difference is considerable. Between the deepest and shallowest it appears to be somewhat more than one fifth. So that supposing large canals and boats and depths of water to bear the same proportions, and that four men or horses would draw a boat in deep water four leagues in four hours, it would require five to draw the same boat in the same time as far in shallow water ; or four would require five hours.

Whether this difference is of consequence enough to justify a greater expence in deepening canals, is a matter of calculation, which our ingenious engineers in that way will readily determine.

         I am, &c.

             B. FRANKLIN.

TO ALPHONSUS LE ROY, AT PARIS.

Read in the American Philosophical Society, December 2, 1785.

Improvements in Navigation.

At Sea, on board the London Packet, Capt. Truxton.

            August 1785.

SIR,

YOUR learned writings on the navigation of the antients, which contain a great deal of curious information, and your

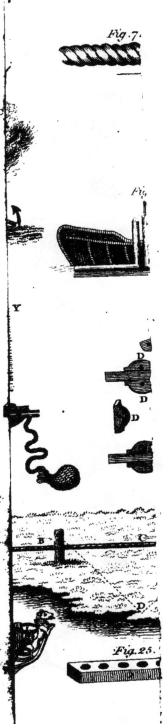

Fig. 7.

Fig.

Fig. 25.

very ingenious contrivances for improving the modern sails, *(voilure)* of which I saw with great pleasure a successful trial on the river Seine, have induced me to submit to your consideration and judgment, some thoughts I have had on the latter subject.

Those mathematicians, who have endeavored to improve the swiftness of vessels, by calculating to find the form of least resistance, seem to have considered a ship as a body moving through one fluid only, the water; and to have given little attention to the circumstances of her moving through another fluid, the air. It is true that when a vessel sails right before the wind, this circumstance is of no importance, because the wind goes with her; but in every deviation from that course, the resistance of the air is something, and becomes greater in proportion as that deviation increases. I wave at present the consideration of those different degrees of resistance given by the air to that part of the hull which is above water, and confine myself to that given to the sails; for their motion through the air is resisted by the air, as the motion of the hull through the water is resisted by the water, though with less force as the air is a lighter fluid. And to simplify the discussion as much as possible, I would state one situation only, to wit, that of the wind upon the beam, the ships course being directly across the wind: and I would suppose the sail set in an angle of 45 degrees with the keel, as in the following figure; in the Plate, Fig 1.

A B represents the body of the vessel, C D the position of the sail, EEE the direction of the wind, MM the line of motion. In observing this figure it will appear, that so much of the body of the vessel as is immersed in the water must, to go forward, remove out of its way what water it meets with between the pricked lines FF. And the sail, to go forward must move out of its way all the air its whole dimension meets with between the pricked lines CG and DG. Thus both the fluids give resistance to the motion, each in proportion to the quantity of matter contained in the dimensions to be removed. And though the air is vastly lighter than the water, and therefore more easily removed, yet the dimension being much greater its effect is very considerable.

It is true that in the case stated, the resistance given by the air between those lines to the motion of the sail is not apparent to the eye, because the greater force of the wind, which strikes it in the direction EEE, overpowers its effect and keeps the sail full in the curve a, a, a, a, a. But suppose the wind to cease, and the vessel in a calm to be impelled with the same swiftness by oars, the sail would then appear filled in the contrary curve b, b, b, b, b, when prudent men would immediately perceive, that the air resisted its motion, and would order it to be taken in.

Is there any possible means of diminishing this resistance, while the same quantity of sail is exposed to the action of the wind, and therefore the same force obtained from it? I think there is, and that it may be done by dividing the sail into a number of parts, and placing those parts in a line one behind the other; thus instead of one sail extending from C to D, figure 2, if four sails containing together the same quantity of canvas, where placed as in figure 3, each having one quarter of the dimensions of the great sail, and exposing a quarter of its surface to the wind, would give a quarter of its force; so that the whole force obtained from the wind would be the same, while the resistance from the air would be nearly reduced to the space between the pricked lines a b and c d, before the foremost sail.

It may perhaps be doubted whether the resistance from the air would be so diminished; since possibly each of the following small sails having also air before it, which must be removed, the resistance on the whole would be the same.

This is then a matter to be determined by experiment. I will mention one that I many years since made with success for another purpose; and I will propose another small one easily made. If that too succeeds, I should think it worth while to make a larger, though at some expense, on a river boat; and perhaps time, and the improvements experience will afford, may make it applicable with advantage to larger vessels.

Having near my kitchen chimney a round whole of eight inches diameter, through which was a constant steady current of air, increasing or diminishing only as the fire increased or diminished, I contrived to place my jack so as to receive the current; and taking off the flyers, I fixed in their stead on the same pivot a round tin plate of nearly the same diameter with the whole; and having cut it in radial lines almost to the centre, so as to have six equal vanes, I gave to each of them the obliquity of forty-five degrees. They moved round, without the weight, by the impression only of the current of air, but two slowly for the purpose of roasting. I suspected that the air struck by the back of each vane might possibly by its resistance retard the motion; and to try this, I cut each of them into two, and I placed the twelve, each having the same obliquity, in a line behind each other, when I perceived a great augmentation in its velocity, which encouraged me to divide them once more, and continuing the same obliquity, I placed the twenty four behind each other in a line, when the force of the wind being the same, and the surface of vane the same, they moved round with much greater rapidity, and perfectly answered my purpose.

The second experiment that I propose, is to take two playing cards of the same dimensions, and cut one of them transversely into eight equal pieces; then with a needle string them upon two threads one near each end, and place them so upon the threads that, when hung up, they may be one exactly over the other, at a distance equal to their breadth, each in a horizontal position; and let a small weight, such as a bird-shot, be hung under them, to make them fall in a straight line when let loose. Suspend also the whole card by threads from its four corners, and hang to it an equal weight, so as to draw it downwards when let fall, its whole breadth pressing against the air. Let those two bodies be attached, one of them to one end of a thread a yard long, the other to the other end. Extend a twine

under the cieling of a room, and put through it at thirty
inches distance two pins bent in the form of fish-hooks.
On these two hooks hang the two bodies, the thread that
connects them extending parallel to the twine, which thread
being cut, they must begin to fall at the same instant. If
they take equal time in falling to the floor, it is a proof
that the resistance of the air is in both cases equal. If the
whole card requires a longer time, it shews that the sum of
the resistances to the pieces of the cut card is not equal to
the resistance of the whole one[8].

This principle so far confirmed, I would proceed to make
a larger experiment, with a shallop, which I would rig in
this manner. Same plate Fig. 4.

A B is a long boom, from which are hoisted seven jibs,
a, b, c, d, e, f, g, each a seventh part of the whole dimensions, and as much more as will fill the whole space when
set in an angle of forty-five degrees, so that they may lap
when going before the wind, and hold more when going
large. Thus rigged, when going right before the wind, the
boom should be brought at right angles with the keel, by
means of the sheet ropes C D, and all the sails hauled flat
to the boom.

These positions of boom and sails to be varied as the wind
quarters. But when the wind is on the beam, or when you
would turn to windward, the boom is to be hauled right fore
and aft, and the sails trimmed according as the wind is
more or less against your course.

It seems to me that the management of a shallop so rigged would be very easy, the sails being run up and down
separately, so that more or less sail may be made at pleasure; and I imagine, that there being full as much sail exposed to the force of the wind which impels the vessel in
its course, as if the whole were in one piece, and the resistance of the dead air against the foreside of the sail being
diminished, the advantage of swiftness would be very con-

8 The motion of the vessel made it inconvenient to try this simple experiment at sea, when the proposal of it was written. But it has been tried since
we came on shore, and succeeded as the other.

siderable; besides that the vessel would lie nearer the wind.

Since we are on the subject of improvements in navigation, permit me to detain you a little longer with a small relative observation. Being, in one of my voyages, with ten merchant-ships under convoy of a frigate at anchor in Torbay, waiting for a wind to go to the westward; it came fair, but brought in with it a considerable swell. A signal was given for weighing, and we put to sea altogether; but three of the ships left their anchors, their cables parting just as their anchors came a-peak. Our cable held, and we got up our anchor; but the shocks the ship felt before the anchor got loose from the ground, made me reflect on what might possibly have caused the breaking of the other cables; and I imagined it might be the short bending of the cable just without the hause-hole, from a horizontal to an almost vertical position, and the sudden violent jerk it receives by the rising of the head of the ship on the swell of a wave while in that position. For example, suppose a vessel hove up so as to have her head nearly over her anchor, which still keeps its hold, perhaps in a tough bottom; if it were calm, the cable still out would form nearly a perpendicular line, measuring the distance between the hause-hole and the anchor; but if there is a swell, her head in the trough of the sea will fall below the level, and when lifted on the wave will be much above it. In the first case the cable will hang loose and bend perhaps as in figure 5. In the second case, figure 6, the cable will be drawn straight with a jerk, must sustain the whole force of the rising ship, and must either loosen the anchor, resist the rising force of the ship, or break. But why does it break at the hause-hole?

Let us suppose it a cable of three inches diameter, and represented by figure 7. If this cable is to be bent round the corner A, it is evident that either the part of the triangle contained between the letters a, b, c, must stretch considerably, and those most that are nearest the surface; or that the parts between d, e, f, must be compressed; or both, which most probably happens. In this case the lower

half of the thickness affords no strength against the jerk, it
not being strained, the upper half bears the whole, and the
yarns near the upper surface being first and most strained,
break first, and the next yarns follow ; for in this bent
situation they cannot bear the strain altogether, and each
contributes its strength to the whole, as they do when the
cable is strained in a straight line.

To remedy this, methinks it would be well to have a kind
of large pulley wheel, fixed in the hause-hole, suppose of
two feet diameter, over which the cable might pass ; and
being there bent gradually to the round of the wheel, would
thereby be more equally strained, and better able to bear
the jerk, which may save the anchor, and by that means in
the course of the voyage to save the ship.

One maritime observation more shall finish this letter. I
have been a reader of news-papers now near seventy years,
and I think few years pass without an account of some vessel met with at sea, with no living soul on board, and so
many feet of water in her hold, which vessel has nevertheless been saved and brought into port: and when not met
with at sea, such forsaken vessels have often come ashore
on some coast.   The crews, who have taken to their boats
and thus abandoned such vessels, are sometimes met with
and taken up at sea by other ships, sometimes reach a coast,
and are sometimes never heard of.   Those that give an account of quitting their vessels generally say, that she sprung
a leak, that they pumped for some time, that the water continued to rise upon them, and that, despairing to save her,
they had quitted her lest they should go down with her. It
seems by the event that this fear was not always well founded, and I have endeavored to guess at the reason of the
people's too hasty discouragement.

When a vessel springs a leak near her bottom, the water
enters with all the force given by the weight of the column
of water, without, which force is in proportion to the difference of level between the water without and that within.
It enters therefore with more force at first and in greater
quantity, than it can afterwards when the water within is

higher. The bottom of the vessel too is narrower, so that the same quantity of water coming into that narrow part, rises faster than when the space for it to flow is larger. This helps to terrify. But as the quantity entering is less and less as the surfaces without and within become more nearly equal in height, the pumps that could not keep the water from rising at first, might afterwards be able to prevent its rising higher, and the people might have remained on board in safety, without hazarding themselves in an open boat on the wide ocean. (Fig. 8.)

Besides the greater equality in the height of the two surfaces, there may sometimes be other causes that retard the farther sinking of a leaky vessel. The rising water within may arrive at quantities of light wooden work, empty chests, and particularly empty water-casks, which if fixed so as not to float themselves may help to sustain her. Many bodies which compose a ship's cargo may be specifically lighter than water, all these when out of water are an additional weight to that of the ship, and she is in proportion pressed deeper into the water; but as soon as these bodies are immersed, they weigh no longer on the ship, but on the contrary, if fixed, they help to support her, in proportion as they are specifically lighter than the water. And it should be remembered, that the largest body of a ship may be so balanced in the water, that an ounce less or more of weight may leave her at the surface or sink her to the bottom. There are also certain heavy cargoes, that, when the water gets at them, are continually dissolving, and thereby lightening the vessel, such as salt and sugar. And as to water-casks mentioned above, since the quantity of them must be great in ships of war where the number of men consume a great deal of water every day, if it had been made a constant rule to bung them up as fast as they were emptied, and to dispose the empty casks in proper situations, I am persuaded that many ships which have been sunk in engagements, or have gone down afterwards, might with the unhappy people have been saved; as well as many of those which in the last war foundered, and were never heard of. While on this topic of sinking, one cannot help recollecting the well known practice of the Chinese, to divide the hold of a great ship into a number of separate chambers by partitions tight caulked (of which you gave a model in your boat upon the Seine) so that if a leak should spring in one of them the others are not affected by it; and though that chamber should fill to a level with the sea, it would not be sufficient to sink the vessel. We have not imitated this practice. Some little disadvantage it might occasion in the stowage is perhaps one reason, though that I think might be more than compensated by an abatement in the insurance that would be reasonable, and by a higher price taken of passengers, who would rather prefer going in such a vessel. But our seafaring people are brave, despise danger, and reject such precautions of safety, being cowards only in one sense, that of *fearing* to be *thought afraid.*

I promised to finish my letter with the last observation, but the garrulity of the old man has got hold of me, and as I may never have another occasion of writing on this subject, I think I may as well now, once for all, empty my nautical budget, and give you all the thoughts that have in my various long voyages occurred to me relating to navigation. I am sure that in you they will meet a candid judge, who will excuse my mistakes on account of my good intention.

There are six accidents that may occasion the loss of ships at sea. We have considered one of them, that of foundering by a leak. The other five are, 1. Oversetting by sudden flaws of wind, or by carrying sail beyond the bearing. 2. Fire by accident or carelessness. 3. A heavy stroke of lightning, making a breach in the ship, or firing the powder. 4. Meeting and shocking with other ships in the night. 5. Meeting in the night with islands of ice.

To that of oversetting, privateers in their first cruize have, as far as has fallen within my knowlege or information, been more subject than any other kind of vessels. The double desire of being able to overtake a weaker flying enemy, or to escape when pursued by a stronger, has induced the owners to overmast their cruizers, and to spread too much canvas; and the great number of men, many of them not seamen, who being upon deck when a ship heels suddenly are huddled down to leeward, and increase by their weight the effect of the wind. This therefore should be more attended to and guarded against, especially as the advantage of lofty masts is problematical. For the upper sails have greater power to lay a vessel more on her side, which is not the most advantageous position for going swiftly through the water. And hence it is that vessels, which have lost their lofty masts, and been able to make little more sail afterwards than permitted the ship to sail upon an even keel, have made so much way, even under jury masts, as to surprise the mariners themselves. But there is besides, something in the modern form of our ships that seems as if calculated expressly to allow their oversetting more easily. The sides of a ship, instead of spreading out as they formerly did in the upper works, are of late years turned in, so as to make the body nearly round, and more resembling a cask. I do not know what the advantages of this construction are, except that such ships are not easily boarded. To me it seems a contrivance to have less room in a ship at nearly the same expence. For it is evident that the same timber and plank consumed in raising the sides from a to b, and from d to c, would have raised them from a to e, and from d to f, fig. 9. In this form all the spaces between e, a, b, and c, d, f, would have been gained, the deck would have been larger, the men would have had more room to act, and not have stood so thick in the way of the enemy's shot; and the vessel, the more she was laid down on her side, the more bearing she would meet with, and more effectual to support her, as being farther from the centre. Whereas in the present form, her ballast makes the chief part of her bearing, without which she would turn in the sea almost as easily as a barrel. More ballast by this means becomes necessary, and that sinking a vessel deeper in the water occasions more

resistance to her going through it.   The Bermudian sloops
still keep with advantage to the old spreading form.   The
islanders in the great Pacific ocean, though they have no
large ships, are the most expert boat-sailors in the world,
navigating that sea safely with their proas, which they prevent oversetting by various means.   Their sailing proas for
this purpose have outriggers, generally to windward, above
the water, on which, one or more men are placed, to move
occasionally further from or nearer to the vessel as the
wind freshens or slackens.   But some have their outriggers
to leeward, which, resting on the water, support the boat so
as to keep her upright when pressed down by the wind.
Their boats moved by oars or rather paddles, are for long
voyages, fixed two together by cross bars of wood that keep
them at some distance from each other, and so render their
oversetting next to impossible.   How far this may be practicable in larger vessels, we have not yet sufficient experience.   I know of but one trial made in Europe, which was
about one hundred years since, by Sir William Petty.   He
built a double vessel, to serve as a packet boat between England and Ireland.   Her model still exists in the museum of
the Royal Society, where I have seen it.   By the accounts
we have of her, she answered well the purpose of her construction, making several voyages; and though wrecked at
last by a storm, the misfortune did not appear owing to her
particular construction, since many other vessels of the common form were wrecked at the same time.   The advantage
of such a vessel is, that she needs no ballast, therefore swims
either lighter or will carry more goods; and that passengers
are not so much incommoded by her rolling: to which may
be added, that if she is to defend herself by her cannon,
they will probably have more effect, being kept more generally in a horizontal position, than those in common vessels.
I think, however, that it would be an improvement of that
model, to make the sides which are opposed to each other
perfectly parallel, though the other sides are formed as in
common thus, figure 10.

The building of a double ship would indeed be more expensive in proportion to her burthen; and that perhaps is sufficient to discourage the method.

The accident of fire is generally well guarded against by the prudent captain's strict orders against smoking between decks, or carrying a candle there out of a lanthorn. But there is one dangerous practice which frequent terrible accidents have not yet been sufficient to abolish; that of carrying store-spirits to sea in casks. Two large ships, the Serapis and the Duke of Athol, one an East-Indiamen, the other a frigate, have been burnt within these two last years, and many lives miserably destroyed, by drawing spirits out of a cask near a candle. It is high time to make it a general rule, that all the ship's store of spirits should be carried in bottles.

The misfortune by a stroke of lightning I have in my former writings endeavored to show a method of guarding against, by a chain and pointed rod, extending, when run up, from above the top of the mast to the sea. These instruments are now made and sold at a reasonable price by Nairne & Co. in London, and there are several instances of success attending the use of them. They are kept in a box, and may be ran up and fixed in about five minutes, on the apparent approach of a thunder gust.

Of the meeting and shocking with other ships in the night I have known two instances in voyages between London and America. In one both ships arrived though much damaged, each reporting their belief that the other must have gone to the bottom. In the other, only one got to port; the other was never afterwards heard of. These instances happened many years ago, when the commerce between Europe and America was not a tenth part of what it is at present, ships of course thinner scattered, and the chance of meeting proportionably less. It has long been the practice to keep a *look-out before* in the channel, but at sea it has been neglected. If it is not at present thought worth while to take that precaution, it will in time become of more consequence; since the number of ships at sea is

continually augmenting.   A drum frequently beat, or a bell
rung in a dark night, might help to prevent such accidents.

Islands of ice are frequently seen off the banks of Newfoundland, by ships going between North America and
Europe.   In the day time they are easily avoided, unless
in a very thick fog.   I remember two instances of ships
running against them in the night. . The first lost her bow-
sprit, but received little other damage.   The other struck
where the warmth of the sea had wasted the ice next to it
and a part hung over above.   This perhaps saved her, for
she was under great way ; but the upper part of the cliff
taking her fore-topmast, broke the shock, though it carried
away the mast.   She disengaged herself with some difficulty, and got safe into port ; but the accident shews the
possibility of other ships being wrecked and sunk by striking those vast masses of ice, of which I have seen one
that we judged to be seventy feet high above the water,
consequently eight times as much under water ; and it is
another reason for keeping a good *look-out before*, though
far from any coast that may threaten danger.

It is remarkable, that the people we consider as savages
have improved the art of sailing and rowing boats in several points beyond what we can pretend to.   We have no
sailing-boats equal to the flying proas of the South Seas, no
rowing or paddling-boat equal to that of the Greenlanders
for swiftness and safety.   The birch canoes of the North-
American Indians have also some advantageous properties.
They are so light that two men may carry one of them over
land, which is capable of carrying a dozen upon the water ;
and in heeling they are not so subject to take in water as
our boats, the sides of which are lowest in the middle
where it is most likely to enter, this being highest in that
part, as in figure 11.

The Chinese are an enlightened people, the most an-
tiently civilized of any existing, and their arts are antient,
a presumption in their favor : their method of rowing their
boats differs from ours, the oars being worked either two
a-stern as we scull, or on the sides with the same kind of

motion, being hung parallel to the keel on a rail, and always acting in the water, not perpendicular to the side as ours are, nor lifted out at every stroke, which is a loss of time, and the boat in the interval loses motion. They see our manner, and we theirs, but neither are disposed to learn of or copy the other.

To the several means of moving boats mentioned above, may be added the singular one lately exhibited at Javelle, on the Seine below Paris, where a clumsy boat was moved across that river in three minutes by rowing, not in the water, but in the air, that is, by whirling round a set of windmill vanes fixed to a horizontal axis, parallel to the keel, and placed at the head of the boat. The axis was bent into an elbow at the end, by the help of which it was turned by one man at a time. I saw the operation at a distance, The four vanes appeared to be about five feet long, and perhaps two and an half wide. The weather was calm. The labor appeared to be great for one man, as the two several times relieved each other. But the action upon the air by the oblique surfaces of the vanes must have been considerable, as the motion of the boat appeared tolerably quick going and returning; and she returned to the same place from whence she first set out, notwithstanding the current. This machine is since applied to the moving of air-balloons: an instrument similar may be contrived to move a boat by turning under water.

Several mechanical projectors have at different times proposed to give motion to boats, and even to ships, by means of circular rowing, or paddles placed on the circumference of wheels to be turned constantly on each side of the vessel; but this method, though frequently tried, has never been found so effectual as to encourage a continuance of the practice. I do not know that the reason has hitherto been given. Perhaps it may be this, that great part of the force employed contributes little to the motion. For instance, (fig. 12) of the four paddles a, b, c, d, all under water, and turning to move a boat from X to Y, c has the most power, be nearly though not quite as much, their motion being nearly horizontal; but the force employed in moving a, is consumed in pressing almost downright upon the water till it comes to the place of b; and the force employed in moving d is consumed in lifting the water till d arrives at the surface; by which means much of the labor is lost. It is true, that by placing the wheels higher out of the water, this waste labor will be diminished in a calm, but where a sea runs, the wheels must unavoidably be often dipt deep in the waves, and the turning of them thereby rendered very laborious to little purpose.

Among the various means of giving motion to a boat, that of M. Bernoulli appears one of the most singular, which was to have fixed in the boat a tube in the form of an L, the upright part to have a funnel-kind of opening at top, convenient for filling the tube with water; which, descending and passing through the lower horizontal part, and issuing in the middle of the stern, but under the surface of the river, should push the boat forward. There is no doubt that the force of the descending water would have a considerable effect, greater in proportion to the height from which it descended; but then it is to be considered, that every bucket full pumped or dipped up into the boat, from its side or through its bottom, must have its *vis inertiæ* overcome so as to receive the motion of the boat, before it can come to give motion by its descent; and that will be a deduction from the moving power. To remedy this, I would propose the addition of another such L pipe, and that they should stand back to back in the boat thus, figure 13, the forward one being worked as a pump, and sucking in the water at the head of the boat, would draw it forward while pushed in the same direction by the force at the stern. And after all it should be calculated whether the labor of pumping would be less than that of rowing. A fire-engine might possibly in some cases be applied in this operation with advantage.

Perhaps this labour of raising water might be spared, and the whole force of a man applied to the moving of a boat by the use of air instead of water; suppose the boat constructed in this form, figure 14. A, a tube round or square, of two feet diameter, in which a piston may move up and down. The piston to have valves in it, opening inwards, to admit air when the piston rises; and shutting, when it is forced down by means of the lever B turning on the centre C. The tube to have a valve D, to open when the piston is forced down, and let the air pass out at E, which striking forcibly against the water abaft must push the boat forward. If there is added an air-vessel F properly valved and placed, the force would continue to act while a fresh stroke is taken with the lever. The boat-man might stand with his back to the stern, and putting his hands behind him, work the motion by taking hold of the cross bar at B, while another should steer; or if he had two such pumps, one on each side of the stern, with a lever for each hand, he might steer himself by working occasionally more or harder with either hand, as watermen now do with a pair of sculls. There is no position in which the body of a man can exert more strength than in pulling right upwards. To obtain more swiftness, greasing the bottom of a vessel is sometimes used, and with good effect. I do not know that any writer has hitherto attempted to explain this. At first sight one would imagine, that though the friction of a hard body, sliding on another hard body, and the resistance occasioned by that friction, might be diminished by putting grease between them, yet that a body sliding on a fluid, such as water, should have no need of, nor receive any advantage from such greasing. But the fact is not disputed. And the reason perhaps may be this—The particles of water have a mutual attraction, called the attraction of adhesion. Water also adheres to wood, and to many other substances, but not to grease: on the contrary they have a mutual repulsion, so that it is a question whether when oil is poured on water, they ever actually touch each other; for a drop of oil upon water, instead of sticking to the spot where it falls, as it would if it fell on a looking-glass, spreads instantly to an immense distance in a film extremely thin, which it could not easily do if it touched and rubbed or adhered even in a small degree to the surface of the water. Now the adhesive force of water to itself, and to other substances, may be estimated from the weight of it necessary to separate a drop, which ádheres, while growing, till it has weight enough to force the separation and break the drop off. Let us suppose the drop to be the size of a pea, then there will be as many of these adhesions as there are drops of that size touching the bottom of a vessel, and these must be broken by the moving power, every step of her motion that amounts to a drop's breadth: and there being no such adhesions to break between the water and a greased bottom, may occasion the difference.

So much respecting the motion of vessels. But we have sometimes occasion to stop their motion; and if a bottom is near enough we can cast anchor: where there are no soundings, we have as yet no means to prevent driving in a storm, but by lying-to, which still permits driving at the rate of about two miles an hour; so that in a storm continuing fifty hours, which is not an uncommon case, the ship may drive one hundred miles out of her course; and should she in that distance meet with a lee shore, she may be lost.

To prevent this driving to leeward in deep water, a swimming anchor is wanting, which ought to have these properties.

1. It should have a surface so large as, being at the end of a hauser in the water, and placed perpendicularly, should hold so much of it, as to bring the ship's head to the wind, in which situation the wind has least power to drive her.

2. It should be able by its resistance to prevent the ship's receiving way.

3. It should be capable of being situated below the heave of the sea, but not below the undertow.

4. It should not take up much room in the ship.

5. It should be easily thrown out, and put into its proper situation.

6. It should be easy to take in again, and stow away.

An ingenious old mariner, whom I formerly knew, proposed, as a swimming anchor for a large ship, to have a stem of wood twenty-five feet long and four inches square, with four boards of 18, 16, 14 and 12, feet long, and one foot wide, the boards to have their substance thickened several inches in the middle by additional wood, and to have each a four inch square hole through its middle, to permit its being slipt on occasionally upon the stem, and at right angles with it; where all being placed and fixed at four feet distance from each other, it would have the appearance of the old mathematical instrument called a forestaff. This thrown into the sea, and held by a hauser veered out at some length, he conceived would bring a vessel up, and prevent her driving, and when taken in might be stowed away by separating the boards from the stem. Figure 15. Probably such a swimming anchor would have some good effect, but it is subject to this objection, that laying on the surface of the sea, it is liable to be hove forward by every wave, and thereby give so much leave for the ship to drive.

Two machines for this purpose have occurred to me, which, though not so simple as the above, I imagine would be more effectual, and more easily manageable. I will endeavour to describe them, that they may be submitted to your judgment, whether either would be serviceable; and if they would, to which we should give the preference.

The first is to be formed, and to be used in the water on almost the same principles with those of a paper kite used in the air. Only as the paper kite rises in the air, this is to descend in the water. Its dimensions will be different for ships of different size.

To make one of suppose fifteen feet high; take a small spar of that length for the back-bone, AB, figure 16, a a smaller of half that length C D, for the cross piece. Let these be united by a bolt at E, yet so as that by turning on the bolt they may be laid parallel to each other. Then make a sail of strong canvas, in the shape of figure 17. To form this, without waste of sail-cloth, sew together pieces of the proper length, and for half the breadth, as in figure 18, then cut the whole in the diagonal lines a, b, c, and turn the piece F so as to place its broad part opposite to that of the piece G, and the piece H in like manner opposite to I, which when all sewed together will appear as in fig. 17. This sail is to be extended on the cross of fig. 16, the top and bottom points well secured to the ends of the long spar; the two side points d, e, fastened to the ends of two cords, which coming from the angle of the loop (which must be similar to the loop of a kite) pass through two rings at the ends of the short spar, so as that on pulling upon the loop the sail will be drawn to its extent. The whole may, when aboard, be furled up, as in figure 19, having a rope from its broad end, to which is tied a bag of ballast for keeping that end downwards when in the water, and at the other end another rope with an empty keg at its end to float on the surface; this rope long enough to permit the kite's descending into the undertow, or if you please lower into still water. It should be held by a hauser. To get it home easily, a small loose rope may be veered out with it, fixed to the keg. Hauling on that rope will bring the kite home with small force, the resistance being small as it will then come end ways.

It seems probable that such a kite at the end of a long hauser would keep a ship with her head to the wind, and, resisting every tug, would prevent her driving so fast as when her side is exposed to it, and nothing to hold her back. If only half the driving is prevented, so as that she moves but fifty miles instead of the hundred during a storm, it may be some advantage, both in holding so much distance as is saved, and in keeping from a lee-shore. If single canvas should not be found strong enough to bear the tug without splitting, it may be doubled, or strengthened by a netting behind it, represented by figure 20.

The other machine for the same purpose, is to be made more in the form of am umbrella, as represented, figure 21. The stem of the umbrella a square spar of proper length, with four moveable arms, of which two are represented C, C. figure 22. These arms to be fixed in four joint cleats, as D, D, &c. one on each side of the spar, but so as that the four arms may open by turning on a pin in the joint. When open they form a cross, on which a four-square can‑ vas sail is to be extended, its corners fastened to the ends of the four arms. Those ends are also to be stayed by ropes fastened to the stem or spar, so as to keep them short of being at right angles with it: and to the end of one of the arms should be hung the small bag of ballast, and to the end of the opposite arm the empty keg. This, on being thrown into the sea, would immediately open; and when it had performed its function, and the storm over, a small rope from its other end being pulled on, would turn it, close it, and draw it easily home to the ship. This machine seems more simple in its operation, and more easily manageable than the first, and perhaps may be as effectual[8].

Vessels are sometimes retarded, and sometimes forward‑ ed in their voyages, by currents at sea, which are often not perceived. About the year 1769, or 70, there was an appli‑ cation made by the board of customs at Boston, to the lords of the treasury in London, complaining that the packets between Falmouth and New-York, were generally a fort‑ night longer in their passages, than merchant-ships from London to Rhode-Island, and proposing that for the future they should be ordered to Rhode-Island instead of New-York. Being then concerned in the management of the American post-office, I happened to be consulted on the occasion; and it appearing strange to me that there should be such a difference between two places, scarce a day's run asunder, especially when the merchant-ships are generally deeper laden, and more weakly manned than the packets, and had from London the whole length of the river and channel to run before they left the land of England, while the packets had only to go from Falmouth, I could not but think the fact misunderstood or misrepresented. There happened then to be in London a Nantucket sea-captain of my acquaint-

8 Captain Truxton, on board whose ship this was written, has executed this proposed machine; he has given six arms to the umbrella, they are joined to the stem by iron hinges, and the canvas is double. He has taken it with him to China. February, 1786.

ance, to whom I communicated the affair. He told me he believed the fact might be true; but the difference was owing to this, that the Rhode-Island captains were acquainted with the gulf-stream, which those of the English packets were not. We are well acquainted with that stream, says he, because in our pursuit of whales, which keep near the sides of it, but are not to be met with in it, we run down along the sides, and frequently cross it to change our side: and in crossing it have sometimes met and spoke with those packets, who were in the middle of it, and stemming it. We have informed them that they were stemming a current, that was against them to the value of three miles an hour; and advised them to cross it and get out of it; but they were too wise to be counselled by simple American fishermen. When the winds are but light, he added, they are carried back by the current more than they are forwarded by the wind : and if the wind be good, the subtraction of 70 miles a day from their course is of some importance. I then observed it was a pity no notice was taken of this current upon the charts, and requested him to mark it out for me, which he readily complied with, adding directions for avoiding it in sailing from Europe to North-America. I procured it to be engraved by order from the general post-office, on the old chart of the Atlantic, at Mount and Page's, Tower-hill; and copies were sent down to Falmouth for the captains of the packets, who slighted it however; but it is since printed in France, of which edition I hereto annex a copy.[9]

This stream is probably generated by the great accumulation of water on the eastern coast of America between the trophics, by the trade-winds which constantly blow there. It is known that a large piece of water ten miles broad and generally only three feet deep, has by a strong wind had its waters driven to one side and sustained so as to become six feet deep, while the windward side was laid dry. This may

9 The map for this edition has been constructed anew, so as to embrace in one view, the theory of the Gulph Stream and the theory of the migration of fish; some attention has been paid also to Volney's suggestions on the subject of the Gulph Stream. See the plate.

give some idea of the quantity heaped up on the American coast, and the reason of its running down in a strong current through the islands into the bay of Mexico, and from thence issuing through the Gulph of Florida, and proceeding along the coast to the banks of Newfoundland, where it turns off towards and runs down through the Western Islands. Having since crossed this stream several times in passing between America and Europe, I have been attentive to sundry circumstances relating to it, by which to know when one is in it; and besides the gulph weed with which it is interspersed, I find that it is always warmer than the sea on each side of it, and that it does not sparkle in the night: I annex hereto the observations made with the thermometer in two voyages, and possibly may add a third. It will appear from them, that the thermometer may be an useful instrument to a navigator, since currents coming from the northward into southern seas, will probably be found colder than the water of those seas, as the currents from southern seas into northern are found warmer. And it is not to be wondered that so vast a body of deep warm water, several leagues wide, coming from between the tropics and issuing out of the gulph into the northern seas, should retain its warmth longer than the twenty or thirty days required to its passing the banks of Newfoundland. The quantity is too great, and it is too deep to be suddenly cooled by passing under a cooler air. The air immediately over it, however, may receive so much warmth from it as to be rarefied and rise, being rendered lighter than the air on each side of the stream ; hence those airs must flow in to supply the place of the rising warm air, and, meeting with each other, form those tornadoes and water-spouts frequently met with, and seen near and over the stream ; and as the vapor from a cup of tea in a warm room, and the breath of an animal in the same room, are hardly visible, but become sensible immediately when out in the cold air, so the vapor from the gulph stream, in warm latitudes is scarcely visible, but when it comes into the cool air from Newfoundland, it is condensed into the fogs, for which those parts are so remarkable.

The power of wind to raise water above its common level in the sea is known to us in America, by the high tides occasioned in all our sea-ports when a strong north-easter blows against the gulph stream.

The conclusion from these remarks is, that a vessel from Europe to North America may shorten her passage by avoiding to stem the stream, in which the thermometer will be very useful; and a vessel from America to Europe may do the same by the same means of keeping in it. It may have often happened accidentally, that voyages have been shortened by these circumstances. It is well to have the command of them.

But may there not be another cause, independent of winds and currents, why passages are generally shorter from America to Europe than from Europe to America? This question I formerly considered in the following short paper.

On board the Pennsylvania Packet, Captain Osborne,

At Sea, April 5, 1775.

" SUPPOSE a ship to make a voyage eastward from a place in lat. 40° north, to a place in lat. 50° north, distance in longitude 75 degrees.

" In sailing from 40 to 50, she goes from a place where a degree of longitude is about eight miles greater than in the place she is going to. A degree is equal to four minutes of time; consequently the ship in the harbour she leaves, partaking of the diurnal motion of the earth, moves two miles in a minute faster, than when in the port she is going to; which is 120 miles in an hour.

" This motion in a ship and cargo is of great force; and if she could be lifted up suddenly from the harbor in which she lay quiet, and set down instantly in the latitude of the port she was bound to, though in a calm, that force contained in her would make her run a great way at a prodigious rate. This force must be lost gradually in her voyage, by gradual impulse against the water, and probably thence shorten the voyage.   Query, In returning does the contrary happen, and is her voyage thereby retarded and lengthened?[1] "

Would it not be a more secure method of planking ships, if, instead of thick single planks laid horizontally, we were to use planks of half the thickness, and lay them double and across, each other as in figure 23?   To me it seems that the difference of expence would not be considerable, and that the ship would be both tighter and stronger.

The securing of the ship is not the only necessary thing; securing the health of the sailors, a brave and valuable order of men, is likewise of great importance.   With this view the methods so successfully practised by captain Cook in his long voyages cannot be too closely studied or carefully imitated.   A full account of those methods is found in sir John Pringle's speech, when the medal of the Royal Society was given to that illustrious navigator.   I am glad to see in his last voyage that he found the means effectual which I had proposed for preserving flour, bread, &c. from moisture and damage.   They were found dry and good after being at sea four years.   The method is described in my printed works, page 452, fifth edition.   In the same, page 469, 470,[2] is proposed a means of allaying thirst in case of want of fresh water.   This has since been practised in two instances with success.   Happy if their hunger, when the other provisions are consumed, could be relieved as commodiously; and perhaps in time this may be found not impossible.   An addition might be made to their present vegetable provision, by drying various roots in slices by the means of an oven.   The sweet potatoe of America and Spain is excellent for this purpose.   Other potatoes, with carrots, parsnips, and turnips, might be prepared and preserved in the same manner.

1 Since this paper was read at the Society, an ingenious member, Mr. Patterson, has convinced the writer that the returning voyage would not, from this cause, be retarded.

2 See the Paper referred to in this volume, page 315.

With regard to make-shifts in cases of necessity, sea-men are generally very ingenious themselves. They will excuse however the mention of two or three. If they happen in any circumstance, such as after ship-wreck, taking to their boat, or the like, to want a compass, a fine sewing-needle laid on clear water in a cup will generally point to the north, most of them being a little magnetical, or may be made so by being strongly rubbed or hammered, lying in a north and south direction. If their needle is too heavy to float by itself, it may be supported by little pieces of cork or wood. A man who can swim, may be aided in a long traverse by his handkerchief formed into a kite, by two cross sticks extending to the four corners; which, being raised in the air when the wind is fair and fresh, will tow him along while lying on his back. Where force is wanted to move a heavy body, and there are but few hands and no machines, a long and strong rope may make a powerful in-strument. Suppose a boat is to be drawn up on a beach, that she may be out of the surf; a stake drove into the beach where you would have the boat drawn, and another to fasten the end of the rope to, which comes from the boat, and then applying what force you have to pull upon the middle of the rope at right angles with it, the power will be augmented in proportion to the length of rope be-tween the posts. The rope being fasted to the stake A, and drawn upon in the direction C D, will slide over the stake B; and when the rope is bent to the angle A D B, represented by the pricked line in figure 24, the boat will be at B.

Some sailors may think the writer has given himself un-necessary trouble in pretending to advise them; for they have a little repugnance to the advice of landmen, whom they esteem ignorant and incapable of giving any worth no-tice; though it is certain that most of their instruments were the invention of landmen. At least the first vessel ever made to go on the water was certainly such. I will therefore add only a few words more, and they shall be addressed to passengers.

When you intend a long voyage, you may do well to keep your intention as much as possible a secret, or at least the time of your departure; otherwise you will be continually interrupted in your preparations by the visits of friends and acquaintance, who will not only rob you of the time you want, but put things out of your mind, so that when you come to sea, you have the mortification to recollect points of business that ought to have been done, accounts you intended to settle, and conveniencies you had proposed to bring with you, &c. all which have been omitted through the effect of these officious friendly visits. Would it not be well if this custom could be changed; if the voyager after having, without interruption, made all his preparations, should use some of the time he has left, in going himself, to take leave of his friends at their own houses, and let them come to congratulate him on his happy return.

It is not always in your power to make a choice in your captain, though much of your comfort in the passage may depend on his personal character, as you must for so long a time be confined to his company, and under his direction; if he is a sensible, sociable, good natured, obliging man, you will be so much the happier. Such there are; but if he happens to be otherwise, and is only skilful, careful, watchful, and active in the conduct of his ship, excuse the rest, for these are the essentials.

Whatever right you may have by agreement in the mass of stores laid in by him for the passengers, it is good to have some particular things in your own possession, so as to be always at your own command.

1. Good water, that of the ship being often bad. You can be sure of having it good only by bottling it from a clear spring or well and in clean bottles. 2. Good tea. 3. Coffee ground. 4. Chocolate. 5. Wine of the sort you particularly like, and cyder. 6. Raisins. 7. Almonds. 8. Sugar. 9. Capillaire. 10. Lemons. 11. Jamaica spirits. 12. Eggs greased. 13. Diet bread. 14. Portable soup. 15. Rusks. As to fowls, it is not worth while to have any called yours, unless you could have the feeding and mana

ging of them according to your own judgment under your own eye. As they are generally treated at present in ships, they are for the most part sick, and their flesh tough and hard as whit-leather. All seamen have an opinion, broached I supposed at first prudently, for saving of water when short, that fouls do not know when they have drank enough, and will kill themselves if you give them too much, so they are served with a little only once in two days. This poured into troughs that lie sloping, and therefore immediately runs down to the lower end. There the fowls ride upon one another's backs to get at it, and some are not happy enough to reach and once dip their bills in it. Thus tantalized, and tormented with thirst, they cannot digest their dry food, they fret, pine, sicken, and die. Some are found dead, and thrown overboard every morning, and those killed for the table are not eatable. Their troughs should be in little divisions, like cups, to hold the water seperately, figure 25. But this is never done. The sheep and hogs are therefore your best dependence for fresh meat at sea, the mutton being generally tolerable and the pork excellent.

It is possible your captain may have provided so well in the general stores, as to render some of the particulars above recommended of little or no use to you. But there are frequently in the ship poorer passengers, who are taken at a lower price, lodge in the steerage, and have no claim to any of the cabin provisions, or to any but those kinds that are allowed the sailors. These people are sometimes dejected, sometimes sick, there may be women and children among them. In a situation where there is no going to market, to purchase such necessaries, a few of these your superfluities distributed occasionally may be of great service, restore health, save life, make the miserable happy, and thereby afford you infinite pleasure.

The worst thing in ordinary merchant ships is the cookery. They have no professed cook, and the worst hand as a seaman is appointed to that office, in which he is not only very ignorant but very dirty. The sailors have therefore a saying, that *God sends meat and the devil cooks*. Passengers more piously disposed, and willing to believe heaven orders all things for the best, may suppose, that, knowing the sea-air and constant exercise by the motion of the vessel would give us extraordinary appetites, bad cooks were kindly sent to prevent our eating too much ; or that, foreseeing we should have bad cooks, good appetites were furnished to prevent our starving. If you cannot trust to these circumstances, a spirit-lamp, with a blaze-pan, may enable you to cook some little things for yourself ; such as a hash, a soup, &c. And it might be well also to have among your stores some potted meats, which if well put up will keep long good. A small tin oven, to place with the open side before the fire, may be another good utensil in which your own servant may roast for you a bit of pork or mutton. You will sometimes be induced to eat of the ship's salt beef, as it is often good. You will find cyder the best quencher of that thirst which salt meat or fish occasions. The ship biscuit is too hard for some sets of teeth. It may be softened by toasting. But rusk is better ; for being made of good fermented bread, sliced and baked a second time, the pieces imbibe the water easily, soften immediately, digest more kindly, and are therefore more wholesome than the unfermented biscuit. By the way, rusk is the true original biscuit, so prepared to keep for sea, *biscuit* in French signifying twice baked. If your dry peas boil hard, a two-pound iron shot put with them into the pot, will by the motion of the ship grind them as fine as mustard.

The accidents I have seen at sea with large dishes of soup upon a table, from the motion of the ship, have made me wish, that our potters or pewterers would make soup-dishes in divisions, like a set of small bowls united together, each containing about sufficient for one person, in some such form as fig. 26 ; for then when the ship should make a sudden heel, the soup would not in a body flow over one side, and fall into people's laps and scald them, as is sometimes the case, but would be retained in the separate divisions, as in figure 27.

After these trifles, permit the addition of a few general reflections. Navigation, when employed in supplying necessary provisions to a country in want, and thereby preventing famines, which were more frequent and destructive before the invention of that art, is undoubtedly a blessing to mankind. When employed merely in transporting superfluities, it is a question whether the advantage of the employment it affords is equal to the mischief of hazarding so many lives on the ocean. But when employed in pillaging merchants and transporting slaves, it is clearly the means of augmenting the mass of human misery. It is amazing to think of the ships and lives risked in fetching tea from China, coffee from Arabia, sugar and tobacco from America, all which our ancestors did well without. Sugar employs near one thousand ships, tobacco almost as many. For the utility of tobacco there is little to be said; and for that of sugar, how much more commendable would it be if we could give up the few minutes gratification afforded once or twice a day by the taste of sugar in our tea, rather than encourage the cruelties exercised in producing it. An eminent French moralist says, that when he considers the wars we excite in Africa to obtain slaves, the numbers necessarily slain in those wars, the many prisoners who perish at sea by sickness, bad provisions, foul air, &c. in the transportation, and how many afterwards die from the hardships of slavery, he cannot look on a piece of sugar without conceiving it stained with spots of human blood! had he added the consideration of the wars we make to take and retake the sugar islands from one another, and the fleets and armies that perish in those expeditions, he might have seen his sugar not merely spotted, but throughly dyed scarlet in grain. It is these wars that make the maritime powers of Europe, the inhabitants of London and Paris, pay dearer for sugar than those of Vienna, a thousand miles from the sea; because their sugar costs not only the price they pay for it by the pound, but all they pay in taxes to maintain the fleets and armies that fight for it.

With great esteem, I am, Sir,

Your most obedient humble servant,

B. FRANKLIN.

ON THE GULPH STREAM.

Remarks upon the Navigation from Newfoundland to New York, in order to avoid the Gulph Stream on one hand, and on the other the Shoals that lie to the Southward of Nantucket and of St. George's Banks.

AFTER you have passed the banks of Newfoundland in about the 44th degree of latitude, you will meet with nothing, till you draw near the Isle of Sables, which we commonly pass in latitude 43. Southward of this isle, the current is found to extend itself as far north as 41° 20′ or 30′, then it turns towards the E. S. E. or S. E. ¼ E.

Having passed the Isle of Sables, shape your course for the St. George's Banks, so as to pass them in about latitude 40°, because the current southward of those banks reaches as far north as 39°. The shoals of those banks lie in 41° 35′.

After having passed St. George's Banks, you must, to clear Nantucket, form your course so as to pass between the latitudes 38° 30′ and 40° 45′.

The most southern part of the shoals of Nantucket lie in about 40° 45′. The northern part of the current, directly to the south of Nantucket, is felt in about latitude 38° 30′.

By observing these directions and keeping between the stream and the shoals, the passage from the Banks of Newfoundland to New York, Delaware, or Virginia, may be considerably shortened; for so you will have the advantage of the eddy current, which moves contrary to the Gulph Stream. Whereas if to avoid the shoals you keep too far to the southward, and get into that stream, you will be retarded by it at the rate of 60 or 70 miles a day,

The Nantucket whale-men being extremely well acquaint-ed with the Gulph Stream, its course, strength, and extent, by their constant practice of whaling on the edges of it, from their island quite down to the Bahamas, this draft of that stream was obtained from one of them, captain Folger, and caused to be engraved on the old chart in London, for the benefit of navigators, by

B. FRANKLIN.

Note, The Nantucket captains who are acquainted with this stream, make their voyages from England to Boston in as short a time generally as others take in going from Boston to England, viz. from twenty to thirty days.

A stranger may know when he is in the Gulph Stream, by the warmth of the water, which is much greater than that of the water on each side of it. If then he is bound to the westward, he should cross the stream to get out of it as soon as possible.

B. FRANKLIN.

Observations *of the* Warmth *of the* Sea-water, *&c. by Fahrenheit's* Thermometer, *in crossing the* Gulph Stream; *with other* Remarks *made on board the* Pennsylvania Packet, *Capt. Osborne, bound from London to Philadelphia, in April and May, 1775.*

Date	Hour	Temp. of Air.	Temp. of Wat.	Wind.	Course.	Distance.	Latitude N.	Longitude W.	Remarks.
April 10			62						
11			61						
12			64						
13			65						
14		60	65						
26		60	70						
27	8 A.M.	70	70	S S E	W b S	34	37° 39	60° 38	Much gulph weed; saw a whale.
28	6 P.M.	67	64	S W	W N W	44	37 13	62 29	Color of water changed.
—	8 A.M.	63	60	N E	W	57	37 48	64 35	No gulph weed.
29	5 P.M.	65	71	N E		69			Sounded, no bottom.
—	11 dit.	66	72	N W b N	W b S	24	37 26	66 0	Much light in the water last night.
—	8 A.M.	64	66	N E	W b N	43			Water again of the usual deep sea color, little or no light in it at night.
30	12	62	70		E b S	25			
—	6 P.M.	64	72	E S E	W b N	60	37 20	68 53	Frequent gulph weed, water continues of sea color, little light.
—	10 dit.	65	65	S		44			Much light.
—	7 A.M.	68	63	S S W	W N W	21	38 13	72 23	Much light all last night.
May 1	12	65	56		W b N	31			Color of water changed.
—	4 P.M.	64	56	S W	W N W	18			
—	10 dit.	64	57			18			
—	8 A.M.	62	53	W S W	N W	15	38 43	74 3	Much light.
2	12	60	53		W S W	10			Much light. Thunder-gust.
—	6 P.M.	64	55	N W	W b N	30			
—	10	65	55						
3	7 A.M.	62	54	N b W			38 30	75 0	

OBSERVATIONS *of the Warmth of the* SEA-WATER, &c. *by Fahrenheit's Thermometer; with other Remarks made on board the Reprisal, Capt. Wycks, bound from Philadelphia to France, in October and November,* 1776.

Date.	Hour A.M.	Hour P.M.	Temp. of Air.	Temp. of Water.	Wind.	Course.	Distance	Lat. N.	Long. W.	Remarks.
Oct. 31	10		76	70	SSE	E b S	135	38 12	70 30	Left the capes Thursday night, October 29, 1776.
Nov. 1	10	4		71	WSW	E ½ N	109	No ob.	68 12	
	8		71	78						
2	12			81	N		141	ditto.	65 23	
	8	4	67	75		ESE ½ E				Some sparks in the water these two last nights.
3	12			78	NW	E b S	160	37 0	62 7	
	9	4	70	76		N b E				
4		1	68	76			194	36 26	58 8	
		4		76		N E				
5	8	8	68	76			163	35 21	55 3	Ditto.
	12			76						
6	8	4	68	76	E b N	S 50 E	75	35 33	53 52	
	12	8	70	78						
7	8			76	SEbE	N30W	108	36 6	52 46	Ditto.
	12			75						
8	9			75	SbE	N 49 E	175	38 2	50 1	
	12	4	75	76						
9	9			77	SW	N 33 E	175	39 39	46 55	
	12	4	75	70						

OBSERVATIONS MADE ON BOARD THE REPRISAL, CONTINUED.

Date.	Hour A.M.	Hour P.M.	Temp. of Air.	Temp. of Water.	Wind.	Course.	Distance.	Latit. N.	Long. W.	Remarks.
Novem. 9	8	4	70	71	E	N 17 E	64	40 39	46 27	
10	12			68						
—	8			64						
11	12		56	63	S E	N 8 E	41	41 19	46 19	
—	8			61						
12	all			59	N N W	N 80 E	120	41 39	43 42	
—		day		69	E	S 82 E	69	41 29	42 10	
13	8		70	68	E S E	N 74 E	111	42 0	39 57	
14		Noon		70						
—		4		72						
15	8		61	71	W S W	N 70 E	186	43 3	35 51	
—		Noon		69						
16		4	65	68	S W	N 67 W	48	43 22	34 50	
—		Noon		67						
17		4		67	E S E	N 19 E	56	44 15	34 25	Some gulph weed.
18	8	all		63	S b W	N 75 E	210	45 6	29 43	
19	all	day		63	S W	N 80 E	238	45 46	24 2	
20		Noon	65	65	N	N 80 E	155	45 19	20 30	
—	8			64						
21		4		62	S	N 88 E	94	45 22	18 17	
22	9		60	60	S S W	S 89 E	133	45 19	15 19	
23	10	Noon		63	W S W	S 86 E	194	45 6	10 35	
24		do.		62	N N E	N 78 E	191	45 46	6 10	
25		do.		61	N E	S 76 E	125	45 4	3 23	Soundings off Bellisle.
26		do.	56	60	E	N 73 E	31	45 13	2 20	
27		do.	54	58						
28		do.		56						

A Journal of a Voyage from the Channel between France and England towards America.

Dates.		Latit. N.	Long. W.	Therm. A. M.		Therm. P. M.		Winds.	Course.	Distance.	Variation of the Needle.	Therm. Noon.	
				Air.	Water.	Air.	Water.					A.	W.
July	29			62	57			These are taken on an					
	30			62	58	63	58	average of 24 hours.					
	31			60	58	62	62			Miles.	West.		
August	1	49 15	4 15	63	62	60	64	East	S W½W	60	22° 0		
	2	48 28	8 58	64	64	64	63	E S E	W b S½S	174			
	3	47 0	12 13	60	67	omit	ted	N E	S W b W	160			
	4	45 0	15 43	66	66	do	66	N W b W	S W½W	190			
	5	43 5	17 25	67	65	65	68	N E	S W b S	131	20 0		
	6	41 3	19 44	70	68	71	69	N E	S W½S	166	16 30		
	7	38 45	21 34	70	70	68	70	N E	S S W¾W	165	11 30		
	8	36 42	23 10	72	71	73	72	N E	S S W¾W	149	11 15		
	9	35 40	25 40	73	73	73	74	N E	W S W¼S	137			
	10	35 0	27 0	71	73	77	75	N W	W S W¾S	76			
	11	33 51	28 42	74	74	76	77	North	S W¾W	112			
	12	33 30	31 30	76	75	76	76	North	W¾S	143			
	13	33 17	33 32	76	76	78	77	N E	W½S	103		77	78
	14	33 22	34 31	76	76	81	79	S S E	W½N	50		81	79
	15	33 45	35 0	78	79	79	78	W N W	S W¼W	35		79	79
	16	34 14	35 30	79	78	81	80	West	N W½N	38		81	80
	17	35 37	36 4	80	79	80	78	W S W	N N W	75		80	78
	18	36 7	37 16	80	78	omit	ted	N W b W	W N W½N	65		80	79
	19	36 38	38 0	78	77	78	77	W S W	N W½W	49		79	77

Journal of a Voyage, &c. continued.

Dates.	Latit. N.		Long. W.		Therm. A. M.		Therm. P. M.		Winds.	Course.	Distance.	Variation of the Needle.	Therm. Noon.	
					Air.	Water.	Air.	Water.					..	W.
August 20	37	38	38	6	78	76	omitted		West	N¼W	62		77	75
21	36	15	38	26	73	74	78	76	W N W	S b W	82		77	75
22	35	40	38	44	77	76	80	77	W b S	S S W	38		80	77
23	35	35	40	52	79	77	78	75	North	W¼S	100		omitted	
24	35	12	41	31	75	73	75	74	W N W	S W b W	41		75	74
25	35	40	42	33	79	76	79	76	W b N	W. N W¼N	60		80	76
26	35	30	42	44	79	76	80	76	S W b W	S W½S	14		80	76
27	35	14	43	23	79	77	81	79	West	W S W¼S	38		81	78
28	34	23	44	0	78	76	78	78	N N E	S W. b S	60		78	78
29	34	12	45	52	77	78	78	78	N E	W¼S	94	8 0	79	78
30	34	5	48	31	78	78	78	78	East	W½S	154		78	78
31	34	20	51	4	80	79	81	79	East	W¼S	129		80	80
Septem. 1	34	20	52	47	81	78	omitted		S S W	W¼N	86		83	80
2	34	55	55	12	81	80	83	80	S W	W b N½W	125		83	80
3	35	30	57	24	83	80	83	80	S W b S	W. b N½N	114	6 0	84	81
4	35	50	59	1	82	80	83	80	S.W ½W	W b N¼N	82		83	81
5	35	55	61	0	81	80	82	81	S S W	W¼N	96		82	81
6	36	20	62	30	80	81	79	80	N W b N	W b N	75		78	80
7	34	50	63	10	87	80	78	81	N W b N	S S W	86		78	81
8	34	45	64	40	75	79	75	79	North	W¼S	74		75	79
9	35	43	66	42	75	79	77	73	N E	W N W	108		78	80
10	37	30	68	40	77	73	77	70	E N E	N W	126		78	72

N. B. Longitude is reckoned from London, and the Thermometer is according to Fahrenheit.

OBSERVATIONS.

July 31. At one P. M. the Start bore W N W. distant six leagues.

August 1. The water appears luminous in the ship's wake.

—2 The temperature of the water is taken at eight in the morning and at eight in the evening.

—6. The water appears less luminous.

—7. Formegas S W. dist. 32½ deg. St. Mary's S W¾S. 33 leagues.

—8. From this date the temperature of the water is taken at eight in the morning and at six in the evening.

—10. Moonlight, which prevents the luminous appearance of the water.

—11. A strong southerly current.

—12. Ditto. From this date the temperature of the air and water was taken at noon, as well as morning and evening.

—16. Northerly current.

—19. First saw gulph weed.

—21. Southerly current.

—22. Again saw gulph weed.

—24. The water appeared luminous in a small degree before the moon rose.

—29. No moon, yet very little light in the water.

—30. Much gulph weed to-day.

—31. Ditto.

Sept. 1. Ditto.

—2. A little more light in the water.

—4. No gulph weed to-day. More light in the water.

—5. Some gulph weed again.

—6. Little light in the water. A very hard thunder-gust in the night.

—7. Little gulph weed.

—8. More light in the water. Little gulph weed.

—9. Little gulph weed. Little light in the water last evening.

—10. Saw some beds of rock-weed ; and we were surprised to observe the water six degrees colder by the thermometer than the preceding noon.

This day (10th) the thermometer still kept descending, and at five in the morning of the 11th, it was in water as low as 70, when we struck soundings. The same evening the pilot came on board, and we found our ship about five degrees of longitude a-head of the reckoning, which our captain accounted for by supposing our course to have been near the edge of the gulph stream, and thus an eddy-current always in our favor. By the distance we ran from Sept. 9, in the evening, till we struck soundings, we must have then been at the western edge of the gulph stream; and the change in the temperature of the water was probably owing to our suddenly passing from that current, into the waters of our own climate.

On the 14th of August the following experiment was made. The weather being perfectly calm, an empty bottle, corked very tight, was sent down 20 fathoms, and it was drawn up still empty. It was then sent down again 35 fathoms, when the weight of the water having forced in the cork, it was drawn up full; the water it contained was immediately tried by the thermometer, and found to be 70, which was six degrees colder than at the surface: the lead and bottle were visible, but not very distinctly so, at the depth of 12 fathoms, but when only 7 fathoms deep they were perfectly seen from the ship. This experiment was thus repeated Sept. 11, when we were in soundings of 18 fathoms. A keg was previously prepared with a valve at each end, one opening inward, the other outward; this was sent to the bottom in expectation that by the valves being both open when going down, and both shut when coming up, it would keep within it the water received at bottom. The upper valve performed its office well, but the under one did not shut quite close, so that much of the water was lost in hauling it up the ship's side. As the water in the keg's passage upwards could not enter at the top, it was concluded that what water remained in it was of that near the ground, and on trying this by the thermometer, it was found to be at 58, which was 12 degrees colder than at the surface.

This last Journal was obligingly kept for me by Mr J. Williams, my fellow-passenger in the London Packet, who made all the experiments with great exactness. [The present colonel Williams of the Engineers.]

The chart given in this edition, has been constructed with a view to give a more comprehensive idea of the course of the Gulph Stream. Volney very plausibly suggests, that the earth deposited by the Gulph Stream S. E. of Newfoundland, has formed the great banks; and that the accumulation there has given the stream a new or more eastwardly direction. This chart also serves to illustrate the long received ideas of the progress of the shoals of fish. May not the glutinous matter seen on the water, and which all persons who have been across the line must have noticed, be another cause of the phenomena of fish shoals. May they not come in search of the food, which the matter seen on the water in such abundance affords? The writer of this note has observed, that on entering the trade winds, the seamen have judged of the change of wind approaching by the direction of the bonetta and other fish, which pass in shoals in the South Atlantic and South-eastern Seas, in a direction opposite to the wind; and when not opposite to the prevailing wind, they conclude a change to be at hand from the direction towards which the fish go. The appearance of luminous floating matter at night is often followed by shoals of fish; the spawn or gluten which the writer has had taken up in a bucket, has been often found as large as two inches diameter, and frequently induced an opinion that it was a species of maritime *cocoon* or egg of an animal; fragments of irregular shaped gluten have been also often seen. An enquiry into the periodical appearance of these luminous substances on voyages to the southward, and remarks on the usual direction of the shoals of bonetta and other fish, might perhaps lead to very interesting discoveries, it might be assumed as a question worthy of examination, whether the direction of shoals of fish is not towards those points from which periodical winds or currents move the waters; and if the shoals of fish which move from the north poles, and by the British isles across the Atlantic, are not led by their instincts in search of these periodical supplies of food; and if the deposits made by the Gulph Stream on the banks of Newfoundland is not the true cause of the great abundance of fish found there.

TO OLIVER NEALE.

On the Art of Swimming.

DEAR SIR,

I CANNOT be of opinion with you that it is too late in
life for you to learn to swim.   The river near the bottom of
your garden affords a most convenient place for the purpose.
And as your new employment requires your being often on
the water, of which you have such a dread, I think you
would do well to make the trial; nothing being so likely to
remove those apprehensions as the consciousness of an
ability to swim to the shore, in case of an accident, or of
supporting yourself in the water till a boat could come to
take you up.

I do not know how far corks or bladders may be useful
in learning to swim, having never seen much trial of them.
Possibly they may be of service in supporting the body
while you are learning what is called the stroke, or that
manner of drawing in and striking out the hands and feet
that is necessary to produce progressive motion.   But you
will be no swimmer till you can place some confidence in
the power of the water to support you; I would therefore
advise the acquiring that confidence in the first place; especially as I have known several who, by a little of the practice necessary for that purpose, have insensibly acquired the
stroke, taught as it were by nature.

The practice I mean is this.   Chusing a place where the
water deepens gradually, walk coolly into into it till it is up
to your breast, then turn round, your face to the shore, and
throw an egg into the water between you and the shore.   It
will sink to the bottom, and be easily seen there, as your
water is clear.   It must lie in water so deep as that you
cannot reach it to take it up but by diving for it.   To encourage yourself in order to do this, reflect that your progress will be from deeper to shallower water, and that at any
time you may, by bringing your legs under you and stand-

ing on the bottom, raise your head far above the water. Then plunge under it with your eyes open, throwing yourself towards the egg, and endeavoring by the action of your hands and feet against the water to get forward till within reach of it. In this attempt you will find, that the water buoys you up against your inclination; that it is not so easy a thing to sink as you imagined; that you cannot but by active force get down to the egg. Thus you feel the power of the water to support you, and learn to confide in that power; while your endeavors to overcome it, and to reach the egg, teach you the manner of acting on the water with your feet and hands, which action is afterwards used in swimming to support your head higher above water, or to go forward through it.

I would the more earnestly press you to the trial of this method, because, though I think I satisfied you that your body is lighter than water, and that you might float in it a long time with your mouth free for breathing, if you would put yourself in a proper posture, and would be still and forbear struggling; yet till you have obtained this experimental confidence in the water, I cannot depend on your having the necessary presence of mind to recollect that posture and the directions I gave you relating to it. The surprise may put all out of your mind. For though we value ourselves on being reasonable knowing creatures, reason and knowlege seem on such occasions to be of little use to us; and the brutes to whom we allow scarce a glimmering of either, appear to have the advantage of us.

I will, however, take this opportunity of repeating those particulars to you, which I mentioned in our last conversation, as, by perusing them at your leisure, you may possibly imprint them so in your memory as on occasion to be of some use to you.

1. That though the legs, arms, and head, of a human body, being solid parts, are specifically something heavier than fresh water, yet the trunk, particularly the upper part, from its hollowness, is so much lighter than water, as that the whole of the body taken together is too light to sink

wholly under water, but some part will remain above, until the lungs become filled with water, which happens from drawing water into them instead of air, when a person in the fright attempts breathing while the mouth and nostrils are under water.

2. That the legs and arms are specifically lighter than salt water, and will be supported by it, so that a human body would not sink in salt-water, though the lungs were filled as above, but from the greater specific gravity of the head.

3. That therefore a person throwing himself on his back in salt water, and extending his arms, may easily lie so as to keep his mouth and nostrils free for breathing ; and by a small motion of his hands may prevent turning, if he should perceive any tendency to it.

4. That in fresh water, if a man throws himself on his back, near the surface, he cannot long continue in that situation but by proper action of his hands on the water. If he uses no such action, the legs and lower part of the body will gradually sink till he comes into an upright position, in which he will continue suspended, the hollow of the breast keeping the head uppermost.

5. But if, in this erect position, the head is kept upright above the shoulders, as when we stand on the ground, the immersion will, by the weight of that part of the head that is out of water, reach above the mouth and nostrils, perhaps a little above the eyes, so that a man cannot long remain suspended in water with his head in that position.

6. The body continuing suspended as before, and upright, if the head be leaned quite back, so that the face looks upwards, all the back part of the head being then under water, and its weight consequently in a great measure supported by it, the face will remain above water quite free for breathing, will rise an inch higher every inspiration, and sink as much every expiration, but never so low as that the water may come over the mouth.

7. If therefore a person unacquainted with swimming and falling accidentally into the water, could have presence of mind sufficient to avoid struggling and plunging, and to

lot the body take this natural position, he might continue long safe from drowning till perhaps help would come. For as to the clothes, their additional weight while immersed is very inconsiderable, the water supporting it, though, when he comes out of the water, he would find them very heavy indeed.

But, as I said before, I would not advise you or any one to depend on having this presence of mind on such an occasion, but learn fairly to swim; as I wish all men were taught to do in their youth; they would, on many occurrences, be the safer for having that skill, and on many more the happier, as freer from painful apprehensions of danger, to say nothing of the enjoyment in so delightful and wholesome an exercise. Soldiers particularly should, methinks, all be taught to swim; it might be of frequent use either in surprising an enemy, or saving themselves. And if I had now boys to educate, I should prefer those schools (other things being equal) where an opportunity was afforded for acquiring so advantageous an art, which once learned is never forgotten.

I am, Sir, &c.

B. FRANKLIN.

ON THE SAME SUBJECT.

In Answer to some Enquiries of M. Dubourg.[3]

... I AM apprehensive that I shall not be able to find leisure for making all the disquisitions and experiments which would be desirable on this subject. I must, therefore, content myself with a few remarks.

The specific gravity of some human bodies, in comparison to that of water, has been examined by Mr. Robinson, in the Philosophical Transactions, volume 50, page 30, for the year 1757. He asserts, that fat persons with small bones float most easily upon the water.

---

3 This and the four following extracts of letters to M. Dubourg, are re-translated from the French edition of Dr. Franklin's works.

The diving-bell is accurately described in the Transactions.

When I was a boy, I made two oval pallets, each about ten inches long, and six broad, with a hole for the thumb, in order to retain it fast in the palm of my hand. They much resembled a painter's pallets. In swimming I pushed the edges of these forward, and I struck the water with their flat surfaces as I drew them back. I remember I swam faster by means of these pallets, but they fatigued my wrists. I also fitted to the soles of my feet a kind of sandals; but I was not satisfied with them, because I observed that the stroke is partly given by the inside of the feet and the ancles, and not entirely with the soles of the feet.

We have here waistcoats for swimming, which are made of double sail-cloth, with small pieces of cork quilted in between them.

I know nothing of the *scaphandre* of M. de la Chapelle.

I know by experience, that it is a great comfort to a swimmer, who has a considerable distance to go, to turn himself sometimes on his back, and to vary in other respects the means of procuring a progressive motion.

When he is seized with the cramp in the leg, the method of driving it away is to give to the parts affected a sudden, vigorous and violent shock; which he may do in the air as he swims on his back.

During the great heats of summer there is no danger in bathing, however warm we may be, in rivers which have been thoroughly warmed by the sun. But to throw oneself into cold spring water, when the body has been heated by exercise in the sun, is an imprudence which may prove fatal. I once knew an instance of four young men, who, having worked at harvest in the heat of the day, with a view of refreshing themselves, plunged into a spring of cold water: two died upon the spot, a third the next morning, and the fourth recovered with great difficulty. A copious draught of cold water, in similar circumstances, is frequently attended with the same effect in North America.

The exercise of swimming is one of the most healthy and agreeable in the world. After having swam for an hour or two in the evening, one sleeps coolly the whole night, even during the most ardent heat of summer. Perhaps the pores being cleansed, the insensible perspiration increases and occasions this coolness. It is certain that much swimming is the means of stopping a diarrhœa, and even of producing a constipation. With respect to those who do not know how to swim, or who are affected with a diarrhœa at a season which does not permit them to use that exercise, a warm bath, by cleansing and purifying the skin, is found very salutary, and often effects a radical cure. I speak from my own experience, frequently repeated, and that of others to whom I have recommended this.

You will not be displeased if I conclude these hasty remarks by informing you, that as the ordinary method of swimming is reduced to the act of rowing with the arms and legs, and is consequently a laborious and fatiguing operation when the space of water to be crossed is considerable; there is a method in which a swimmer may pass to great distances with much facility, by means of a sail. This discovery I fortunately made by accident, and in the following manner.

When I was a boy I amused myself one day with flying a paper kite; and approaching the bank of a pond, which was near a mile broad, I tied the string to a stake, and the kite ascended to a very considerable height above the pond, while I was swimming. In a little time, being desirous of amusing myself with my kite, and enjoying at the same time the pleasure of swimming, I returned; and loosing from the stake the string with the little stick which was fastened to it, went again into the water, where I found, that, lying on my back and holding the stick in my hands, I was drawn along the surface of the water in a very agreeable manner. Having then engaged another boy to carry my clothes round the pond, to a place which I pointed out to him on the other side, I began to cross the pond with my kite, which carried me quite over without the least fatigue, and with the greatest pleasure imaginable. I was only obliged occasionally to

halt a little in my course, and resist its progress, when it appeared that, by following too quick, I lowered the kite too
much; by doing which occasionally I made it rise again.
I have never since that time practised this singular mode of
swimming though I think it not impossible to cross in this
manner from Dover to Calais.   The packet-boat, however,
is still preferable.

B. FRANKLIN.

TO M. DUBOURG.

On the free Use of Air.

London, July 28, 1760.

.......I GREATLY approve the epithet which you give,
in your letter of the 8th of June, to the new method of treat-
ing the small-pox, which you call the *tonic* or bracing method; I will take occasion, from it, to mention a practice to
which I have accustomed myself.   You know the cold bath
has long been in vogue here as a tonic; but the shock of the
cold water has always appeared to me, generally speaking,
as too violent, and I have found it much more agreeable to
my constitution to bathe in another element, I mean cold air.
With this view I rise almost every morning, and sit in my
chamber without any clothes whatever, half an hour or an
hour, according to the season, either reading or writing.
This practice is not in the least painful, but, on the contrary,
agreeable; and if I return to bed afterwards, before I dress
myself, as sometimes happens, I make a supplement to my
night's rest of one or two hours of the most pleasing sleep
that can be imagined.   I find no ill consequences whatever
resulting from it, and that at least it does not injure my
health, if it does not in fact contribute much to its preserva-
tion.   I shall therefore call it for the future a *bracing* or
tonic bath.

B. FRANKLIN.

On the Causes of Colds.

March 10, 1773.

........I shall not attempt to explain why damp clothes oc-casion colds, rather than wet ones, because I doubt the fact ; I imagine that neither the one nor the other contribute to this effect, and that the causes of colds are totally independ-ent of wet and even of cold. I propose writing a short paper on this subject, the first moment of leisure I have at my disposal. In the mean time I can only say, that having some suspicions that the common notion, which attributes to cold the property of stopping the pores and obstructing perspiration, was ill founded, I engaged a young physician, who is making some experiments with Sanctorius's balance, to estimate the different proportions of his perspiration, when remaining one hour quite naked, and another warmly clothed. He pursued the experiment in this alternate manner for eight hours successively, and found his perspi-ration almost double during those hours in which he was naked.

B. FRANKLIN.

TO MR. HOPKINSON.

On the Vis Inertiæ of Matter.

Philadelphia, 1748.

SIR,

ACCORDING to my promise, I send you *in writing* my observations on your book[4] : you will be the better able to consider them ; which I desire you to do at your leisure, and set me right where I am wrong.

I stumble at the threshold of the building, and therefore have not read farther. The author's *vis inertiæ essential to matter*, upon which the whole work is founded, I have not been able to comprehend. And I do not think he demon-strates at all clearly (at least to me he does not) that there is really *such a property in matter*.

4 Baxter's inquiry into the Nature of the Human Soul.

He says, No. 2. "Let a given body or mass of matter be called a, and let any given celerity be called c. That *celerity* doubled, tripled, &c. or halved, thirded, &c. will be 2 c, 3 c, &c. or $\frac{1}{2}$ c, $\frac{1}{3}$ c, &c. respectively : also the *body* doubled, tripled, or halved, thirded, will be 2 a, 3 a, or $\frac{1}{2}$ a, $\frac{1}{3}$ a, respectively." Thus far is clear.—But he adds, " Now to move the body a with the celerity c, requires a certain force to be impressed upon it ; and to move it with a celerity as 2 c, requires *twice that force* to be impressed upon it, &c." Here I suspect some mistake creeps in by the author's not distinguishing between a great force applied at once, or a small one continually applied, to a mass of matter, in order to move it. I think it is generally allowed by the philosophers, and, for ought we know, is certainly true, that there is no mass of matter, how great soever, but may be moved by any force how small soever (taking friction out of the question) and this small force continued, will in time bring the mass to move with any velocity whatsoever.—Our author himself seems to allow this towards the end of the same No. 2, when he is sub-dividing his celerities and forces : for as in continuing the division to eternity by his method of $\frac{1}{2}$ c, $\frac{1}{3}$ c, $\frac{1}{4}$ c, $\frac{1}{5}$ c, &c. you can never come to a fraction of velocity that is equal to c, or no celerity at all ; so dividing the force in the same manner, you can never come to a fraction of force that will not produce an equal fraction of celerity.—Where then is the mighty *vis inertiæ*, and what is its strength ; when the greatest assignable mass of matter will give to, or be moved by the *least* assignable force ? Suppose two globes, equal to the sun and to one another, exactly equipoised in Jove's balance ; suppose no friction in the centre of motion, in the beam or elsewhere : if a musketo then were to light on one of them, would he not give motion to them both, causing one to descend and the other to rise ? If it is objected, that the force of gravity helps one globe to descend, I answer, the same force opposes the other's rising : here is an equality that leaves the whole motion to be produced by the musketo : without whom those globes would not be moved at all. What then

does *vis inertiæ* do in this case? and what other effect could
we expect *if there were no such thing?* Surely if it were any
thing more than a phantom, there might be enough of it in
such *vast* bodies, to annihilate so trifling a force by its opposition to motion!

Our author would have reasoned more clearly, I think,
if, as he has used the letter *a* for a certain quantity of
matter, and *c* for a certain quantity of celerity, he had
employed one letter more, and put *f* perhaps, for a certain
quantity of force. This let us suppose to be done; and
then as it is a maxim that the force of bodies in motion is
equal to the quantity of matter multiplied by the celerity,
(or $f = c \times a$); and as the force received by and subsisting in
matter, when it is put in motion, can never exceed the
force given; so if *f* moves *a* with *c*, there must needs be
required 2 *f* to move *a* with 2 *c;* for *a* moving with 2 *c*
would have a force equal to 2 *f*, which it could not receive
from 1 *f*; and this, not because there is such a thing as *vis
inertiæ*, for the case would be the same *if that had no existence;* but because nothing *can* give more than it has, if
1 *f* can to 1 *a* give 1 *c*, which is the same thing as giving
it 1 *f;* (i. e. if force applied to matter at rest, can put it in
motion, and give it *equal* force) where then is *vis inertiæ?*
If it existed at all in matter, should we not find the quantity of its resistance subtracted from the force given?

In No. 4. our author goes on and says, "the body *a* requires a certain force to be impressed on it to be moved
with a celerity as *c*, or such a force is necessary; and therefore makes a certain resistance, &c. A body as 2 *a* requires *twice* that force to be moved with the *same celerity*,
or it makes twice that resistance; and so on.—This I think
is not true; but that the body 2 *a* moved by the force 1 *f*
(though the eye may judge otherwise of it) does really
move with the same celerity as it did when impelled by the
same force; for 2 *a* is compounded of 1 *a* $\times$ 1 *a:* and if
each of the 1 *a*'s or each part of the compound were made
to move with 1 *c* (as they might be by 2 *f*) then the whole
would move with 2 *c*, and not with 1 *c*, as our author sup-

poses.   But 1 f applied to 2 a, makes each a move with $\frac{1}{2}$
c; and so the whole moves with 1 c; exactly the same as 1
a was made to do by 1 f before.   What is equal celerity
but a *measuring the same space by moving bodies in the same
time?*—Now if 1 a impelled by 1 f measures 100 yards in
a minute; and in 2 a impelled by 1 f, each a measures 50
yards in a minute, which added make 100; are not the celerities as the forces equal? and since force and celerity in
the same quantity of matter are always in *proportion* to
each other, why should we, when the quantity of matter is
doubled, allow the force to continue unimpaired, and yet
suppose one half of the celerity to be lost?—I wonder the
more at our author's mistake in this point, since in the
same number I find him observing: "We may easily conceive that a body as 3 a, 4 c, &c. would make 3 or 4 bodies
equal to once a, each of which would require once the first
force to be moved with the celerity c." If then in 3 a, each
a requires once the first force f to be moved with the celerity c, would not each move with the force f and celerity c;
and consequently the whole be 3 a moving with 3 f and 3
c? After so distinct an observation, how could he miss of
the consequence, and imagine that 1 c and 3 c were the
same? Thus as our author's abatement of celerity in the
case of 2 a moved by 1 f is imaginary, so must be his additional resistance.—And here again, I am at a loss to discover any effect of the vis inertiæ.

In No. 6, he tells us, that all this is likewise certain
when taken the contrary way, viz. *from motion to rest;* for
the body a moving with a certain velocity, as c, requires a
certain degree of force or resistance to stop that motion,
&c." that is, in other words, equal force is necessary to
destroy force.   It may be so.   But how does this discover
a *vis inertiæ?* Would not the effect be the same *if there
were no such thing?* A force 1 f strikes a body 1 a, and
moves it with the celerity 1 c, i. e. with the force 1 f: It
requires, even according to our author, only an opposing 1
f to stop it.   But ought it not (if there were a *vis inertiæ*)
to have not only the force 1 f, but an additional force equal

to the force of *vis inertiæ*, that *obstinate power by which a body endeavors with* all its might *to continue in its present state, whether of motion or rest* ? I say, ought there not to be an opposing force equal to the sum of these ?—The truth however is, that there is no body, how large soever, moving with any velocity, how great soever, but may be stopped by any opposing force, how small soever, continually applied.' At least all our modern philosophers agree to tell us so.

Let me turn the thing in what light I please, I cannot discover the *vis inertiæ*, nor any effect of it. It is allowed by all, that a body 1 *a* moving with a velocity 1 *c*, and a force 1 *f striking another* body 1 *a* at rest, they will afterwards *move on together*, each with $\frac{1}{2}c$ and $\frac{1}{2}f$; which, as I said before, is equal in the whole to 1 *c* and 1 *f*. If *vis inertiæ*, as in this case, neither abates the force nor the velocity of bodies, what does it, or how does it discover itself ?

I imagine I may venture to conclude my observations on this piece, almost in the words of the author ; that if the doctrines of the immateriality of the soul and the existence of God and of divine providence are demonstrable from no plainer principles, the *deist* [i. e. *theist*] has a desperate cause in hand. I oppose *my theist* to his atheist, because I think they are diametrically opposite ; and not near of kin, as Mr. Whitfield seems to suppose ; where (in his journal) he tells us, " *M. B. was a deist, I had almost said an atheist ;*" that is *chalk*, I had almost said *charcoal.*

The din of the market[5] increases upon me ; and that, with frequent interruptions, has, I find, made me say some things twice over ; and, I suppose, forget some others I intended to say. It has, however, one good effect, as it obliges me to come to the relief of your patience with

Your humble servant,

B. FRANKLIN.

---

5 Dr. Franklin lived in Market street, opposite the market.

TO DR. JOHN PRINGLE.

On the different Strata of the Earth.

Craven-Street, Jan. 6, 1758.

SIR,

I RETURN you Mr. Mitchell's paper on the strata of the earth[6] with thanks. The reading of it, and perusal of the dr aft that accompanies it, have reconciled me to those convulsions which all naturalists agree this globe has suffered. Had the different strata of clay, gravel, marble, coals, lime-stone, sand, minerals, &c. continued to lie level, one under the other, as they may be supposed to have done before those convulsions, we should have had the use only of a few of the uppermost of the strata, the others lying too deep and too difficult to be come at; but the shell of the earth being broke, and the fragments thrown into this oblique position, the disjointed ends of a great number of strata of different kinds are brought up to day, and a great variety of useful materials put into our power, which would otherwise have remained eternally concealed from us. So that what has been usually looked upon as a *ruin* suffered by this part of the universe, was, in reality, only a preparation, or means of rendering the earth more fit for use, more capable of being to mankind a convenient and comfortable habitation.

I am, Sir,

With great esteem,

Yours, &c.

B. FRANKLIN.

---

6 The paper of Mr. Mitchell, here referred to was published, afterwards in the Philosophical Transactions of London.

TO THE ABBE SOULAVIE.

Occasioned by his sending me some notes he had taken of what I had said to him in conversation on the Theory of the Earth. I wrote it to set him right in some points wherein he had mistaken my meaning.   B. F.

THEORY OF THE EARTH.

Read in the American Philosophical Society, November 21, 1788.

Passy, September 22, 1782.

SIR,

I RETURN the papers with some corrections, I did not find coal mines under the calcareous rock in Derbyshire. I only remarked, that at the lowest part of that rocky mountain which was in sight, there were oyster shells mixed in the stone ; and part of the high county of Derby being probably as much above the level of the sea, as the coal mines of Whitehaven were below it, it seemed a proof, that there had been a great *boulversement* in the surface of that island, some part of it having been depressed under the sea, and other parts, which had been under it, being raised above it. Such changes in the superficial parts of the globe, seemed to me unlikely to happen, if the earth were solid to the centre. I therefore imagined, that the internal parts might be a fluid more dense, and of greater specific gravity than any of the solids we are acquainted with, which therefore might swim in or upon that fluid. Thus the surface of the globe would be a shell, capable of being broken and disordered by the violent movements of the fluid on which it rested. And as air has been compressed by art so as to be twice as dense as water, in which case, if such air and water could be contained in a strong glass vessel, the air would be seen to take the lowest place, and the water to float above and upon it; and as we know not yet the degree of density to which air may be compressed, and M. Amontons calculated, that its density increasing as it approached the centre, in the same proportion as above the surface, it would

at the depth of   leagues, be heavier than gold ; possibly
the dense fluid occupying the internal parts of the globe
might be air compressed. And as the force of expansion in
dense air when heated, is in proportion to its density, this
central air might afford another agent to move the surface,
as well as be of use in keeping alive the subterraneous fires ;
though, as you observe, the sudden rarefaction of water
coming into contact without those fires, may also be an
agent sufficiently strong for that purpose, when acting between the incumbent earth and the fluid on which it rests.

If one might indulge imagination in supposing how such
a globe was formed, I should conceive, that all the elements in separate particles being originally mixed in confusion, and occupying a great space, they would (as soon
as the almighty fiat ordained gravity, or the mutual attraction of certain parts, and the mutual repulsion of others, to
'exist) all move to their common centre: that the air being
a fluid whose parts repel each other, though drawn to the
common centre by their gravity, would be densest towards
the centre, and rarer as more remote ; consequently all matters lighter than the central parts of that air, and immersed
in it, would recede from the centre, and rise till they arrived at that region of the air which was of the same specific
gravity with themselves, where they would rest; while other
matter, mixed with the lighter air, would descend, and the
two meeting would form the shell of the first earth, leaving
the upper atmosphere nearly clear. The original move-
ment of the parts towards their common centre would naturally form a whirl there ; which would continue upon the
turning of the new-formed globe upon its axis, and the
greatest diameter of the shell would be in its equator. If
by any accident afterwards the axis should be changed, the
dense internal fluid, by altering its form, must burst the
shell, and throw all its substance into the confusion in which
we find it. I will not trouble you at present with my fancies concerning the manner of forming the rest of our system. Superior beings smile at our theories, and at our
presumption in making them. I will just mention, that

your observation of the ferruginous nature of the lava which is thrown out from the depths of our volcanoes, gave me great pleasure. It has long been a supposition of mine that the iron contained in the surface of the globe has made it capable of becoming, as it is, a great magnet; that the fluid of magnetism perhaps exists in all space; so that there is a magnetical north and south of the universe, as well as of this globe, and that if it were possible for a man to fly from star to star, he might govern his course by the compass; that it was by the power of this general magnetism this globe became a particular magnet. In soft or hot iron the fluid of magnetism is naturally diffused equally; when within the influence of the magnet it is drawn to one end of the iron, made denser there and rarer at the other. While the iron continues soft and hot, it is only a temporary magnet; if it cools or grows hard in that situation, it becomes a permanent one, the magnetic fluid not easily resuming its equilibrium. Perhaps it may be owing to the permanent magnetism of this globe, which it had not at first, that its axis is at present kept parallel to itself, and not liable to the changes it formerly suffered, which occasioned the rupture of its shell, the submersions and emersions of its lands, and the confusion of its seasons. The present polar and equatorial diameters differing from each other near ten leagues, it is easy to conceive, in case some power should shift the axis gradually, and place it in the present equator, and make the new equator pass through the present poles, what a sinking of the waters would happen in the present equatorial regions, and what a rising in the present polar regions; so that vast tracts would be discovered, that now are under water, and others covered, that are now dry, the water rising and sinking in the different extremes near five leagues. Such an operation as this possibly occasioned much of Europe, and among the rest this Mountain of Passy on which I live, and which is composed of limestone, rock and sea-shells, to be abandoned by the sea, and to change its ancient climate, which seems to have been a hot one, The globe being now become a perfect magnet, we are, perhaps, safe

from any change of its axis. But we are still subject to
the accidents on the surface, which are occasioned by a wave
in the internal ponderous fluid; and such a wave is producible by the sudden violent explosion you mention, happening from the junction of water and fire under the earth,
which not only lifts the incumbent earth that is over the
explosion, but impressing with the same force the fluid
under it, creates a wave, that may run a thousand leagues,
lifting, and thereby shaking, successively, all the countries
under which it passes. I know not, whether I have expressed myself so clearly, as not to get out of your sight in
these reveries. If they occasion any new enquiries, and
produce a better hypothesis, they will not be quite useless.
You see I have given a loose to imagination; but I approve
much more your method of philosophising, which proceeds
upon actual observation, makes a collection of facts, and
concludes no farther than those facts will warrant. In my
present circumstances, that mode of studying the nature of
the globe is out of my power, and therefore I have permitted myself to wander a little in the wilds of fancy. With
great esteem,

I have the honor to be, Sir, &c.

B. FRANKLIN.

P. S. I have heard, that chemists can by their art decompose stone and wood, extracting a considerable quantity of water from the one, and air from the other. It
seems natural to conclude from this, that water and air were
ingredients in their original composition : for men cannot
make new matter of any kind. In the same manner may
we not suppose, that when we consume combustibles of all
kinds, and produce heat or light, we do not create that heat
or light; but only decompose a substance, which received
it originally as a part of its composition? Heat may be thus
considered as originally in a fluid state; but attracted by
organised bodies in their growth, becomes a part of the
solid. Besides this, I can conceive, that in the first assem-

blage of the particles of which this earth is composed, each brought its portion of the loose heat that had been connected with it, and the whole, when pressed together, produced the internal fire that still subsists.

TO DAVID RITTENHOUSE.

New and curious Theory of Light and Heat.

Read in the American Philosophical Society, November 20, 1788.

UNIVERSAL space, as far as we know of it, seems to be filled with a subtle fluid, whose motion, or vibration, is called light.

This fluid may possibly be the same with that, which being attracted by, and entering into other more solid matter, dilates the substance by separating the constituent particles, and so rendering some solids fluid, and maintaining the fluidity of others ; of which fluid, when our bodies are totally deprived, they are said to be frozen ; when they have a proper quantity, they are in health, and fit to perform all their functions ; it is then called natural heat ; when too much, it is called fever ; and when forced into the body in too great a quantity from without, it gives pain, by separating and destroying the flesh, and is then called burning, and the fluid so entering and acting is called fire.

While organised bodies, animal or vegetable, are augmenting in growth, or are supplying their continual waste, is not this done by attracting and consolidating this fluid called fire, so as to form of it a part of their substance ? And is it not a separation of the parts of such substance, which, dissolving its solid state, sets that subtle fluid at liberty, when it again makes its appearance as fire ?

For the power of man relative to matter, seems limited to the separating or mixing the various kinds of it, or changing its form and appearance by different compositions of it ; but does not extend to the making or creating new matter, or annihilating the old. Thus, if fire be an origi-

nal element or kind of matter, its quantity is fixed and permanent in the universe.   We cannot destroy any part of it,
or make addition to it ; we can only separate it from that
which confines it, and so set it at liberty ; as when we put
wood in a situation to be burnt, or transfer it from one solid
to another, as when we make lime by burning stone, a part
of the fire dislodged in the fuel being left in the stone. May
not this fluid, when at liberty, be capable of penetrating and
entering into all bodies, organised or not, quitting easily
in totality those not organised, and quitting easily in part
those which are ; the part assumed and fixed remaining till
the body is dissolved ?

Is it not this fluid which keeps asunder the particles of
air, permitting them to approach, or separating them more,
in proportion as its quantity is diminished or augmented ?

Is it not the greater gravity of the particles of air, which
forces the particles of this fluid to mount with the matters
to which it is attached, as smoke or vapor ?

Does it not seem to have a greater affinity with water,
since it will quit a solid to unite with that fluid, and go off
with it in vapor, leaving the solid cold to the touch, and the
degree measurable by the thermometer ?

The vapor rises attached to this fluid, but at a certain
height they separate, and the vapor descends in rain, retaining but little of it, in snow or hail less.   What becomes of
that fluid ? Does it rise above our atmosphere, and mix
with the universal mass of the same kind ?

Or does a spherical stratum of it, denser, as less mixed
with air, attracted by this globe, and repelled or pushed up
only to a certain height from its surface, by the greater
weight of air, remain there surrounding the globe, and proceeding with it round the sun ?

In such case, as there may be a continuity or communication of this fluid through the air quite down to the earth,
is it not by the vibrations given to it, by the sun, that light
appears to us ? And may it not be, that every one of the
infinitely small vibrations, striking common matter with a
certain force, enters its substance, is held there by attrac-

tion, and augmented by succeeding vibrations, till the matter has received as much as their force can drive into it ?

Is it not thus, that the surface of this globe is continually heated by such repeated vibrations in the day, and cooled by the escape of the heat when those vibrations are discontinued in the night, or intercepted and reflected by clouds ?

Is it not thus, that fire is amassed and makes the greatest part of the substance of combustible bodies ?

Perhaps, when this globe was first formed, and its original particles took their place at certain distances from the centre, in proportion to their greater or less gravity, the fluid fire, attracted towards that centre, might in great part be obliged, as lightest, to take place above the rest, and thus form the sphere of fire above supposed, which would afterwards be continually diminishing by the substance it afforded to organised bodies, and the quantity restored to it again, by the burning or other separating of the parts of those bodies.

Is not the natural heat of animals thus produced, by separating in digestion the parts of food, and setting their fire at liberty?

Is it not this sphere of fire which kindles the wandering globes that sometimes pass through it in our course round the sun, have their surface kindled by it, and burst when their included air is greatly rarefied by the heat on their burning surfaces?

May it not have been from such considerations that the ancient philosophers supposed a sphere of fire to exist above the air of our atmosphere ?

B. FRANKLIN.

Queries and Conjectures relating to Magnetism and the Theory of the Earth.

Read in the American Philosophical Society, January 15, 1790.

DEAR SIR,

I RECEIVED your favors by Messrs. Gore, Hilliard, and Lee, with whose conversation I was much pleased, and wished for more of it; but their stay with us was too short. Whenever you recommend any of your friends to me, you oblige me.

I want to know whether your Philosophical Society received the second volume of our Transactions. I sent it, but never heard of its arriving. If it miscarried, I will send another. Has your Society among its books the French work *Sur les Arts, et les Metiers?* It is voluminous, well executed, and may be useful in our country. I have bequeathed it them in my will; but if they have it already, I will substitute something else.

Our ancient correspondence used to have something philosophical in it. As you are now more free from public cares, and I expect to be so in a few months, why may we not resume that kind of correspondence? Our much regretted friend Winthrop once made me the compliment, that I was good at starting game for philosophers, let me try if I can start a little for you.

Has the question, how came the earth by its magnetism, ever been considered?

Is it likely that *iron ore* immediately existed when this globe was first formed; or may it not rather be supposed a gradual production of time?

If the earth is at present magnetical, in virtue of the masses of iron ore contained in it, might not some ages pass before it had magnetic polarity?

Since iron ore may exist without that polarity, and by being placed in certain circumstanes may obtain it, from an external cause, is it not possible that the earth received its magnetism from some such cause?

In short, may not a magnetic power exist throughout our system, perhaps through all systems, so that if men could make a voyage in the starry regions, a compass might be of use? And may not such universal magnetism, with its uniform direction, be serviceable in keeping the diurnal revolution of a planet more steady to the same axis?

Lastly, as the poles of magnets may be changed by the presence of stronger magnets, might not, in ancient times, the near passing of some large comet of greater magnetic power than this globe of ours have been a means of changing its poles, and thereby wrecking and deranging its surface, placing in different regions the effect of centrifugal force, so as to raise the waters of the sea in some, while they were depressed in others?

Let me add another question or two, not relating indeed to magnestism, but, however, to the theory of the earth.

Is not the finding of great quantities of shells and bones of animals (natural to hot climates) in the cold ones of our present world, some proof that its poles have been changed? Is not the supposition that the poles have been changed, the easiest way of accounting for the deluge, by getting rid of the old difficulty how to dispose of its waters after it was over? Since if the poles were again to be changed, and placed in the present equator, the sea would fall there about fifteen miles in height, and rise as much in the present polar regions; and the effect would be proportionable if the new poles were placed any where between the present and the equator.

Does not the apparent wreck of the surface of this globe, thrown up into long ridges of mountains, with strata in various positions, make it probable, that its internal mass is a fluid; but a fluid so dense as to float the heaviest of our substances? Do we know the limit of condensation air is capable of? Supposing it to grow denser *within* the surface, in the same proportion nearly as it does *without*, at what depth may it be equal in density with gold?

Can we easily conceive how the strata of the earth could have been so deranged, if it had not been a mere shell supported by a heavier fluid? Would not such a supposed internal fluid globe be immediately sensible of a change in the situation of the earth's axis, alter its form, and thereby burst the shell, and throw up parts of it above the rest? As if we would alter the position of the fluid contained in the shell of an egg, and place its longest diameter where the shortest now is, the shell must break; but would be much harder to break; if the whole internal substance were as solid and hard as the shell.

Might not a wave, by any means raised in this supposed internal ocean of extremely dense fluid, raise in some degree, as it passes, the present shell of incumbent earth, and break it in some places, as in earthquakes? And may not the progress of such wave, and the disorders it occasions among the solids of the shell, account for the rumbling sound being first heard at a distance, augmenting as it approaches, and gradually dying away as it proceeds? A circumstance observed by the inhabitants of South America in their last great earthquake, that noise coming from a place, some degrees north of Lima, and being traced by enquiry quite down to Buenos Ayres, proceeded regularly from north to south at the rate of   leagues per minute, as I was informed by a very ingenious Peruvian whom I met with at Paris.

B. FRANKLIN.

TO M. DUBOURG.

On the Nature of Sea Coal.[7]

..... I AM persuaded, as well as you, that the sea coal has a vegetable origin, and that it has been formed near the surface of the earth; but as preceding convulsions of nature had served to bring it very deep in many places, and covered it with many different strata, we are indebted to subsequent convulsions for having brought within our view

---

[7] Translated from the French edition of Dr. Franklin's works.

the extremities of its veins, so as to lead us to penetrate the
earth in search of it. I visited last summer a large coal-
mine at Whitehaven, in Cumberland; and in following the
vein and descending by degrees towards the sea, I penetrated below the ocean, where the level of its surface was
more than eight hundred fathom above my head, and the
miners assured me, that their works extended some miles
beyond the place where I then was, continually and gradually descending under the sea. The slate, which forms the
roof of this coal mine, is impressed in many places with the
figures of leaves and branches of fern, which undoubtedly
grew at the surface when the slate was in the state of sand
on the banks of the sea. Thus it appears that this vein of
coal has suffered a prodigious settlement.

B. FRANKLIN.

DR. PERKINS OF BOSTON, TO DR. FRANKLIN.

Respecting the Number of Deaths in Philadelphia by Inoculation.

Boston, August 3, 1752,

SIR,

THIS comes to you on account of Dr. Douglass: he
desired me to write to you for what you know of the number
that died of the inoculation in Philadelphia, telling me he
designed to write something on the small-pox shortly. We
shall both be obliged to you for a word on this affair.

The chief particulars of our visitation, you have in the
public prints. But the less degree of mortality than usual
in the common way of infection, seems chiefly owing to the
purging method designed to prevent the secondary fever; a
sixth, but had we been experienced in this way, at the first
method first begun and carried on in this town, and with
success beyond expectation. We lost one in eleven one-
coming of the distemper, probably the proportion had been
but one in thirteen or fourteen. In the year 1730 we lost
one in nine, which is more favorable than ever before with

us. The distemper pretty much the same then as now, but some circumstances not so kind this time.

If there be any particulars which you want to know, please to signify what they are, and I shall send them.

The number of our inhabitants decreases.[8] On a strict inquiry, the overseers of the poor find but fourteen thousand one hundred and ninety whites, and one thousand five hundred and forty-four blacks, including those absent, on account of the small-pox, many of whom, it is probable, will never return.

I pass this opportunity without any particulars of my old theme. One thing, however, I must mention, which is, that perhaps my last letters contained something that seemed to militate with your doctrine of the *Origin*, &c. But my design was only to relate the phenomena as they appeared to me. I have received so much light and pleasure from your writings, as to prejudice me in favor of every thing from your hand, and leave me only liberty to observe, and a power of dissenting when some great probability might oblige me : and if at any time that be the case, you will certainly hear of it.

I am, Sir, &c.

---

8 Boston was then an old town, and had been the seat of all the trade of the country, that was carried on by sea. New towns and ports, at this period, divided the trade with it, and diminished its inhabitants, though the inhabitants of the country, in general, had greatly increased.

DR. FRANKLIN, TO DR. PERKINS.

In Answer to the preceding.

Philadelphia, Aug. 13, 1752.

SIR,

I RECEIVED your favor of the 3d instant. Some time last winter I procured from one of our physicians an account of the number of persons inoculated during the five visitations of the small-pox we have had in twenty-two years; which account I sent to Mr. W. V. of your town, and have no copy. If I remember right, the number exceeded eight hundred, and the deaths were but four. I suppose Mr. V. will show you the account, if he ever received it. Those four were all that our doctors allow to have died of the small-pox by inoculation, though I think there were two more of the inoculated who died of the distemper; but the eruptions appearing soon after the operation, it is supposed they had taken the infection before, in the common way.

I shall be glad to see what Dr. Douglass may write on the subject. I have a French piece printed at Paris, 1724, entitled, *Observations sur la Saignée du Pied, et sur la Purgation au commencement de la Petite Verole, et Raisons de doubte contre l'Inoculation.*—A letter of the doctor's is mentioned in it. If he or you have it not, and desire to see it, I will send it.—Please to favor me with the particulars of your purging method, to prevent the secondary fever.

I am indebted for your preceding letter, but business sometimes obliges me to postpone philosophical amusements. Whatever I have wrote of that kind, are really, as they are intitled, but *Conjectures* and *Suppositions;* which ought always to give place, when careful observation militates against them. I own I have too strong a penchant to the building of hypotheses; they indulge my natural indolence: I wish I had more of your patience and accuracy in making observations, on which, alone, true philosophy can be founded. And, I assure you, nothing ean be more obliging to me, than your kind communication of those you make, however they may disagree with my pre-conceived notions.

I am sorry to hear that the number of your inhabitants decreases. I some time since, wrote a small paper of *Thoughts on the peopling of Countries*[9], which, if I can find, I will send you, to obtain your sentiments. The favorable opinion you express of my writings, may, you see, occasion you more trouble than you expected from,

Sir, yours, &c.

B. FRANKLIN.

TO BENJAMIN VAUGHAN.

On the Effects of Lead upon the human Constitution.[1]

Philadelphia, July 31, 1786.

DEAR FRIEND,

I RECOLLECT that when I had last the pleasure of seeing you at Southampton, now a twelvemonth since, we had some conversation on the bad effects of lead taken inwardly ; and that at your request I promised to send you in writing a particular account of several facts I then mentioned to you, of which you thought some good use might be made. I now sit down to fulfil that promise.

The first thing I remember of this kind was a general discourse in Boston when I was a boy, of a complaint from North Carolina against New England rum, that it poisoned their people, giving them the dry-belly-ache, with a loss of the use of their limbs. The distilleries being examined on the occasion, it was found, that several of them used leaden still-heads and worms, and the physicians were of opinion, that the mischief was occasioned by that use of lead. The

---

9 This paper will be found in another volume of this edition.

1 This letter was published in a work by Dr. John Hunter, entitled *Observations on the Diseases of the Army.*

legislature of Massachusetts thereupon passed an act, prohibiting, under severe penalties, the use of such still-heads and worms thereafter.

In 1724, being in London, I went to work in the printing-house of Mr. Palmer, Bartholomew-close, as a compositor. I there found a practice, I had never seen before, of drying a case of types (which are wet in distribution) by placing it sloping before the fire. I found this had the additional advantage, when the types were not only dried but heated, of being comfortable to the hands working over them in cold weather. I therefore sometimes heated my case when the types did not want drying. But an old workman observing it, advised me not to do so, telling me I might lose the use of my hands by it, as two of our companions had nearly done, one of whom, that used to earn his guinea a week, could not then make more than ten shillings, and the other, who had the *dangles*, but seven and sixpence. This, with a kind of obscure pain, that I had sometimes felt, as it were, in the bones of my hand when working over the types made very hot, induced me to omit the practice. But talking afterwards with Mr. James, a letter-founder in the same close, and asking him if his people, who worked over the little furnaces of melted metal, were not subject to that disorder; he made light of any danger from the effluvia, but ascribed it to particles of the metal swallowed with their food by slovenly workmen, who went to their meals after handling the metal, without well washing their fingers, so that some of the metalline particles were taken off by their bread and eaten with it. This appeared to have some reason in it. But the pain I had experienced made me still afraid of those effluvia.

Being in Derbyshire at some of the furnaces for smelting of lead ore, I was told, that the smoke of those furnaces was pernicious to the neighboring grass and other vegetables; but I do not recollect to have heard any thing of the effect of such vegetables eaten by animals. It may be well to make the enquiry.

In America I have often observed, that on the roofs of our shingled-houses, where moss is apt to grow in northern exposures, if there be any thing on the roof painted with white lead, such as balusters, or frames of dormant windows, &c. there is constantly a streak on the shingles from such paint down to the eaves, on which no moss will grow, but the wood remains constantly clean and free from it. We seldom drink rain-water that fall on our houses ; and if we did, perhaps the small quantity of lead descending from such paint might not be sufficient to produce any sensible ill-effect on our bodies. But I have been told of a case in Europe, I forget the place, where a whole family was afflicted with what we call the dry-belly-ache, or *colica pictorum*, by drinking rain-water. It was at a country-seat, which, being situated too high to have the advantage of a well, was supplied with water from a tank, which received the water from the leaded roofs. This had been drank several years without mischief, but some young trees planted near the house growing up above the roof, and shedding their leaves upon it, it was supposed, that an acid in those leaves had corroded the lead they covered, and furnished the water of that year with its baneful particles and qualities.

When I was in Paris with sir John Pringle in 1767, he visited *La Charité*, an hospital particularly famous for the cure of that malady, and brought from thence a pamphlet, containing a list of the names of persons, specifying their professions or trades, who had been cured there. I had the curiosity to examine that list, and found, that all the patients were of trades, that some way or other use or work in lead ; such as plumbers, glaziers, painters, &c. excepting only two kinds, stone-cutters, and soldiers. In them, I could not reconcile it to my notion, that lead was the cause of that disorder. But on my mentioning it to a physician of that hospital, he informed me, that the stone-cutters are continually using melted lead to fix the ends of iron balustrades in stone ; and that the soldiers had been employed by painters as laborers in grinding of colors.

This, my dear friend, is all I can at present recollect on the subject. You will see by it, that the opinion of this mischievous effect from lead, is at least above sixty years old ; and you will observe with concern how long a useful truth may be known and exist, before it is generally received and practised on.

I am, ever, yours most affectionately,

B. FRANKLIN.

TO M. DUBOURG[2].

Observations on the prevailing Doctrines of Life and Death.

......YOUR observations on the causes of death, and the experiments which you propose for recalling to life those who appear to be killed by lightning, demonstrate equally your sagacity and your humanity. It appears, that the doctrines of life and death, in general, are yet but little understood.

A toad buried in sand will live, it is said, till the sand becomes petrified : and then, being inclosed in the stone, it may still live for we know not how many ages. The facts which are cited in support of this opinion are too numerous, and too circumstantial, not to deserve a certain degree of credit. As we are accustomed to see all the animals, with which we are acquainted, eat and drink, it appears to us difficult to conceive, how a toad can be supported in such a dungeon : but if we reflect, that the necessity of nourishment, which animals experience in their ordinary state, proceeds from the continual waste of their substance by perspiration, it will appear less incredible, that some animals in a torpid state, perspiring less because they use no exercise, should have less need of aliment ; and that others, which are covered with scales or shells, which stop perspiration, such as land and sea-turtles, serpents, and some species of fish, should be able to subsist a considerable time without any nourishment whatever.——A plant, with its flow-

2 Translated from the French edition of Dr. Franklin's works. It has no date, but the letter to which it is an answer is dated April 15, 1773.

ers, fades and dies immediately, if exposed to the air without having its root immersed in a humid soil, from which it may draw a sufficient quantity of moisture to supply that which exhales from its substance and is carried off continually by the air. Perhaps, however if it were buried in quicksilver, it might preserve for a considerable space of time its vegetable life, its smell, and color. If this be the case, it might prove a commodious method of transporting from distant countries those delicate plants, which are unable to sustain the inclemency of the weather at sea, and which require particular care and attention. I have seen an instance of common flies preserved in a manner somewhat similar. They had been drowned in Madeira wine, apparently about the time when it was bottled in Virginia, to be sent hither (to London). At the opening of one of the bottles, at the house of a friend where I then was, three drowned flies fell into the first glass that was filled. Having heard it remarked, that drowned flies were capable of being revived by the rays of the sun, I proposed making the experiment upon these: they were therefore exposed to the sun upon a sieve, which had been employed to strain them out of the wine. In less than three hours, two of them began by degress to recover life. They commenced by some convulsive motions of the thighs, and at length they raised themselves upon their legs, wiped their eyes with their fore-feet, beat and brushed their wings with their hind-feet, and soon after began to fly, finding themselves in Old England, without knowing how they came thither. The third continued lifeless till sunset, when, losing all hopes of him, he was thrown away.

I wish it were possible, from this instance, to invent a method of embalming drowned persons, in such a manner that they may be recalled to life at any period, however distant; for having a very ardent desire to see and observe the state of America an hundred years hence, I should prefer to any ordinary death, the being immersed in a cask of Madeira wine, with a few friends till that time, to be then recalled to life by the solar warmth of my dear country ! But since in all probability we live in an age too early and too near the infancy of science, to hope to see such an art brought in our time to its perfection, I must for the present content myself with the treat, which you are so kind as to promise me, of the resurrection of a fowl or a turkey-cock.

I am, &c.

B. FRANKLIN.

An Account of the new-invented Pennsylvanian Fire-Places : wherein their Construction and Manner of Operation is particularly explained ; their Advantages above every other Method of warming Rooms demonstrated ; and all Objections that have been raised against the Use of them answered and obviated. With Directions for putting them up, and for using them to the best Advantage. And a Copper-Plate, in which the several parts of the Machine are exactly laid down, from a Scale of Equal Parts.

BY B. FRANKLIN.

(First printed at Philadelphia in 1745.)

IN these northern colonies the inhabitants keep fires to sit by generally seven months in the year ; that is, from the beginning of October, to the end of April ; and, in some winters, near eight months, by taking in part of September and May.

Wood, our common fuel, which within these hundred years might be had at every man's door, must now be fetched near one hundred miles to some towns, and makes a very considerable article in the expence of families.

As therefore so much of the comfort and conveniency of our lives, for so great a part of the year, depends on the article of *fire ;* since fuel is become so expensive, and (as the country is more cleared and settled) will of course grow scarcer and dearer, any new proposal for saving the wood, and for lessening the charge, and augmenting the benefit of fire, by some particular method of making and managing it, may at least be thought worth consideration.

The new fire-places are a late invention to that purpose, of which this paper is intended to give a particular account.

That the reader may the better judge whether this method of managing fire has any advantage over those heretofore in use, it may be proper to consider both the old and
new methods separately and particularly, and afterwards
make the comparison.

In order to this, it is necessary to understand well, some
few of the properties of air and fire, viz.

1. Air is rarefied by *heat*, and condensed by *cold*, *i. e.* the
same quantity of air takes up more space when warm than
when cold. This may be shown by several very easy experiments. Take any clear glass bottle (a Florence flask
stript of the straw is best) place it before the fire, and as
the air within is warmed and rarefied, part of it will be
driven out of the bottle ; turn it up, place its mouth in a
vessel of water, and remove it from the fire ; then, as the
air within cools and contracts, you will see the water rise in
the neck of the bottle, supplying the place of just so much
air as was driven out. Hold a large hot coal near the side
of the bottle, and as the air within feels the heat, it will
again distend and force out the water.——Or, fill a bladder
not quite full of air, tie the neck tight, and lay it before a
fire as near as may be without scorching the bladder ; as the
air within heats, you will perceive it to swell and fill the
bladder, till it becomes tight, as if full blown : remove it
to a cool place, and you will see it fall gradually, till it becomes as lank as at first.

2. Air rarefied and distended by heat is specifically[3]
lighter than it was before, and will rise in other air of greater density. As wood, oil, or any other matter specifically
lighter than water, if placed at the bottom of a vessel of
water, will rise till it comes to the top ; so rarefied air will
rise in common air, till it either comes to air of equal
weight, or is by cold reduced to its former density.

A fire then being made in any chimney, the air over the
fire is rarified by the heat, becomes lighter, and therefore

3 Body or matter of any sort, is said to be *specifically* heavier or lighter than
other matter, when it has more or less substance or weight in the same dimensions.

immediately rises in the funnel, and goes out; the other air in the room (flowing towards the chimney) supplies its place, is rarefied in its turn, and rises likewise; the place of the air thus carried out of the room, is supplied by fresh air coming in through doors and windows, or, if they be shut, through every crevice with violence, as may be seen by holding a candle to a key-hole: If the room be so tight as that all the crevices together will not supply so much air as is continually carried off, then, in a little time, the current up the funnel must flag, and the smoke being no longer driven up, must come into the room.

1. Fire (*i. e.* common fire) throws out light, heat, and smoke (or fume.) The two first move in right lines, and with great swiftness, the latter is but just separated from the fuel, and then moves only as it is carried by the stream of rarefied air: and without a continual accession and recession of air, to carry off the smoky fumes, they would remain crouded about the fire, and stifle it.

2. Heat may be separated from the smoke as well as from the light, by means of a plate of iron, which will suffer heat to pass through it without the others.

3. Fire sends out its rays of heat as well as rays of light equally every way; but the greatest sensible heat is over the fire, where there is, besides the rays of heat shot upwards, a continual rising stream of hot air, heated by the rays shot round on every side.

These things being understood, we proceed to consider the fire-places heretofore in use, *viz.*

1. The large open fire-places used in the days of our fathers, and still generally in the country, and in kitchens.

2. The newer-fashioned fire places, with low breasts, and narrow hearths.

3. Fire-places with hollow backs, hearths, and jambs of iron (described by M. Gauger, in his tract entitled, *La Mechanique de Feu*) for warming the air as it comes into the room.

4. The Holland stoves, with iron doors opening into the room.

5. The German stoves, which have no opening in the room where they are used, but the fire is put in from some other room, or from without.

6. Iron pots, with open charcoal fires, placed in the middle of a room.

1. The first of these methods has generally the conveniency of two warm seats, one in each corner; but they are sometimes too hot to abide in, and, at other times, incommoded with the smoke; there is likewise good room for the cook to move, to hang on pots, &c. Their inconveniencies are, that they almost always smoke, if the door be not left open; that they require a large funnel, and a large funnel carries off a great quantity of air, which occasions what is called a strong draft to the chimney, without which strong draft the smoke would come out of some part or other of so large an opening, so that the door can seldom be shut; and the cold air so nips the backs and heels of those that sit before the fire, that they have no comfort till either screens or settles are provided (at a considerable expence) to keep it off, which both cumber the room, and darken the fire-side. A moderate quantity of wood on the fire, in so large a hearth, seems but little; and, in so strong and cold a draught, warms but little; so that people are continually laying on more. In short, it is next to impossible to warm a room with such a fire-place: and I suppose our ancestors never thought of warming rooms to sit in; all they purposed was, to have a place to make a fire in, by which they might warm themselves when cold.

2. Most of these old-fashioned chimneys in towns and cities, have been, of late years, reduced to the second sort mentioned, by building jambs within them, narrowing the hearth, and making a low arch or breast. It is strange, methinks, that though chimneys have been so long in use, their construction should be so little understood till lately, that no workman pretended to make one which should always carry off all smoke, but a chimney-cloth was looked upon as essential to a chimney. This improvement, however, by small openings and low breasts, has been made in

our days; and success in the first experiments has brought
it into general use in cities, so that almost all new chimneys
are now made of that sort, and much fewer bricks will
make a stack of chimneys now than formerly. An improvement, so lately made, may give us room to believe,
that still farther improvements may be found to remedy the
inconveniencies yet remaining. For these new chimneys,
though they keep rooms generally free from smoke, and
the opening being contracted, will allow the door to be
shut, yet the funnel still requiring a considerable quantity
of air, it rushes in at every crevice so strongly, as to make
a continual whistling or howling; and it is very uncomfortable, as well as dangerous, to sit against any such crevice.
Many colds are caught from this cause only, it being safer
to sit in the open street, for then the pores do all close together and the air does not strike so sharply against any particular part of the body.

The Spaniards have a proverbial saying,

> If the wind blows on you through a hole,
> Make your will, and take care of your soul.

Women particularly, from this cause, as they sit much in
the house, get colds in the head, rheums and defluctions,
which fall into their jaws and gums, and have destroyed
early many a fine set of teeth in these northern colonies.
Great and bright fires do also very much contribute to damage the eyes, dry and shrivel the skin, and bring on early
the appearances of old age. In short, many of the diseases
proceeding from colds, as fevers, pleuresies, &c. fatal to very
great numbers of people, may be ascribed to strong drawing chimneys, whereby, in severe weather, a man is scorched before while he is froze behind.[4] In the mean time,

4 As the writer is neither physician nor philosopher, the reader may expect
he should justify these his opinions by the authority of some that are so. M.
Clare, F. R. S. in his treatise of *The Motion of Fluids*, says, page 246, &c.
" And here it may be remarked, that it is more prejudicial to health to sit
near a window or door, in a room where there are many candles and a fire, than
in a room without; for the consumption of air thereby occasioned, will always
be very considerable, and this must necessarily be replaced by cold air from
without. Down the chimney none can enter, the stream of warm air always
arising therein absolutely forbids it, the supply must therefore come in where-

very little is done by these chimneys towards warming the room; for the air round the fire-place, which is warmed by the direct rays from the fire, does not continue in the room, but is continually crouded and gathered into the chimney by the current of cold air coming behind it, and so is presently carried off.

ever other openings shall be found. If these happen to be small, *let those who sit near them beware;* the smaller the floodgate, the smarter will be the stream. Was a man, even in a sweat, to leap into a cold bath, or jump from his warm bed, in the intensest cold, even in a frost, provided he do not continue overlong therein, and be in health when he does this, we see by experience that he gets no harm. If he sits a little while against a window, into which a successive current of cold air comes, his pores are closed, and he gets a fever. In the first case, the shock the body endures, is general, uniform, and therefore less fierce; in the other, a single part, a neck, or ear perchance, is attacked, and that with the greater violence probably, as it is done by a successive stream of cold air. And the cannon of a battery, pointed against a single part of a bastion, will easier make a breach than were they directed to play singly upon the whole face, and will admit the enemy much sooner into the town."

That warm rooms, and keeping the body warm in winter, are means of preventing such diseases, take the opinion of that learned Italian physician Antonino Parcio, in the preface to his tract *de Militis Sanitate tuenda,* where speaking of a particular wet and cold winter, remarkable at Venice for its sickliness, he says, " Popularis autem pleuritis quæ Venetiis sæviit mensibus *Dec. Jan. Feb.* ex cæli, aërisque inclementia facta est, quod non habeant hypocausta [*stove-rooms*] & quod non soliciti sunt Itali omnes de auribus, temporibus, collo, totoque corpore defendendis ab injuriis aëris; et tegmina domorum Veneti disponant parum inclinata, ut nives diutius permaneant super tegmina. E contra, Germani, qui experiuntur cæli inclementiam, perdidicere sese defendere ab aëris injuria. Tecta construunt multum inclinata, ut decidant nives. Germani abundant lignis, domusque *hypocaustis;* foris autem incedunt pannis pellibus, gossipio, bene mehercule loricati atque muniti. In Bavaria interrogabam (curiositate motus videndi Germaniam) quot nam elapsis mensibus pleuritide vel peripneumonia fuissent absumti : dicebant vix unus aut alter illis temporibus pleuritide fuit correptus.

The great Dr. Boerhaave, whose authority alone might be sufficient, in his *Aphorisms,* mentions, as one antecedent cause of pleurisies, " A cold air, driven violently through some narrow passage upon the body, overheated by labor or fire."

The eastern physicians agree with the Europeans in this point; witness the Chinese treatise entitled, *Tschang seng;* i. e. *The Art of procuring Health and long Life,* as translated in Pere Du Halde's account of China, which has this passage. " As, of all the passions which ruffle us, anger does the most mischief, so of all the malignant affections of the air, a wind that comes through any narrow passage, which is cold and piercing, is most dangerous; and coming upon us unawares insinuates itself into the body, often causing grievous diseases. It should therefore be avoided, according to the advice of the ancient proverb, as carefully as the point of an arrow." These mischiefs are avoided by the use of the new-invented fire-places, as will be shewn hereafter.

In both these sorts of fire-places, the greatest part of the heat from the fire is lost; for as fire naturally darts heat every way, the back, the two jambs, and the hearth, drink up almost all that is given them, very little being reflected from bodies so dark, porous, and unpolished; and the upright heat, which is by far the greatest, flies directly up the chimney. Thus five-sixths at least of the heat (and consequently of the fuel) is wasted, and contributes nothing towards warming the room.

3. To remedy this, the sieur Gauger gives, in his book entitled, La Mechanique de Feu, published in 1709, seven different constructions of the third sort of chimneys mentioned above, in which there are hollow cavities made by iron plates in the back, jambs, and hearths, through which plates the heat passing warms the air in those cavities, which is continually coming into the room fresh and warm. The invention was very ingenious, and had many inconveniencies: the room was warmed in all parts, by the air flowing into it through the heated cavities: cold air was prevented rushing through the crevices, the funnel being sufficiently supplied by those cavities: much less fuel would serve, &c. But the first expence, which was very great, the intricacy of the design, and the difficulty of the execution, especially in old chimneys, discouraged the propagation of the invention; so that there are, I suppose, very few such chimneys now in use. The upright heat, too, was almost all lost in these, as in the common chimneys.

4. The Holland iron stove, which has a flue proceeding from the top, and a small iron door opening into the room, comes next to be considered. Its conveniencies are, that it makes a room all over warm; for the chimney being wholly closed, except the flue of the stove, very little air is required to supply that, and therefore not much rushes in at crevices, or at the door when it is opened. Little fuel serves, the heat being almost all saved; for it rays out almost equally from the four sides, the bottom and the top, into the room, and presently warms the air around it, which, being rarefied, rises to the ceiling, and its place is supplied by the

3 F

lower air of the room, which flows gradually towards the stove, and is there warmed, and rises in its turn, so that there is a continual circulation till all the air in the room is warmed. The air, too, is gradually changed, by the stove-door's being in the room, through which part of it is continually passing, and that makes these stoves wholesomer, or at least pleasanter than the German stoves, next to be spoken of. But they have these inconveniencies. There is no sight of the fire, which is in itself a pleasant thing. One cannot conveniently make any other use of the fire but that of warming the room. When the room is warm, people, not seeing the fire, are apt to forget supplying it with fuel till it is almost out, then growing cold, a great deal of wood is put in, which soon makes it too hot. The change of air is not carried on quite quick enough, so that if any smoke or ill smell happens in the room, it is a long time before it is discharged. For these reasons the Holland stove has not obtained much among the English (who love the sight of the fire) unless in some workshops, where people are obliged to sit near windows for the light, and in such places they have been found of good use.

5. The German stove is like a box, one side wanting. It is composed of five iron plates screwed together, and fixed so as that you may put the fuel into it from another room, or from the outside of the house. It is a kind of oven reversed, its mouth being without, and body within the room that is to be warmed by it. This invention certainly warms a room very speedily and thoroughly with little fuel: no quantity of cold air comes in at any crevice, because there is no discharge of air which it might supply, there being no passage into the stove from the room. These are its conveniencies. Its inconveniencies are, that people have not even so much sight or use of the fire as in the Holland stoves, and are, moreover, obliged to breathe the same unchanged air continually, mixed with the breath and perspiration from one another's bodies, which is very disagreeable to those who have not been accustomed to it.

Plate IX.

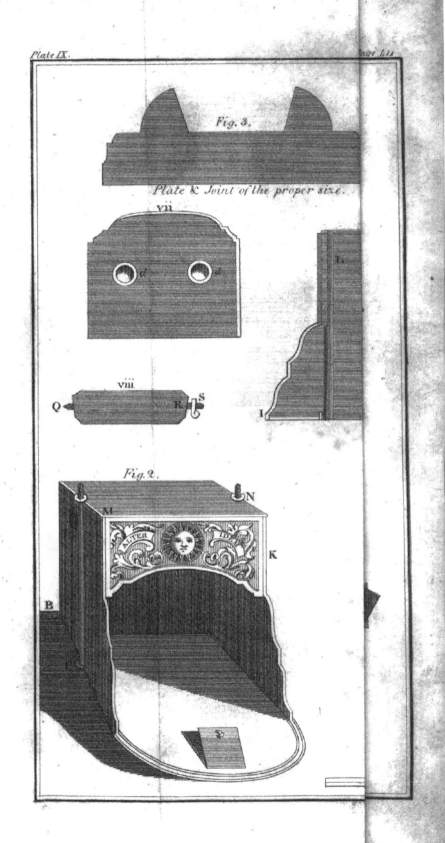

Fig. 3.

Plate & Joint of the proper size.

6. Charcoal fires in pots are used chiefly in the shops of handicraftsmen. They warm a room (that is kept close, and has no chimney to carry off the warmed air) very speedily and uniformly; but there being no draught to change the air, the sulphurous fumes from the coals, [be they ever so well kindled before they are brought in, there will be some,] mix with it, render it disagreeable, hurtful to some constitutions, and sometimes, when the door is long kept shut, produce fatal consequences.

To avoid the several inconveniences, and at the same time retain all the advantages of other fire-places, was contrived the Pennsylvanian fire-place, now to be described.

This machine consists of

A bottom-plate, (i) *(See the Plate annexed.)*

A back plate, (ii)

Two side plates, (iii iii)

Two middle plates, (iv iv) which, joined together, form a tight box, with winding passages in it for warming the air.

A front plate, (v)

A top plate (vi)

These are all cast of iron, with mouldings or ledges where the plates come together, to hold them fast, and retain the mortar used for pointing to make tight joints. When the plates are all in their places, a pair of slender rods, with screws, are sufficient to bind the whole very firmly together, as it appears in Fig. 2.

There are, moreover, two thin plates of wrought iron, viz. the shutter, (vii) and the register, (viii); besides the screw-rods O P, all which we shall explain in their order.

(i) The bottom plate, or hearth-piece, is round before, with a rising moulding, that serves as a fender to keep coals and ashes from coming to the floor, &c. It has two ears, F G, perforated to receive the screw-rods O P; a long air-hole, *a a*, through which the fresh outward air passes up into the air-box; and three smoke-holes B C, through which the smoke descends and passes away; all represented by dark squares. It has also double-ledges to receive between them the bottom edges of the back plate, the two side-plates, and the two middle plates. These ledges are about an inch asunder, and about half an inch high; a profile of two of them, joined to a fragment of plate, appears in Fig. 3.

(ii) The back plate is without holes, having only a pair of ledges on each side, to receive the back edges of the two.

(iii iii) Side-plates: These have each a pair of ledges to receive the side-edges of the front-plate, and a little shoulder for it to rest on; also two pair of ledges to receive the side-edges of the two middle plates which form the air-box; and an oblong air-hole near the top, through which is discharged into the room the air warmed in the air-box. Each has also a wing or bracket, H and I, to keep in falling brands, coals, &c. and a small hole, Q and R, for the axis of the register to turn in.

(iv iv) The air-box is composed of the two middle plates, D E and F G. The first has five thin ledges or partitions cast on it, two inches deep, the edges of which are received in so many pair of ledges cast in the other. The tops of all the cavities formed by these thin deep ledges, are also covered by a ledge of the same form and depth, cast with them; so that when the plates are put together, and the joints luted, there is no communication between the air-box and the smoke. In the winding passages of this box, fresh air is warmed as it passes into the room.

(v) The front plate is arched on the under side, and ornamented with foliages, &c. it has no ledges.

(vi) The top plate has a pair of ears, M N, answerable to those in the bottom plate, and perforated for the same purpose: It has also a pair of ledges running round the under side, to receive the top edges of the front, back, and side-plates. The air-box does not reach up to the top plate by two inches and a half.

(vii) The shutter is of thin wrought iron and light, of such a length and breadth as to close well the opening of the fire-place. It is used to blow up the fire, and to shut up and secure it at nights. It has two brass knobs for handles, ·

PROFILE OF THE PENNSYLVANIA CHIMNEY &c.FIREPLACE

Plate X.   Vol. III. p. 452.

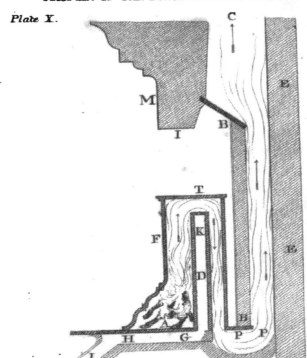

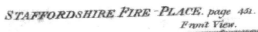

STAFFORDSHIRE FIRE-PLACE. page 451.

Side View.   Front View.

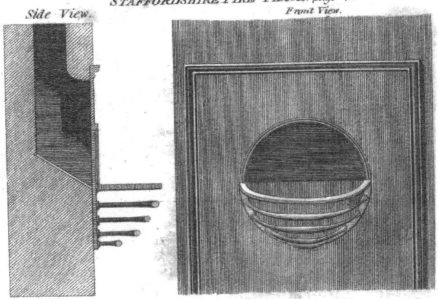

J. Akin fc.

d d, and commonly slides up and down in a groove, left, in putting up the fire-place, between the foremost ledge of the side-plates, and the face of the front plate ; but some chuse to set it aside when it is not in use, and apply it on occasion.

(viii) The register is also of thin wrought iron. It is placed between the back plate and air-box, and can, by means of the key S, be turned on its axis so as to lie in any position between level and upright.

The screw-rods O P are of wrought iron, about a third of an inch thick, with a button at bottom, and a screw and nut at top, and may be ornamented with two small brasses screwed on above the nuts.

To put this machine to work,

1. A false back of four inch (or, in shallow small chimneys, two inch) brick work is to be made in the chimney, four inches or more from the true back : from the top of this false back a closing is to be made over to the breast of the chimney, that no air may pass into the chimney, but what goes under the false back, and up behind it.

2. Some bricks of the hearth are to be taken up, to form a hollow under the bottom plate ; across which hollow runs a thin tight partition, to keep apart the air entering the hollow and the smoke ; and is therefore placed between the air-hole and smoke-holes.

3. A passage is made, communicating with the outward air, to introduce that air into the fore part of the hollow under the bottom plate, whence it may rise through the air-hole into the air-box.

4. A passage is made from the back part of the hollow, communicating with the flue behind the false back : through this passage the smoke is to pass.

The fire-place is to be erected upon these hollows, by putting all the plates in their places, and screwing them together.

Its operation may be conceived by observing the plate entitled, Profile of the Chimney and Fire-Place.

M The mantle-piece, or breast of the chimney.

C The funnel.

B The false back and closing.

E True back of the chimney.

T Top of the fire-place.

F The front of it.

A The place where the fire is made.

D The air-box.

K The hole in the side-plate, through which the warmed air is discharged out of the air-box into the room.

H The hollow filled with fresh air, entering at the passage *I*, and ascending into the air-box through the air-hole in the bottom plate near.

G The partition in the hollow to keep the air and smoke apart.

P The passage under the false back and part of the hearth for the smoke.

The arrows show the course of the smoke.

The fire being made at **A**, the flame and smoke will ascend and strike the top T, which will thereby receive a considerable heat. The smoke, finding no passage upwards, turns over the top of the air-box, and descends between it and the back plate to the holes in the bottom plate, heating, as it passes, both plates of the air-box, and the said back plate ; the front plate, bottom and side plates are also all heated at the same time. The smoke proceeds in the passage that leads it under and behind the false back, and so rises into the chimney. The air of the room, warmed behind the back plate, and by the sides, front, and top plates, becoming specifically lighter than the other air in the room, is obliged to rise ; but the closure over the fire-place hindering it from going up the chimney, it is forced out into the room, rises by the mantle-piece to the ceiling, and spreads all over the top of the room, whence being crouded down gradually by the stream of newly-warmed air that follows and rises above it, the whole room becomes in a short time equally warmed.

At the same time the air, warmed under the bottom plate, and in the air-box, rises and comes out of the holes in the side-plates, very swiftly, if the door of the room be shut, and joins its current with the stream before-mentioned, rising from the side, back, and top plates.

The air that enters the room through the air-box is fresh, though warm ; and, computing the swiftness of its motion with the areas of the holes, it is found that near ten barrels of fresh air are hourly introduced by the air-box ; and by this means the air in the room is continually changed, and kept, at the same time, sweet and warm.

It is to be observed, that the entering air will not be warm at first lighting the fire, but heats gradually as the fire increases.

A square opening for a trap-door should be left in the closing of the chimney, for the sweeper to go up : the door may be made of slate or tin,' and commonly kept close shut, but so placed as that, turning up against the back of the chimney when open, it closes the vacancy behind the false back, and shoots the soot, that falls in sweeping, out upon the hearth.   This trap-door is a very convenient thing.

In rooms where much smoking of tobacco is used, it is also convenient to have a small hole, about five or six inches square, cut near the ceiling through into the funnel : this hole must have a shutter, by which it may be closed or opened at pleasure.   When open, there will be a strong draught of air through it into the chimney, which will presently carry off a cloud of smoke, and keep the room clear : if the room be too hot likewise, it will carry off as much of the warm air as you please, and then you may stop it entirely, or in part, as you think fit.   By this means it is, that the tobacco smoke does not descend among the heads of the company near the fire, as it must do before it can get into common chimneys.

The Manner of using this Fire-Place.

Your cord-wood must be cut into three lengths ; or else a short piece, fit for the fire-place, cut off, and the longer left for the kitchen or other fires.   Dry hickory, or ash, or any woods that burn with a clear flame are rather to be

chosen, because such are less apt to foul the smoke-passages
with soot: and flame communicates with its light, as well as
by contact, greater heat to the plates and room. But where
more ordinary wood is used, half a dry faggot of brush-
wood, burnt at the first making the fire in the morning, is
very advantageous, as it immediately, by its sudden blaze,
heats the plates, and warms the room (which with bad wood
slowly kindling would not be done so soon) and at the same
time by the length of its flame, turning in the passages, consumes and cleanses away the soot that such bad smoky
wood had produced therein the preceding day, and so keeps
them always free and clean. When you have laid a little
back log, and placed your billets on small dogs, as in common chimneys, and put some fire to them, then slide down
your shutter as low as the dogs, and the opening being by
that means contracted, the air rushes in briskly, and presently blows up the flames. When the fire is sufficiently
kindled, slide it up again[5]. In some of these fire-places
there is a little six-inch square trap-door of thin wrought
iron or brass, covering a hole of like dimensions near the
fore-part of the bottom plate, which being by a ring lifted
up towards the fire, about an inch, where it will be retained
by two springing sides fixed to it perpendicularly *(See the
plate, Fig.* 4.) the air rushes in from the hollow under the
bottom plate, and blows the fire. Where this is used, the
shutter serves only to close the fire at nights. The more
forward you can make your fire on the hearth-plate, not to
be incommoded by the smoke, the sooner and more will the
room be warmed. At night, when you go to bed, cover the
coals or brands with ashes as usual; then take away the
dogs, and slide down the shutter close to the bottom-plate,
sweeping a little ashes against it, that no air may pass under

---

5 The shutter is slid up and down in this manner, only in those fire-places
which are so made as that the distance between the top of the arched opening,
and the bottom plate, is the same as the distance between it and the top plate.
Where the arch is higher, as it is in the draught annexed (which is agreeable to
late improvements) the shutter is set by, and applied occasionally; because if it were made deep enough to close the whole opening when slid down,
it would hide part of it when up.

it; then turn the register, so as very near to stop the flue behind. If no smoke then comes out at crevices into the room, it is right: if any smoke is perceived to come out, move the register, so as to give a little draught, and it will go the right way. Thus the room will be kept warm all night; for the chimney being almost entirely stopt, very little cold air, if any, will enter the room at any crevice. When you come to re-kindle the fire in the morning, turn open the register before you lift up the slider, otherwise, if there be any smoke in the fire-place, it will come out into the room. By the same use of the shutter and register, a blazing fire may be presently stifled, as well as secured, when you have occasion to leave it for any time; and at your return you will find the brands warm, and ready for a speedy rekindling. The shutter alone will not stifle a fire, for it cannot well be made to fit so exactly but that air will enter, and that in a violent stream, so as to blow up and keep alive the flames, and consume the wood, if the draught be not checked by turning the register to shut the flue behind. The register has also two other uses. If you observe the draught of air into your fire-place to be stronger than is necessary (as in extreme cold weather it often is) so that the wood is consumed faster than usual; in that case, a quarter, half, or two-thirds, turn of the register, will check the violence of the draught, and let your fire burn with the moderation you desire: and at the same time both the fire-place and the room will be the warmer, because less cold air will enter and pass through them. And if the chimney should happen to take fire (which indeed there is very little danger of, if the preceding direction be observed in making fires, and it be well swept once a year; for, much less wood being burnt, less soot is proportionably made; and the fuel being soon blown into flame by the shutter, or the trap-door bellows, there is consequently less smoke from the fuel to make soot; then, though the funnel should be foul, yet the sparks have such a crooked up and down round about way to go, that they are out before they get at it). I say, if ever it should be on fire, a turn of the register shuts all close, and prevents any air going into the chimney, and so the fire may easily be stifled and mastered.

The Advantages of this Fire-place.

Its advantages above the common fire-places are,

1. That your whole room is equally warmed, so that people need not croud so close round the fire, but may sit near the window, and have the benefit of the light for reading, writing, needle-work, &c. They may sit with comfort in any part of the room, which is a very considerable advantage in a large family, where there must often be two fires kept, because all cannot conveniently come at one.

2. If you sit near the fire, you have not that cold draught of uncomfortable air nipping your back and heels, as when before common fires, by which many catch cold, being scorched before, and, as it were, froze behind.

3. If you sit against a crevice, there is not that sharp draught of cold air playing on you, as in rooms where there are fires in the common way; by which many catch cold, whence proceed coughs[6], catarrhs, tooth-aches, fevers, pleuresies, and many other diseases.

4. In case of sickness, they make most excellent nursing rooms; as they constantly supply a sufficiency of fresh air, so warmed at the same time as to be no way inconvenient or dangerous. A small one does well in a chamber; and, the chimneys being fitted for it, it may be removed from one room to another, as occasion requires, and fixed in half an hour. The equal temper too, and warmth of the air of the room, is thought to be particularly advantageous in some distempers; for it was observed in the winters of 1730 and 1736, when the small-pox spread in Pennsylvania, that very few children of the Germans died of that distemper in proportion to those of the English; which was ascribed, by some,

---

6 Lord Molesworth, in his account of Denmark, says, "That few or none of the people there are troubled with coughs, catarrhs, consumptions, or such like diseases of the lungs; so that in the midst of winter in the churches, which are very much frequented, there is no noise to interrupt the attention due to the preacher. I am persuaded (says he) their *warm stoves* contribute to their freedom from these kinds of maladies." page 91.

to the warmth and equal temper of air in their stove-rooms, which made the disease as favorable as it commonly is in the West Indies. But this conjecture we submit to the judgment of physicians.

5. In common chimneys, the strongest heat from the fire, which is upwards, goes directly up the chimney, and is lost; and there is such a strong draught into the chimney that not only the upright heat, but also the back, sides, and downward heats are carried up the chimney by that draught of air; and the warmth given before the fire, by the rays that strike out towards the room is continually driven back, crouded into the chimney, and carried up by the same draught of air. But here the upright heat strikes and heats the top plate, which warms the air above it, and that comes into the room. The heat likewise, which the fire communicates to the sides, back, bottom, and air-box, is all brought into the room; for you will find a constant current of warm air coming out of the chimney-corner into the room. Hold a candle just under the mantle-piece, or breast of your chimney, and you will see the flame bent outwards: by laying a piece of smoking paper on the hearth, on either side, you may see how the current of air moves, and where it tends, for it will turn and carry the smoke with it.

6. Thus, as very little of the heat is lost, when this fire-place is used, *much less wood*[7] will serve you, which is a considerable advantage where wood is dear.

7. When you burn candles near this fire-place, you will find that the flame burns quite upright, and does not blare and run the tallow down, by drawing towards the chimney, as against common fires.

---

7 People who have used these fire-places, differ much in their accounts of the wood saved by them. Some say five-sixths, others three-fourths, and others much less. This is owing to the great difference there was in their former fires; some (according to the different circumstances of their rooms and chimneys) having been used to make very large, others middling, and others, of a more sparing temper, very small ones: while in these fire-places (their size and draught being nearly the same, the consumption is more equal. I suppose, taking a number of families together, that two-thirds, or half the wood, at least, is saved. My common room, I know, is made twice as warm as it used to be, with a quarter of the wood I formerly consumed there.

8. This fire-place cures most smoky chimneys, and thereby preserves both the eyes and furniture.

9. It prevents the fouling of chimneys; much of the lint and dust that contributes to foul a chimney, being, by the low arch, obliged to pass through the flame, where it is consumed. Then, less wood being burnt, there is less smoke made. Again, the shutter, or trap-bellows, soon blowing the wood into a flame, the same wood does not yield so much smoke as if burnt in a common chimney: for as soon as flame begins, smoke in proportion ceases.

10. And if a chimney should be foul, it is much less likely to take fire. If it should take fire, it is easily stifled and extinguished.

11. A fire may be very speedily made in this fire-place by the help of the shutter, or trap-bellows, as aforesaid.

12. A fire may be soon extinguished, by closing it with the shutter before, and turning the register behind, which will stifle it, and the brands will remain ready to rekindle.

13. The room being once warm, the warmth may be retained in it all night.

14. And lastly, the fire is so secured at night, that not one spark can fly out into the room to do damage.

With all these conveniences, you do not lose the pleasing sight nor use of the fire, as in the Dutch stoves, but may boil the tea-kettle, warm the flat-irons, heat heaters, keep warm a dish of victuals by setting it on the top, &c.

Objections answered.

There are some objections commonly made by people that are unacquainted with these fire-places, which it may not be amiss to endeavor to remove, as they arise from prejudices which might otherwise obstruct, in some degree, the general use of this beneficial machine. We frequently hear it said, *They are of the nature of Dutch stoves; stoves have an unpleasant smell; stoves are unwholesome; and, warm rooms make people tender, and apt to catch cold.*——As to the first, that they are of the nature of Dutch stoves, the description of those stoves, in the beginning of this paper, compared with that of these machines, shows, that there is a most material difference, and that these have vastly the advantage, if it were only in the single article of the admission and circulation of the fresh air. But it must be allowed there may have been some cause to complain of the offensive smell of iron stoves. This smell, however, never proceeded from the iron itself, which, in its nature, whether hot or cold, is one of the sweetest of metals, but from the general uncleanly manner of using those stoves. If they are kept clean, they are as sweet as an ironing-box, which, though ever so hot, never offends the smell of the nicest lady: but it is common to let them be greased, by setting candlesticks on them, or otherwise; to rub greasy hands on them; and, above all, to spit upon them, to try how hot they are, which is an inconsiderate filthy unmannerly custom; for the slimy matter of spittle drying on, burns and fumes when the stove is hot, as well as the grease, and smells most nauseously; which makes such close stove-rooms, where there is no draught to carry off those filthy vapors, almost intolerable to those that are not from their infancy accustomed to them. At the same time nothing is more easy than to keep them clean; for when by any accident they happen to be fouled, a lee made of ashes and water, with a brush, will scour them perfectly: as will also a little strong soft soap and water.

That hot iron of itself gives no offensive smell, those know very well who have (as the writer of this has) been present at a furnace when the workmen were pouring out the flowing metal to cast large plates, and not the least smell of it to be perceived. That hot iron does not, like lead, brass, and some other metals, give out unwholesome vapors, is plain from the general health and strength of those who constantly work in iron, as furnace-men, forge-men, and smiths; that it is in its nature a metal perfectly wholesome to the body of man, is known from the beneficial use of chalybeate or iron-mine-waters; from the good done by taking steel filings in several disorders; and that even the smithy water in which hot irons are quenched, is found advantageous to the human constitution.——The ingenious and learned Dr. Desaguliers, to whose instructive writings the contriver of this machine acknowleges himself much indebted, relates an experiment he made, to try whether heated iron would yield unwholesome vapors: he took a cube of iron, and having given it a very great heat, he fixed it so to a receiver, exhausted by the air-pump, that all the air rushing in to fill the receiver, should first pass through a hole in the hot iron. He then put a small bird into the receiver, who breathed that air without any inconvenience, or suffering the least disorder. But the same experiment being made with a cube of hot brass, a bird put into that air died in a few minutes. Brass, indeed, stinks even when cold, and much more when hot; lead, too, when hot, yields a very unwholesome steam; but iron is alwsys sweet and every way taken is wholesome and friendly to the human body—except in weapons.

That warmed rooms make people tender, and apt to catch cold, is a mistake as great as it is (among the English) general. We have seen in the preceding pages how the common rooms are apt to give colds; but the writer of this paper may affirm from his own experience, and that of his family and friends who have used warm rooms for these four winters past, that by the use of such rooms, people are rendered *less liable* to take cold, and, indeed, *actually hardened.* If sitting warm in a room made one subject to take cold on going out, lying warm in bed, should by a parity of reason, produce the same effect when we rise. Yet we find we can leap out of the warmest bed naked, in the coldest morning, without any such danger; and in the same manner out of warm clothes into a cold bed. The reason is, that in these cases the pores all close at once, the cold is shut out, and the heat within augmented, as we soon after feel by the glowing of the flesh and skin. Thus no one was ever known to catch cold by the use of the cold bath: and are not cold baths allowed to harden the bodies of those that use them? Are they not therefore frequently prescribed to the tenderest constitutions? Now every time you go out of a warm room into the cold freezing air, you do as it were plunge into a cold bath, and the effect is in proportion the same; for (though perhaps you may feel somewhat chilly at first) you find in a little time your bodies hardened and strengthened, your blood is driven round with a brisker circulation, and a comfortable steady uniform inward warmth succeeds that equal outward warmth you first received in the room. Farther to confirm this assertion, we instance the Swedes, the Danes, and the Russians: these nations are said to live in rooms, compared to ours, as hot as ovens;[8] yet where are the hardy soldiers, though bred in their boasted cool houses, that can, like these people, bear the fatigues of a winter campaign in so severe a climate, march whole days to the neck in snow, and at night entrench in ice as they do?

The mentioning of those northern nations, puts me in mind of a considerable *public advantage* that may arise from the general use of these fire-places. It is observable, that though those countries have been well inhabited for many ages, wood is still their fuel, and yet at no very great price; which could not have been, if they had not universally used stoves, but consumed it as we do, in great quantities, by open fires. By the help of this saving invention our wood may grow as fast as we consume it, and our posterity may warm themselves at a moderate rate, without being obliged to fetch their fuel over the Atlantic; as, if pit-coal should not

---

8 Mr. Boyle, in his experiments and observations upon cold, *Shaw's Abridgement*, Vol. F. p. 684, says, "It is remarkable, that while the cold has strange and tragical effects at Moscow and elsewhere; the Russians and Livonians should be exempt from them, who accustom themselves to pass immediately from a great degree of heat, to as great an one of cold, without receiving any visible prejudice thereby. I remember being told by a person of unquestionable credit, that it was a common practice among them, to go from a hot stove, into cold water; the same was also affirmed to me by another who resided at Moscow. This tradition is likewise abundantly confirmed by Olearius."—"It is a surprising thing," says he, "to see how far the Russians can endure heat; and how, when it makes them ready to faint, they can go out of their stoves, start naked, both men and women, and throw themselves into cold water; and even in winter wallow in the snow."

be here discovered (which is an uncertainty) they must ne-
cesarily do.[9]

We leave it to the *political arithmetician* to compute how
much money will be saved to a country, by its spending two-
thirds less of fuel; how much labor saved in cutting and
carriage of it; how much more land may be cleared by
cultivation; how great the profit by the additional quantity
of work done, in those trades particularly that do not exercise the body so much, but that the workfolks are obliged
to run frequently to the fire to warm themselves: and to
physicians to say, how much healthier thick-built towns and
cities will be, now half-suffocated with sulphury smoke,
when so much less of that smoke shall be made; and the air
breathed by the inhabitants be consequently so much purer.
These things it will suffice just to have mentioned; let us
proceed to give some necessary directions to the workman
who is to fix or set up these fire-places.

Directions to the Bricklayer.

The chimney being first well swept and cleansed from
soot, &c. lay the bottom plate down on the hearth, in the
place where the fire-place is to stand, which may be as forward as the hearth will allow. Chalk a line from one of
its back corners round the plate to the other corner, that
you may afterwards know its place when you come to fix it;
and from those corners, two parallel lines to the back of
the chimney: make marks also on each side, that you may
know where the partition is to stand, which is to prevent
any communication between the air and smoke. Then, removing the plate, make a hollow under it and beyond it, by
taking up as many of the bricks or tiles as you can, within
your chalked lines, quite to the chimney-back. Dig out
six or eight inches deep of the earth or rubbish, all the
breadth and length of your hollow; then make a passage of
four inches square (if the place will allow so much) leading

---

9 Pitcoal has been discovered since in great abundance in various parts of the
United States. The mountains of Pennsylvania contain vast treasures, which
only require canals and roads to convey them in quantities sufficient for the
supply of the whole continent.

from the hollow to some place communicating with the outer air ; by *outer air* we mean air without the room you intend to warm. This passage may be made to enter your hollow on either side, or in the fore part, just as you find most convenient, the circumstances of your chimney considered. If the fire-place is to be put up in a chamber, you may have this communication of outer air from the stair-case ; or sometimes more easily from between the chamber floor, and the ceiling of the lower room, making only a small hole in the wall of the house entering the space betwixt those two joists with which your air-passage in the hearth communicates. If this air passage be so situated as that mice may enter it, and nestle in the hollow, a little grate of wire will keep them out. This passage being made, and, if it runs under any part of the earth, tiled over securely, you may proceed to raise your false back. This may be of four inches or two inches thickness, as you have room, but let it stand at least four inches from the true chimney-back. In narrow chimneys this false back runs from jamb to jamb, but in large old-fashioned chimneys, you need not make it wider than the back of the fire-place. To begin it, you may form an arch nearly flat, of three bricks end to end, over the hollow, to leave a passage the breadth of the iron fire-place, and five or six inches deep, rounding at bottom, for the smoke to turn and pass under the false back, and so behind it up the chimney. The false back is to rise till it is as high as the breast of the chimney, and then to close over the breast ;[9] always observing, if there is a wooden mantle-tree, to close above it. If there is no wood in the breast, you may arch over and close even with the lower part of the breast. By this closing the chimney is made tight, that no air or smoke can pass up it, without going under the false back. Then from side to side of your hollow, against the marks you made with chalk, raise a tight partition, brick-on-edge, to separate the air from the smoke, bevelling

9 See page 415, where the trap-door is described that ought to be in this closing.

away to half an inch the brick that comes just under the
air-hole, th t the air may have a free passage up into the
air-box: lastly, close the hearth over that part of the hollow that is between the false back and the place of the bottom plate, coming about half an inch under the plate, which
piece of hollow hearth may be supported by a bit or two of
old iron-hoop; then is your chimney fitted to receive the
fire-place.

To set it, lay first a little bed of mortar all round the
edges of the hollow, and over the top of the partition:
then lay down your bottom plate in its place (with the rods
in it) and tread it till it lies firm.   Then put a little fine
mortar (made of loam and lime, with a little coarse hair)
into its joints, and set in your back plate, leaning it for
the present against the false back: then set in your air-box,
with a little mortar in its joints; then put in the two sides,
closing them up against the air-box, with mortar in their
grooves, and fixing at the same time your register: then
bring up your back to its place, with mortar in its grooves,
and that will bind the sides together.   Then put in your
front plate, placing it as far back in the groove as you can,
to leave room for the sliding plate: then lay on your top
plate, with mortar in its grooves also, screwing the whole
firmly together by means of the rods.   The capital letters
A B D E, &c. in the annexed cut, shew the corresponding
parts of the several plates.   Lastly, the joints being pointed
all round on the outside, the fire-place is fit for use.

When you make your first fire in it, perhaps if the chimney be thoroughly cold, it may not draw, the work too being all cold and damp.   In such case, put first a few shovels
of hot coals in the fire-place, then lift up the chimney-
sweeper's trap-door, and putting in a sheet or two of flaming paper, shut it again, which will set the chimney a
drawing immediately, and when once it is filled with a
column of warm air, it will draw strongly and continually.

The drying of the mortar and work by the first fire may
smell unpleasantly, but that will soon be over.

In some shallow chimneys, to make more room for the false back and its flue, four inches or more of the chimney back may be picked away.

Let the room be made as tight as conveniently it may be, so will the outer air, that must come in to supply the room and draught of the fire, be all obliged to enter through the passage under the bottom plate, and up through the air-box, by which means it will not come cold to your backs, but be warmed as it comes in, and mixed with the warm air round the fire-place, before it spreads in the room.

But as a great quantity of cold air, in extreme cold weather especially, will presently enter a room if the door be carelessly left open, it is good to have some contrivance to shut it, either by means of screw hinges, a spring, or a pulley.

When the pointing in the joints is all dry and hard, get some powder of black lead (broken bits of black lead crucibles from the silver-smiths, pounded fine, will do) and mixing it with a little rum and water, lay it on, when the plates are warm, with a hard brush, over the top and front-plates, part of the side and bottom-plates, and over all the pointing; and, as it dries, rub it to a gloss with the same brush, so the joints will not be discerned, but it will look all of a piece, and shine like new iron. And the false back being plaistered and white-washed, and the hearth reddened, the whole will make a pretty appearance. Before the black lead is laid on, it would not be amiss to wash the plates with strong lee and a brush, or soap and water, to cleanse them from any spots of grease or filth that may be on them. If any grease should afterwards come on them, a little wet ashes will get it out.

If it be well set up, and in a tolerable good chimney, smoke will draw in from as far as the fore part of the bottom plate, as you may try by a bit of burning paper.

People are at first apt to make their rooms too warm, not imagining how little a fire will be sufficient. When the plates are no hotter than that one may just bear the hand on them, the room will generally be as warm as you desire it.

Soon after the foregoing piece was published, some persons in England, in imitation of Dr. Franklin's invention, made what they call Pennsylvanian Fire-Places, *with improvements ; the principal of which pretended improvements is, a contraction of the passages in the air-box, originally designed for admitting a quantity of fresh air, and warming it as it entered the room. The contracting these passages gains indeed more room for the grate, but in a great measure defeats their intention. For if the passages in the air-box do not greatly exceed in dimensions the amount of all the crevices by which cold air can enter the room, they will not considerably prevent, as they were intended to do, the entry of cold air through these crevices.*

TO DR. INGENHAUSZ, PHYSICIAN TO THE EMPEROR, AT VIENNA[1].

On the Causes and Cure of Smoky Chimnies.

Read in the American Philosophical Society, Oct. 21, 1785.

At Sea, Aug. 28, 1785.

DEAR FRIEND,

IN one of your letters, a little before I left France, you desired me to give you in writing my thoughts upon the construction and use of chimneys, a subject you had sometimes heard me touch upon in conversation. I embrace willingly this leisure afforded by my present situation to comply with your request, as it will not only show my regard to the desires of a friend, but may at the same time be of some utility to others ; the doctrine of chimneys appearing not to be as yet generally well understood, and mistakes respecting them being attended with constant inconvenience, if not remedied, and with fruitless expence, if the true remedies are mistaken.

1 This letter, has been published in a separate pamphlet, in Germany, England, and America ; it has also appeared in the Transactions of the American Philosophical Society.

Those who would be acquainted with this subject should begin by considering on what principle smoke ascends in any chimney. At first many are apt to think that smoke is in its nature and of itself specifically lighter than air, and rises in it for the same reason that cork rises in water. These see no case why smoke should not rise in the chimney, though the room be ever so close. Others think there is a power in chimneys to *draw* up the smoke, and that there are different forms of chimneys which afford more or less of this power. These amuse themselves with searching for the best form. The equal dimensions of a funnel in its whole length is not thought artificial enough, and it is made, for fancied reasons, sometimes tapering and narrowing from below upwards, and sometimes the contrary, &c. A simple experiment or two may serve to give more correct ideas. Having lit a pipe of tobacco, plunge the stem to the bottom of a decanter half filled with cold water; then putting a rag over the bowl, blow through it and make the smoke descend in the stem of the pipe, from the end of which it will rise in bubbles through the water; and being thus cooled, will not afterwards rise to go out through the neck of the decanter, but remain spreading itself and resting on the surface of the water. This shows that smoke is really heavier than air, and that it is carried upwards only when attached to, or acted upon, by air that is heated, and thereby rarefied and rendered specifically lighter than the air in its neighborhood.

Smoke being rarely seen but in company with heated air, and its upward motion being visible, though that of the rarefied air that drives it is not so, has naturally given rise to the error.

I need not explain to you, my learned friend, what is meant by rarefied air; but if you make the public use you propose of this letter, it may fall into the hands of some, who are unacquainted with the term and with the thing. These then may be told, that air is a fluid which has weight as well as others, though about eight hundred times lighter than water. That heat makes the particles of air recede

from each other and take up more space; so that the same
weight of air heated will have more bulk, than equal
weights of cold air which may surround it, and in that case
must rise, being forced upwards by such colder and heavier
air, which presses to get under it and take its place. That
air is so rarefied or expanded by heat may be proved to their
comprehension, by a lank blown bladder, which, laid before
a fire, will soon swell, grow tight, and burst.

Another experiment may be to take a glass tube about
an inch in diameter, and twelve inches long, open at both
ends and fixed upright on legs, so that it need not be han-,
dled, for the hands might warm it. At the end of a quill
fasten five or six inches of the finest light filament of silk,
so that it may be held either above the upper end of the
tube or under the lower end, your warm hand being at a
distance by the length of the quill. (See the plate fig. 1.) If
there were any motion of air through the tube, it would
manifest itself by its effect on the silk; but if the tube and
the air in it are of the same temperature with the surrounding air, there will be no such motion, whatever may be the
form of the tube, whether crooked or strait, narrow below
and widening upwards, or the contrary; the air in it will
be quiescent. Warm the tube, and you will find, as long
as it continues warm, a constant current of air entering
below and passing up through it, till discharged at the top;
because the warmth of the tube being communicated to the
air it contains, rarefies that air and makes it lighter than
the air without, which therefore presses in below, forces it
upwards, and follows and takes its place, and is rarefied in
its turn. And, without warming the tube, if you hold under it a knob of hot iron, the air thereby heated will rise
and fill the tube, going out at its top, and this motion in
the tube will continue as long as the knob remains hot, because the air entering the tube below is heated and rarefied
by passing near and over that knob.

That this motion is produced merely by the difference of
specific gravity between the fluid within and that without
the tube, and not by any fancied form of the tube itself,

may appear by plunging it into water contained in a glass jar a foot deep, through which such motion might be seen. The water within and without the tube being of the same specific gravity, balance each other, and both remain at rest. But take out the tube, stop its bottom with a finger and fill it with olive oil, which is lighter than water, then stopping the top, place it as before, its lower end under water, its top a very little above. As long as you keep the bottom stopt, the fluids remain at rest, but the moment it is unstopt, the heavier enters below, forces up the lighter, and takes its place. And the motion then ceases, merely because the new fluid cannot be successively made lighter, as air may be by a warm tube.

In fact, no form of the funnel of a chimney has any share in its operation or effect respecting smoke, except its height. The longer the funnel, if erect, the greater its force when filled with heated and rarefied air, to *draw* in below and drive up the smoke, if one may, in compliance with custom, use the expression *draw*, when in fact it is the superior weight of the surrounding atmosphere that *presses* to enter the funnel below, and so *drives up* before it the smoke and warm air it meets with in its passage.

I have been the more particular in explaining these first principles, because, for want of clear ideas respecting them, much fruitless expence has been occasioned ; not only single chimnies, but in some instances, within my knowlege, whole stacks having been pulled down and rebuilt with funnels of different forms, imagined more powerful in *drawing* smoke ; but having still the same height and the same opening below, have performed no better than their predecessors.

What is it then which makes a *smoky chimney*, that is, a chimney which, instead of conveying up all the smoke, discharges a part of it into the room, offending the eyes and damaging the furniture ?

The casues of this effect, which have fallen under my observation, amount to *nine*, differing from each other, and therefore requiring different remedies.

1. *Smoky chimnies in a new house, are such, frequently from mere want of air.* The workmanship of the rooms being all good, and just out of the workman's hand, the joints of the boards of the flooring, and of the pannels of wainscotting are all true and tight, the more so as the walls, perhaps not yet thoroughly dry, preserve a dampness in the air of the room which keeps the wood-work swelled and close. The doors and the sashes too, being worked with truth, shut with exactness, so that the room is as tight as a snuff box, no passage being left open for air to enter, except the key-hole, and even that is sometimes covered by a little dropping shutter. Now if smoke cannot rise but as connected with rarefied air, and a column of such air, suppose it filling the funnel, cannot rise, unless other air be admitted to supply its place; and if, therefore, no current of air enter the opening of the chimney, there is nothing to prevent the smoke coming out into the room. If the motion upwards of the air in a chimney that is freely supplied, be observed by the raising of the smoke or a feather in it, and it be considered that in the time such feather takes in rising from the fire to the top of the chimney, a column of air equal to the content of the funnel must be discharged, and an equal quantity supplied from the room below, it will appear absolutely impossible that this operation should go on if the tight room is kept shut; for were there any force capable of drawing constantly so much air out of it, it must soon be exhausted like the receiver of an air-pump, and no animal could live in it. Those therefore who stop every crevice in a room to prevent the admission of fresh air, and yet would have their chimney carry up the smoke, require inconsistencies, and expect impossibilities. Yet under this situation, I have seen the owner of a new house, in despair, and ready to sell it for much less than it cost, conceiving it uninhabitable, because not a chimney in any one of its rooms would carry off the smoke, unless a door or window were left open. Much expence has also been made, to alter and amend new chimneys which had really no fault; in one house particularly that I knew, of a nobleman in Westmin-

ster, that expence amounted to no less than three hundred pounds, *after* his house had been, as he thought, finished and all charges paid. And after all, several of the alterations were ineffectual, for want of understanding the true principles.

Remedies. When you find on trial, that opening the door or a window, enables the chimney to carry up all the smoke, you may be sure that want of air *from without*, was the cause of its smoking. I say *from without*, to guard you against a common mistake of those who may tell you, the room is large, contains abundance of air, sufficient to supply any chimney, and therefore it cannot be that the chimney wants air. These reasoners are ignorant, that the largeness of a room, if tight, is in this case of small importance, since it cannot part with a chimney full of air without occasioning so much vacuum; which it requires a great force to effect, and could not be borne if effected.

It appearing plainly, then, that some of the outward air must be admitted, the question will be, how much is *absolutely necessary;* for you would avoid admitting more, as being contrary to one of your intentions in having a fire, viz. that of warming your room. To discover this quantity, shut the door gradually while a middling fire is burning, till you find that, before it is quite shut, the smoke begins to come out into the room, then open it a little till you perceive the smoke comes out no longer. There hold the door, and observe the width of the open crevice between the edge of the door and the rabbit it should shut into. Suppose the distance to be half an inch, and the door eight feet high, you find thence that your room requires an entrance for air equal in area to ninety-six half inches, or forty-eight square inches, or a passage of six inches by eight. This however is a large supposition, there being few chimneys, that, having a moderate opening and a tolerable height of funnel, will not be satisfied with such a crevice of a quarter of an inch; and I have found a square of six by six, or thirty-six square inches, to be a pretty good medium, that will serve for most chimneys. High

3 I

funnels, with small and low openings, may indeed be supplied through a less space, because for reasons that will appear hereafter, the *force of levity*, if one may so speak, being greater in such funnels, the cool air enters the room with greater velocity, and consequently more enters in the same time. This however has its limits, for experience shows, that no increased velocity, so occasioned, has made the admission of air through the key-hole equal in quantity to that through an open door; though through the door the current moves slowly, and through the key-hole with great rapidity.

It remains then to be considered how and where this necessary quantity of air from without is to be admitted so as to be least inconvenient. For if at the door, left so much open, the air thence proceeds directly to the chimney, and in its way comes cold to your back and heels as you sit before your fire. If you keep the door shut, and raise a little the sash of your window, you feel the same inconvenience. Various have been the contrivances to avoid this, such as bringing in fresh air through pipes in the jambs of the chimney, which, pointing upwards, should blow the smoke up the funnel; opening passages into the funnel above, to let in air for the same purpose. But these produce an effect contrary to that intended; for as it is the constant current of air passing from the room *through the opening of the chimney* into the funnel which prevents the smoke coming out into the room, if you supply the funnel by other means or in other ways with the air it wants, and especially if that air be cold, you diminish the force of that current, and the smoke in its effort to enter the room finds less resistance.

The wanted air must then *indispensibly* be admitted into the room, to supply what goes off through the opening of the chimney. M. Gauger, a very ingenious and intelligent French writer on the subject, proposes with judgment to admit it *above* the opening of the chimney; and to prevent inconvenience from its coldness, he directs its being made to pass in its entrance through winding cavities made behind the iron back and sides of the fire-place, and under the iron hearth-plate; in which cavities it will be warmed, and even heated, so as to contribute much, instead of cooling, to the warming of the room. This invention is excellent in itself, and may be used with advantage in building new houses; because the chimneys may then be so disposed, as to admit conveniently the cold air to enter such passages: but in houses built without such views, the chimneys are often so situated, as not to afford that convenience, without great and expensive alterations. Easy and cheap methods, though not quite so perfect in themselves, are of more general utility; and such are the following.

In all rooms where there is a fire, the body of air warmed and rarefied before the chimney is continually changing place, and making room for other air that is to be warmed in its turn. Part of it enters and goes up the chimney, and the rest rises and takes place near the ceiling. If the room be lofty, that warm air remains above our heads as long as it continues warm, and we are little benefited by it, because it does not descend till it is cooler. Few can imagine the difference of climate between the upper and lower parts of such a room, who have not tried it by the thermometer, or by going up a ladder till their heads are near the ceiling. It is then among this warm air that the wanted quantity of outward air is best admitted, with which being mixed, its coldness is abated, and its inconvenience diminished so as to become scarce observable. This may be easily done, by drawing down about an inch the upper sash of a window; or, if not moveable, but cutting such a crevice through its frame; in both which cases, it will be well to place a thin shelf of the length, to conceal the opening, and sloping upwards to direct the entering air horizontally along and under the ceiling. In some houses the air may be admitted by such a crevice made in the waincost, cornish, or plastering, near the ceiling and over the opening of the chimney. This, if practicable, is to be chosen, because the entering cold air will there meet with the warmest rising air from before the fire, and be soonest tempered by the mixture. The same kind of shelf should also be placed here. Another way, and not a very difficult one, is to take out an upper pane of glass in one of your sashes, set in a tin frame, (Plate, Fig. 2.) giving it two springing angular sides, and then replacing it, with hinges below on which it may be turned to open more or less above. It will then have the appearance of an internal sky light. By drawing this pane in, more or less, you may admit what air you find necessary. Its position will naturally throw that air up and along the ceiling. This is what is called in France a *Was ist das?* As this is a German question, the invention is probably of that nation, and takes its name from the frequent asking of that question when it first appeared. In England, some have of late years cut a round hole about five inches diameter in a pane of the sash and placed against it a circular plate of tin hung on an axis, and cut into vanes, which, being separately bent a little obliquely, are acted upon by the entering air, so as to force the plate continually round like the vanes of a windmill. This admits the outward air, and by the continual whirling of the vanes, does in some degree disperse it. The noise only, is a little inconvenient.

2. A second cause of the smoking of chimneys is, *their openings in the room being too large;* that is, too wide, too high, or both. Architects in general have no other ideas of proportion in the opening of a chimney, than what relate to symmetry and beauty, respecting the dimensions of the room:[2] while its true proportion, respecting its function and utility depends on quite other principles; and they might as properly proportion the step in a stair-case to the height of the story, instead of the natural elevation of men's legs in mounting. The proportion then to be regarded, is what relates to the height of the funnel. For as the funnels in the different stories of a house are necessarily of different heights or lengths, that from the lowest floor being the highest or longest, and those of the other floors shorter

2 See Notes at the end of this paper, No. I.

and shorter, till we come to those in the garrets, which are of course the shortest; and the force of draft being, as already said, in proportion to the height of funnel filled with rarefied air; and a current of air from the room into the chimney, sufficient to fill the opening, being necessary to oppose and prevent the smoke coming out into the room; it follows, that the openings of the longest funnels may be larger, and that those of the shorter funnels should be smaller. For if there be a large opening to a chimney that does not draw strongly, the funnel may happen to be furnished with the air it demands by a partial current entering on one side of the opening, and, leaving the other side free of any opposing current, may permit the smoke to issue there into the room. Much too of the force of draft in a funnel depends on the degree of rarefaction in the air it contains, and that depends on the nearness to the fire of its passage in entering the funnel. If it can enter far from the fire on each side, or far above the fire, in a wide or high opening, it receives little heat in passing by the fire, and the contents of the funnel is by that means less different in levity from the surrounding atmosphere, and its force in drawing consequently weaker. Hence if too large an opening be given to chimneys in upper rooms, those rooms will be smoky: on the other hand, if too small openings be given to chimneys in the lower rooms, the entering air, operating too directly and violently on the fire, and afterwards strengthening the draft as it ascends the funnel, will consume the fuel too rapidly.

Remedy. As different circumstances frequently mix themselves in these matters, it is difficult to give precise dimensions for the openings of all chimneys. Our fathers made them generally much too large; we have lessened them; but they are often still of greater dimension than they should be, the human eye not being easily reconciled to sudden and great changes. If you suspect that your chimney smokes from the too great dimension of its opening, contract it by placing moveable boards so as to lower and narrow it gradually, till you find the smoke no longer issues into the room. The proportion so found will be that which is proper for that chimney, and you may employ the bricklayer or mason to reduce it accordingly. However, as, in building new houses, something must be sometimes hazarded, I would make the openings in my lower rooms about thirty inches square and eighteen deep, and those in the upper, only eighteen inches square and not quite so deep; the intermediate ones diminishing in proportion as the height of funnel diminished. In the larger openings, billets of two feet long, or half the common length of cordwood, may be burnt conveniently; and for the smaller, such wood may be sawed into thirds. Where coals are the fuel, the grates will be proportioned to the openings. The same depth is nearly necessary to all, the funnels being all made of a size proper to admit a chimney-sweeper. If in large and elegant rooms custom or fancy should require the appearance of a large chimney, it may be formed of extensive marginal decorations, in marble, &c. In time perhaps, that which is fittest in the nature of things may come to be thought handsomest. But at present, when men and women in different countries show themselves dissatisfied with the forms God has given to their heads, waists and feet, and pretend to shape them more perfectly, it is hardly to be expected that they will be content always with the best form of a chimney. And there are some, I know, so bigotted to the fancy of a large noble opening, that rather than change it, they would submit to have damaged furniture, sore eyes, and skins almost smoked to bacon.

3. Another cause of smoky chimneys is, *too short a funnel.* This happens necessarily in some cases, as where a chimney is required in a low building; for, if the funnel be raised high above the roof, in order to strengthen its draft, it is then in danger of being blown down, and crushing the roof in its fall.

Remedies. Contract the opening of the chimney, so as to oblige all the entering air to pass through or very near the fire; whereby it will be more heated and rarefied, the funnel itself be more warmed, and its contents have more of what may be called the force of levity, so as to rise strongly and maintain a good draft at the opening.

Or you may in some cases, to advantage, build additional stories over the low building, which will support a high funnel.

If the low building be used as a kitchen, and a contraction of the opening therefore inconvenient, a large one being necessary, at least when there are great dinners, for the free management of so many cooking utensils; in such case I would advise the building of two more funnels joining to the first, and having three moderate openings, one to each funnel, instead of one large one. When there is occasion to use but one, the other two may be kept shut by sliding plates, hereafter to be described;[3] and two or all of them may be used together when wanted. This will indeed be an expence, but not an useless one, since your cooks will work with more comfort, see better than in a smoky kitchen what they are about, your victuals will be cleaner dressed, and not taste of smoke, as is often the case; and to render the effect more certain, a stack of three funnels may be safely built higher above the roof than a single funnel.

The case of too short a funnel is more general than would be imagined, and often found where one would not expect it. For it is not uncommon, in ill-contrived buildings, instead of having a funnel for each room or fire-place, to bend and turn the funnel of an upper room so as to make it enter the side of another funnel that comes from below. By this means the upper room funnel is made short of course, since its length can only be reckoned from the place where it enters the lower room funnel; and that funnel is also shortened by all the distance between the entrance of the second funnel and the top of the stack; for all that part being readily supplied with air through the second funnel, adds no strength to the draught, especially as that air is cold where there is no fire in the second chimney. The only easy

---

3 See Notes at the end of this paper, No. II.

remedy here is, to keep the opening shut of that funnel in which there is no fire.

4. Another very common cause of the smoking of chimneys, is, *their overpowering one another.* For instance, if there be two chimneys in one large room, and you make fires in both of them, the doors and windows close shut, you will find that the greater and stronger fire shall overpower the weaker, and draw air down its funnel to supply its own demand; which air descending in the weaker funnel will drive down its smoke, and force it into the room. If, instead of being in one room, the two chimneys are in two different rooms, communicating by a door, the case is the same whenever that door is open. In a very tight house, I have known a kitchen chimney on the lowest floor, when it had a great fire in it, overpower any other chimney in the house, and draw air and smoke into its room, as often as the door was opened communicating with the staircase.

Remedy. Take care that every room has the means of supplying itself from without, with the air its chimney may require, so that no one of them may be obliged to borrow from another, nor under the necessity of lending. A variety of these means have been already described.

5. Another cause of smoking is, *when the tops of chimneys are commanded by higher buildings,* or *by a hill,* so that the wind blowing over such eminences falls like water over a dam, sometimes almost perpendicularly on the tops of the chimneys that lie in its way, and beats down the smoke contained in them.

Remedy. That commonly applied to this case, is a turn-cap made of tin or plate iron, covering the chimney above and on three sides, open on one side, turning on a spindle, and which, being guided or governed by a vane, always presents its back to the current. This I believe may be generally effectual, though not certain, as there may be cases in which it will not succeed. Raising your funnels, if practicable, so as their tops may be higher, or at least equal with the commanding eminence, is more to be depended on. But the turning cap, being easier and cheaper, should first be tried. If obliged to build in such a situation, I would chuse to place my doors on the side next the hill, and the backs of my chimneys on the furthest side; for then the column of air falling over the eminence, and of course pressing on that below, and forcing it to enter the doors, or *Was-ist-dases* on that side, would tend to balance the pressure down the chimneys, and leave the funnels more free in the exercise of their functions.

6. There is another case of command, the reverse of that last mentioned. It is where the commanding eminence is farther from the wind than the chimney commanded. To explain this a figure may be necessary. Suppose then a building whose side A, happens to be exposed to the wind, and forms a kind of dam against its progress. (Plate, Figure 3.) The air obstructed by this dam will, like water, press and search for passages through it; and finding the top of the chimney B, below the top of the dam, it will force itself down that funnel, in order to get through by some door or window open on the side of the building. And if there be a fire in such chimney, its smoke is of course beat down, and fills the room.

Remedy. I know of but one, which is to raise such funnel higher than the roof, supporting it, if necessary, by iron bars. For a turn-cap in this case has no effect, the dammed up air pressing down through it in whatever position the wind may have placed its opening.

I know a city in which many houses are rendered smoky by this operation. For their kitchens being built behind, and connected by a passage with the houses, and the tops of the kitchen chimneys lower than the top of the houses, the whole side of a street, when the wind blows against its back, forms such a dam as above described; and the wind, so obstructed, forces down those kitchen chimneys (especially when they have but weak fires in them) to pass through the passage and house into the street. Kitchen chimneys, so formed and situated, have another inconvenience. In summer, if you open your upper room windows

3 K

for air, a light breeze blowing over your kitchen chimney towards the house, though not strong enough to force down its smoke as aforesaid, is sufficient to waft it into your windows, and fill the rooms with it; which, besides the disagreeableness, damages your furniture.

7. Chimneys, otherwise drawing well, are sometimes made to smoke by *the improper and inconvenient situation of a door*. When the door and chimney are on the same side of the room as in the figure, if the door A, being in the corner, is made to open against the wall (Plate, Figure 4) which is common, as being there, when open, more out of the way, it follows, that when the door is only opened in part, a current of air rushing in passes along the wall into and across the opening of the chimney B, and flirts some of the smoke out into the room. This happens more certainly when the door is shutting, for then the force of the current is augmented, and becomes very inconvenient to those who, warming themselves by the fire, happen to sit in its way.

The *remedies* are obvious and easy. Either put an intervening skreen from the wall round great part of the fireplace; or, which is perhaps preferable, shift the hinges of your door, so as it may open the other way, and when open throw the air along the other wall.

8. A room, that has no fire in its chimney, is sometimes filled with *smoke which is received at the top of its funnel and descends into the room*. In a former paper[4] I have already explained the descending currents of air in cold funnels; it may not be amiss however to repeat here, that funnels without fires have an effect, according to their degree of coldness or warmth, on the air that happens to be contained in them. The surrounding atmosphere is frequently changing its temperature; but stacks of funnels, covered from winds and sun by the house that contains them, retain a more equal temperature. If, after a warm season, the outward air suddenly grows cold, the empty warm fun-

---

4 See Notes at the end of this paper, No. II.

nels begin to draw strongly upward; that is, they rarefy the air contained in them, which of course rises, cooler air enters below to supply its place, is rarefied in its turn and rises; and this operation continues till the funnel grows cooler, or the outward air warmer, or both, when the motion ceases. On the other hand, if after a cold season, the outward air suddenly grows warm and of course lighter, the air contained in the cool funnels, being heavier, descends into the room; and the warmer air which enters their tops being cooled in its turn, and made heavier, continues to descend; and this operation goes on, till the funnels are warmed by the passing of warm air through them, or the air itself grows cooler. When the temperature of the air and of the funnels is nearly equal, the difference of warmth in the air between day and night is sufficient to produce these currents, the air will begin to ascend the funnels as the cool of the evening comes on, and this current will continue till perhaps nine or ten o'clock the next morning, when it begins to hesitate; and as the heat of the day approaches, it sets downwards, and continues so till towards evening, when it again hesitates for some time, and then goes upwards constantly during the night, as before mentioned. Now when smoke issuing from the tops of neighboring funnels passes over the tops of funnels which are at the time drawing downwards, as they often are in the middle part of the day, such smoke is of necessity drawn into these funnels, and descends with the air into the chamber.

The *remedy* is to have a sliding plate, hereafter described[5], that will shut perfectly the offending funnel.

9. Chimneys which generally draw well, do nevertheless sometimes give smoke into the rooms, *it being driven down by strong winds passing over the tops of their funnels,* though not descending from any commanding eminence. This case is most frequent where the funnel is short, and the opening turned from the wind. It is the more grievous, when it happens to be a cold wind that produces the effect,

---

5 See Notes at the end of this paper, No. II.

because when you most want your fire, you are sometimes obliged to extinguish it. To understand this, it may be considered that the rising light air, to obtain a free issue from the funnel, must push out of its way or oblige the air that is over it to rise. In a time of calm or of little wind this is done visibly, for we see the smoke that is brought up by that air rise in a column above the chimney. But when a violent current of air, that is, a strong wind, passes over the top of a chimney, its particles have received so much force, which keeps them in a horizontal direction and follow each other so rapidly, that the rising light air has not strength sufficient to oblige them to quit that direction and move upwards to permit its issue. Add to this, that some of the current passing over that side of the funnel which it first meets with, viz. at A, (Plate, Figure 5.) having been compressed by the resistance of the funnel, may expand itself over the flue, and strike the interior opposite side at B, from whence it may be reflected downwards and from side to side in the direction of the pricked lines c c c.

Remedies. In some places, particularly in Venice, where they have not stacks of chimneys but single flues, the custom is, to open or widen the top of the flue rounding in the true form of a funnel ; (Plate, Figure 6) which some think may prevent the effect just mentioned, for that the wind blowing over one of the edges into the funnel may be slanted out again on the other side by its form. I have had no experience of this ; but I have lived in a windy country, where the contrary is practised, the tops of the flues being *narrowed* inwards, so as to form a slit for the issue of the smoke, long as the breadth of the funnel, and only four inches wide. This seems to have been contrived on a supposition, that the entry of the wind would thereby be obstructed, and perhaps it might have been imagined, that the whole force of the rising warm air being condensed, as it were, in the narrow opening, would thereby be strengthened, so as to overcome the resistance of the wind. This however did not always succeed ; for when the wind was at north-east and blew fresh, the smoke was forced down by fits into the room I commonly sat in, so as to oblige me to shift the fire into another. The position of the slit of this funnel was indeed north-east and south-west. Perhaps if it had lain across the wind, the effect might have been different. But on this I can give no certainty. It seems a matter proper to be referred to experiment. Possibly a turn-cap might have been serviceable, but it was not tried.

Chimneys have not been long in use in England. I formerly saw a book printed in the time of queen Elizabeth, which remarked the then modern improvements of living, and mentioned among others the convenience of chimneys. " Our forefathers," said the author, " had no chimneys. There was in each dwelling house only one place for a fire, and the smoke went out through a hole in the roof; but now there is scarce a gentleman's house in England that has not at least one chimney in it."—When there was but one chimney, its top might then be opened as a funnel, and perhaps, borrowing the form from the Venetians, it was then the flue of a chimney got that name. Such is now the growth of luxury, that in both England and France we must have a chimney for every room, and in some houses every possessor of a chamber, and almost every servant, will have a fire; so that the flues being necessarily built in stacks, the opening of each as a funnel is impracticable. This change of manners soon consumed the firewood of England, and will soon render fuel extremely scarce and dear in France, if the use of coals be not introduced in the latter kingdom as it has been in the former, where it at first met with opposition; for there is extant in the records of one of queen Elizabeth's parliaments, a motion made by a member, reciting, "That many dyers, brewers, smiths, and other artificers of London, had of late taken to the use of pitcoal for their fires, instead of wood, which filled the air with noxious vapors and smoke, very prejudicial to the health, particularly of persons coming out of the country; and therefore moving that a law might pass to prohibit the use of such fuel (at least during the session of parliament) by those artificers."—It seems it was not then commonly used in private houses. Its supposed unwholesomeness was an objection. Luckily the inhabitants of London have got over that objection, and now think it rather contributes to render their air salubrious, as they have had no general pestilential disorder since the general use of coals, when, before it, such were frequent. Paris still burns wood at an enormous expence, continually augmenting, the inhabitants having still that prejudice to overcome. In Germany you are happy in the use of stoves, which save fuel wonderfully: your people are very ingenious in the management of fire; but they may still learn something in that art from the Chinese[6], whose country being greatly populous and fully cultivated, has little room left for the growth of wood, and having not much other 'fuel that is good, have been forced upon many inventions during a course of ages, for making a little fire go as far as possible.

I have thus gone through all the common causes of the smoking of chimneys that I can at present recollect as having fallen under my observation; communicating the remedies that I have known successfully used for the different cases, together with the principles on which both the disease and the remedy depend, and confessing my ignorance wherever I have been sensible of it. You will do well, if you publish, as you propose, this letter, to add in notes, or as you please, such observations as may have occurred to your attentive mind; and if other philosophers will do the same, this part of science, though humble, yet of great utility, may in time be perfected. For many years past, I have rarely met with a case of a smoky chimney, which has not been solvable on these principles, and cured by these remedies, where people have been willing to apply them; which is indeed not always the case; for many have prejudices in favor of the nostrums of pretending chimneydoctors and fumists, and some have conceits and fancies of their own, which they rather chuse to try, than to lengthen a funnel, alter the the size of an opening, or admit air into

6 See Notes at the end of this paper, No. III.

a room, however necessary; for some are as much afraid
of fresh air as persons in the hydrophobia are of fresh water. I myself had formerly this prejudice, this *aerophobia*,
as I now account it, and dreading the supposed dangerous
effects of cool air, I considered it as an enemy, and closed
with extreme care every crevice in the rooms I inhabited.
Experience has convinced me of my error. I now look
upon fresh air as a friend: I even sleep with an open window. I am persuaded that no common air from without,
is so unwholesome as the air within a close room that has
been often breathed and not changed. Moist air too, which
formerly I thought pernicious, gives me now no apprehensions: for considering that no dampness of air applied to
the outside of my skin can be equal to what is applied to
and touches it within, my whole body being full of moisture,
and finding that I can lie two hours in a bath twice a week,
covered with water, which certainly is much damper than
any air can be, and this for years together, without catching
cold, or being in any other manner disordered by it, I no longer dread mere moisture, either in air or in sheets or shirts:
and I find it of importance to the happiness of life, the being
freed from vain terrors, especially of objects that we are
every day exposed inevitably to meet with. You physicians have of late happily discovered, after a contrary opinion had prevailed some ages, that fresh and cool air does
good to persons in the small pox and other fevers. It is to
be hoped, that in another century or two we may all find
out, that it is not bad even for people in health. And as
to moist air, here I am at this present writing in a ship with
above forty persons, who have had no other but moist air
to breathe for six weeks past; every thing we touch is
damp, and nothing dries, yet we are all as healthy as we
should be on the mountains of Switzerland, whose inhabitants are not more so than those of Bermuda or St. Helena,
islands on whose rocks the waves are dashed into millions
of particles, which fill the air with damp, but produce no
diseases, the moisture being pure, unmixed with the poi-
sonous vapors arising from putrid marshes and stagnant

pools, in which many insects die and corrupt the water. These places only, in my opinion (which however I submit to yours) afford unwholesome air; and that it is not the mere water contained in damp air, but the volatile particles of corrupted animal matter mixed with that water, which renders such air pernicious to those who breathe it. And I imagine it a cause of the same kind that renders the air in close rooms, where the perspirable matter is breathed over and over again by a number of assembled people, so hurtful to health. After being in such a situation, many find themselves affected by that *febricula*, which the English alone call *a cold*, and, perhaps from the name, imagine that they caught the malady by *going out* of the room, when it was in fact by being in it.

You begin to think that I wander from my subject, and go out of my depth. So I return again to my chimneys.

We have of late many lecturers in experimental philosophy. I have wished that some of them would study this branch of that science, and give experiments in it as a part of their lectures. The addition to their present apparatus need not be very expensive. A number of little representations of rooms composed each of five panes of sash glass, framed in wood at the corners, with proportionable doors, and moveable glass chimneys, with openings of different sizes, and different lengths of funnel, and some of the rooms so contrived as to communicate on occasion with others, so as to form different combinations, and exemplify different cases; with quantities of green wax taper cut into pieces of an inch and half, sixteen of which stuck together in a square, and lit, would make a strong fire for a little glass chimney, and blown out would continue to burn and give smoke as long as desired. With such an apparatus all the operations of smoke and rarefied air in rooms and chimneys might be seen through their transparent sides; and the effect of winds on chimneys, commanded or otherwise, might be shown by letting the entering air blow upon them through an opened window of the lecturer's chamber, where it would be constant while he kept a good fire in his chimney.

By the help of such lectures our fumists would become better instructed. At present they have generally but one remedy, which perhaps they have known effectual in some one case of smoky chimnies, and they apply that indiscriminately to all the other causes, without success,—but not without expence to their employers.

With all the science, however, that a man shall suppose himself possessed of in this article, he may sometimes meet with cases that may puzzle him. I once lodged in a house at London, which, in a little room, had a single chimney and funnel. The opening was very small, yet it did not keep in the smoke, and all attempts to have a fire in this room were fruitless. I could not imagine the reason, till at length observing that the chamber over it, which had no fire-place in it, was always filled with smoke when a fire was kindled below and that the smoke came through the cracks and crevices of the wainscot; I had the wainscot taken down, and discovered that the funnel which went up behind it, had a crack many feet in length, and wide enough to admit my arm, a breach very dangerous with regard to fire, and occasioned probably by an apparent irregular settling of one side of the house. The air entering this breach freely, destroyed the drawing force of the funnel. The remedy would have been, filling up the breach or rather rebuilding the funnel: but the landlord rather chose to stop up the chimney.

Another puzzling case I met with at a friend's country house near London. His best room had a chimney in which, he told me, he never could have a fire, for all the smoke came out into the room. I flattered myself I could easily find the cause, and prescribe the cure. I had a fire made there, and found it as he said. I opened the door, and perceived it was not want of air. I made a temporary contraction of the opening of the chimney, and found that it was not its being too large that caused the smoke to issue. I went out and looked up at the top of the chimney: its funnel was joined in the same stack with others, some of them shorter, that drew very well, and I saw nothing to prevent its doing the same. In fine, after every other examination I could think of, I was obliged to own the insufficiency of my skill. But my friend, who made no pretentions to such kind of knowlege, afterwards discovered the cause himself. He got to the top of the funnel by a ladder, and looking down, found it filled with twigs and straw cemented by earth, and lined with feathers. It seems the house, after being built, had stood empty some years before he occupied it; and he concluded that some large birds had taken advantage of its retired situation to make their nest there. The rubbish, considerable in quantity, being removed, and the funnel cleared, the chimney drew well and gave satisfaction.

In general, smoke is a very tractable thing, easily governed and directed when one knows the principles, and is well informed of the circumstances. You know I made it *descend* in my Pennsylvania stove. I formerly had a more simple construction, in which the same effect was produced, but visible to the eye (Plate, Figure 7.) It was composed of two plates A B and C D, placed as in the figure. The lower plate A B rested with its edge in the angle made by the hearth with the back of the chimney. The upper plate was fixed to the breast, and lapped over the lower about six inches wide and the length of the plates (near two feet) between them. Every other passage of air into the funnel was well stopped. When therefore a fire was made at E, for the first time with charcoal, till the air in the funnel was a little heated through the plates, and then wood laid on, the smoke would rise to A, turn over the edge of that plate, descend to D, then turn under the edge of the upper plate, and go up the chimney. It was pretty to see, but of no great use. Placing therefore the under plate in a higher situation, I removed the upper plate C D, and placed it perpendicularly (Plate, Figure 8) so that the upper edge of the lower plate A B came within about three inches of it, and might be pushed farther from it, or suffered to come nearer to it, by a moveable wedge between them. The flame then ascending from the fire at E, was carried to

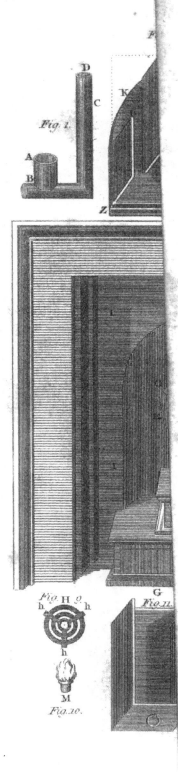

Plate XII.

Fig. 1.

Fig. 2.

Fig. 10.

Fig. 11.

strike the upper plate, made it very hot, and its heat rose and spread with the rarefied air into the room.

I believe you have seen in use with me, the contrivance of a sliding-plate over the fire, seemingly placed to oppose the rising of the smoke, leaving but a small passage for it, between the edge of the plate and the back of the chimney. It is particularly described, and its uses explained, in my former printed letter, and I mention it here only as another instance of the tractability of smoke[7].

What is called the Staffordshire chimney (see the Plate, facing page 314) affords an example of the same kind. The opening of the chimney is bricked up, even with the fore-edge of its jambs, leaving open only a passage over the grate of the same width, and perhaps eight inches high. The grate consists of semicircular bars, their upper bar of the greatest diameter, the others under it smaller and smaller, so that it has the appearance of half a round basket. It is, with the coals it contains, wholly without the wall that shuts up the chimney, yet the smoke bends and enters the passage above it, the draft being strong, because no air can enter that is not obliged to pass near or through the fire, so that all that the funnel is filled with is much heated, and of course much rarefied.

Much more of the prosperity of a winter country depends on the plenty and cheapness of fuel, than is generally imagined. In travelling I have observed, that in those parts where the inhabitants can have neither wood, nor coal, nor turf, but at excessive prices, the working people live in miserable hovels, are ragged, and have nothing comfortable about them. But when fuel is cheap (or where they have the art of managing it to advantage) they are well furnished with necessaries, and have decent habitations. The obvious reason is, that the working hours of such people are the profitable hours, and they who cannot afford sufficient fuel have fewer such hours in the twenty-four, than those who have it cheap and plenty: for much of the domestic work

7 See Notes at the end of this paper, No. II.

of poor women, such as spinning, sewing, knitting; and
of the men in those manufactures that require little bodily
exercise, cannot well be performed where the fingers are
numbed with cold, those people therefore, in cold weather,
are induced to go to bed sooner, and lie longer in a morning than they would do if they could have good fires or
warm stoves to sit by; and their hours of work are not
sufficient to produce the means of comfortable subsistence.
Those public works, therefore, such as roads, canals, &c.
by which fuel may be brought cheap into such countries
from distant places, are of great utility; and those who
promote them may be reckoned among the benefactors of
mankind.

I have great pleasure in having thus complied with your
request, and in the reflection, that the friendship you honor
me with, and in which I have ever been so happy, has continued so many years without the smallest interruption.
Our distance from each other is now augmented, and nature
must soon put an end to the possibility of my continuing
our correspondence: but if consciousness and memory remain in a future state, my esteem and respect for you, my
dear friend, will be everlasting.

                                   B. FRANKLIN.

─────────────────

Notes for the Letter upon Chimnies.

No. I.

THE latest work on architecture that I have seen, is that
entitled *Nutshells*, which appears to be written by a very
ingenious man, and contains a table of the proportions of
the openings of chimneys; but they relate solely to the
proportions he gives his rooms, without the smallest regard
to the funnels.   And he remarks, respecting those proportions, that they are similar to the harmonic divisions of a
monochord[8].   He does not indeed lay much stress on this;

─────────────────

8 " It may be just remarked here, that upon comparing these proportions
with those arising from the common divisions of the monochord, it happens
that the first answers to unisons, and although the second is a discord, the

but it shows that we like the appearance of principles; and where we have not true ones, we have some satisfaction in producing such as are imaginary.

No. II.

The description of the sliding plates here promised, and which hath been since brought into use under various names, with some immaterial changes, is contained in a former letter to James Bowdoin, Esq. as follows:

TO JAMES BOWDOIN, BOSTON.

London, December 2, 1758.

DEAR SIR,

I HAVE executed here an easy simple contrivance, that I have long since had in speculation, for keeping rooms warmer in cold weather than they generally are, and with less fire. It is this: the opening of the chimney is contracted, by brick-work faced with marble slabs, to about two feet between the jambs, and the breast brought down to within about three feet of the hearth. An iron frame is placed just under the breast, and extending quite to the back of the chimney, so that a plate of the same metal may slide horizontally backwards and forwards in the grooves on each side of the frame. This plate is just so large as to fill the whole space, and shut the chimney entirely when thrust quite in, which is convenient when there is no fire. Drawing it out, so as to leave a space between its further edge and the back, of about two inches; this space is sufficient for the smoke to pass; and so large a part of the funnel being stopt by the rest of the plate, the passage of warm air out of the room, up the chimney, is obstructed and retarded, and by that means much cold air is prevented from coming in through crevices, to supply its place. This effect is made manifest three ways. First, when the fire burns briskly in cold weather, the howling or whistling

third answers to the third minor, the fourth to the third major, the fifth to the fourth, the sixth to the fifth, and the seventh to the octave." NUTSHELLS, page 85.

noise made by the wind, as it enters the room through the
crevices, when the chimney is open as usual, ceases as soon
as the plate is slid in to its proper distance. Secondly, opening the door of the room about half an inch, and holding
your hand against the opening, near the top of the door, you
feel the cold air coming in against your hand, but weakly,
if the plate be in. Let another person suddenly draw it out,
so as to let the air of the room go up the chimney, with its
usual freedom where chimnies are open, and you immediately feel the cold air rushing in strongly. Thirdly, if
something be set against the door, just sufficient, when the
plate is in, to keep the door nearly shut, by resisting the
pressure of the air that would force it open: then, when
the plate is drawn out, the door will be forced open by the
increased pressure of the outward cold air endeavoring to
get in to supply the place of the warm air, that now passes
out of the room to go up the chimney. In our common
open chimnies, half the fuel is wasted, and its effect lost;
the air it has warmed being immediately drawn off. Several of my acquaintance, having seen this simple machine in
my room, have imitated it at their own houses, and it seems
likely to become pretty common. I describe it thus particularly to you, because I think it would be useful in Boston, where firing is often dear.

Mentioning chimnies puts me in mind of a property I
formerly had occasion to observe in them, which I have
not found taken notice of by others ; it is, that in the summer time, when no fire is made in the chimneys, there is,
nevertheless, a regular draft of air through them, continually passing upwards, from about five or six o'clock in
the afternoon, till eight or nine o'clock the next morning,
when the current begins to slacken and hesitate a little, for
about half an hour, and then sets as strongly down again,
which it continues to do till towards five in the afternoon,
then slackens and hesitates as before, going sometimes a
little up, then a little down, till, in about half an hour, it
gets into a steady upward current for the night, which continues till eight or nine the next day ; the hours varying a

little as the days lengthen and shorten, and sometimes varying from sudden changes in the weather ; as if, after being long warm, it should begin to grow cool about noon, while the air was coming down the chimney, the current will then change earlier than the usual hour, &c.

This property in chimnies I imagine we might turn to some account, and render improper, for the future, the old saying, *as useless as a chimney in summer.* If the opening of the chimney, from the breast down to the hearth, be closed by a slight moveable frame or two, in the manner of doors, covered with canvas, that will let the air through, but keep out the flies ; and another little frame set within upon the hearth, with hooks on which to hang joints of meat, fowls, &c. wrapt well in wet linen cloths, three or four fold, I am confident, that if the linen is kept wet, by sprinkling it once a day, the meat would be so cooled by the evaporation, carried on continually by means of the passing air, that it would keep a week or more in the hottest weather. Butter and milk might likewise be kept cool, in vessels or bottles covered with wet cloths. A shallow tray, or keeler, should be under the frame to receive any water that might drip from the wetted cloths. I think, too, that this property of chimneys might, by means of smoke-jack vanes, be applied to some mechanical purposes, where a small but pretty constant power only is wanted.

If you would have my opinion of the cause of this changing current of air in chimnies, it is, in short, as follows. In summer time there is generally a great difference in the warmth of the air at mid-day and mid-night, and, of course, a difference of specific gravity in the air, as the more it is warmed the more it is rarefied. The funnel of a chimney, being for the most part surrounded by the house, is protected, in a great measure, from the direct action of the sun's rays and also from the coldness of the night air. It thence preserves a middle temperature between the heat of the day and the coldness of the night. This middle temperature it communicates to the air contained in it. If the state of the outward air be cooler than that in the funnel of the chimney, it will, by being heavier, force it to rise, and go out at the top. What supplies its place from below, being warmed, in its turn, by the warmer funnel, is likewise forced up by the colder and weightier air below, and so the current is continued till the next day, when the sun gradually changes the state of the outward air, makes it first as warm as the funnel of the chimney can make it (when the current begins to hesitate) and afterwards warmer. The funnel, being cooler than the air that comes into it, cools that air, makes it heavier than the outward air, of course it descends; and what succeeds it from above being cooled in its turn, the descending current continues till towards evening, when it again hesitates and changes its course, from the change of warmth in the outward air, and the nearly remaining same middle temperature in the funnel.

Upon this principle, if a house were built behind Beacon-hill, an adit carried from one of the doors into the hill horizontally, till it meet with a perpendicular shaft sunk from its top, it seems probable to me, that those who lived in the house would constantly, in the heat even of the calmest day, have as much cool air passing through the house, as they should chuse ; and the same, though reversed in its current, during the stillest night.

I think, too, this property might be made of use to miners ; as, where several shafts or pits are sunk perpendicularly into the earth, communicating at bottom by horizontal passages, which is a common case, if a chimney of thirty or forty feet high were built over one of the shafts, or so near the shaft, that the chimney might communicate with the top of the shaft, all air being excluded but what should pass up or down by the shaft, a constant change of air would by this means, be produced in the passages below, tending to secure the workmen from those damps, which so frequently incommode them. For the fresh air would be almost always going down the open shaft, to go up the chimney, or down the chimney, to go up the shaft. Let me add one observation more, which is, that if that part of the funnel of a chimney, which appears above the roof of a house, be pretty long, and have three of its sides exposed to the heat of the sun successively, viz. when he is in the east, in the south, and in the west, while the north side is sheltered by the building from the cool northerly winds; such a chimney will often be so heated by the sun, as to continue the draft strongly upwards, through the whole twenty-four hours, and often for many days together. If the outside of such a chimney be painted black, the effect will be still greater, and the current stronger.

No. III.

IT is said the northern Chinese have a method of warming their ground floors, which is ingenious. Those floors are made of tiles, a foot square and two inches thick, their corners being supported by bricks set on end, that are a foot long and four inches square; the tiles, too, join into each other, by ridges and hollows along their sides. This forms a hollow under the whole floor, which on one side of the house has an opening into the air, where a fire is made, and it has a funnel rising from the other side to carry off the smoke. The fuel is a sulphurous pitcoal, the smell of which in the room is thus avoided, while the floor, and of course the room, is well warmed. But as the underside of the floor must grow foul with soot, and a thick coat of soot prevents much of the direct application of the hot air to the tiles, I conceive that burning the smoke, by obliging it to descend through red coals, would in this construction be very advantageous, as more heat would be given by the flame than by the smoke, and the floor being thereby kept free from soot would be more heated with less fire. For this purpose I would propose erecting the funnel close to the grate, so as to have only an iron plate between the fire and the funnel, through which plate, the air in the funnel being heated, it will be sure to draw well, and force the smoke to descend, as in the figure (Plate, Figure 9.) where A is the funnel or chimney, B the grate on which the fire is placed, C one of the apertures through which the descending smoke is drawn into the channel D of figure 10, along which channel it is conveyed by a circuitous route, as designated by the arrows, until it arrives at the small aperture E, figure 10,

3 M

through which it enters the funnel **F.** **G** in both figures is the iron plate against which the fire is made, which being heated thereby, will rarefy the air in that part of the funnel, and cause the smoke to ascend rapidly. The flame thus dividing from the grate to the right and left, and turning in passages, disposed, as in figure 13, so as that every part of the floor may be visited by it before it enters the funnel **F,** by the two passages **E E,** very little of the heat will be lost, and a winter room thus rendered very comfortable.

No. IV.

PAGE 435. *Few can imagine,* &c. It is said the Icelanders have very little fuel, chiefly drift wood that comes upon their coast. To receive more advantage from its heat, they make their doors low, and have a stage round the room above the door, like a gallery, wherein the women can sit and work, the men read or write, &c. The roof being tight, the warm air is confined by it and kept from rising higher and escaping; and the cold air, which enters the house when the door is opened, cannot rise above the level of the top of the door, because it is heavier than the warm air above the door, and so those in the gallery are not incommoded by it. Some of our too lofty rooms might have a stage so constructed as to make a temporary gallery above, for the winter, to be taken away in summer. Sedentary people would find much comfort there in cold weather.

No. V.

PAGE 451. *Where they have the art of managing it,* &c. In some houses of the lower people among the northern nations of Europe, and among the poorer sort of Germans in Pennsylvania, I have observed this construction, which appears very advantageous. (Plate Figure 11.) A is the kitchen with its chimney; B an iron stove in the stove-room. In a corner of the chimney is a hole through the back into the stove, to put in fuel, and another hole above it to let the smoke of the stove come back into the chimney. As soon as the cooking is over, the brands in the kitchen chimney are put through the hole to supply the stove, so that there is seldom more than one fire burning at a time. In the floor over the stove-room, is a small trap door, to let the warm air rise occasionally into the chamber. Thus the whole house is warmed at little expence of wood, and the stove-room kept constantly warm; so that in the coldest winter nights, they can work late, and find the room still comfortable when they rise to work early. An English farmer in America, who makes great fires in large open chimneys, needs the constant employment of one man to cut and haul wood for supplying them; and the draft of cold air to them is so strong, that the heels of his family are frozen while they are scorching their faces, and the room is never warm, so that little sedentary work can be done by them in winter. The difference in this article alone of economy shall, in a course of years, enable the German to buy out the Englishman, and take possession of his plantation.

Miscellaneous Observations.

CHIMNIES, whose funnels go up in the north wall of a house and are exposed to the north winds, are not so apt to draw well as those in a south wall; because, when rendered cold by those winds, they draw downwards.

, Chimnies, enclosed in the body of a house, are better than those whose funnels are exposed in cold walls.

Chimnies in [stacks are apt to draw better than separate funnels, because the funnels, that have constant fires in them warm the others, in some degree, that have none.

One of the funnels, in a house I once occupied, had a particular funnel joined to the south side of the stack, so that three of its sides were exposed to the sun in the course of the day, viz. (Plate Figure 12.) the east side E during the morning, the south side S in the middle part of the day, and the west side W during the afternoon, while its north side was sheltered by the stack from the cold winds. This funnel which came from the ground-floor, and had a considerable height above the roof, was constantly in a strong drawing state day and night, winter and summer.

Blacking of funnels, exposed to the sun, would probably make them draw still stronger.

In Paris I saw a fire-place so ingeniously contrived as to serve conveniently two rooms, a bedchamber and a study. The funnel over the fire was round. The fire-place was of cast iron (Plate, Figure 13.) having an upright back A, and two horizontal semicircular plates B C, the whole so ordered as to turn on the pivots D E. The plate B always stopped that part of the round funnel that was next to the room without fire, while the other half of the funnel over the fire was always open. By this means a servant in the morning could make a fire on the hearth C, then in the study, without disturbing the master by going into his chamber; and the master, when he rose, could, with a touch of his foot, turn the chimney on its pivots, and bring the fire into his chamber, keep it there as long as he wanted it, and turn it again, when he went out, into his study. The room which had no fire in it was also warmed by the heat coming through the back plate, and spreading in the room, as it could not go up the chimney.

Description of a new Stove for burning of Pitcoal, and consuming all its Smoke.

Read in the American Philosophical Society, January 28, 1786.

TOWARDS the end of the last century an ingenious French philosopher, whose name I am sorry I cannot recollect, exhibited an experiment to show, that very offensive things might be burnt in the middle of a chamber, such as woollen rags, feathers, &c. without creating the least smoke or smell. The machine in which it was made, if I remember right, was of this form (see plate Figure 1.) made of plate iron. Some clear burning charcoals were put into the opening of the short tube A, and supported there by the grate B. The air, as soon as the tubes grew warm, would ascend in the longer leg C and go out at D, consequently air must enter at A descending to B. In this course it must be heated by the burning coals through which it passed, and rise more forcibly in the longer tube, in proportion to its degree of heat or rarefaction, and length of that tube. For such a machine is a kind of inverted syphon; and as the greater weight of water in the longer leg of a common syphon in descending is accompanied by an ascent of the same fluid in the shorter; so, in this inverted syphon, the greater quantity of levity of air in the longer leg, in rising is accompanied by the descent of air in the shorter. The things to be burned being laid on the hot coals at A, the smoke must descend through those coals, be converted into flame, which, after destroying the offensive smell, came out at the end of the longer tube as mere heated air.

Whoever would repeat this experiment with success must take care that the part A, B, of the short tube, be quite full of burning coals, so that no part of the smoke may descend and pass by them without going through them, and being converted into flame; and that the longer tube be so heated as that the current of ascending hot air is established in it before the things to be burnt are laid on the coals; otherwise there will be a disappointment.

It does not appear either in the Memoirs of the Academy of Sciences, or Philosophical Transactions of the English Royal Society, that any improvement was ever made of this ingenious experiment, by applying it to useful purposes. But there is a German book, entitled *Vulcanus Famulans*, by John George Leutmann, P. D. printed at Wirtemberg in 1723, which describes, among a great variety of other stoves for warming rooms, one, which seems to have been formed on the same principle, and probably from the hint thereby given, though the French experiment is not mentioned. This book being scarce, I have translated the chapter describing the stove, viz.

" *Vulcanus Famulans, by John George Leutmann, P. D.*
Wirtemberg, 1723.

" CHAP. VII.

" *On a Stove. which draws downwards.*

" HERE follows the description of a sort of stove, which
can easily be removed and again replaced at pleasure. This
drives the fire down under itself, and gives no smoke, but
however a very unwholesome vapor.

" In the figure, A is an iron vessel like a funnel, (Plate,
Figure 20.) in diameter at the top about twelve inches,
at the bottom near the grate about five inches; its height
twelve inches. This is set on the barrel C, which is ten
inches diameter and two feet long, closed at each end E E.
From one end rises a pipe or flue about four inches diameter,
on which other pieces of pipe are set, which are gradually
contracted to D, where the opening is but about two inches.
Those pipes must together be at least four feet high. B is
an iron grate. F F are iron handles guarded with wood,
by which the stove is to be lifted and moved. It stands on
three legs. Care must be taken to stop well all the joints,
that no smoke may leak through.

" When this stove is to be used, it must first be carried
into the kitchen and placed in the chimney near the fire.
There burning wood must be laid and left upon its grate till
the barrel C is warm, and the smoke no longer rises at A,
but descends towards C. Then it is to be carried into the
room which it is to warm. When once the barrel C is
warm, fresh wood may be thrown into the vessel A as often as one pleases, the flame descends and without smoke,
which is so consumed that only a vapor passes out at D.

" As this vapor is unwholesome, and affects the head,
one may be freed from it, by fixing in the wall of the room
an inverted funnel, such as people use to hang over lamps,
through which their smoke goes out as through a chimney.
This funnel carries out all the vapor cleverly, so that one
finds no inconvenience from it, even though the opening D
be placed a span below the mouth of the said funnel G.

The neck of the funnel is better when made gradually bending, than if turned in a right angle.

" The cause of the draft downwards in the stove is the pressure of the outward air, which, falling into the vessel A in a column of twelve inches diameter, finds only a resisting passage at the grate B, of five inches, and one at D, of two inches, which are much too weak to drive it back again; besides, A stands much higher than B, and so the pressure on it is greater and more forcible, and beats down the frame to that part where it finds the least resistance. Carrying the machine first to the kitchen fire for preparation, is on this account, that in the beginning the fire and smoke naturally ascend, till the air in the close barrel C is made thinner by the warmth. When that vessel is heated, the air in it is rarefied, and then all the smoke and fire descends under it.

" The wood should be thoroughly dry, and cut into pieces five or six inches long, to fit it for being thrown into the funnel A." Thus far the German book.

It appears to me, by Mr. Leutmann's explanation of the operation of this machine, that he did not understand the principles of it, whence I conclude he was not the inventor of it; and by the description of it, wherein the opening at A is made so large, and the pipe E, D, so short, I am persuaded he never made nor saw the experiment, for the first ought to be much smaller and the last much higher, or it hardly will succeed. The carrying it in the kitchen, too, every time the fire should happen to be out, must be so troublesome, that it is not likely ever to have been in practice, and probably has never been shown but as a philosophical experiment. The funnel for conveying the vapor out of the room would besides have been uncertain in its operation, as a wind blowing against its mouth would drive the vapor back.

The stove I am about to describe was also formed on the idea given by the French experiment, and completely carried into execution before I had any knowlege of the German invention; which I wonder should remain so many years in a country, where men are so ingenious in the management of fire, without receiving long since the improvements I have given it.

Description of the Parts.

A, the bottom plate which lies flat upon the hearth, with its partitions, 1, 2, 3, 4, 5, 6, (Plate, Figure 2.) that are cast with it, and a groove Z Z, in which are to slide, the bottom edges of the small plates Y, Y, figure 12; which plates meeting at X close the front.

B 1, figure 3, is the cover plate shewing its under side, with the grooves 1, 2, 3, 4, 5, 6, to receive the top edges of the partitions that are fixed to the bottom plate. It shews also the grate W W, the bars of which are cast in the plate, and a groove V. V. which comes right over the groove Z Z, figure 2, receiving the upper edges of the small sliding plates Y Y, figure 12.

B 2, figure 4, shows the upper side of the same plate, with a square impression or groove for receiving the bottom mouldings T T T T of the three-sided box C, figure 5, which is cast in one piece.

D, figure 6, its cover, showing its under side with grooves to receive the upper edges S S S of the sides of C, figure 5, also a groove R, R, which when the cover is put on comes right over another Q Q in C. figure 5, between which it is to slide.

E, figure 7, the front plate of the box.

P, a hole three inches diameter through the cover D, figure 6, over which hole stands the vase F, figure 8, which has a corresponding hole two inches diameter through its bottom.

The top of the vase opens at O, O, O, figure 8, and turns back upon a hinge behind when coals are to be put in ; the vase has a grate within at N N of cast iron H, figure 9, and a hole in the top, one and a half inches diameter, to admit air, and to receive the ornamental brass gilt flame M, figure 10, which stands in that hole, and, being itself hollow and open, suffers air to pass through it into the fire.

G, figure 11, is a drawer of plate iron, that slips in between in the partitions 2 and 3, figure 2, to receive the fal-

ling ashes. It is concealed when the small sliding plates
Y Y, figure 12, are shut together.

I, I, I, I, figure 8, is a niche built of brick in the chimney
and plastered. It closes the chimney over the vase, but
leaves two funnels, one in each corner, communicating
with the bottom box K K, figure 2.

Dimensions of the Parts.	Feet.	In.
Front of the bottom box,	2	0
Height of its partitions,	0	$4\frac{1}{4}$
Length of No. 1, 2, 3, and 4, each,	1	3
Length of No. 5 and 6, each,	0	$8\frac{1}{4}$
Breadth of the passage between No. 2 and 3,	0	6
Breadth of the other passages each,	0	$3\frac{1}{2}$
Breadth of the grate,	0	$6\frac{5}{8}$
Length of ditto,	0	8
Bottom moulding of box, C, square,	1	0
Height of the sides of ditto,	0	4
Length of the back side,	0	10
Length of the right and left sides, each,	0	$9\frac{1}{2}$
Length of the front plate E, where longest,	0	11
The cover D, square,	0	12
Hole in ditto, diameter,	0	3
Sliding plates Y Y, their length, each,	1	0
.... their breadth, each,	0	$4\frac{1}{4}$
Drawer G. its length,	0	1
.... breadth,	0	$5\frac{5}{8}$
.... depth,	0	4
.... depth of its further end only,	0	1
Grate H in the vase, its diameter to the extremity of its knobs,	0	5
Thickness of the bars at top,	0	$0\frac{1}{4}$
.... at bottom, less,	0	0
Depth of the bars at the top,	0	$0\frac{3}{4}$
Height of the vase,	1	6
Diameter of the opening O, O, in the clear,	0	8
Diameter of the air-hole at top,	0	$1\frac{1}{3}$
.... of the flame hole at bottom,	0	2

To fix this Machine.

Spread mortar on the hearth to bed the bottom plate A, then lay that plate level, equally distant from each jamb, and projecting out as far as you think proper. Then putting some Windsor loam in the grooves of the cover B, lay that on: trying the sliding plates Y Y, to see if they move freely in the grooves Z Z, V V, designed for them.

Then begin to build the niche, observing to leave the square corners of the chimney unfilled; for they are to be funnels. And observe also to leave a free open communication between the passages at K K, and the bottom of those funnels, and mind to close the chimney above the top of the niche, that no air may pass up that way. The concave back of the niche will rest on the circular iron partition 1 A 4, figure 2, then with a little loam, put on the box C over the grate, the open side of the box in front.

Then, with loam in three of its grooves, the grooves R R being left clean, and brought directly over the groove Q Q in the box, put on the cover D, trying the front plate E. to see if it slides freely in those grooves.

Lastly, set on the vase, which has small holes in the moulding of its bottom to receive two iron pins that rise out of the plate D at I I, for the better keeping it steady.

Then putting in the grate H, which rests on its three knobs h h h against the inside of the vase, and slipping the drawer into its place; the machine is fit for use.

To use it.

Let the first fire be made after eight in the evening or before eight in the morning, for at those times and between those hours all night, there is usually a draft up a chimney, though it has long been without fire; but between those hours in the day there is often, in a cold chimney, a draft downwards, when, if you attempt to kindle a fire, the smoke will come into the room.

But to be certain of your proper time, hold a flame over the air-hole at the top. If the flame is drawn strongly down for a continuance, without whiffling, you may begin to kindle a fire.

First put in a few charcoals on the grate H.

Lay some small sticks on the charcoals.

Lay some pieces of paper on the sticks.

Kindle the paper with a candle.

Then shut down the top, and the air will pass down through the air-hole, blow the flame of the paper down through the sticks, kindle them, and their flame passing lower kindles the charcoal.

When the charcoal is well kindled, lay on it the seacoals, observing not to choak the fire by putting on too much at first.

The flame descending through the hole in the bottom of the vase, and that in plate D into the box C, passes down farther through the grate W W in plate B 1, then passes horizontally towards the back of the chimney; there dividing, and turning to the right and left, one part of it passes round the far end of the partition 2, then coming forward it turns round the near end of partition 1, then moving backward it arrives at the opening into the bottom of one of the upright corner funnels behind the niche, through which it ascends into the chimney, thus heating that half of the box and that side of the niche. The other part of the divided flame passes round the far end of partition 3, round the near end of partition 4, and so into and up the other corner funnel, thus heating the other half of the box, and the other side of the niche. The vase itself, and the box C will also be very hot, and the air surrounding them being heated, and rising, as it cannot get into the chimney, it spreads into the room, colder air succeeding is warmed in its turn, rises and spreads, till by the continual circulation the whole is warmed.

If you should have occasion to make your first fire at hours not so convenient as those above mentioned, and when the chimney does not draw, do not begin it in the vase, but in one or more of the passages of the lower plate, first covering the mouth of the vase. After the chimney has drawn a while with the fire thus low, and begins to be a little warm, you may close those passages and kindle another fire in the box C, leaving its silding shutter a little open; and when you find after some time that the chimney being warmed draws forcibly, you may shut that passage, open your vase, and kindle your fire there, as above directed. The chimney well warmed by the first day's fire will continue to draw constantly all winter, if fires are made daily.

You will, in the management of your fire, have need of the following implements:

A pair of small light tongs, twelve or fifteen inches long, plate, figure 13.

A light poker about the same length with a flat broad point, figure 14.

A rake to draw ashes out of the passages of the lower plate, where the lighter kind escaping the ash-box will gather by degrees, and perhaps once more in a week or ten days require being removed, figure 15.

And a fork with its prongs wide enough to slip on the neck of the vase cover, in order to raise and open it when hot, to put in fresh coals, figure 16.

In the managment of this stove there are certain precautions to be observed, at first with attention, till they become habitual. To avoid the inconvenience of smoke, see that the grate H be clear before you begin to light a fresh fire. If you find it clogged with cinders and ashes, turn it up with your tongs and let them fall upon the grate below; the ashes will go through it, and the cinders may be raked off and returned into the vase when you would burn them. Then see that all the sliding plates are in their places and and close shut, that no air may enter the stove but through the round opening at the top of the vase. And to avoid the inconvenience of dust from the ashes, let the ash drawer be taken out of the room to be emptied: and when you rake the passages, do it when the draft of the air is strong inwards, and put the ashes carefully into the ash-box, that remaining in its place.

If, being about to go abroad, you would prevent your fire burning in your absence, you may do it by taking the brass flame from the top of the vase, and covering the passage with a round tin plate, which will prevent the entry of more air than barely sufficient to keep a few of the coals alive. When you return, though some hours absent, by taking off the tin plate and admitting the air, your fire will soon be recovered.

The effect of this machine, well managed, is to burn not only the coals, but all the smoke of the coals, so that while the fire is burning, if you go out and observe the top of your chimney, you will see no smoke issuing, nor any thing but clear warm air, which as usual makes the bodies seen through it appear waving.

But let none imagine from this, that it may be a cure for bad or smoky chimneys, much less, that as it burns the smoke it may be used in a room that has no chimney. It is by the help of a good chimney, the higher, the better, that it produces its effect; and though a flue of plate iron sufficiently high might be raised in a very lofty room, the management to prevent all disagreeable vapor would be too nice for common practice, and small errors would have unpleasing consequences.

It is certain that clean iron yields no offensive smell when heated. Whatever of that kind you perceive where there are iron stoves, proceeds therefore from some foulness burning or fuming on their surface. They should therefore never be spit upon, or greased, nor should any dust be suffered to lie upon them. But as the greatest care will not always prevent these things, it is well once a week to wash the stove with soap lees and a brush, rinsing it with clean water.

The Advantages of this Stove.

1. The chimney does not grow foul, nor ever need sweeping; for as no smoke enters it, no soot can form in it.

2. The air heated over common fires instantly quits the room and goes up the chimney with the smoke; but in the stove, it is obliged to descend in flame and pass through the long winding horizontal passages, communicating its heat to a body of iron plate, which, having thus time to re-

ceive the heat, communicates the same to the air of the room, and thereby warms it to a greater degree.

3. The whole of the fuel is consumed by being turned into flame, and you have the benefit of its heat, whereas in common chimneys a great part goes away in smoke which you see as it rises, but it affords you no rays of warmth. One may obtain some notion of the quantity of fuel thus wasted in smoke, by reflecting on the quantity of soot that a few weeks firing will lodge against the sides of the chimney, and yet this is formed only of those particles of the column of smoke that happen to touch the sides in its ascent. How much more must have passed off in the air? And we know that this soot is still fuel: for it will burn and flame as such, and when hard caked together is indeed very like and almost as solid as the coal it proceeds from. The destruction of your fuel goes on nearly in the same quantity whether in smoke or in flame: but there is no comparison in the difference of heat given. Observe when fresh coals are first put on your fire, what a body of smoke arises. This smoke is for a long time too cold to take flame. If you then plunge a burning candle into it, the candle instead of inflaming the smoke will instantly be itself extinguished. Smoke must have a certain degree of heat to be inflammable. As soon as it has acquired that degree, the approach of a candle will inflame the whole body, and you will be very sensible of the difference of the heat it gives. A still easier experiment may be made with the candle itself. Hold your hand near the side of its flame, and observe the heat it gives; then blow it out, the hand remaining in the same place, and observe what heat may be given by the smoke that rises from the still burning snuff. You will find it very little. And yet. that smoke has in it the substance of so much flame, and will instantly produce it, if you hold another candle above it so as to kindle it. Now the smoke from the fresh coals laid on this stove, instead of ascending and leaving the fire while too cold to burn, being obliged to descend through the burning coals, receives among them that degree of heat

which converts it into flame, and the heat of that flame is communicated to the air of the room, as above explained.

4. The flame from the fresh coals laid on in this stove, descending through the coals already ignited, preserves them long from consuming, and continues them in the state of red coals as long as the flame continues that surrounds them, by which means the fires made in this stove are of much longer duration than in any other, and fewer coals are therefore necessary for a day. This is a very material advantage indeed. That flame should be a kind of pickle, to preserve burning coals from consuming, may seem a paradox to many, and very unlikely to be true, as it appeared to me the first time I observed the fact. I must therefore relate the circumstances, and shall mention an easy experiment, by which my reader may be in possession of every thing necessary to the understanding of it. In the first trial I made of this kind of stove, which was constructed of thin plate iron, I had instead of the vase a kind of inverted pyramid like a mill-hopper; and fearing at first that the small grate contained in it might be clogged by cinders, and the passage of the flame sometimes obstructed, I ordered a little door near the grate, by means of which I might on occasion clear it: though after the stove was made, and before I tried it, I began to think this precaution superfluous, from an imagination, that the flame being contracted in the narrow part where the grate was placed, would be more powerful in consuming what it should there meet with, and that any cinders between or near the bars would be presently destroyed and the passage opened. After the stove was fixed and in action, I had a pleasure now and then in opening that door a little, to see through the crevice how the flame descended among the red coals, and observing once a single coal lodged on the bars in the middle of the focus, a fancy took me to observe with my watch in how short a time it would be consumed. I looked at it long without perceiving it to be at all diminished, which surprised me greatly. At length it occurred to me, that I and many others had seen the same thing thousands of times, in the

conservation of the red coal formed in the snuff of a burning candle, which while enveloped in flame, and thereby
prevented from the contact of passing air, is long continued,
and augments instead of diminishing, so that we are often
obliged to remove it by the snuffers, or bend it out of the
flame into the air, where it consumes presently to ashes.
I then supposed, that to consume a body by fire, passing
air was necessary to receive and carry off the separated
particles of the body : and that the air passing in the flame
of my stove, and in the flame of a candle, being already
saturated with such particles, could not receive more, and
therefore left the coal undiminished as long as the outward
air was prevented from coming to it by the surrounding
flame, which kept it in a situation somewhat like that of charcoal in a well luted crucible, which, though long kept in a
strong fire, comes out unconsumed.

An easy experiment will satisfy any one of this conserv-
ing power of flame enveloping red coal.　Take a small
stick of deal or other wood the size of a goose quill, and
hold it horizontally and steadily in the flame of the candle
above the wick, without touching it, but in the body of the
flame.　The wood will first be inflamed, and burn beyond
the edge of the flame of the candle, perhaps a quarter of
an inch.　When the flame of the wood goes out, it will
leave a red coal at the end of the stick, part of which will
be in the flame of the candle and part out in the air.　In a
minute or two you will perceive the coal in the air diminish
gradually, so as to form a neck ; while the part in the flame
continues of its first size, and at the neck being quite consumed it drops off; and by rolling it between your fingers
when extinguished you will find it still a solid coal.

However, as one cannot be always putting on fresh fuel
in this stove to furnish a continual flame as is done in a candle, the air in the intervals of time gets at the red coals
and consumes them.　Yet the conservation while it lasted,
so much delayed the consumption of the coals, that two
fires, one made in the morning, and the other in the afternoon, each made by only a hatful of coals, were sufficient to

keep my writing room, about sixteen feet square and ten high, warm a whole day. The fire kindled át seven in the morning would burn till noon; and all the iron of the machine with the walls of the niche being thereby heated, the room kept warm till evening, when another smaller fire kindled, kept it warm till midnight.

Instead of the sliding plate E, which shuts the front of the box C, I sometimes used another which had a pane of glass, or, which is better, of Muscovy talc, that the flame might be seen descending from the bottom of the vase and passing in a column through the box C, into the cavities of the bottom plate, like water falling from a funnel, admirable to such as are not acquainted with the nature of the machine, and in itself a pleasing spectacle.

Every utensil, however properly contrived to serve its purpose, requires some practice before it can be used adroitly. Put into the hands of a man for the first time a gimblet or a hammer (very simple instruments) and tell him the use of them, he shall neither bore a hole nor drive a nail with the dexterity and success of another who has been accustomed to handle them. The beginner therefore in the use of this machine, will do well not to be discouraged with little accidents that may arise at first from his want of experience. Being somewhat complex, it requires, as already said, a variety of attentions; habit will render them unnecessary. And the studious man who is much in his chamber, and has a pleasure in managing his own fire, will soon find this a machine most comfortable and delightful. To others who leave their fires to the care of ignorant servants, I do not recommend it. They will with difficulty acquire the knowlege necessary, and will make frequent blunders that will fill your room with smoke. It is therefore by no means fit for common use in families. It may be adviseable to begin with the flaming kind of stone coal, which is large, and, not caking together, is not so apt to clog the grate. After some experience, any kind of coal may be used, and with this advantage, that no smell, even from the most sulphurous kind can come into your room, the current of air being constantly into the vase, where too that smell is all consumed.

The vase form was chosen as being elegant in itself, and very proper for burning of coals: where wood is the usual fuel, and must be burned in pieces of some length, a long square chest may be substituted, in which A is the cover opening by a hinge behind, B the grate, C the hearth-box with its divisions as in the other, D the plan of the chest, E the long narrow grate. (Plate, Figure 17.) This I have not tried, but the vase machine was completed in 1771, and used by me in London three winters, and one afterwards in America, much to my satisfaction; and I have not yet thought of any improvement it may be capable of, though such may occur to others. For common use, while in France, I have contrived another grate for coals, which has in part the same property of burning the smoke and preserving the red coals longer by the flame, though not so completely as in the vase, yet sufficiently to be very useful, which I shall now describe as follows.

A, is a round grate, one foot (French) in diameter, and eight inches deep between the bars and the back; (Plate, Figure 18.) the sides and back of the plate iron; the sides having holes of half an inch diameter distant three or four inches from each other, to let in air for enlivening the fire. The back without holes. The sides do not meet at top nor at bottom by eight inches: that square is filled by grates of small bars crossing front to back to let in air below, and let out the smoke or flame above. The three middle bars of the front grate are fixed, the upper and lower may be taken out and put in at pleasure, when hot, with a pair of pincers. This round grate turns upon an axis, supported by the crotchet B, the stem of which is an inverted conical tube five inches deep, which comes on as many inches upon a pin that fits it, and which is fixed upright in a cast iron plate D, that lies upon the hearth; in the middle of the top and bottom grates are fixed small upright pieces E E about an inch high, which, as the whole is turned on its axis, stop it when the grate is perpendicular. Figure 19 is another view of the same machine.

In making the first fire in a morning with this grate, there is nothing particular to be observed. It is made as in other grates, the coals being put in above, after taking out the upper bar, and replacing it when they are in. The round figure of the fire when thoroughly kindled is agreeable, it represents the great giver of warmth to our system. As it burns down and leaves a vacancy above, which you would fill with fresh coals, the upper bar is to be taken out, and afterwards replaced. The fresh coals, while the grate continues in the same position, will throw up as usual a body of thick smoke. But every one accustomed to coal fires in common grates must have observed, that pieces of fresh coal stuck in below among the red coals have their smoke so heated as that it becomes flame as fast as it is produced, which flame rises among the coals and enlivens the appearance of the fire. Here then is the use of this swivel grate. By a push with your tongs or poker, you turn it on its pin till it faces the back of the chimney, then turn it over on its axis gently till it again faces the room, whereby all the fresh coals will be found under the live coals, and the greater part of the smoke arising from the fresh coals will in its passage through the live ones be heated so as to be converted into flame: whence you have much more heat from them, and your red coals are longer preserved from consuming. I conceive this construction, though not so complete a consumer of all the smoke as the vase, yet to be fitter for common use, and very advantageous. It gives too a full sight of the fire, always a pleasing object, which we have not in the other. It may with a touch be turned more or less from any one of the company that desires to have less of its heat, or presented full to one just come out of the cold. And supported in a horizontal position, a tea-kettle may be boiled on it.

The author's description of his Pennsylvania fire-place, first published in 1744, having fallen into the hands of workmen in Europe, who did not, it seems, well comprehend the principles of that machine, it was much disfigured in their imitations of it; and one of its main intentions, that of admitting a sufficient quantity of fresh air warmed in entering through the air-box, nearly defeated, by a pretended improvement, in lessening its passages to make more room for coals in a grate. On pretence of such improvements, they obtained patents for the invention, and for a while made great profits by the sale, till the public became sensible of that defect, in the expected operation. If the same thing should be attempted with this vase stove, it will be well for the buyer to examine thoroughly such pretended improvements, lest, being the mere productions of ignorance, they diminish or defeat the advantages of the machine, and produce inconvenience and disappointment.

The method of burning smoke, by obliging it to descend through hot coals, may be of great use in heating the walls of a hot-house. In the common way, the horizontal passages or flues that are made to go and return in those walls, lose a great deal of their effect when they come to be foul with soot; for a thick blanket-like lining of soot prevents much of the hot air from touching and heating the brick work in its passage, so that more fire must be made as the flue grows fouler: but by burning the smoke they are kept always clean. The same method may also be of great advantage to those businesses in which large coppers or caldrons are to be heated.

Written at Sea, 1785.

TO MISS STEPHENSON.

Method of Contracting Chimneys. Modesty in Disputation.

Craven-Street, Saturday Evening, past 10.

THE question you ask me is a very sensible one, and I shall be glad if I can give you a satisfactory answer. There are two ways of contracting a chimney; one, by contracting the opening *before* the fire; the other, by contracting the funnel *above* the fire. If the funnel above the fire is left open in its full dimensions, and the opening before the fire is contracted; then the coals, I imagine, will burn faster, because more air is directed through the fire, and in a stronger stream; that air which before passed over it, and on each side of it, now passing *through* it. This is seen in narrow stove chimneys, when a *sacheverell* or blower is used, which still more contracts the narrow opening.——But if the funnel only *above* the fire is contracted, then, as a less stream of air is passing up the chimney, less must pass through the fire, and consequently it should seem that the consuming of the coals would rather be checked than augmented by such contraction. And this will also be the case, when both the opening *before* the fire, and the funnel *above* the fire are contracted, provided the funnel above the fire is more contracted in proportion than the opening before the fire.——So you see I think you had the best of the argument; and as you notwithstanding gave it up in complaisance to the company, I think you had also the best of the dispute. There are few, though convinced, that know how to give up, even an error, they have been once engaged in maintaining; there is therefore the more merit in dropping a contest where one thinks one's self right; it is at least respectful to those we converse with. And indeed all our knowlege is so imperfect, and we are from a thousand causes so perpetually subject to mistake and error, that positiveness can scarce ever become even the most knowing; and modesty in advancing any opinion, however plain and true we may suppose it, is always decent, and generally more likely to procure assent. Pope's rule

> To speak, though sure, with seeming diffidence,

is therefore a good one; and if I had ever seen in your conversation the least deviation from it, I should earnestly recommend it to your observation.

I am, &c.

B. FRANKLIN.

END OF THE VOLUME.